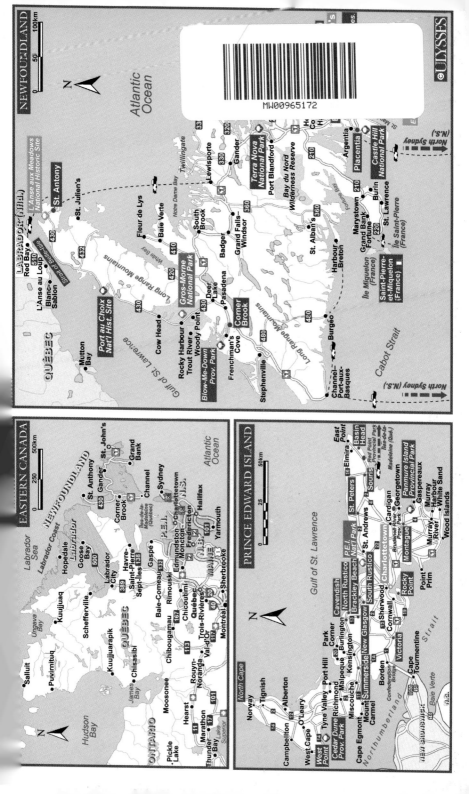

In Bouctouch, New Brunswick, a charming fishing village was modelled after the one featured in Antonine Maillet's, *La Sagouine*. - *Perry Mastrovito*

Atlantic Canada

3rd Edition

Benoit Prieur

Travel better, enjoy more

ULYSSES

Travel Guides

Author
Benoit Prieur

Editor
Stéphane G. Marceau

Publisher
Pascale Couture

Copy Editing
Jacqueline Grekin
Anne Joyce
Tara Salman

Translation
Myles McKelvey
Natalie Philpot
Tracy Kendrick
Sarah Kresh
Andrea Szakos

Page Layout
Typesetting
Anne Joyce
Julie Brodeur
Alexandra Gilbert
Visuals
Caroline Béliveau
Anne Joyce

Cartographers
André Duchesne
Patrick Thivierge
Yanik Landreville

Computer Graphics
Stéphanie Routhier

Artistic Director
Patrick Farei (Atoll)

Illustrations
Myriam Gagné
Lorette Pierson

Photography
Cover Page
Derk Trask
(Superstock)
Inside Pages
Tibor bognár
P.Couture
Michel julien
(Reflexion)
Perry Mastrovito
(Réflexion)
Roger Michel
P. Quittemelle
(Megapress Images)
B. Terry (Reflexion)

Distributors

AUSTRALIA: Little Hills Press, 11/37-43 Alexander St., Crows Nest NSW 2065, ☎ (612) 437-6995, Fax: (612) 438-5762

CANADA: Ulysses Books & Maps, 4176 Saint-Denis, Montréal, Québec, H2W 2M5, ☎ (514) 843-9882, ext.2232, 800-748-9171, Fax: 514-843-9448, info@ulysses.ca, www.ulyssesguides.com

GERMANY and **AUSTRIA**: Brettschneider, Fernreisebedarf, Feldfirchner Strasse 2, D-85551 Heimstetten, München, ☎ 89-99 02 03 30, Fax: 89-99 02 03 31, cf@brettschneider.de

GREAT BRITAIN and **IRELAND**: World Leisure Marketing, Unit 11, Newmarket Court, Newmartket Drive, Derby DE24 8NW, ☎ 1 332 57 37 37, Fax: 1 332 57 33 99, office@wlmsales.co.uk

ITALY: Centro Cartografico del Riccio, Via di Soffiano 164/A, 50143 Firenze, ☎ (055) 71 33 33, Fax: (055) 71 63 50

PORTUGAL: Dinapress, Lg. Dr. Antonio de Sousa de Macedo, 2, Lisboa 1200, ☎ (1) 395 52 70, Fax: (1) 395 03 90

SCANDINAVIA: Scanvik, Esplanaden 8B, 1263 Copenhagen K, DK, ☎ (45) 33.12.77.66, Fax: (45) 33.91.28.82

SPAIN: Altaïr, Balmes 69, E-08007 Barcelona, ☎ 454 29 66, Fax: 451 25 59, altair@globalcom.es

SWITZERLAND: OLF, P.O. Box 1061, CH-1701 Fribourg, ☎ (026) 467.51.11, Fax: (026) 467.54.66

U.S.A.: The Globe Pequot Press, 246 Goose Lane, Guilford, CT 06437-0480, ☎ 1-800-243-0495, Fax: 800-820-2329, sales@globe-pequot.com

OTHER COUNTRIES: Ulysses Books & Maps, 4176 Saint-Denis, Montréal, Québec, H2W 2M5, ☎ (514) 843-9882, ext.2232, 800-748-9171, Fax: 514-843-9448, info@ulysses.ca, www.ulyssesguides.com

No part of this publication may be reproduced in any form or by any means, including photocopying, without the written permission of the publisher.

Canadian Cataloguing in Publication Data (see page 7)
© May 2000, Ulysses Travel Guides.
All rights reserved
Printed in Canada
ISBN 2-8946-4275-X

"There was a freshness in the air as of a wind that had blown over the honey-sweet fields of clover... Beyond lay the sea, misty and purple with its haunting, unceasing murmur."

Lucy Maud Montgomery, *Anne of the Green Gables*

Table of Contents

Portrait 11
  Geography 11
  History 13
  Politics and the Economy . . . 19
  Architecture 20
  Arts and Culture 25

Practical Information 27
  Entrance Formalities 27
  Customs 27
  Embassies and Consulates . . 28
  Tourist Information 30
  Finding Your Way Around . . 30
  Money and Banking 34
  Taxes and Tipping 35
  Time Difference 36
  Climate and Clothing 36
  Health 37
  Safety 37
  Telecommunications 38
  Gay and Lesbian Life 38
  Exploring 38
  Accommodations 38
  Restaurants 40
  Bars and Danceclubs 40
  Wine, Beer and Alcohol 40
  Advice for Smokers 40
  Children 40
  Shopping 40
  Miscellaneous 41

Outdoors 43
  Parks 43
  Summer Activities 45
  Beaches 46
  Winter Activities 47

Fredericton 53
  Finding Your Way Around . . 53
  Practical Information 54
  Exploring 54
  Outdoor Activities 58
  Accommodations 58
  Restaurants 60
  Entertainment 61
  Shopping 62

St. John River Valley 63
  Finding Your Way Around . . 63
  Practical Information 64
  Exploring 64
  Outdoor Activities 70
  Accommodations 71
  Restaurants 73
  Entertainment 74
  Shopping 74

Southern New Brunswick 77
  Finding Your Way Around . . 77
  Practical Information 78
  Exploring 78
  Outdoor Activities 92
  Accommodations 94
  Restaurants 100
  Entertainment 103
  Shopping 104

Acadian Coast 107
  Finding Your Way Around . 107
  Practical Information 108
  Exploring 108
  Beaches 116
  Outdoor Activities 117
  Accommodations 119
  Restaurants 124
  Entertainment 127
  Shopping 127

Halifax **131**
 Finding Your Way Around . 132
 Practical Information 132
 Exploring 132
 Outdoor Activities 140
 Accommodations 140
 Restaurants 143
 Entertainment 145
 Shopping 146

Isthmus of Chignecto **149**
 Finding Your Way Around . 149
 Practical Information 150
 Exploring 150
 Beaches 154
 Outdoor Activities 154
 Accommodations 154
 Restaurants 156
 Shopping 156
 Finding Your Way Around . 158
 Practical Information 158
 Exploring 158
 Accommodations 167
 Restaurants 170
 Entertainment 172

Lighthouse Route **173**
 Practical Information 173
 Exploring 173
 Beaches 181
 Outdoor Activities 181
 Accommodations 182
 Restaurants 187
 Entertainment 189
 Shopping 189

Cape Breton Island **191**
 Finding Your Way Around . 191
 Practical Information 192
 Beaches 199
 Outdoor Activities 199
 Accommodations 201
 Restaurants 204
 Entertainment 206
 Shopping 206

Prince Edward Island **207**
 Finding Your Way Around . 208
 Practical Information 210
 Exploring 212
 Outdoor Activities 230
 Accommodations 233
 Restaurants 240
 Entertainment 247
 Shopping 248

Newfoundland and Labrador **251**
 Finding Your Way Around . 253
 Practical Information 254
 Exploring 254
 Parks 269
 Outdoor Activities 270
 Accommodations 272
 Restaurants 278
 Entertainment 281
 Shopping 281

Symbols

🌴	Ulysses's Favourite
☎	Telephone Number
⇄	Fax Number
≡	Air Conditioning
⊗	Fan
≈	Pool
fb	Full board
ℜ	Restaurant
ℑ	Fireplace
◉	Whirlpool
ℝ	Refrigerator
K	Kitchenette
△	Sauna
⊘	Exercise Room
tv	Colour Television
pb	Private Bathroom
sb	Shared Bathroom
bkfst	Breakfast Included
♠	Casino
♿	Wheelchair Access
✿	Health Centre

ATTRACTION CLASSIFICATION

★	Interesting
★★	Worth a visit
★★★	Not to be missed

The prices listed in this guide are for the admission of one adult.

HOTEL CLASSIFICATION

The prices in this guide are for one room, double occupancy in high season.

RESTAURANT CLASSIFICATION

$	$10 or less
$$	$10 to $20
$$$	$20 to $30
$$$$	$30 and more

The prices in the guide are for a meal for one person, not including drinks and tip.

All prices in this guide are in Canadian dollars.

Write to Us

The information contained in this guide was correct at press time. However, mistakes can slip in, omissions are always possible, places can disappear, etc. The authors and publisher hereby disclaim any liability for loss or damage resulting from omissions or errors.

We value your comments, corrections and suggestions, as they allow us to keep each guide up to date. The best contributions will be rewarded with a free book from Ulysses Travel Guides. All you have to do is write us at the following address and indicate which title you would be interested in receiving (see the list at the end of guide).

Ulysses Travel Guides
4176 Rue Saint-Denis
Montréal, Québec
Canada H2W 2M5
www.ulyssesguides.com
E-mail: text@ulysses.ca

Thanks to: Department of Economic Development and Tourism (N.B.); Department of Tourism (N.S.); Visitors Centre (P.E.I); Destination Newfoundland and Labrador; Parks Canada (Nancy McLachlan and Deanna Wilmshurst).

We acknowledge the financial support of the Government of Canada through the Book Publishing Industry Development Program (BPIDP) for our publishing activities.

We would also like to thank SODEC (Québec) for its financial support.

Cataloguing

Canadian Cataloguing in Publication Data

Prieur, Benoit, 1965-

    Atlantic Canada

    3rd ed.
    (Ulysses travel guide)
    Translation of: Provinces atlantiques du Canada
    Includes index.

    ISBN 2-89464-275-X

    1. Atlantic Provinces - Guidebooks. 2. Prince Edward Island - Guidebooks. 3. New Brunswick - Guidebooks. 4. Nova Scotia - Guidebooks. 5. Newfoundland - Guidebooks. I. Title. II. Series.

FC2004.P7413 2000   917.1504'4   C00-940269-1

List of Maps

Where is Atlantic Canada? 10
Table of distances 26
Symbols 6
New Brunswick 51
Fredericton 52
Downtown Fredericton 55
The St. John River Valley 65
Southern New Brunswick 79
Saint John and Surrounding 83
Saint John 85
Moncton 89
The Acadian Coast 106
Shediac 109
St. Andrews by-the-Sea 79
Nova Scotia 130
Halifax 137
The Halifax Area 133
The Old Acadia 159
The Lighthouse Route 175
Cape Breton Island 193
Isthmus of Chignecto 148
Prince Edward Island 207
Charlottetown 211
Charlettetown and Suroundings 213
Cavendish and Suroundings 217
Newfoundland 250
St. John's 255

Map Symbols

	Tourist Information		Mountain
	Car Ferry		Golf Course
	Passenger Ferry		Beach
	Provincial Capital		Lookout

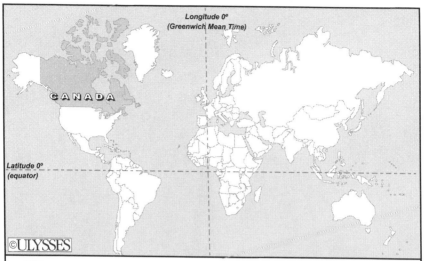

 ## *Where is Atlantic Canada?*

Nova Scotia
Capital: Halifax Population: 944,800 inhab. Area: 55,490 km²

New Brunswick	Prince Edward Island	Newfoundland
Capital: Fredericton Population: 754,700 inhab. Area: 73,437 km²	Capital: Charlottetown Population: 137,800 inhab. Area: 5,657 km²	Capital: St. John's Population: 541,200 inhab. Area: 406,000 km²

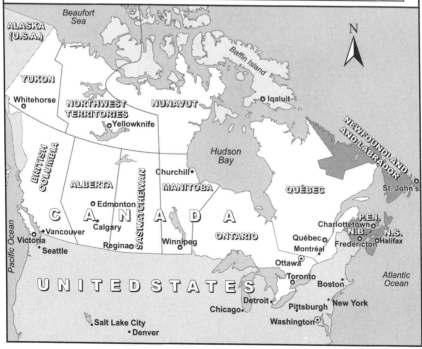

Portrait

New Brunswick,

Nova Scotia, Prince Edward Island and New-foundland make up a picturesque region that com-bines thousands of kilometres of splendid coastal scenery with rich local tradition and a fascinating way of life.

The Atlantic prov-inces boast some of the most beautiful natu-ral sites in eastern North America, includ-ing the spectacular Cape Breton Highlands, the magnificent sand dunes and beaches on Prince Edward Island, the cliffs and fjords of Newfoundland's Gros Morne National Park, and the stunning land-scapes along the Bay of Fundy, sculpted by the highest and most pow-erful tides in the world. The area's unique charm, however, is also largely due to the sim-ple scenes of everyday life, like the sight of a fleet of colourful ships heading out in the morning fog from a little fishing port along the coast.

A trip to Atlantic Canada thus offers visitors an opportunity to view the region's magnificent scenery, while getting to know the rich local culture and history. These are not the area's only pleasures, however. Among the most de-lightful memories will certainly be the beaches, washed by the warmest waters north of Virginia (U.S.A.), and the feasts of lobster and of other fresh seafood.

Geography

Canada covers 9,959,400km². The At-lantic provinces lie in the eastern part of this immense country. These four provinces, New Brunswick, Nova Scotia, Prince Edward Island and Newfound-land all have shorelines along the Gulf of St. Lawrence, the Atlantic Ocean or the Bay of Fundy.

New Brunswick covers an area of 73,436km² and shares a border with Québec to the west and the north and Maine (U.S.A.) to the west; its coast is linked to Nova Scotia by the Chignecto

Isthmus. To the east, the province is separated from Prince Edward Island by the Northumberland Strait. New Brunswick is bound by water on two sides; its northern and northeastern shores look out on Baie des Chaleurs and the Gulf of St. Lawrence, its south shore on the Bay of Fundy. There are two major waterways that run through the heart of the territory – the St. John and Miramichi Rivers. The north of New Brunswick has highlands reaching up to 820m that constitute the end of the Appalachians, and its centre is studded by several hills. A dense forest, consisting mostly of coniferous and some deciduous trees, covers approximately 85% of the territory and constitutes an important natural resource, enabling the province to become an exporter of pulp and paper.

Nova Scotia is only linked to the rest of Canada by a narrow strip of land, the Chignecto Isthmus. Its shores are washed by the Bay of Fundy to the northwest, the Atlantic Ocean in the south and the Gulf of St. Lawrence to the northeast. The province also boasts no fewer than 3,000 lakes and many little streams and rivers. It covers an area of 54,565km², about 10% of which is arable land. Like New Brunswick, Nova Scotia originally had a dense forest consisting mainly of conifers.

Prince Edward Island, which has an area of only 5,657km², is the smallest but most densely populated province in Canada, with an average of 21 inhabitants per km². Its economy, unlike that of the other two Maritime provinces, is based largely on agriculture; nearly 50% of the territory is covered with extremely fertile soil. The potato is one of the islaned's most important crops. Vast fields stretch across land once occupied by a forest of beech, birch, maple, oak and pine trees. This island, separated from Nova Scotia and New Brunswick by the Northumberland Strait, lies in the Gulf of St. Lawrence. Its inland waters are limited to small ponds and narrow rivers.

The province of **Newfoundland** is made up of two distinct parts: the island of Newfoundland and the immense territory of Labrador. The island covers an area of 110,681km². As North America's easternmost island, Newfoundland started playing a pivotal role in communications between Europe and the New World at a very early date. It is separated from the mainland by the Strait of Belle Isle and also has shores on the Gulf of St. Lawrence and on the Atlantic Ocean. Unlike the other Atlantic provinces, Newfoundland is almost entirely unfit for farming. Its population is thus concentrated along the shore, where fishing is the mainstay of the economy, and in a few inland urban centres, where the cutting and processing of wood are the main activities. The west part of the island is rimmed by the Long Range Mountains, whose highest summit rises to an altitude of 815m; the rest is either flat or has a gently rolling landscape. Spectacular cliffs tower over the coastline in many spots. Labrador, nearly three times the size of the island of Newfoundland, covers 295,039km². Most of this territory has a gently undulating landscape strewn with countless lakes and rivers, which is typical of the Canadian Shield.

Farther north, the terrain is shaped by the Torngat Mountains, which soar 1,729m into the sky at their highest point. Labrador is covered with subarctic forest and, in its northernmost part, with tundra. Its shoreline stretches nearly 8,000km along the Strait of Belle Isle and the Atlantic Ocean. To the east and south, Labrador shares a long border with Quebec.

History

The arrival of European explorers in the 15th and 16th centuries did not mark the beginning of human history in the region now known as the Atlantic provinces. It was actually a moment of rupture, since the territory had already been inhabited for over 10,000 years by descendants of nomads who crossed the Bering Strait at the end of the ice age. Furthermore, John Cabot and Jacques Cartier were not the first Europeans to come to this part of North America. Legend has it that at the end of the fifth century, St. Brendan, an Irish abbot, crossed the Atlantic in search of new peoples to convert to Christianity and came ashore on this island. The first Europeans whose presence here can actually be proved, however, are the Vikings, who, toward the year 1000, apparently used the island as a base for exploring the continent. Leif's Camp, in L'Anse-aux-Meadows (Newfoundland), is the oldest known European settlement in North America. It wasn't until several centuries later that Europeans rediscovered Newfoundland.

In the 15th century, Europeans learned of the teeming waters around the island from Basque fishers. Each summer, the Basques would come to this region to fish cod in the Grand Banks and hunt whales in the Strait of Belle Isle. The voyages of Cabot and Cartier nevertheless represented a decisive moment in history, heralding an era of European colonization in this region and in the rest of North America.

In 1497, after finding financial support in England, John Cabot (born Giovanni Caboto) set out from Bristol in search of a direct route to the riches of the Orient. On June 24, 1497, he reached the coast of North America, most probably the northern shores of the island of Newfoundland, then returned to England. His voyage was not in vain, however, as he helped spread the word about the tremendous natural riches in this part of the world – an apparently inexhaustible supply of cod off the northern coasts of the New World. From that moment on, even larger numbers than before of English, French, Basque and Spanish fishers started heading out from the ports of Europe to fish cod off the coast of Newfoundland and Nova Scotia.

In 1534, Breton navigator Jacques Cartier launched the first of his three voyages to North America. Commissioned by King Francis I of France to seek out gold and a passage to Asia, he found neither. These expeditions did, however, enable Cartier to discover the shoreline of a huge territory. On his first voyage, he explored the coast of the Atlantic provinces, from the west point of present-day Prince Edward Island to the mouth of the Miramichi River (in New Brunswick). Farther along, in Baie des Chaleurs (Québec), he met the local Aboriginal people. He erected a cross here, symbolically claiming this land in the name of the King of France.

Micmac Cradle

The Aboriginals Cartier encountered in Baie des Chaleurs belonged to the Algonquian-speaking Micmac tribe. The Micmacs inhabited not only this region but also, in greater numbers, what is now Nova Scotia, New Brunswick and Prince Edward Island, territories they shared with another Algonquian-speaking nation, the Malecites. The direct ancestors of these Aboriginal people settled in the region - about 2,500 years ago. In the summer, the Micmacs and Malecites lived in fairly large groups along the coast, surviving mainly on fish. In winter, they would leave the coast and head into the forest to hunt game. The island of Newfoundland, for its part, has been inhabited since the second century by the Beothuk, whose lifestyle was similar to that of the Micmac and the Malecite. This traditional way of life was greatly disrupted by the arrival of the explorers and European fishers.

In the second half of the 16th century, the Europeans began trading more and more with the Aboriginal people. Fur garments were becoming fashionable in Europe and created an extremely lucrative market. In response to this trend, many European fishers became merchants, trading metal objects, for the most part, for furs. The Micmacs, Malecites and Beothuks, who lived near the shore, profited the most from this activity. However, they were also the first to succumb to various illnesses transmitted by the Europeans, which their immune system could not combat. Before long, these diseases had claimed the lives of vast numbers of Aboriginals. Around the year 1600, for example, it is estimated that a mere 3,500 Micmacs remained in the Maritimes; a century earlier, before their first contact with Europeans, their population was 10 times that size.

Acadia and Early Settlement

The development of fisheries prompted the Europeans to establish **trading posts** on the shores of Newfoundland. The English founded their first outpost in Trinity in 1558 on the Bonavista Peninsula, then officially took possession of the port of St. John's in 1583. The French also started establishing footholds on the shores of Newfoundland to support their seasonal fishing activities. However, the fur trade being carried out with Aboriginal suppliers required a much more permanent European presence on the continent.

Most efforts to set up trading posts along the coast of this part of North America were made by the French. - Several fruitless attempts were made, namely on Sable Island (Nova Scotia) and in Tadoussac (Québec). Then, in 1604, one year after receiving authorization from King Henry IV of France, Pierre de Gua, Sieur de Monts, founded the first real French colony in North America. It was christened Acadia *(Acadie)*, a term probably derived from the word "Arcadia" (the name of a region in ancient Greece), which the explorer Verrazano had already used to designate this part of the North American coast.

In March 1604, De Monts set out from the port of Le Havre, in France, for Acadia accompanied by about 80 men, including Samuel de Champlain who founded the settlement of Québec a few years later. De Monts and his men decided to spend their first winter on the little island of Sainte-Croix, at the mouth of the Sainte-Croix River (in the present-day state of Maine), in the Bay of Fundy. This proved to be an error in judgment, because as soon as winter set in, the men could no longer cross the strait between the island and the continent to go hunting, cut firewood or find potable water. At least 35 of the original colonists perished before spring arrived.

As soon as the ice melted, the survivors hurried off to make another attempt at colonization somewhere else. They crossed the Bay of Fundy and settled at the mouth of the river now known as the Annapolis, where they founded the colony of Port-Royal (in what is now Nova Scotia). The site had a safe, natural harbour and the advantage of being located on the territory of a Micmac community that was friendly towards French settlers. Its chief, Membertou, was in favour of trading

The Beothuks

Before the arrival of the European colonists, Newfoundland was inhabited by the Beothuks, an Aboriginal people that settled in the area around AD 200. Unfortunately, this language group perished in the early 19th century.

First weakened by diseases brought by Europeans, they were then forced out of their ancestral lands by the arrival of the Micmac, themselves pushed by the colonists. The Beothuks found themselves with limited access to the sea, their primary means of subsistence, and they slowly died out. Shawnawdithit, the last known Beothuk, died of tuberculosis in 1829, and with her, the last of their secrets.

with France, believing that his people could thereby increase their power by acting as commercial intermediaries between the Europeans and other Aboriginal peoples. Before long, a close personal relationship had developed between Membertou and one of the colony's most important officers, Baron Jean de Biencourt de Poutrincourt. Without the direct assistance of the Micmac, Port-Royal probably never would have existed.

In France, however, the settlers' efforts made little impression on Henry IV, who, in the spring of 1607, cancelled the fur-trading monopoly he had granted de Monts. In the wake of this royal decree,

Port-Royal was temporarily abandoned only to be re-inhabited some time later, mainly as a result of Baron de Poutrincourt's efforts. In order to start colonizing Port-Royal again, De Poutrincourt joined forces with wealthy French Catholics, promising to try to convert the Aboriginals to Christianity. In 1610, he left the French port of Dieppe accompanied by a priest named Jessé Flesché and about 20 men. Upon arriving at Port-Royal in June, he found the settlement he had abandoned three years earlier almost entirely intact. In an effort to satisfy the baron's Catholic allies, Jessé Flesché baptised about 20 Micmacs, including Membertou, who were quite cooperative, apparently considering their conversion to be a mere adjunct to their own traditional religious beliefs. In France, however, news of the Aboriginals' conversion was greeted with such great enthusiasm that Jesuit missionaries Pierre Biard and Edmond Massé, along with about 40 men, came to bolster the population of Port-Royal the following year.

Nevertheless, sustaining the French presence along this part of the North American coast was never an easy task. Due to its location, isolated from both France and New France (present-day Québec), the settlement was particularly vulnerable to attacks from Great Britain and from its fledgling colonies farther south along the Atlantic coast. In 1613, an adventurer from Virginia named Samuel Argall seized Port-Royal and drove out most of the colonists. It wasn't until 1632, with the Treaty of Saint-Germain-en-Laye, that France was able to regain possession of Acadia.

This episode was but the first of a long series in which the Acadians were often the primary victims of the rivalry between the French and British empires. Acadia fell into British hands again in 1654, and was returned to the French in 1667 under the Treaty of Breda. The British seized Acadia once more in 1690, in the wake of a naval attack led by General Phips, and then again relinquished it to the French in 1697, under the Treaty of Ryswick. Finally, in 1710, Acadia was appropriated by the British once and for all. In 1713, its status as a British colony was confirmed by the Treaty of Utrecht.

During this time, the little colony continued to grow. Most of the original settlers, who arrived in the 1630s, 1640s and 1670s, came from the southern part of the Loire valley, mainly from Poitou. The Acadians quickly became self-sufficient, supporting themselves through farming, livestock, fishing and hunting as well as through business. They initially remained in the immediate vicinity of Port-Royal, but were then attracted by the excellent farmlands along the Bay of Fundy, where they established new settlements in the 1670s and 1680s. The most important of these was Grand-Pré, on the Minas Basin. The Acadians were successful as farmers because they managed to develop an ingenious system of dykes and aboiteaux that made it possible to drain excellent farmlands and protect them from the tides in the Bay of Fundy.

The Deportation

With the signing of the Treaty of Utrecht in 1713, Acadia came under British rule once and for all. This loss, along with that of the port of Plaisance in Newfoundland and Britain's control of Hudson Bay, weakened France's position in North America considerably. To counterbalance the British presence on the Atlantic coast, French authorities decided to develop Île Saint-Jean (Prince Edward Island) and Île Royale (Cape Breton Island), which they still controlled. The first became a settlement devoted solely to agriculture. On Île Royale, however, France erected the largest network of fortifications in its North American possessions – the fortified city of Louisbourg, which had 10,000 inhabitants at its peak.

The struggle between Great Britain and France for control over North America put the Acadians in a difficult position. Having French roots, they were subjected to increasing pressure from colonial authorities anxious to make them swear an unconditional vow of allegiance to Great Britain. The Acadian leaders were willing to accept British authority, provided that they would be allowed to remain neutral in the event of a conflict between the two colonial powers. British governor Philips (1729-1731) accepted the Acadians' neutrality. Life went on under the British regime, and the Acadian population grew from about 2,500 inhabitants in 1713 to some 14,000 by 1755.

During the first half of the 18th century, however, there continued to be a great deal of tension between the two colonial powers, and a face-off for control of North America was clearly imminent. In 1745, troops from New England scored a decisive blow with the swift and stunning capture of the fortress of Louisbourg on Île Royale. To the great disappointment of British colonists, however, Louisbourg was returned to France three years later under the Treaty of Aix-la-Chapelle. In 1749, in an effort to reinforce their hold over Nova Scotia (formerly Acadia), whose population was still mostly Acadian, 2,500 British soldiers landed on the Atlantic coast and built the citadel of Halifax. The French accelerated their own war preparations by erecting Fort Beauséjour (New Brunswick) on the Chignecto Isthmus in 1750. The British responded the following year by building Fort Lawrence just 3km east of Fort Beauséjour.

Given the context, British authorities found the Acadians' neutrality increasingly troubling. They feared that the Acadians would help the French in one way or another in the event of a conflict. In 1755, The Legislative Council of Nova Scotia, led by Charles Lawrence, decided to settle the issue once and for all by ordering the deportation of all Acadians. Between 1755 and 1762, the majority of Acadian villages were destroyed: houses and churches were burned and livestock was confiscated. About half of the 14,000 Acadians were put on boats and deported to England, France and other parts of North America. The others managed to escape, seeking refuge in the woods. When the signing of the Treaty of Paris brought the war between France and Britain to an end in 1763, Acadia had already been wiped from the map. Under the terms of the treaty, France ceded New France and its other North American possessions, including Saint-Jean and Île Royale, to Great Britain. Of her empire in North America, France kept only the two small islands of Saint-Pierre and Miquelon, as well as fishing rights on the coasts of Newfoundland.

The deportation scattered the Acadians, and in many cases split up families. Many took up residence along the eastern and northeastern coast of New Brunswick, which now has the highest proportion of Acadians in the Maritimes. Others settled elsewhere in the Maritimes, in Québec, in Louisiana, where they would become the ancestors of today's Cajuns, and elsewhere in North America or Europe. It would take the Acadians of the Maritimes more than a century to establish their own institutions once again.

The Arrival of the Loyalists

Following the Franco-British wars for control of North America, another conflict had significant repercussions on the Atlantic provinces. The American Revolution, in the beginning at least, was a veritable civil war that pitted supporters of independence against Loyalists wishing to maintain colonial ties with Great Britain. Over 350,000 of these Loyalists became active participants in the conflict by joining the British forces. In 1783, after a long, agonizing battle, the British admitted defeat. The victory of the American revolutionary forces prompted about 100,000 Loyalists to leave the United States to seek refuge elsewhere. Of this number, approximately 35,000 chose the

Atlantic provinces as their new home.

Within a few months, the impact of this massive influx of new colonists was felt all over the region, whose population had previously been no more than 20,000. The major ports of entry for the Loyalists were Shelburne, on the Atlantic coast of Nova Scotia, and the mouth of the St. John River, on the Bay of Fundy. Shelburne suddenly became one of the most populated towns in North America, with about 9,000 inhabitants. More than 14,000 Loyalists headed up the St. John River in New Brunswick, most settling in the valley, on the fertile lands upriver. Several other ports, including St. Andrews, St. Stephen, Annapolis Royal and Halifax, were also flooded by large numbers of Loyalists.

The political and economic repercussions of this influx of Loyalists varied from one region to another, depending on the size of the local population. For example, the several hundred Loyalists who settled on Île Saint-Jean (renamed Prince Edward Island in 1798) and on Cape Breton Island quickly blended into the existing population, causing very few changes. In New Brunswick, however, the Loyalists represented more than three quarters of the population

and soon occupied positions of political and economic power. In Nova Scotia, where they made up about half of the population, their integration caused a certain degree of friction for the first few years. Be that as it may, the arrival of the Loyalists was a key moment in the history of the Atlantic provinces and radically transformed the profile of region with a sudden increase in the local population.

The Golden Age and Canadian Confederation

For the first half of the 19th century, the Atlantic provinces experienced an economic boom, as well as a remarkable growth in population. In less than a century, the natural growth of the population, combined with substantial immigration (mainly from the British Isles) caused a 10-fold increase in the number of inhabitants.

This population explosion was sustained by a dramatic increase in the region's economic activity, due in large part to the export value of local products. Many people profited from this boom, but merchants, shipowners and shipbuilders were especially well-positioned to amass immense fortunes. Foreign markets were found for many products, including agricul-

tural produce from Prince Edward Island, coal ore from Cape Breton and the Chignecto Isthmus, wooden billets from the area around the Miramichi River and fish from Nova Scotia and Newfoundland. All this exportation was made possible by the large fleet of Atlantic Canada's merchant navy, which crisscrossed seas all over the world. There were Shipyards found in many towns and villages along the coast. This was a glorious era for the region.

The second half of the 19th century, however, proved less prosperous for the region, whose economy gradually slowed down. This decline was caused by a number of different factors, an important one being the development of new technologies in the transport industry. Traditional vessels, until then one of the mainsprings of the local economy, began to face fierce competition from steamships. The era also witnessed the development of the railway, a new, highly efficient transportation network, in which Atlantic Canada played only a minor role. The decline of the region's economy and political powers was probably accentuated by Canadian Confederation (1867), which Nova Scotia and New Brunswick joined immediately, despite considerable controversy, followed by Prince Edward Island in 1873. The province of Newfoundland didn't join the Confederation until 1949. Confederation soon led to the creation of a large domestic market stretching from the Atlantic to the Pacific. The central regions were at an advantage, since they served as transportation and communication centres for the entire country. The political powers of the Atlantic provinces greatly diminished with Canadian confederation, and their economies became controlled by the central provinces.

The 20th Century

The 20th century was marked by several bursts of economic growth, particularly during the two World Wars, in which the region played an important role. Most of the military convoys transporting Canadian troops to Europe set out from the city of Halifax, which is still the Canadian Navy's principal home port in the eastern part of the country. Newfoundland, for its part, was used as a base for the Allied naval and air forces defending the North Atlantic. The period between the two wars was much more difficult for Atlantic Canada, however. The Great Depression

of the 1930s dealt a crushing blow to the local economy, perhaps hitting harder here than elsewhere in the country, given the region's dependence on the decision-makers in central Canada.

The most significant political event in the post-war period took place in New Brunswick in the 1960s and 1970s, when the Acadian community was accorded more rights and began to advance economically. In 1968, in the heat of this campaign to promote equality, the New Brunswick government passed the Official Languages Law, which required public services to be available in both French and English. The government's efforts had a concrete effect, for Acadians now play a very active role in the economy and in politics. In the last decade of the 20th century, however, current events were above all marked by difficulties encountered in certain traditional and important sectors of the local economy. This was particularly true for fisheries, where poor management of resources forced authorities to declare a moratorium on the fishing of certain species, such as cod. The local economy was seriously affected, especially in Newfoundland, a province heavily dependent on fishing. The Atlantic provinces have reacted

and are making concerted efforts to diversify their economy and develop new areas of expertise.

Politics and the Economy

Politically speaking, New Brunswick is different from the other Maritime provinces because of its Official Languages Law, which makes it the only officially bilingual province in Canada. French-speakers make up about 33% of the province's total population, and government services are available here in both French and English. This law, along with the promotion of equality for Acadians in general, has been upheld by every provincial government since the 1960s. However, the Confederation of Regions, a political party opposed to official bilingualism in New Brunswick, has had eight deputies in the province's Legislative Assembly since 1991.

New Brunswick's economy revolves around forestry, the chemical and oil industries, farming, fishing, mining and tourism. Premier from 1987 to 1997, Frank McKenna, has managed to energize the economy through an effective public relations strategy aimed at foreign businesses. The province's extremely efficient telephone sys-

Portrait

tem and skilled workforce have allowed McKenna to persuade several large companies to set up their telephone exchanges here. Also, in recent years, the province's Acadian community has demonstrated a dynamic entrepreneurial spirit. Bernard Lord, of the Progressive Conservative Party, is presently premier of the province. The population of New Brunswick totals about 754,700 inhabitants.

Of the three Atlantic provinces, Nova Scotia is the most prosperous and has the most diversified economy. Its capital, Halifax, is the region's main seaport, as well as its most important financial and commercial centre. Halifax is also the Canadian Navy's principal home port on the east coast. The fishing, mining and shipbuilding industries, cornerstones of the local economy for many years, now represent only a small share of the province's gross national product. Today, the service and manufacturing sectors predominate. In 1995, the city of Halifax was chosen to host the delegates of the G-7, a union of the seven most economically powerful countries in the world. The premier of Nova Scotia is John F. Hamm, of the Progressive Conservative Party. Nova Scotia is the most populated of

the Atlantic provinces, with a population of 944,800.

Industrialization only began in Prince Edward Island at the end of the Second World War. Located far from the big urban centres and cut off from the major transportation networks, the island has always been slow to develop a strong manufacturing industry. Hopefully, the newly inaugurated Confederation Bridge, which joins the island to New Brunswick, will remedy some of its problems. Presently, a large portion of the economy is based on agriculture (especially potato farming) as well as the fishing, tourist and service industries. Prince Edward Island is the least populated province of Canada, with 137,800 inhabitants. The current premier is Patrick George Binns, of the Progressive Conservative Party.

Newfoundland's economy, still largely dependent on the fisheries, has been hard hit since the government imposed a moratorium on cod fishing. Years of commercial fishing had nearly exhausted the supply of cod in the Grand Banks. Newfoundlanders are frustrated by this situation, since it is difficult for them to exercise control over fishing activities in the Grand Banks, which lie in

both Canadian and international waters.

In addition to fishing, the province has a large wood-cutting and -processing industry and one of the biggest iron mines in the world, located in Labrador. Newfoundlanders have also started to capitalize on Labrador's tumultuous rivers by building huge hydroelectric dams. Furthermore, they have high hopes about a planned offshore drilling operation over 300km from the coast of the island. The Hibernia platform, the biggest ever built, will exploit this oilfield, estimated to contain over 600 million barrels of petroleum. The total population of Newfoundland, including Labrador, is 541,200. The province is led by Premier Brian Tobin, of the Liberal Party.

Architecture

Aided by favourable winds, a few Viking boats reached the shores of Newfoundland in the year 1000, carrying hale and hearty fellows with thick, blond mustaches. Before long, these men had built villages near the beaches. Their houses, made of wood and stone, were roofed with thick layers of earth and thick blankets of wild grass sprouting out of them. Around 1950, archaeologists excavated one of these villages, L'Anse-aux-Meadows, in the northern part of Newfoundland. The village then became the object of a restoration campaign and was equipped with its own interpretation centre. Thanks to this discovery, the Atlantic provinces can justly take pride in being home to the oldest European settlement in all of North America.

When the Vikings arrived, Newfoundland's hinterland was inhabited by Aboriginal peoples. Iron objects left by the Vikings were later discovered here. In those days, many nations, such as the Beothuk, survived on fishing and hunting. These nomads would move from one region to another depending on the season and the availability of food, rebuilding their camp each time. They used lightweight materials, like branches and birch bark to make wigwams. The Labrador Inuit, for their part, lived in dome-shaped igloos made of ice and snow during winter and in tents made of animal hides during summer. Nowadays, these traditional dwellings are reconstructed periodically for folk festivals. In the 19th century, missionaries encouraged Aboriginals to settle in one place. They now live in the west, in small aluminum-roofed wooden houses, clus-

tered in villages on federal reserves.

Once the Vikings left, there were no new European settlements in North America for over 500 years, at which point the Spanish and the Portuguese started establishing a foothold in the south, and Basque and French fishers set up camp on the coast of Newfoundland and in the St. Lawrence River Valley. The few remaining traces of their annual summer stays are few, and little effort has been made to turn them into attractions. It wasn't until 1605, with the founding of the colony of Port-Royal, that any permanent architecture was erected in the Atlantic provinces.

The Abitation de Port-Royal has been successfully reconstructed (Annapolis Royal, Nova Scotia, see p 163). Its main buildings, with their walls made of squared-off tree trunks, are grouped around a courtyard with a drinking well in the middle. They have few doors and windows and are clustered together to combat the cold, the wind coming off the sea and possible attacks by Aboriginal or the British. These buildings fall into the medieval tradition, with their high–boarded roofs, and their massive chimneys made of big stones, and are gathered in the surrounding fields. A palisade ran

along one edge of the site, so that the men could safely leave the central courtyard to watch out for the enemy. The peasants who worked the surrounding land lived in hovels with walls made of posts planted straight into the ground instead of foundations. The only stone portion of these structures was a central hearth.

The 18th century saw the emergence of much more substantial buildings. The French, after losing part of Acadia to the British in 1713, consolidated their position in their remaining territory along the coast. Meanwhile, the British wasted no time founding villages in Acadia, thus reinforcing their own hold. The French built the fortress of Louisbourg at the mouth of the Gulf of St. Lawrence. Much more than a simple fort, Louisbourg was a veritable fortified town with a large harbour. Begun under the French Regency, it was not completed until 1745. The Royal Treasury spent over three million livres on the project, the largest ever undertaken in New France. At its peak, in 1745, the town had some 10,000 inhabitants – 2,000 more than Québec City, the capital of the French colony. Vauban-style ramparts with bastions and baroque gates made of hewn stone hemmed in a town that was not just

Portrait

a cluster of half-timbered houses; it had some prestigious buildings, like the king's barracks, a long rectangle of rubble stone and French bricks in the spirit of Louis XV. Unfortunately, Louisbourg was destroyed by the English army during the French and Indian War (or Seven Years' War). Thanks to archaeological excavations begun in 1960, a portion of the fortress has been reconstructed and is now open to the public (see p 195).

To counterbalance Louisbourg, the British founded Halifax in 1749. Right from its first few years of existence, its civilian architecture was far more impressive than its meagre fortifications, thus conveying the confidence and strength of the British colonies, who had little fear of the feeble flotillas sent out by the French. The landscape was dominated by several white, wooden, Georgian-style churches similar to those already scattered across New England. These buildings are as elegant as they are simple. St. Paul Church in Halifax, built in 1750, is representative of this era (see p 135). The comfortable houses, for their part, all had sash windows subdivided into little squares.

With the massive influx of Loyalists in 1783, the population of the mainland maritime territories doubled. These new arrivals, who came from urban areas, sought to refine the local architecture even further, by adorning the facades with Palladian decorations made of carved wood, for example. Palladian windows (a central arched window with a small, rectangular window on either side) are definitely the most characteristic feature of this style, known as the Federal Style in the United States. St. George's, in Halifax, built between 1800 and 1827, is one of the most original buildings of this period.

In the early 19th century, the region's economic prosperity, accompanied by a demographic and political weight it has since lost, led to the construction of huge public and government buildings with freestone facades.

Province House, in Halifax (Nova Scotia) and Government House, in Charlottetown (Prince Edward Island) are among the handsomest buildings from this era in Canadian history. These edifices, which would belong in Dublin or Edinburgh, feature a harmonious blend of Georgian, Palladian and neoclassical styles. During this same period, wealthy shipowners and ship's captains built luxurious houses in the countryside (Prescott House Museum in Starrs Point, Nova Scotia, see p 162).

Isolated Newfoundland marched to its own beat. Ill-suited to farming, its territory remained largely uninhabited, with only a few fishing villages founded by Irish immigrants punctuating its rocky shores. The first stone houses here, topped by gambrel roofs covered with bluish slate, are reminiscent of those of the Emerald Isle.

Province House – Halifax

In 1830, after a brief period of economic diversification, the Maritimes turned once and for all toward the sea and its resources, leading to the emergence of a vernacular architecture that reflected the region's close ties to the Atlantic Ocean. Wooden fishing shacks covered with cedar shingles or clapboard sprang up along the beaches. These buildings often stood on piles made out of tree trunks, which are pounded by the surf at high tide. Lighthouses shaped like truncated pyramids were built on the capes to help cope with the rise in maritime traffic. These high towers covered with white clapboards punctuate the shoreline from the U.S. border to southern Labrador.

Finally, the attics of houses were modified to accommodate bow windows and wide dormer windows shaped like triptychs. The widow's walk – a railed rooftop platform – also became a fairly common feature. These modifications made it easier for local residents to observe the comings and goings of the boats. The lady of the house would thus know if her husband, the captain, would be home for dinner or not.

In the second half of the 19th century, Victorian architecture quickly came into fashion in towns inhabited by recent British immigrants. These people's affection for their beloved Albion was reflected in their choice of styles and architects. Gothic Revival was the style par excellence for churches, as evidenced so beautifully by Christ Church Cathedral (1853) in Fredericton, New Brunswick (see p 57), with its ogival arches and tall steeple atop its transept. It was designed by Frank Wills, a native of Salisbury, England, and is not unlike the cathedral of the same name he designed for the Anglican community of Montréal.

Christ Church Cathedral

The Anglican Cathedral of St. John's, Newfoundland, for its part, is in a class of its own, having been designed by the celebrated English architect Sir George Gilbert Scott, whose many other credits include the Albert Memorial and the Foreign Office, both in London.

The Renaissance Revival style managed to hold its own in the company of all these impressive Gothic Revival buildings. The projecting cornices, varied rustications and little columns adorning many of the commercial buildings in St. John, New Brunswick and Halifax, Nova Scotia (the Historic Properties, see p 136). The Second Empire style, for its part, was used to lend a certain Parisian chic to mansions in wealthy neighbourhoods. Their mansard roofs, topped with wrought- or cast-iron ornamentation, are visible between the stately trees lining the peaceful streets of Fredericton, New Brunswick and Charlottetown, Prince Edward Island.

The influence of the late 19th-century institutional architecture of Québec is clearly evident in those areas inhabited by Acadians – mainly in the northern part of New Brunswick. The rusticated limestone facing of the colleges, the silvery steeples of the churches and the wraparound

Portrait

porches of the presbyteries are the major distinguishing features of this kind of architecture. Around the same time, the Nova Scotians of Cape Breton Island were importing a style of architecture with a strong Scottish flavour, characterized by red and beige sandstone facing, stepped gables and fanciful gargoyles.

As the 19th century marched on, American architecture gained more and more ground in the Atlantic provinces. The designs of Downing and Davis, published in the middle of the century, inspired more than one builder. These catalogs prompted homeowners to adopt the tastes of Midwestern Americans, adorning their cornices and verandas with charming, lacy woodwork of medieval or Italian inspiration.

It should be noted that Atlantic Canada (New Brunswick, Nova Scotia and Prince Edward Island) was attracting more and more summer visitors from both the United States and from the other Canadian provinces.

Starting in 1880, the region saw the emergence of architecture modelled on the seaside resorts along the east coast of the United States. St. Andrews by-the-Sea (New Brunswick) and Summerside (Prince Edward Island) boast the finest examples. These villages suddenly found themselves graced with huge wooden summer homes in the Queen Anne, Shingle or Stick style, designed by Montréal architects like brothers Edward and William S. Maxwell or local architects like William Crithlow Harris. These houses had multiple gables and wide, wraparound porches that served as additional rooms during warm weather.

The harsh climate of Newfoundland, however, did not attract summer vacationers. Furthermore, the islanders had to be quite creative in their efforts to protect themselves from the wind and cold. They designed easy-to-build, cube-shaped houses, which were covered with multicoloured clapboards.

Most of these houses were built right up against the sidewalk. Some have bow-windows, lending the windy, sloping streets of St. John's a friendly air.

The first half of the 20th century was a difficult period for all the Atlantic provinces, which no longer saw the sort of large-scale development taking place elsewhere in Canada. Still, a few significant Tudor Revival (the Algonquin Resort in St. Andrews-by-the-Sea, New Brunswick), Arts and Crafts (the Hydrostone quarter in Halifax, Nova Scotia), and Art Deco (John M. Lyle's Bank of Nova Scotia in Halifax) buildings were erected during this time.

Between 1960 and 1980, a massive investment of provincial and federal funds, combined with a profound malaise induced by the success of big Canadian cities like Montréal and Toronto, led the region to squander its precious architectural heritage.

Algonquin Resort

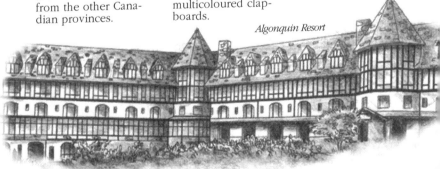

Many old buildings were replaced by nondescript modern structures designed to house regional branches of companies whose real interests lay elsewhere. Fortunately, this trend started to reverse itself in 1980, as residents of the Maritimes started to become aware of the treasure they possessed in their old architecture. Since then, the focus has been on smaller-scale projects that can be integrated into the existing framework. Some of the finest examples of this new approach are Market Square in St. John, New Brunswick, and the Historic Properties in Nova Scotia.

Arts and Culture

Over the years, the three Maritime provinces have established prestigious institutions in order to encourage local artistic expression and promote greater public awareness of the arts. Thanks to the patronage of Lord Beaverbrook in 1958, Fredericton was endowed with the remarkable Beaverbrook Art Gallery, which houses the works of some of the greatest artists from the Maritimes, as well as from elsewhere in Canada and abroad. Particularly noteworthy is an impressive painting by Salvador Dalí. Fredericton also has a theatre, where the excellent New Brunswick Theatre Company performs regularly.

In 1984, the Confederation Arts Centre, a large arts complex made up of theatres, an art gallery and a public library, was inaugurated in Charlottetown, the capital of Prince Edward Island. Concerts, plays and dance productions are presented here, and a number of works by local and national artists, including portrait artist Robert Harris, are exhibited in the gallery. In 1975, the Nova Scotia Art Gallery, which houses the most impressive art collection in the Maritimes, was founded in Halifax. The city also boasts the Neptune Theatre and a symphony orchestra. The Maritimes have produced many artists, one of the most illustrious being the painter Alex Colville. Lucy Maud Montgomery, author of *Anne of Green Gables*, is undoubtedly the most widely renowned of local writers. Most of her stories take place on Prince Edward Island, where she was born.

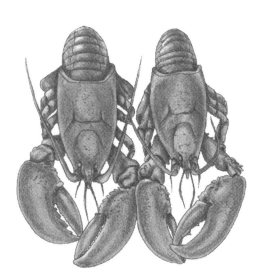

Table of Distances (km)
Via the Shortest Route

© ULYSSES

	Augusta (Maine)	Charlottetown (P.E.I.)	Corner Brook (Nfld)	Edmundston (N.B.)	Fredericton (N.B.)	Halifax (N.S.)	Labrador City (Nfld.)	Moncton (N.B.)	Montréal (Que.)	Québec (Que.)	St. Anthony (Nfld.)	Saint John (N.B.)	St. John's (Nfld.)	Souris (P.E.I.)	Summerside (P.E.I.)	Sydney (N.S.)
Charlottetown (P.E.I.)	820															
Corner Brook (Nfld)	1530	772														
Edmundston (N.B.)	520	676	1389													
Fredericton (N.B.)	434	373	1095	289												
Halifax (N.S.)	904	280	835	760	415											
Labrador City (Nfld.)	1454	1345	2055	944	12234	2240										
Moncton (N.B.)	622	175	901	475	200	275	1153									
Montréal (Que.)	484	1200	1916	540	835	1250	1284	1025								
Québec (Que.)	352	960	1694	313	585	982	1062	785	270/162							
St. Anthony (Nfld.)	1989	1231	468	1850	1554	629	2513	1359	2375	2153						
Saint John (N.B.)	402	344	1054	400	111	315	1334	146	931	709	1512					
St. John's (Nfld.)	1715	957	687	1572	1281	1020	2240	1086	2101	1879	629	1239				
Souris (P.E.I.)	898	77	795	755	463	288	1422	268	1284	1062	1253	421	980			
Summerside (P.E.I.)	785	78	849	639	350	325	1310	156	1171	949	1308	308	1034	154		
Sydney (N.S.)	1152	367	429	1008	695	422	1676	497	1520	1280	888	675	614	416	476	
Yarmouth (N.S.)	363	574	1144	577	288	344	1511	323	711	606	1602	177	1329	597	486	766

Example: the distance between Halifax (NS) and St. John (NB) is 315 km.

Practical Information

Information in this chapter will help visitors better plan their trip to Canada's Atlantic provinces.

Entrance Formalities

Passport

A valid passport is usually sufficient for most visitors planning to stay less than three months in Canada; visas are not required. American residents do not need a passport, but it is, however, a good form of identification. A three-month extension is possible, but a return ticket and proof of sufficient funds to cover this extension may be required.

Note: some countries do not have an agreement with Canada concerning health and accident insurance, so it is advisable to have the appropriate coverage. For more information, see the section entitled "Health" on page 37.

Extended Visits

Visitors must submit a request **in writing** to extend their visit and **before** the expiration of the first three months of their visit or of their visa (the date is usually written in your passport) to an Immigration Canada office. To make a request you must have a valid passport, a return ticket, proof of sufficient funds to cover the stay, as well as the $65 non-refundable filing-fee. In some cases (work, study), however, the request must be made **before** arriving in Canada.

Customs

If you are bringing gifts into Canada, remember that certain restrictions apply:

Smokers (minimum age is 16) can bring in a maximum of 200 cigarettes, 50 cigars, 400 of tobacco, and 400 tobacco sticks.

Wine and alcohol: the limit is 1.1 litres; in practice, however, two bottles per person are usually allowed. The limit for beer is 24 cans or bottles, the 355 ml size.

Plants, vegetation, and food: there are very strict rules regarding the importation of plants, flowers, and other vegetation; it is therefore not advisable to bring any of these types of products into the country. If it is absolutely necessary, contact the Customs-Agriculture service of the Canadian embassy **before** leaving.

Pets: if you are travelling with your pet, you will need a health certificate (available from your veterinarian) as well as a rabies vaccination certificate. It is important to remember that the vaccination must be carried out **at least** 30 days **before** your departure and should not have been administered more than one year ago.

Tax reimbursements for visitors: it is possible to get reimbursed for certain taxes paid on purchases made while in Atlantic Canada (see p 35).

Embassies and Consulates

Canadian Embassies and Consulates Abroad

AUSTRALIA
Canadian Consulate General
Level 5, Quay West, 111 Harrington Rd., Sydney, N.S.W. Australia 2000
☎ *(61) 2364-3000*
⇒ *(61) 2364-3098*

BELGIUM
Canadian Embassy
2 Ave. de Tervueren
1040 Brussels
(Métro Mérode)
☎ *(2) 741.06.11*
⇒ *(2) 741.06.19*

DENMARK
Canadian Embassy
Kr. Bernikowsgade 1, DK=1105 Copenhagen K, Denmark
☎ *(45) 12.22.99*
⇒ *(45) 14.05.85*

FINLAND
Canadian Embassy
Pohjos Esplanadi 25 B, 00100 Helsinki, Finland
☎ *(9) 171-141*
⇒ *(9) 601-060*

GERMANY
Canadian Consulate General
Internationales Handelszentrum
Friedrichstrasse 95, 23rd floor
10117 Berlin, Germany
☎ *(30) 261.11.61*
⇒ *(30) 262.92.06*

GREAT BRITAIN
Canada High Commission
Macdonald House, One Grosvenor Sq., London
W1X 0AB, England
☎ *(171) 258-6600*
⇒ *(171) 258-6384*

ITALY
Canadian Embassy
Via Zara 30, 00198 Rome
☎ *(6) 44.59.81*
⇒ *(6) 44.59.87*

NETHERLANDS
Canadian Embassy
Parkstraat 25, 2514JD
The Hague, Netherlands
☎ *(70) 361-4111*
⇒ *(70) 365-6283*

NORWAY
Canadian Embassy
Oscars Gate 20, Oslo 3, Norway
☎ *(47) 46.69.55*
⇒ *(47) 69.34.67*

PORTUGAL
Canadian Embassy
MCB Buildin, Avenida Liberdade no. 144, 2nd and 3rd floors
1200 Lisboa
☎ *213474892*
⇒ *213476466*

SPAIN
Canadian Embassy
Edificio Goya, Calle Nunez de Balboa 35, 28001 Madrid
☎ *(1) 423.32.50*
⇒ *(1) 423.32.51*

SWEDEN
Canadian Embassy
Tegelbacken 4, 7th floor
Stockholm, Sweden
☎ *(8) 613-9900*
⇒ *(8) 24.24.91*

SWITZERLAND
Canadian Embassy
Kirchenfeldstrasse 88
3000 Berne 6
☎ *(31) 357.32.00*
⇒ *(31) 357.32.10*

UNITED STATES
Canadian Embassy
501 Pennsylvania Ave. NW
Washington, DC, 20001
☎ *(202) 682-1740*
⇒ *(202) 682-7726*

Canadian Consulate General
Suite 400 South Tower
One CNN Center, Atlanta
Georgia, 30303-2705
☎(404) 577-6810
☎(404) 577-1512
⇌(404) 524-5046

Canadian Consulate General
Three Copley Pl., Suite 400
Boston, Massachusetts, 02116
☎(617) 262-3760
⇌(617) 262-3415

Canadian Consulate General
Two Prudential Plaza, 180 N.
Stetson Ave., Suite 2400, Chicago, Illinois, 60601
☎(312) 616-1860
⇌(312) 616-1877

Canadian Consulate General
St. Paul Place, Suite 1700
750 N. St. Paul St.
Dallas, Texas, 75201
☎(214) 922-9806
⇌(214) 922-9815

Canadian Consulate General
600 Renaissance Center
Suite 1100, Detroit, Michigan
48234-1798
☎(313) 567-2085
⇌(313) 567-2164

Canadian Consulate General
300 South Grande Ave.
10th floor, California Plaza
Los Angeles, California, 90071
☎(213) 687-7432
⇌(213) 620-8827

Canadian Consulate General
Suite 900, 701 Fourth Ave.
South, Minneapolis, Minnesota
55415-1899
☎(612) 333-4641
⇌(612) 332-4061

Canadian Consulate General
1251 Ave. of the Americas, New York, NY, 10020-1175
☎(212) 596-1600
⇌(212) 596-1793

Canadian Consulate General
One Marine Midland Center
Suite 3000, Buffalo, New York
14203-2884
☎(716) 852-1247
⇌(716) 852-4340

Canadian Consulate General
412 Plaza 600, Sixth and Stewart Streets, Seattle, Washington
98101-1286
☎(206) 442-1777
⇌(206) 443-1782

Foreign Consulates in Atlantic Canada

Not all countries are represented in the Atlantic provinces. Those that are not generally have offices in Montréal, Toronto or Ottawa.

AUSTRALIA
Australian High Commission
50 O'Connor St., Ottawa Ontario, K1N 5R2
☎(613) 236-0841
⇌(613) 236-4376

BELGIUM
Honourary Consulate
1050 Bellevue Ave., Halifax
Nova Scotia, B3H 3L9
☎(902) 468-1030

DENMARK
Consulate General
One Pl.-Ville-Marie, 35th floor
Montréal, H3B 4M4
☎(514) 877-3060

FINLAND
Consulate General
800 Carré Victoria, Suite 3400
Montréal, H4Z 1A1
☎(514) 397-7437

GERMANY
Honourary Consulate
22 Poplar Ave., St John's, NF
A1B 1C8
☎(709) 753-7777
⇌(709) 739-6666

GREAT BRITAIN
Consulate General
1000 de la Gauchetiere
Suite 4200, Montreal, QC
H3B 4W5
☎(514) 866-5863

ITALY
Consulate General
496 Huron St., Toronto, ON
M5R 2R3
☎(416) 921-3802
⇌(416) 962-2503

NETHERLANDS
Consulate General
1002 Rue Sherbrooke O.
Suite 2201, Montréal, QC
H3A 3L6
☎(514) 849-4247
⇌(514) 849-8260

NORWAY
Consulate General
1155 Boul. René-Lévesque O.
Suite 3900, Montréal H3B 3V2
☎(514) 874-9087

SPAIN
Consulate General
One Westmount Sq., Suite 1546
Montréal, QC., H3Z 2P9
☎(514) 935-5235
⇌(514) 935-4655

SWEDEN
Consulate General
800 Carré Victoria, 34th floor
box 242, Montréal, QC
H4Z 1E9
☎(514) 866-4019

Practical Information

SWITZERLAND
Consulate General
1572 Ave. Dr Penfield
Montréal H3G 1C4
☎*(514) 985-0666*
⇋*(514) 932-9028*

UNITED STATES
Consulate General
Suite 910, Cogswell Tower
Scotia Square, 200 Barrington
St., Halifax, NS., B3J 3K1
☎*(902) 429-2480*

Tourist Information

This guide covers four distinct regions: New Brunswick (N.B.), Nova Scotia (N.S.), Prince Edward Island (P.E.I.) and Newfoundland (Nfld.). Within each province you will find tourist information offices which can provide brochures concerning attractions, restaurants and hotels. You can also pick up listings of bed and breakfasts in the area.

Information is available by mail for these three provinces by writing to the following addresses:

New Brunswick

Department of Economic Development and Tourism
P.O. Box 6000, Fifth floor Centennial Bldg., Fredericton E3B 5H1
☎*(506) 453-3984*
⇋*(506) 444-4586*

Nova Scotia

Department of Tourism and Culture
World Trade Centre, Sixth floor
P.O. Box 456, 1800 Argyle St.
Halifax, B3J 2R5
☎*(902) 424-5000*

Prince Edward Island

Department of Tourism
P.O. Box 2000, Charlottetown C1A 7N8
☎*(902) 368-6410*
⇋*(902) 368-5277*

Tourist information on the Internet

about New Brunswick
www.gov.nb.ca

about Nova Scotia
www.gov.ns.ca

www.tians.org (Nova Scotia Bed & Breakfast Association)

about Prince Edward Island
www.gov.pe.ca
www.peiplay.com

about Newfoundland
www.gov.nf.ca

On the National Parks of Canada
http://parkscanada.pch.gc.ca

Newfoundland

Department of Tourism
P.O. Box 8700, St. John's A1B 4J6
☎*800-563-6353*

Finding Your Way Around

By Plane

European visitors will arrive in the Atlantic provinces in Halifax, since it is the only airport that regularly receives international flights; in New Brunswick, Prince Edward Island and Newfoundland, the airports occasionally receive flights from the United States. **Iceland Air** also offers direct flights from Reykjavik. **American Airlines** (☎*800-433-7300*) offer flights through Montréal to Halifax, (N.S.) while **Delta Airlines** (☎*800-221-1212*) offer direct flights from Boston to Halifax (N.S.), with connections to St. John (N.B.). Charter flights to Montréal, and then a Montréal-Halifax flight can be cheaper. It is strongly recommended to compare prices several weeks before your departure.

Air Canada offers direct flights from London, England, to Halifax and from Newark, New Jersey, to Halifax. Otherwise European and American travellers must stop-over in Montréal or Toronto.

From Montréal, Air Canada and its partner **Air Nova** offer direct flights to Halifax (N.S.), Fredericton (N.B.), Moncton (N.B.) and Saint John (N.B.), and a flight with a stop-over for Charlottetown (P.E.I.). For information: ☎800-361-8620.

Canadian does not offer direct flights between Atlantic Canada and Europe. European travellers must stop-over in Montréal or Toronto. From Montréal, Canadian and its partner **Air Atlantic** offer direct flights to Halifax (N.S.), Fredericton (N.B.), Moncton (N.B.) and Saint John (N.B.), and a flight with a stop-over for Charlottetown (P.E.I.) and St. John's (Nfld.). For information: ☎800-426-7000.

For more information:

Air Canada
☎800-222-6596

American Airlines
☎800-433-7300

British Airways
☎888-334-3448

Canadian International
☎800-665-1177

Continental Airlines
☎800-231-0856

Delta Airlines
☎800-221-1212

Japan Airlines
☎800-525-3663

KLM Royal Dutch
☎800-361-1887

Lufthansa German Airlines
☎800-563-5954

Northwest Airlines
☎800-225-2525

Quantas Airways
☎800-227-4500

US Airways
☎800-428-4322

Inter-Provincial Flights

Flying within the Atlantic Provinces is by far the most expensive mode of transportation; however, some airline companies, especially the regional ones, regularly offer special rates (off season, short stays). Once again, it is wise to shop around and compare prices.

Airports

Nova Scotia

Halifax International Airport
40 km north of the city
Rte. 102, Exit 6
☎(902) 873-2091

The Halifax airport is the largest airport in the Atlantic provinces. There is an exchange office open everyday from 6am to 9pm. Six car-rental companies have offices in the airport. Taxis and limousines offer transportation to downtown for about $30. A shuttle bus makes the trip from the airport to downtown about once an hour ($11). The airport is mostly served by Air

Canada-Air Nova (☎429-7111) and by Canadian-Air Atlantic (☎427-5500)

Sydney Airport
PO Box 670
Sydney, Nova Scotia
B1P 6h7
☎(902) 564-7720
≈(902) 564-2726

The Sydney Airport is another entry point to Atlantic Canada from Europe. Four scheduled air carriers – Air Nova, Air Atlantic, Royal Airlines and Air St. Pierre – fly in and out of Sydney as do two charter operations: Provincial Airlines and Prince Edward Air.

New Brunswick

Fredericton Airport
16 km from the city
Lincoln Rd.
☎(506) 444-6202

The Fredericton airport does not have an exchange office. Four car-rental companies have offices here. Taxis offer transportation to downtown. The airport is mostly served by Air Canada-Air Nova (☎458-8561) and by Canadian-Air Atlantic (☎458-4089).

Moncton Airport
12 km east of the city
Champlain St., Dieppe
☎(506) 851-2200

The Moncton airport does not have an exchange office. Four car rental companies have offices here. Taxis offer transportation to downtown for less than $10.

Practical Information

The airport is mostly served by Air Canada-Air Nova (☎857-1044) and by Canadian-Air Atlantic (☎857-0620).

Saint John Airport
4180 Loch Lemond
☎(506) 636-3950

The Saint John airport does not have an exchange office. Five car-rental companies have offices here. Taxis offer transportation to downtown for less than $10. The airport is mostly served by Air Canada - Air Nova (☎652-1517) and by Canadian - Air Atlantic (☎696-2630).

Prince Edward Island

Charlottetown Airport
Sherwood
☎(902) 566-7992

The Charlottetown airport does not have an exchange office. Four car-rental companies have offices here. Taxis offer transportation to downtown for less than $10. The airport is mostly served by Air Canada - Air Nova (☎894-8825) and by Canadian - Air Atlantic (☎892-5358).

Newfoundland

St. John's has the largest airport in the province, located 6km from downtown. There are regular direct flights between St. John's and some of the major Canadian cities such as Halifax, Montréal and Toronto, among others.

The two main airline companies servicing the island are Air Canada with its partner, Air Nova (☎800-463-8620) as well as Canadian Airlines and its partner, Air Atlantic (☎709-576-0274).

By Car

Considering the large distances to be covered and lack of good public transportation systems, the easiest way to tour the Atlantic provinces is by car. Also, the roads are generally in good condition.

Things to Consider

Driver's License: As a general rule, foreign driver's licenses are valid for six months from the arrival date in Canada.

Pedestrians: Drivers in the Atlantic provinces are very respectful of pedestrians, and willingly stop to give them the right of way even in the big cities. Crosswalks are usually indicated by a yellow sign. When driving, pay special attention that there is no one about to cross near these signs.

Turning **right on a red** when the way is clear is permitted in the Atlantic provinces.

When a **school bus** (usually yellow in colour) has stopped and has its signals flashing, you must come to a complete stop, no matter

what direction you are travelling in. Failing to stop at the flashing signals is considered a serious offense, and carries a heavy penalty.

Wearing of **seatbelts** in the front and back seats is mandatory at all times.

There are no **tolls** on highways in Atlantic Canada. There is an occasional toll for bridges.

The **speed limit** on highways is 100km/h. The speed limit on secondary highways is 90km/h, and 50km/h in urban areas.

Gas Stations: Because Canada produces its own crude oil, gasoline prices are less expensive than in Europe. However, due to hidden taxes, gas prices are considerably higher than those in the United States and in Western Canada. Some gas stations (especially in the downtown areas) might ask for payment in advance as a security measure, especially after 11pm.

Car Rentals

The best way to get a good price for car rental is to reserve well in advance. Many travel agencies have agreements with the major car-rental companies (Avis, Budget, Hertz, etc.) and offer good values; contracts often include added bonuses (reduced ticket prices for shows, etc.).

When renting a car, find out if the contract includes unlimited kilometres, and check that the insurance provides full coverage (accident, property damage, hospital costs for you and passengers, theft).

Note: To rent a car you must be at least 21 years of age and have had a driver's license for **at least** one year. If you are between 21 and 25, certain companies (for example Avis, Thrifty, Budget) will ask for a $500 deposit, and in some cases they will also charge an extra sum for each day you rent the car. These conditions do not apply for those over 25 years of age.

A credit card is extremely useful for the deposit to avoid tying up large sums of money, and can in some cases (gold cards) cover the collision and theft insurance.

Most rental cars come with an automatic transmission, however you can request a car with a manual shift.

Child safety seats cost extra.

Accidents and Emergencies

If you run into trouble on the highway, pull onto the shoulder of the road and turn the hazard lights on. If it is a rental car, contact the rental company as soon as possible. Always file an accident report. If a disagreement arises over who was at fault in an accident, ask for police help.

If you are a member of an automobile association (Canada: Canadian Automobile Association; U.S.A.: American Automobile Association; Switzerland: Automobile Club de Suisse; Belgium: Royal Automobile Touring Club de Belgique; Great-Britain: Automobile Association; Australia: Royal Australian Automobile Association), you have access to some free services provided in Canada by the C.A.A.

By Bus

Besides the car, travelling by bus is the best way to get around. Buses cover most of the major routes and highways of the Atlantic provinces and are relatively inexpensive. Except for public transportation, there is no government run service; several companies service the region.

Smoking is forbidden on almost all lines. Pets are not allowed. Generally, children five years old or younger travel for free and seniors and students are eligible for discounts.

By Train

Travelling by train is not always the cheapest way to get around, however it is a comfortable alternative for long distances. VIA Rail Canada offers trips east to New Brunswick and Nova Scotia. A few years ago passenger train travel in Prince Edward Island became a thing of the past. The only way to get around the island these days is by bus or car.

When coming from the United States, your best option is to take Amtrak to Montréal and then VIA Rail to the Maritimes since Amtrak does not provide service through Maine. Make your reservations through a travel agent that can reserve with both companies.

Travel Times

Montréal-Halifax
20hrs
Moncton-Halifax
5hrs
Toronto-Halifax
25hrs

Ferries

The biggest ferry company in the Atlantic provinces is **Marine Atlantic** (☎800-341-7981). To reach Newfoundland, many crossings are possible: North-Sydney (Cape Breton Island, N.S.) to Port-aux-Basques (Nfld.); North-Sydney to Argentia

Practical Information

(Nfld.); Goose Bay (Labrador) to Lewisporte (Nfld.). For Nova Scotia, certain crossings greatly cut down on driving time: Saint John (N.B.) to Digby (N.S.); Bar Harbour (Maine, U.S.A.) to Yarmouth (N.S.); Portland (Maine, U.S.A.) to Yarmouth (N.S.). Since the construction of the Confederation Bridge in 1997, there is no more ferry service between Cape Tourmentine (N.B.) and Borden (P.E.I.); however, there is service to the Wood Islands (P.E.I.) from Pictou (N.S.).

Bicycling

Bicycling is very popular and is a great way to see the countryside. Tranquil backroads are numerous in each province but caution is always advised, even on these quiet roads.

Hitchhiking

Hitchhiking is common, especially in the summer, and much easier outside the big centres. Nevertheless do not forget that hitchhiking is actually illegal on the highways.

Money and Banking

Currency

The monetary unit is the dollar ($), which is divided into cents (¢). One dollar=100 cents.

Bills come in 5, 10, 20, 50, 100, 500 and 1000 dollar denominations, and coins come in 1 (pennies), 5 (nickels), 10 (dimes), 25 (quarters) cent pieces and in 1 (loonies) and 2 (twoonies) dollar coins.

Exchange

Most banks readily exchange U.S. and European currencies but almost all will charge **commission**. There are, however, exchange offices that do not charge commissions and have longer hours. Just remember to **ask about fees** and **to compare rates**.

Traveller's Cheques

Traveller's cheques are accepted in most large stores and hotels, however, it is easier and to your advantage to change your cheques at an exchange office. For a better exchange rate buy your traveller's cheques in Canadian dollars before leaving.

Credit Cards

Most major credit cards are accepted at stores, restaurants and hotels. While the main advantage of credit cards is that they allow visitors to avoid carrying large sums of money, using a credit card also makes leaving a deposit for car rental much easier; some cards, gold cards for example, automatically insure you when you rent a car (check with your credit card company to see what coverage it provides). In addition, the exchange rate with a credit card is generally better. The most commonly accepted credit cards are Visa, Master Card, and American Express.

Banks

Banks can be found almost everywhere and most offer the standard services to tourists. Visitors who choose to stay in Canada for a long period of time should note that **nonresidents** cannot open bank accounts. If this is the case, the best way to have money readily available is to use traveller's cheques. Withdrawing money from foreign accounts is expensive. However, several automatic teller machines accept foreign bank cards, so that you can withdraw directly from your account. Money orders are another means of having money sent from abroad. No commission is charged but it takes time. People who have residence status, permanent or not (such as landed-immigrants, students), can open a bank account. A passport and proof of residence status are required.

Exchange Rates

$1 CAN	=	$0.68 US	$1 US	=	$1.45 CAN
$1 CAN	=	0.43 £	1£	=	$2.29 CAN
$1 CAN	=	$1.13 Aust	$1 Aust	=	$0.88 CAN
$1 CAN	=	$1.41 NZ	$1 NZ	=	$0.71 CAN
$1 CAN	=	$0.71 EURO	$1 EURO	=	$1.40 CAN
$1 CAN	=	1.57 fl.	1 fl.	=	$0.64 CAN
$1 CAN	=	1.14 SF	1 SF	=	$0.87 CAN
$1 CAN	=	118 BF	10 BF	=	$0.37 CAN
$1 CAN	=	1.39 DM	1 DM	=	$0.71 CAN
$1 CAN	=	118 PTA	100 ITL	=	$0.84 CAN
$1 CAN	=	1376 ITL	1000 PTA	=	$0.73 CAN

Practical Information

Taxes and Tipping

Taxes

The ticket price on items usually **does not include tax**. There are two taxes, the G.S.T., federal Goods and Services Tax, of 7 % and the P.S.T., Provincial Sales Tax (New Brunswick, 11%; Nova Scotia, 11%; and Prince Edward Island, 10%; Newfoundland and Labrador 12%). You must therefore add between 17 and 19% to the price of most items and to restaurant and hotel prices.

Some exceptions to this taxation system are books, which are only taxed 7% and food (except for ready-made meals), which is not taxed at all.

Tax Refunds

Non-residents can obtain refunds for the tax paid on purchases. To obtain a refund, it is important to keep your receipts. Refunds are made at the border or by filling out and returning a special form.

For information, call: ☎800-668-4748.

Tipping

In general, tipping applies to all service at a table: restaurants, bars and nightclubs (therefore no tipping in fast-food restaurants). Tips are also given in taxis and in hair salons.

The tip is usually about 15 % of the bill before taxes, but varies, of course, depending on the quality of service.

Business Hours and Public Holidays

Business Hours

Stores

The law respecting business hours allows stores to be open the following hours:

Mon to Fri
10am to 6pm
Thu and Fri
10am to 9pm
Sat
9am or 10am to 5pm
Sun
noon to 5pm

Well-stocked convenience stores that sell food are found throughout the Atlantic provinces and are open later, sometimes 24hrs a day.

Banks

Banks are open Monday to Friday from 10am to 3pm. Most are open on Thursdays and Fridays, until 6pm or even 8pm. Automatic teller machines are widely available and are open night and day.

Post Offices

Large post offices are open from 9am to 5pm. There are several smaller post offices throughout Eastern Canada located in shopping malls, convenience stores, and even pharmacies; these post offices are open much later than the larger ones.

Holidays and Public Holidays

The following are public holidays in Atlantic Canada. Most administrative offices and banks are closed on these days.

New Year's Day
January 1

Easter Monday

Victoria Day
3rd Monday in May

Canada Day
July 1

Labour Day
1st Monday in September

Thanksgiving
2nd Monday in October

Remembrance Day
November 11; only banks and federal government services are closed

Christmas
December 25

Boxing Day
December 26

Time Difference

Atlantic Canada spans two time zones: Atlantic Standard Time, which is four hours behind Greenwich Mean Time, and Newfoundland time, which is three and a half hours behind GMT and which is only observed on the island of Newfoundland. When it is noon in Montreal and New York City it is 1pm in Halifax, Moncton and Charlottetown and 1:30pm in St. John's.

Climate and Clothing

Climate

The sea air makes for milder temperatures, especially close to the Bay of Fundy which is warmed by the Gulf Stream. Temperature ranges are however quite significant. Summer temperatures are around 25°C, and in the winter around -2°C. Temperatures vary on the coasts where it is colder in summer and winter. Finally the coasts are often shrouded by a thick fog, especially along the Bay of Fundy and in Newfoundland.

Winter

From December to March is the best season for skiing, snowmobiling, skating, snowshoeing and other winter sports. Temperatures remain low, and warm clothing (coats, scarves, hats, gloves or mittens, wool sweaters and boots) is a neccessity. On the coast, it remains quite humid in winter.

Spring and Fall

Spring is short, lasting roughly from the end of March to the end of May. Everything thaws and streets are often slushy. In fall, it's time to watch the colours change. it can get quite cool in both these seasons so be sure to pack a sweater, scarf, gloves, wind-breaker and an umbrella.

Summer

From the end of May to the end of August it can get very hot. Bring t-shirts, lightweight shirts and pants, shorts and sunglasses. A jacket or sweater will still come in handy in the evening. In certain regions of Atlantic Canada, notably near the Bay of Fundy, on the Atlantic coast of Nova Scotia and on the island of Newfoundland, rain and fog are frequent; an umbrella and raincoat are a good idea.

Health

Vaccinations are not necessary for people coming from Europe, the United States, Australia and New Zealand. On the other hand, it is strongly suggested, particularly for medium or long-term stays, that visitors take out health and accident insurance. There are different types so it is best to shop around. Bring along all medication, especially prescription medicine. Unless otherwise stated, the water is drinkable throughout Atlantic Canada.

In the winter, moisturizing lotion and lip balm are useful for people with sensitive skin, since the air in many buildings is very dry.

During the summer, always protect yourself against sunburn. It is often hard to feel your skin getting burned by the sun on windy days. Do not forget to bring sun screen!

Emergencies

The *911* emergency number is available throughout the Atlantic provinces.

Safety

There is far less violence in Atlantic Canada, compared to the United States. A genuine non-violence policy is advocated throughout the area.

By taking the normal precautions, there is no need to worry about your personal security. If trouble should arise, remember that *911* is the emergency telephone number.

Insurance

Cancellation Insurance

Your travel agent will usually offer you cancellation insurance when you buy your airline ticket or vacation package. This insurance allows you to be reimbursed for the ticket or package deal if your trip must be cancelled due to serious illness or death. Healthy people are unlikely to need this protection, which is therefore only of relative use.

Theft Insurance

Most residential insurance policies protect some of your goods from theft, even if the theft occurs in a foreign country. To make a claim, you must fill out a police report. It may

not be necessary to take out further insurance, depending on the amount covered by your current home policy. As policies vary considerably, you are advised to check with your insurance company. European visitors should take out baggage insurance.

Life Insurance

Several airline companies offer a life insurance plan included in the price of the airplane ticket. However, many travellers already have this type of insurance and do not require additional coverage.

Health Insurance

This is the most useful kind of insurance for travellers, and should be purchased before your departure. Your insurance plan should be as complete as possible because health care costs add up quickly. When buying insurance, make sure it covers all types of medical costs, such as hospitalization, nursing services and doctor's fees. Make sure your limit is high enough, as these expenses can be costly. A repatriation clause is also vital in case the required care is not available on site. Furthermore, since you may have to pay immediately, check your policy to see what provisions it includes for such situations. To avoid any problems during your vacation, always keep proof of your insurance policy on you.

Telecommunications

Local area codes are clearly indicated in the "Practical Information" section of each chapter. Dialling these codes is unnecessary if the call is local. For long distance calls, dial *1* for the United States and Canada, followed by the appropriate area code and the number. Phone numbers preceded by *800* or *888* allow you call without charge from Canada, and often from the United States as well. If you wish to contact an operator, dial *0*.

When calling abroad you can use a local operator and pay local phone rates. First dial *011* then the international country code and then the phone number.

Country Codes

United Kingdom	*44*
Ireland	*353*
Australia	*61*
New Zealand	*64*
Belgium	*32*
Switzerland	*41*
Italy	*39*
Spain	*34*
Netherlands	*31*
Germany	*49*

For example, to call the U.K., dial *011-44*, followed by the area code and the subscriber's number.

Another way to call abroad is by using the direct access numbers below to contact an operator in your home country.

United States
AT&T
☎*800-CALL ATT*
MCI
☎*800-888-8000*

British Telecom Direct
☎*800-408-6420*
☎*800-363-4144*

Australia Telstra Direct
☎*800-663-0683*

New Zealand Telecom Direct
☎*800-663-0684*

Considerably less expensive than in Europe, public phones are scattered throughout the city and are easy to use. Local calls cost $0.25 for unlimited time. For long distance calls, equip yourselves with quarters ($0.25 coins). It is now possible to pay by credit card or with a pre-paid calling card; take note, however, that these methods are more expensive.

Gay and Lesbian Life

In general, Canadians have an open and tolerant attitude towards homosexuality. Over the years, federal legis-

lation has updated laws concerning gay rights, reflecting favourable a public opinion.

However, in the Atlantic provinces, structured gay communities exist only in Halifax.

Exploring

Each chapter in this guide leads you through a region or province of Atlantic Canada, including major tourist attractions, followed by an historical and cultural description. Attractions are classified according to a star system, allowing you to quickly determine what are the must-sees.

★	Interesting
★★	Worth a visit
★★★	Not to be missed

The name of each attraction is followed by its address and phone number. Prices included are admission fees for one adult. It is best to make inquiries, for several places offer discounts for children, students, senior citizens and families. Several are only open during the summer. Even in the off-season, however, some of these places welcome groups upon request.

Accommodations

A wide choice of types of accommodation to fit every budget is available in most regions of Atlantic Canada. Most places are very comfortable and can offer a number of extra services. Prices vary according to the type of accommodation and the value for the money is generally good, but remember to add 15% tax. This tax is refundable for non-residents (see p 35). When reserving in advance, which is strongly recommended during the summer months, a credit card is indispensable for the deposit, as payment for the first night is often required.

Hotels

Hotels rooms abound in the Atlantic provinces, and range from modest to luxurious. Most hotel rooms come equipped with a private bathroom. Atlantic Canada has several internationally reputed hotels, four of them being part of the Canadian Pacific chain.

Inns

Often set up in beautiful historic houses, inns offer quality lodging. There are a lot of these establishments which are more charming and usually more picturesque than hotels. Many are furnished with beautiful period pieces. Breakfast is often included.

Bed and Breakfasts

Unlike hotels, rooms in private homes are not always equipped with a private bathroom. Bed and Breakfasts are found throughout Atlantic Canada, in the country as well as the city. Besides the obvious price advantage, is the unique family atmosphere. Credit cards are not always accepted in bed and breakfasts.

The following associations can arrange accommodation in a bed and breakfast:

New Brunswick

N.B. Bed & Breakfast Association
5662 King St., Riverside, Albert County, New Brunswick
E4H 4B1
☎ *(506) 882-2079*

Nova Scotia

N.S. Bed & Breakfast Association
1800 Argyle St., Suite 402 Halifax, B3J 3N8
☎ *(902) 423-4480*
☎ *800-948-4267*

Prince Edward Island

Visitors' Services P.E.I.
Box 940, Charlottetown, P.E.I.
C1A 7N5
☎ *(902) 368-4444*
☎ *800-565-0267*

Motels

There are many motels throughout the prov-

inces, and though they tend to be cheaper they are also lacking in atmosphere. These are particularly useful when pressed for time.

Youth Hostels

Youth hostel addresses are listed in the "Accommodations" section for the cities in which they are located.

University Residences

Due to certain restrictions, this can be a complicated alternative. Residences are only available during the summer (mid-May to mid-August); reservations must be made several months in advance, usually by paying the first night with a credit card.

However, this type of accommodation is less costly than the "traditional" alternatives, and making the effort to reserve early can be worthwhile. Visitors with valid student cards can expect to pay approximately $25 plus tax. Bedding is included in the price, and there is usually a cafeteria in the building (meals are not included in the price).

Camping

Next to staying with friends, camping is the most inexpensive form of accommodation.

Practical Information

Unfortunately, unless you have winter-camping gear, camping is limited to a short period of the year, from June to August. Services provided and prices vary considerably, from $8 to $20 or more per night, depending on whether the site is private or public.

Restaurants

There are several excellent restaurants in Atlantic Canada. The big specialty is without a doubt fish and seafood, notably lobster.

Prices in this guide are for a meal for one person, **before taxes and tip** (See "Taxes and Tipping", p 35).

$	$10 or less
$$	$10 to $20
$$$	$20 to $30
$$$$	$30 or more

These prices are often based on the cost of set dinner menus, but remember that lunchtime meals are often considerably less expensive.

Bars and Danceclubs

In most cases there is no cover charge, aside from the occasional mandatory coat-check. However, expect to pay a few dollars to get into nightclubs on weekends.

Wine, Beer and Alcohol

The legal drinking age in Atlantic Canda is 19. Beer, wine and alcohol can only be purchased in liquor stores run by the provincial governments. Very little wine-producing goes on in Atlantic Canada. Several good beers are brewed, however, including Moosehead.

Advice for Smokers

As in the United States, cigarette smoking is considered taboo, and it is being prohibited in more and more public places:

in most shopping centres;
in buses;
in government offices.

Most public places (restaurants, cafés) have smoking and non-smoking sections. Cigarettes are sold in bars, grocery stores, newspaper and magazine shops.

Children

As in the rest of Canada, facilities exist in Atlantic Canada that make travelling with children quite easy, whether it be for transportation or when enjoying the sights. Generally, children under five travel for free, and those under 12 are eligible for fare reductions. The same rules apply for various leisure activities and shows. Find out before you purchase tickets. High chairs and children's menus are available in most restaurants, while a few of the larger stores provide a babysitting service while parents shop.

Shopping

What to Buy

Lobster and salmon: you'll find these for sale on piers and docks for good prices. Most merchants can also sell you a hermetically sealed container (*about $6*) for transporting your catch on a plane.

Books: books by local authors are widely available.

Local crafts: paintings, sculptures, woodwork, ceramics, copper-based enamels and weaving, among other crafts, are readily available in all the Atlantic provinces.

Aboriginal Arts & Crafts: There are beautiful native sculptures made from different types of stone that are generally quite expensive. Make sure the sculpture is authentic by asking for a certificate of authenticity issued by the Canadian government. Good quality imitations are everywhere and are much less expensive.

Weights and Measures

Although the metric system has been in use in Canada for more than 10 years, some people continue to use the Imperial system in casual conversation. Here are some equivalents:

Weights
1 pound (lb) = 454 grams (g)
1 kilogram (kg) = 2.2 pounds (lbs)

Linear Measure
1 inch = 2.54 centimetres (cm)
1 foot (ft) = 30 centimetres (cm)
1 mile = 1.6 kilometres (km)
1 kilometre (km) = 0.63 miles
1 metre (m) = 39.37 inches

Land Measure
1 acre = 0.4 hectare
1 hectare = 2.471 acres

Volume Measure
1 U.S. gallon (gal) = 3.79 litres
1 U.S. gallon (gal) = 0.83 imperial gallons

Temperature
To convert °F into °C: subtract 32, divide by 9, multiply by 5
To convert °C into °F: multiply by 9, divide by 5, add 32

Practical Information

Miscellaneous

Drugs

Recreational drugs are against the law and not tolerated (even "soft" drugs). Drug users and dealers caught with drugs in their possession risk severe consequences.

Electricity

Voltage is 110 volts throughout Canada, the same as in the United States. Electricity plugs have two parallel, flat pins, and adaptors are available here.

Hairdressers

As in restaurants, a tip of 15% before taxes is standard.

Laundromats

Laundromats are found almost everywhere in urban areas. In most cases, detergent is sold on site. Although change machines are sometimes provided, it is best to bring plenty of quarters ($0.25) with you.

Movie theatres

There are no ushers and therefore no tips.

Newspapers

Each big city has its own local newspaper.
Fredericton: *Gleaner*
Saint John: *Telegraph Journal* and *Times-Globe*
Moncton: *Times-Transcript*
Halifax: *Chronicle Herald* and *Daily News*
Charlottetown: *The Guardian* and *Evening Post*
St. John's (Nfld.): *Evening Telegram*
The larger newspapers, for example *The Globe and Mail*, are widely available. Many international newspapers are also for sale in Halifax.

Religion

Almost all religions are represented. Most of the Francophone population are Catholic and the Anglophone, Protestant.

Restrooms

Public restrooms can be found in most shopping centres. If you cannot find one, it usually is not a problem to use one in a bar or restaurant.

Nova Scotia,

New Brunswick, Prince Edward Island and Newfoundland all boast vast, untouched stretches of wilderness protected by national and provincial parks that visitors can explore on foot or by bicycle.

Red sand beaches and cliffs overhanging the sea (Prince Edward Island National Park), shoreline with tides as high as 18m (Fundy National Park, N.B.), mountains that tower over the rough waters of the Atlantic Ocean (Cape Breton Highlands National Park, N.S.) and rigged, rocky terrain (Gros Morne National Park, Nfld.) all await discovery. The following pages contain a description of the various outdoor activities that can be enjoyed in these parks.

Parks

In Atlantic Canada, there are both national parks, run by the federal government, and provincial parks, each administered by their province's government. Most national parks offer services such as information centres, nature programs, guides, accommodation (B&Bs, inns, equipped and primitive camping sites) and dining facilities. Not all of these services are available in every park (and some vary by season) so it is best to contact park authorities before setting off on a trip. Provincial parks are usually smaller and generally have fewer services.

A number of parks are crisscrossed by marked trails several kilometres long, perfect for hiking, cycling and cross-country skiing. Primitive camp-sites or shelters can be found along some of these paths. Some of these camp-sites are very rudimentary, and a few don't even have water; it is therefore essential to be well equipped. Since some of the trails lead deep into the forest, far from human habitation, visitors are strongly advised to heed all signs. Useful maps showing trails, camp-sites and shelters are available for most parks.

Respect the Forest!

As a hiker, it is important to realize your role in preserving and respecting the fragility of the ecosystem and to comprehend your impact on your surroundings. Here are a few guidelines:

First of all, stay on the trails even if they are covered in snow or mud in order to protect the ground vegetation and avoid widening the trail.

Unless you're heading off on a long trek, wear lightweight hiking boots; they do less damage to vegetation. When in a group in alpine regions, spread out and walk on rocks as much as possible to avoid damaging vegetation.

It is just as important to protect waterways, bodies of water and the ground water when in mountainous regions. When digging back-country latrines, place them at least 30m from all water sources, and cover everything (paper included) with earth.

Never clean yourself in lakes or streams.

At campsites dispose of waste water only in designated areas.

The water in mountain regions is not always potable and therefore should be boiled for at least 10min before drinking.

Never leave any garbage behind. Bags for this are provided at park offices.

Certain types of flowers are endangered, so do not pick anything.

Leave everything as you find it, so that those who follow can enjoy the beauty of nature as you did.

For safety reasons, always keep your dog on a leash or leave it at home. Dogs that roam free have a tendency to wander off and chase wild animals. They have even been known to chase down bears and then take refuge with their masters.

National Parks

There are seven national parks in Atlantic Canada: Fundy National Park (Alma, N.B.), Kouchibouguac National Park (along the Acadian coast of New Brunswick), Prince Edward Island National Park (Cavendish, P.E.I.), Cape Breton Highlands National Park (Baddeck, N.S.), Kejimkujik National Park (Maitland Bridge, N.S.), Terra Nova National Park (centre of Newfoundland) and Gros Morne National Park (western Newfoundland). In addition to these parks, Park Canada also operates a number of national historic sites, which are described in the "Exploring" section of each chapter.

For more information on national parks, contact:

Parks Canada Atlantic Service Center
1869 Upper Water Street, Halifax, Nova Scotia, B3J 1S9
☎ *(902) 426-3436*
= *(902) 426-6881*
http://parkscanada.pch.gc.ca

Provincial Parks

Each of the four Atlantic provinces manages a wide variety of parks. Some of these are small and open only during the day, while the larger ones offer a broader scope of activi

ties. There are no fewer than 23 provincial parks in New Brunswick, 29 on Prince Edward Island, over 100 in Nova Scotia and more than 20 in Newfoundland and Labrador. These parks provide visitors with access to beaches, camp-sites, golf courses and hiking trails. Throughout this guide, the most important parks are described in the "Exploring" section of each chapter.

New Brunswick is a true paradise for nature lovers and for those seeking fresh air and wilderness, since 85% of the province's 74,437km² is forested. The province is also blessed with around 1000km of coastline along the Bay of Fundy and the Atlantic Ocean, as well as numerous lakes and rivers, of which the St. John and Miramichi rivers are the major ones.

For more information on provincial parks, write to:

New Brunswick

New Brunswick Ministry of Natural Resources and Energy, Park Services
P.O. Box 6000, Fredericton E3B 5H1

Nova Scotia

Department of Natural Resources
R.R. 1, Belmont, B0M 1C0
☎*(902) 662-3030*

Prince Edward Island

Department of Economic Development and Tourism
R.R.3, O'Leary, C0B 1D0

Newfoundland

Department of Tourism, Culture and Recreation, Parks and Natural Areas Division
P.O. Box 8700, St. John's A1B 4J6

Summer Activities

In mild weather, visitors can enjoy the activities listed below. Anyone deciding to spend more than a day in a park should remember that the nights are cool (often even in July and August) and that long-sleeved shirts or sweaters will be very practical in some regions. In June, an effective insect repellent is almost indispensable for an outing in the forest.

Hiking

Hiking is an activity open to everyone, and can be enjoyed in all national and most provincial parks. Before setting out, plan your excursion well by checking the length and level of difficulty of each trail. Some parks have long trails that require more than a

day of hiking and lead deep into the wilderness. When taking one of these trails, which can stretch tens of kilometres, it is crucial to respect all signs.

To make the most of a hike, make sure to bring along the right equipment. Remember a good pair of walking shoes, all appropriate maps, sufficient food and water and a small first-aid kit containing a pocket knife and bandages.

Bicycling

Bicycling is practised throughout Eastern Canada, whether along the usually quiet secondary roads or the trails within the parks. The roads offer prudent cyclists one of the most enjoyable means possible of visiting these picturesque regions. Keep in mind, however, that even though these are Canada's smallest provinces, distances here can still seem very long.

If you wish to bring your own bicycle, you are allowed to bring it on any bus; just be sure it is properly protected in an suitable box. Another option is to rent one on site. For bike rental locations, look under the heading *Bicycling* in the "Outdoor Activities" section of each chapter, contact

Outdoors

a tourist information centre or check under "Bicycles-Rentals" in the *Yellow Pages*. Adequate insurance is a good idea when renting a bicycle. Some places include insurance against theft in the cost of the rental, so inquire before renting.

Canoeing

Many parks are studded with lakes and rivers that offer canoe-trippers a day or more of exploring. Simple camp-sites have been laid out to accommodate canoers during long excursions. Canoe rentals and maps of possible routes are usually available at the park's information centre.

If you're heading out for adventure on Nova Scotia's waterways, maps and information are available at:

Canoe Nova Scotia
5516 Spring Garden Rd.
Box 3010, South Halifax
B3J 3G6
☎ *(902)425-5450*

Beaches

White and red sand beaches, shores washed by 18m tides, sand dunes inhabited by fascinating animal life, endless beaches with no sign of human life and others located near charming villages... without question, these are some of Atlantic Canada's most precious natural attractions. Each province takes care to offer visitors clean, well maintained beaches that are perfect for swimming. A visit to Atlantic Canada would not be complete without a stop at one of the region's many beaches.

Its beaches alone merit a trip to New Brunswick. Particularly popular are the beautiful white-sand beaches on the Acadian coast, especially in the southeast of the province near Shédiac. Aside from their beauty, their waters are the warmest north of Virginia, perfect for swimming and aquatic activities.

Fishing

Fishing is permitted in the Atlantic provinces, but visitors should remember that it is a regulated activity. Fishing laws are complicated, so it is wise to request information from the Ministry of Natural Resources of each province and obtain the brochure stating key fishing regulations (see p 45).

As a general rule, however, keep in mind that:

● it is necessary to obtain a permit from the provincial government before going fishing;

● a special permit is usually required for salmon fishing;

● fishing seasons are established by the ministry and must be respected at all times; the seasons vary depending on the species;

● fishing is permitted in parks, but it is necessary to obtain a permit from park officials beforehand; for more information, look under the "Fishing" heading in the "Outdoor Activities" section of the relevant chapter.

Bird-watching

The shores of the Atlantic provinces attract all sorts of birds, which can easily be observed with a pair of binoculars. Among the species frequenting this region are cormorants, kingfishers, a wide variety of ducks (including the mallard) and great blue herons. If you're lucky, you might catch a glimpse of an Atlantic puffin, a piping plover or a bald eagle. For help identifying various birds, get a copy of *Peterson's Field Guide: All the Birds of Eastern and Central North America*, published by Houghton Mifflin. Although parks are often the best places to observe certain species, bird-watching is an activity that can be enjoyed all over Atlantic Canada.

Whale-watching

Whales swim near the coasts of Atlantic Canada, in the Gulf of St. Lawrence, the Bay of Fundy and in the Strait of Belle Isle.

Visitors wishing a closer view of these impressive and harmless sea mammals can take part in a whale-watching cruise. Most often, you can sight the humpback whale, the finback whale, the minke whale, the blue roqual and, occasionally, the bowhead whale. These excursions usually start near St. Andrews in New Brunswick, Digby and Cape Breton in Nova Scotia and in many places along the Newfoundland coast.

Seal-watching

Seals also swim off the coasts of Nova Scotia, New Brunswick and Prince Edward Island, and anyone wishing to observe them up close can take part in seal-watching. Occasionally, attracted by the boats, these curious mammals will pop their heads out of the water to gaze at the passengers with their big black eyes. Other times, they can be spotted sunning on a deserted beach. The best place for seal-watching is along the eastern shore of Prince Edward Island.

Golf

All over Eastern Canada, there are magnificent golf courses, renowned for their remarkable settings. Stretched out along the seashore, they offer stunning views. Golf lovers can enjoy unforgettable vacations here, as some courses lie in the heart of provincial parks, in the most tranquil surroundings imaginable, with luxurious hotels just a short distance away.

Winter Activities

In winter, the Atlantic provinces are covered with a blanket of snow. Most parks with summer hiking trails adapt for the season, welcoming cross-country skiers. New Brunswick also features an extensive network of snowmobile trails. Finally, although there are only a few mountains in this region, visitors can downhill ski in New Brunswick, Nova Scotia and Newfoundland.

Outdoors

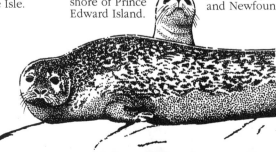

Cross-country Skiing

Some parks, such as Kejimkujik, Cape Breton Highlands, Mount Sugarloaf and Kouchibouguac, are renowned for their long cross-country ski trails. Daily ski rentals are available at a number of resorts.

Downhill Skiing

Although this region is not really known for downhill skiing, there are a few noteworthy mountains. New Brunswick has some lovely ski resorts, most importantly Mount Sugarloaf and Mount Crabbe. Though the mountains in Nova Scotia are lower, Keltic Cape Smokey is worth mentioning.

The best place for downhill skiing in the region, however, is in Newfoundland: Marble Mountain, near Corner Brook, in the west of the island, has excellent runs and a lengthy ski season.

Snowmobiling

Snowmobiling is gaining popularity in the Atlantic provinces. - Visitors can explore the region by snowmobile, but should take care to heed all regulations. Don't forget, though, that a permit is required. It is also advisable to take out liability insurance.

The following rules should always be obeyed:

- stay on the snow-mobile trails;

- always drive on the right side of the trail;

- wear a helmet;

- all snowmobiles must have head-lights.

To help you plan a snowmobile excursion in New Brunswick, contact:

F.C.M.N.B.
P.O. Box 536, Newcastle
E1V 3T7
☎ *(506) 325-2625*
⇋ *(506) 325-2627*

or in Nova Scotia:

Snowmobile Association
Box 3010, South Halifax
B3J 3G6
☎ *(902) 425-5450*

New Brunswick

N ew Brunswick, gateway to Atlantic Canada, is enchanting in its diversity. Geographically, it is remarkably varied, combining more than a thousand kilometres of shoreline and seascapes with picturesque farmlands and endless stretches of often mountainous wilderness.

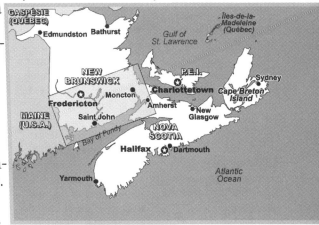

Forests cover a full 85% of the territory, which is traversed from north to south by the majestic St. John River, whose source lies in the Appalachian foothills. This river has always been essential to the province's development, and charming towns and villages have sprung up along its richly fertile banks.

Among these are Fredericton, New Brunswick's pretty capital, with its old-fashioned feel, and Saint John, the province's chief port city and industrial centre.

After winding its way through a pastoral landscape, the St. John River empties into the Bay of Fundy, whose often spectacularly steep shores mark the southern border of New Brunswick. An amazing natural phenomenon occurs in this bay twice a day when the highest, most powerful tides in the world surge up onto the shores, reshaping the landscape in sometimes unusual ways, and actually reversing the current of the rivers! Without question, the

Bay of Fundy's giant tides constitute one of the greatest natural attractions in the eastern part of the continent.

The bay's shoreline, furthermore, is of incomparable beauty. Be that as it may, New Brunswick's other coast, on the Atlantic Ocean, has charms of its own. It is here, from the border of Nova Scotia to that of Québec, that visitors will find the province's most beautiful sandy beaches, washed by uncommonly warm waters that are perfect for swimming. Most importantly, however, this is the Acadian coast. It is here, in towns and villages like Caraquet, Shippagan and Shediac, that visitors can learn about Acadia and its warm, hospitable inhabitants.

In addition to its varied scenery, New Brunswick offers a rich medley of strong, distinct cultures. In fact, after a past scarred by rivalry between the French and British for control of the continent in the 18th century, New Brunswick is now Canada's only officially bilingual province. Originally inhabited by natives of the Micmac and Malecite Nations, the territory corresponding to present-day New Brunswick was first visited by envoys of the King of France.

In 1604, a trading post was established on Île Sainte-Croix, right near the city of St. Stephen, marking the birth of Acadia. The following year, the French moved the trading post to the opposite shore of the Bay of Fundy, founding Port-Royal in what is now Nova Scotia. For a century and a half, Acadia developed mainly along the shores of the Bay of Fundy. In 1755, however, a tragic event took place: the Deportation of the Acadians by the British. Approximately half of the 14,000 Acadians were put on boats and deported, while the others hid or escaped into the woods. Many of these eventually took up residence on the Atlantic coast of New Brunswick.

A little more than two decades later, another event, the end of the American Revolution, would have a tremendous influence on the course of history in this region. From 1783 on, when American revolutionary forces finally defeated the British, thousands of soldiers and civilians wishing to remain loyal to Great Britain sought refuge in Atlantic Canada; many settled on the banks of the St. John River.

Later, a heavy flow of immigrants from the British Isles added to the province's population. Today, English is the mother tongue of the majority of New Brunswick's inhabitants, although French-speakers still make up a third of the population. The Acadians still live, for the most part, on the Atlantic coast, while another group of French-speakers, known as Brayons, may be found along the St. John and Madawaska Rivers, in the northwestern part of the province.

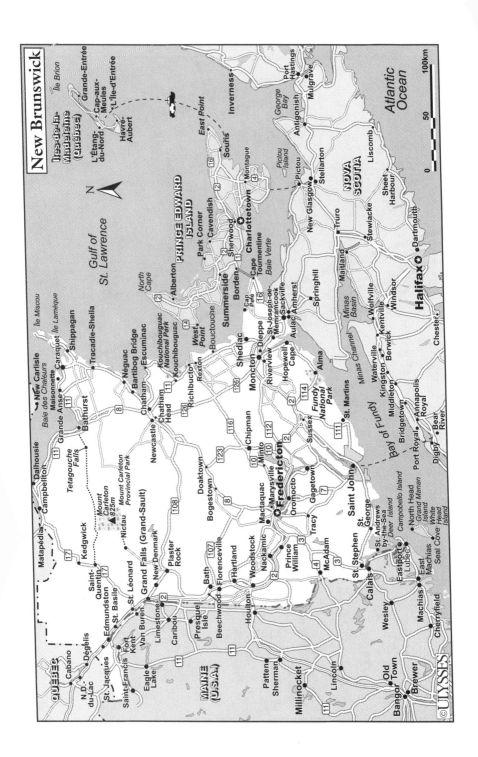

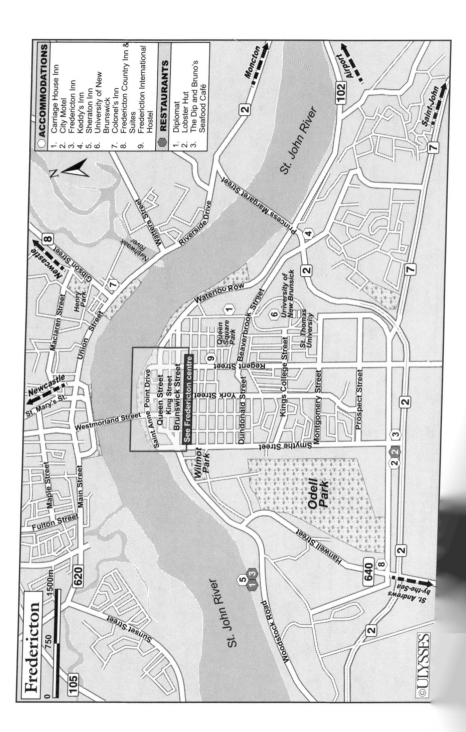

Fredericton

ACCOMMODATIONS
1. Carriage House Inn
2. City Motel
3. Fredericton Inn
4. Keddy's Inn
5. Sheraton Inn
6. University of New Brunswick
7. Colonel's Inn
8. Fredericton Country Inn & Suites
9. Frederiction International Hostel

RESTAURANTS
1. Diplomat
2. Lobster Hut
3. The Dip and Bruno's Seafood Café

St. John River

Princess Margaret Street

Moncton

102

Airport

Saint-John

7

2

7

University of New Brunswick

St. Thomas University

Waterloo Row

Queen Square Park

Beaverbrook Street

Regent Street

Kings College Street

Montgomery Street

Prospect Street

York Street

Dundonald Street

Smythe Street

2 2

2

3

See Fredericton centre

Brunswick Street

King Street

Queen Street

Saint Anne Point Drive

Westmorland Street

Wilmot Park

Odell Park

Hanwell Street

640

8

St. Andrews by-the-Sea

2

Woodstock Road

St. John River

5 113

Sunset Street

620

105

0   750   1500m

Fulton Street

Main Street

Maple Street

Maclaren Street

Henry Park

Union Street

7

Gibson Street

8

Newcastle

Nashwaak River

Waterloo Street

St. Mary's St.

Newcastle

Riverside Drive

N

©ULYSSES

Fredericton

Fredericton ★★ is definitely one of the most precious jewels in the province's crown.

Capital of New Brunswick, it has managed to preserve the remarkable historical legacy and architectural harmony handed down to it from the previous century, giving it a subtle elegance and old-fashioned character. Adorned with magnificent churches and government buildings, as well as large green spaces, some of which lie alongside the St. John River, Fredericton is one of those cities that charms visitors at first sight. Its quiet streets, lined with stately elms, are graced with vast, magnificent Victorian residences. These pretty houses, with their invariably well-tended front gardens, abound in Fredericton, contributing greatly to the city's charm.

The site now occupied by the city was originally an Acadian trading post named

Sainte-Anne that was founded in the late 17th century. Acadians lived here until 1783, when they were driven away by arriving Loyalists. The city of Fredericton was founded the following year. It became the provincial capital and was named Fredericton in honour of the second son of George III, Great Britain's king at the time. Over the years, very few industries have set up shop here, opting instead for Saint John. Today, Fredericton's chief employers are the

provincial government and the universities.

Finding Your Way Around

The city of Fredericton grew up on either side of the St. John River, but the downtown area and most tourist attractions lie on the west bank. Visitors will have no difficulty finding their way around the small city centre, which may be explored on foot. The two main downtown arteries are Queen and King Streets, both of which run parallel to the river. Most attractions, as well as many restaurants and businesses, lie on one or the other of these streets.

By Plane

Fredericton's Airport is located about 16km southeast of the city, on Lincoln Road (☎451-8011); it is served mainly by Air Canada (☎458-8561) and its partner, Air Nova, and Canadian Airlines (☎446-6034 or 800-665-1177) and its partner, Air Atlantic. Visitors can take a taxi to the downtown area.

Bus Station

The bus station (☎458-6000) is located at the corner of Brunswick and Regent Streets.

Practical Information

Area Code: **506**

Tourist Information Offices

Frediction Tourism
CB 130 Fredericton, N.B.
E3B 4Y7
☎*(506) 460-2129*
☎*888-888-4768*
≈*(506) 460-2474*
www.city.fredericton.nb.ca

On the Trans-Canada Highway
☎*460-2191*

City Hall
Queen Street
☎*460-2129 or 888-888-4768*

Exploring

The best place to start off a tour of downtown Fredericton is at the excellent tourist office located inside City Hall (*at the corner of Queen and York Sts.,* ☎452-9616), which also offers very good guided bus tours of the city. The oldest part of the **City hall** ★ *(free admission; mid-May to early Sep, every day 8am to 7:30pm; early Sep to mid-May, by appointment)* was built in 1876, at which time it included not only the municipal offices and council rooms, but also an opera house, a farmer's market and a number of prison cells. The fountain in front of City Hall dates from 1885; the building's second wing was erected between 1975 to 1977. The Council Chamber, open to the public during summer, makes for an interesting visit.

On the other side of York Street, visitors will see the **courthouse** *(no tours; at the corner of Queen and York Sts.),* a large stone building erected in the late 1930s.

The edifice was used as a high school before being adopted for its present purpose in 1970. Right next to the courthouse stands the **New Brunswick College of Craft and Design** *(no tours),* the only post-secondary school in Canada to offer a program devoted entirely to training artisans.

A little farther, visitors will see the **Military Compound and Guard House** ★★ *(free admission; Jun to early Sep, every day 10am to 6pm; at the corner of Queen and Carleton Sts.,* ☎453-3747). These stone buildings, erected in 1827 as replacements for the city's original wooden military buildings, served as barracks for British troops until 1869. One room has been restored to illustrate the building's initial use, and a soldier in period dress serves as a guide. A sundial was reconstructed on the barracks wall. Up until the beginning of this century, residents of Fredericton could check the time by referring to devices such as this one.

Head up Carleton Street to the corner of King Street, where **Wilnot United Church** ★★ *(at the corner of Carleton and King Sts.)* is located. Its rather austere facade conceals a superb, exceptionally colourful interior abounding in hand-carved woodwork.

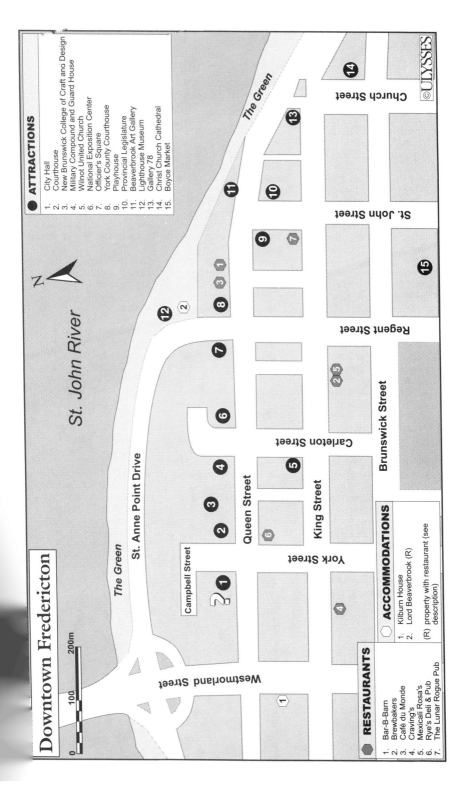

Downtown Fredericton

0   100   200m

St. John River

St. Anne Point Drive

The Green

N

Campbell Street

Queen Street

York Street

King Street

Carleton Street

Regent Street

St. John Street

Brunswick Street

Church Street

The Green

Westmorland Street

● **ATTRACTIONS**

1. City Hall
2. Courthouse
3. New Brunswick College of Craft and Design
4. Military Compound and Guard House
5. Wilmot United Church
6. National Exposition Center
7. Officier's Square
8. York County Courthouse
9. Playhouse
10. Provincial Legislature
11. Beaverbrook Art Gallery
12. Lighthouse Museum
13. Gallery 78
14. Christ Church Cathedral
15. Boyce Market

◇ **ACCOMMODATIONS**

1. Kilburn House
2. Lord Beaverbrook (R)

(R) property with restaurant (see description)

◆ **RESTAURANTS**

1. Bar-B-Barn
2. Brewbakers
3. Café du Monde
4. Craving's
5. Mexicali Rosa's
6. Rye's Deli & Pub
7. The Lunar Rogue Pub

©ULYSSES

This church was built in 1852, although the Fredericton Methodist Society, which joined the United Church of Canada in 1925, was founded back in 1791.

A beautiful Second-Empire-style building erected in 1881 houses the **New Brunswick Sports Hall of Fame** *(free admission, early Jun to early Sep, every day 10am to 6pm; early Sep to Jun, Mon to Fri noon to 4pm; ☎453-3747)*, dedicated to New Brunswick's finest athletes.

Also on Queen Street, **Officer's Square** ★★ *($2; Jun 1 to Sep 30, Tues to Sat 10am to 5pm, Sun noon to 5pm; rest of the year, Tue to Sat 10am to 5pm; 571 Queen St., near Regent St., ☎455-6041)* is an attractive park. Facing it is the building once used as officers' quarters, erected in two stages, from 1839 to 1840 and in 1851. Its bow-shaped stone columns, railings and iron stairs are typical of architecture designed by royal engineers during the colonial era. The former quarters now house the **York-Sunbury Museum**, devoted to the province's military and domestic history.

Continue along Queen Street to the pretty **York County Courthouse** ★ *(no tours; Queen St., after Regent St.)*, erected in 1855. In those years, there was a market on the ground floor. Today, the building hou-

ses the services of the Ministry of Justice, as well as a courtroom.

A little farther along Queen Street, on the opposite side of the street, stands the **Playhouse** *(Queen St., at the corner of St. John St., ticket sales: ☎506-458-8344)*, built in 1964. Since 1969, it has served as home base for the only English-speaking theatre company in the province, The New Brunswick Theatre. Construction of the Playhouse was financed by Lord Beaverbrook, a British newspaper tycoon who lived in New Brunswick as a child.

Not far from the Playhouse, visitors will see the **Provincial Legislature** ★★ *(free admission; Jun to Aug, every day 9am to 7pm; late Aug to early Jun, Mon to Fri 9am to 4pm; Queen St., at the corner of St. John St., ☎453-2527)*.

This legislature has been seat of the provincial government since 1882. Inside, an impressive spiral wooden staircase leads to the library, which contains over 35,000 volumes, some of which are very rare. Of particular interest are the Assembly Chamber, where the members of Parliament gather, and the portraits of King George III and Queen Charlotte, by British painter Joshua Reynolds, hang.

Across from the Legislative Building stands the **Beaverbrook Art Gallery** ★★★ *($3; Jun and Sep, Mon to Fri 9am to 6pm, Sat and Sun 10am to 5pm, guided tours at 11am; Queen St., ☎458-8545)*, another of Lord Beaverbrook's gifts to the city of Fredericton. The gallery houses, among other things, a superb collection of works by highly renowned British painters, as well as a number of other lovely canvases by Canadian artists such as Cornelius Krieghoff and James Wilson Morrice.

Provincial Legislature

Without question, however, the most impressive piece on display is Catalan artist Salvador Dali's *Santiago el Grande*.

After touring the fascinating Beaverbrook Art Gallery, summer visitors can enjoy a delightful stroll on Fredericton's splendid **Green ★** (see p 58 in "Hiking"), which stretches 4km alongside the St. John River, enabling both walkers and cyclists to explore the banks of the river. The Green contributes greatly to the quality of life in the city. Visitors can stop at the **Lighthouse Museum** *($2; May to Jun, Mon to Fri 10am to 4pm, Sat and Sun 10am to 9pm, Jul to Aug every day 10am to 9pm; ☎459-2515)*, which presents a historical exhibit.

Back on Queen Street, the pretty silhouette of Crocket House, which now houses **Gallery 78**, is visible. Built at the end of the 19th century, Croquet House is a magnificent three-storey Queen Anne-style home. It was named after the Crocket family, who lived here from the 1930s, and in 1963, it was given to New Brunswick Heritage. Since 1989, it has been home to Gallery 78, one of the best galleries in the province, which features works by renowned Canadian artists. In addition to viewing the works in the gallery, visitors can admire the beautiful interior of the home.

Take Queen Street to Church Street in order to visit the Gothic style **Christ Church Cathedral ★★** *(at the corner of Queen St. and Church St., ☎506-450-8500)*, whose construction, completed in 1853, was largely due to the efforts of Fredericton's first Anglican bishop, John Medley.

Located in the former York county prison, which was built in 1909, the **Centre Scientifique de Science Est** (Science East) offers over 100 interactive exhibits that allow visitors to explore fundamental scientific principles through experiments. At the entrance, there's also a small exhibit on the history of the prison.

From the cathedral, take Brunswick Street to Regent Street. On the left-hand side stands **Boyce Market** *(Sat 6am to 1pm; 665 George St., at the corner of Brunswick and Regent Sts., ☎506-451-1815)*, a public market where farmers, artisans and artists sell their products every Saturday morning. Right next door, on the left side of Brunswick Street, lies Fredericton's **Old Loyalist Cemetery**. It was here that the most notable figures in Fredericton's early history were buried from 1787 to 1878.

Outside Downtown

Situated outside the downtown area, the **Old Government House** *(free admission, Jun to Oct, every day 10am to 6pm, ☎453-6440)* once served as the official residence of the lieutenant-governor of the province

The **University of New Brunswick** *(at the end of University St.)*, founded in 1785 by newly arrived Loyalists, is made up of several different edifices. Its arts building is the oldest university building still in use in Canada.

On the same site, visitors will also find **St. Thomas University**, a Catholic institution originally located in Chatham, on the Miramichi River. Together, the two universities have 8,000 students. This is a wonderful spot from which to view the city below.

Odell Park ★ *(Rockwood Ave., northwest of the city)* covers over 175ha and includes 16km of trails. This beautifully preserved, peaceful natural area has been enhanced by the addition of an enclosure for deer, duck ponds, picnic tables and a play area for children.

Outdoor Activities

Cycling

Cycling is not only a great sport, but also a fantastic means of exploring New Brunswick, which abounds in peaceful roads and bike paths. Fredericton, the pretty provincial capital, is a marvellous city to tour by bicycle. In addition to its often quiet streets, Fredericton has a magnificent bicycle trail that runs along the river for 4km

Bicycle Rental

Kawack
Fredericton
☎*458-8985*

Radical Edge
☎*459-3478*

Hiking

A good way to explore Fredericton's beauty is on foot: it has 12 trails that meander through the outskirts of the town. The longest trail, the **North Side**, follows the north shore of the St. John River for about 10km. The **Green**, which

snakes through the southwest shore for 4km through the prettiest areas of the town, is probably the most scenic trail. It links up with other shorter trails, which are equally beautiful. All of the trails offer interesting hiking. You can obtain a copy of the *Trail Guide* by contacting the **New Brunswick Trails Council Inc.** *(235 Main St.,* ☎*459-1931, www.sentierNBtrail.com).*

Canoeing and Kayaking

After strolling along the streets of Fredericton, there's nothing like a guided river tour in a canoe or kayak. You say you don't know how to paddle? Not to worry: this business offers short training sessions on handling these crafts and trips that offer a chance to explore the river and see its beautiful flora and fauna.

Small Craft Aquatic Centre
$15
Woodstock Rd.
☎*460-2260*

Accommodations

University of New Brunswick
May to mid-Aug
200 beds
20 Bailey Dr., end of University Ave.
☎*453-4891*
≈*453-3585*
During the summer, rooms in the student residence can be rented at the University of New Brunswick. Expect to pay around $41.50 for a double-occupancy room, or $28.40 for a single room.

Youth Hostel
$18 member
$20 non-member
ℂ
621 Churchill Row, E3B 1M3
☎*450-4417*
Located in a gigantic house, this youth hostel is undoubtedly one of the best choices for those on a tight budget. It offers a perfect location, only 5min by foot from the centre of town. What's more, unlike most facilities of its kind, which have dormitories, it offers rooms of different sizes. Guests have access to a kitchenette and a game room. In winter, there are fewer rooms available, since a part of the building serves as a students' residence.

Kilburn House
$60 bkfst incl
3 rooms
80 Northumberland St.
E3B 3H8
☎/≈*455-7078*
Located close to the
centre of town, this
reasonably priced facil-
ity offers a few simply
decorated, but clean
rooms. The down side,
however, is that Kil-
burn house is situated
on a busy street.

City Motel
$54
tv, ℜ, ≡
56 rooms
1216 Regent St., E3B 3Z4
☎*450-9900 or 800-268-2858*
≈*452-1915*
It would be difficult to
find a more boring
decor than the one
used in the rooms of
the City Motel, located
next to the Trans-
Canada. For visitors
aiming to see the main
sights of Fredericton,
this hotel is a little out
of the way. Neverthe-
less, it is clean, not too
expensive and there is
a good seafood restau-
rant next door.

🛶 **Carriage House Inn**
$60
tv
10 rooms
230 University Ave., E3C 4H7
☎*452-9924 or 800-267-6068*
≈*458-0799*
The many opulent Vic-
torian residences lining
the streets of Frederic-
ton provide much of its
charm. The Carriage
House Inn is one of
these magnificent
houses, built in 1875
and transformed into
an inn with a unique
atmosphere that trans-

ports guests to another
era. There are several
large rooms including a
ballroom, a library and
a solarium, as well as
10 guest rooms fur-
nished with antiques.
The inn looks out onto
a quiet, well-to-do
street shaded by large
elm trees and lies just a
few minutes' walk from
downtown. It is best to
reserve in advance,
regardless of the sea-
son. Breakfast is served
in a cheerful solarium
frequented by
businesspeople.

The Colonel's Inn
$80 bkfst incl.
2 rooms
843 Union St., E3A 3P6
☎*452-2802*
A charming B&B with
only a few rooms, The
Colonel's Inn is a beau-
tiful century-old home.
Its welcoming hosts,
who offer information
about the region, en-
sure an enjoyable stay.
To get here from the
town centre, you must
take a scenic drive on
the north shore of the
St. John River rather
than from Carleton
Park.

Fredericton Inn
$79
tv, ℜ, ≈, K, ☺
200 rooms
1315 Regent St., E3B 1A1
☎*455-1430 or 800-561-8777*
≈*458-5448*
Located just outside the
downtown area and
close to several shop-
ping malls along the
Trans-Canada, the Fred-
ericton Inn offers a
large choice of rooms,
from suites to motel-
style accommodation.

The latter offers good
value for the money.

Keddy's Inn
$84
K, tv, ≈, ℜ, △
115 rooms
368 Forest Hill Road, E3B 5G1
☎*454-4461 or 800-561-7666*
≈*452-6915*
Keddy's Inn is a large,
two-storey building
with clean, relatively
reasonably priced mo-
tel rooms. Of the estab-
lishments in this cate-
gory, Keddy's Inn is
closest to downtown
Fredericton, which is
just a 10min stroll
away.

**Fredericton Country Inn &
Suites**
$94 bkfst incl
tv, K
445 Prospect St. W., E3B 6B8
☎*459-0035*
≈*458-1011*
Located outside of
town, this hotel offers
decent rooms. Guests
enjoy many little extras,
such as free newspa-
pers and all-day coffee
long, which make the
stay quite enjoyable.
For longer stays in
Fredericton, travellers
can rent a room with a
kitchenette and living
room.

Lord Beaverbrook Hotel
$108
tv, ℜ, ℑ, ≡, △, ✿, ☺, P, ≈
175 rooms
659 Queen St., E3B 5A6
☎*455-3371 or 800-561-7666*
≈*455-1441*
You won't find a hotel
more centrally located
than the Lord
Beaverbrook Hotel –
which has been a land-
mark in downtown
Fredericton for half a

century. With its back to the St. John River, it faces the Legislative Assembly of New Brunswick. The hotel's prestigious history is evident in the richly decorated entrance hall and the aristocratic air about the Governor's Room, a small dining room tucked away. Despite renovations, the rooms are not as luxurious as you might expect.

 Sheraton Inn
$109
tv, K, △, ☉,ℜ, ≈
223 rooms
225 Woodstock Road, E3B 2H8
☎*457-7000 or 800-325-3535*
≠*457-4000*
The elegant Sheraton Inn is beautifully located on the shore of the St. John River, just outside of downtown Fredericton. It is by far the most luxurious hotel in the capital and one of the nicest in the province. The architects made the most of the location including a superb terrace looking out over the river, the ideal spot for cocktails, a dip in the pool or a relaxed meal while taking in the scenery. The rooms are very comfortable, pretty and functional, and several offer great views. As you might expect, the recently built Sheraton is equipped with an indoor pool and exercise facilities, a very good restaurant, a bar and conference rooms. It has clearly been designed to please both business people and travellers.

Restaurants

Craving's
$
384 King St.
☎*452-7482*
If you feel like a healthy meal, head to Craving's, which offers attentive service and a laid-back atmosphere. Sample its specialities, such as chicken pitas, quiches or salads.

Rye's Deli & Pub
$$
422 Queen St.
☎*453-0582*
Rye's Deli & Pub is a favourite with smoked-meat fans, and according to their advertisements they follow the original Montreal recipe. What the decor lacks in atmosphere is more than made up for by the terrace when the warm weather arrives. Rye's is particularly popular among employees of the neighbouring offices and shops.

Mexicali Rosa's
$$
546 King St.
☎*451-0686*
Mexicali Rosa's is a good spot for fans of Mexican food. Servings are usually quite large, and a small terrace allows for outdoor dining.

Diplomat
$$
next to the Sheraton
☎*454-2400*
Open 24hrs a day, seven days a week, the Diplomat is a favourite perch for night owls. The menu is varied but simple, consisting essentially of typical delicatessen fare. Chinese food is one of its specialties. The Diplomat also serves copious breakfasts at very good prices.

The Lunar Rogue Pub
$$
625 King St.
☎*450-2065*
This is a great place to go to on beautiful sunny days when guests can enjoy the terrace. Although fairly predictable, the food here is worth the trip. Enjoy generous portions of hamburgers, sandwiches and steak.

 The Lobster Hut
$$
1216 Regent St., City Motel
☎*455-4413*
The Lobster Hut could almost be listed as a Fredericton attraction, due to its bizarre, almost psychedelic decor, made up of an eclectic collection of photos, posters and gadgets all having to do with maritime life. The restaurant is as friendly as can be and, as you may have guessed, specializes in fish and seafood. The food is good and relatively inexpensive.

Brewbakers
$$-$$$
546 King St.
☎*450-0067*
Brewbakers has something for everyone. Those who like to chat over a scrumptious dessert and coffee will enjoy its main floor. The second floor is a pleasant mezzanine, and the third floor has a dining room and a terrace, where guests can enjoy hearty portions of delicious pasta, pizza, steak, chicken and seafood. Convivial ambience.

Governor's Room
$$$
Lord Beaverbrook Hotel
☎*455-3371*
The Lord Beaverbrook Hotel (see above) boasts a dining room and a terrace looking out over the St. John River. For a fancier dinner, however, make reservations at the Governor's Room, two private dining rooms with an antiquated decor and a slightly aristocratic atmosphere. The chef specializes in French cuisine.

The Dip
$$-$$$
Sheraton Inn
During mild, summertime weather, it would be hard to imagine a better spot for a drink, light snack or meal than The Dip, a terrace restaurant with a bistro menu. Besides the attentive and courteous service, The Dip offers an absolutely unbeatable view of the St. John River.

Bruno's Seafood Café
$$$
Sheraton Inn
If the weather proves prohibitive, you can always take shelter at Bruno's Seafood Café, the indoor restaurant at the Sheraton Inn (see p 60). The cuisine is just as good, the service, impeccable and the ambiance, cozy. The highlights of the menu are excellent scallops Florentine and pepper shrimp. There is also a children's menu. In addition, Bruno's usually offers a seafood buffet on Friday evenings for about $20 per person.

Entertainment

Bars and Pubs

The Upper Deck Sports Bar
2nd floor, Queen St.
Always hopping, even on a Sunday night, The Upper Deck Sports Bar is one of the most popular spots with young Frederictonians. The place features pool tables and regular live music. This bar has a large back patio where people can eat and sip drinks in a relaxing atmosphere.

Social Club
University of New Brunswick Student Union Building
The students may come and go, but the Social Club at the University of New Brunswick remains a sure bet year after year. It is packed just about every night in winter, while in the summer, most of the action is limited to weekends.

The Lunar Rogue Pub
625 King St.
☎*450-2065*
There's nothing like a night out at The Lunar Rogue Pub. It offers a lively terrace, which is overflowing on weekend evenings. It also has great beer on tap.

Picaroons Brewing Co. & Taprooms
366 Queen St.
☎*455-TAPS*
Picaroons is first and foremost a microbrewery, but it is also a place to sample homemade beer served in its bar. It has quickly become a popular local hangout, and crowds now flock here to enjoy its pretty terrace and delicious, basic fare.

Dolar's Pub
349 King St.
☎*450-IRIS*
The 25-plus clientele at this pub is serenaded by live music, mainly courtesy of Maritime musicians.

Festivals and Cultural Activities

The **Playhouse** *(Queen St.)* is a lovely hall that presents the productions of the New Brunswick Theatre, the only professional English-language theatre company in the province. It also regularly hosts other cultural events

(Programme information: ☎458-8345*)*.

During summer months, **outdoor concerts** are presented on Tuesdays and Thursdays at 7:30pm at Officer's Square on Queen Street.

The first few days in September are the time for jazz and blues in Fredericton. The **Harvest Jazz & Blues Festival** *(early Sep,* ☎622-5837, *www.harvestjazzblues.nb. ca)* is a special occasion for those who love these two musical styles. Shows are presented in bars, parks, restaurants and theatres in town.

Film

Empire Theatre
Regent Mall
☎*458-9704*

Shopping

The Regent Mall, which has 95 shops, is the largest shopping centre in town.

No visit to Fredericton would be complete without a stop at **Gallery 78** *(796 Queen St.)*, which exhibits and sells works by some of the best-known New Brunswick artists. It is also a wonderful way to visit a sumptuous Victorian house overlooking the St. John River. With its high ceilings, large rooms,

hardwood floors and stately staircase, you'll be wishing it was for sale too!

The **Arts Council of New Brunswick** *(103 Church St.,* ☎*450-8989)* Gallery exhibits and sells a superb collection of high quality products created by the province's artists and craftspeople. It is one of the best craft boutiques in New Brunswick.

Crafts and Books

By the Light of the Moon
385 Mazzuca Lane
☎**455-2878**
By the Light of the Moon offers magnificent and unusual fabrics, all of which are hand-painted and made from natural fibres.

Beaverbrook Gallery Gift Shop
Queen St.
☎**458-8545**
The Beaverbrook Gallery Gift Shop sells reproductions, art books, decorations, and the like. A great place to find a quality souvenir.

Soldiers' Barracks Crafts Shops
458 Queen St.
In summertime, soldiers' barracks are transformed into charming little boutiques. A few of them also have workshops, which offer a great opportunity to see the artists at work.

Cultures
383 Masochist Lane
Cultures is an innovative shop selling crafts and products made in developing nations. There are several beautiful objects. The boutique is located at what is probably one of the most difficult corners to find in Fredericton: a small alley ending at York Street, between King and Queen Streets.

Westminister Books
445 King St.
☎**454-1442**
Without a doubt one of the best bookstores in Fredericton, Westminister Books offers an excellent selection of English-language novels and essays. The staff is particularly helpful and more than willing to point out the works of authors from this region and from Atlantic Canada in general.

Kingfisher Books
358 Queen St.
☎**458-5531**
If you haven't yet found the book you're looking for at the Westminster bookstore, you can always browse Kingfisher Books, which has an excellent selection.

St. John River Valley

Fr</br>om the République de Madawaska, in the northwestern part of the province, to the industrial city of Saint John, where it empties into the Bay of Fundy, the majestic St. John River is the keystone of New Brunswick's most continental region.

Each bend in the river reveals new scenery and different facets of a land full of contrasts. Around Edmundston and Grand Falls (Grand-Sault) – French-speaking areas graced with flamboyant Catholic churches – visitors will discover a lovely, gently rolling landscape, where the local economy centres on lumbering and potato farming. Farther south, as the valley widens, the rivers runs through an entirely different region, studded with towns and villages boasting a rich architectural heritage.

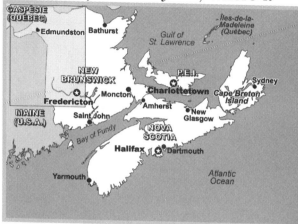

Among these is Fredericton, the province's capital. Two centuries ago, this entire portion of the St. John valley became a veritable "promised land" for thousands of Loyalists (American colonists wishing to remain loyal to the British crown after the Revolutionary War). In spite of these cultural and social differences, the valley is united by one force: an endless fascination with the mighty St. John, from its source to its estuary.

Finding Your Way Around

By Car

From the Québec border, visitors can take Highway 2 (the Trans-Canada Highway) or any other parallel road to the province's capital, Fredericton. After passing through Fredericton, take Highway 7, then Route 102 to Gagetown, the last stop on the tour. By continuing south, visitors will soon reach the city of

Saint John, on the shores of the Bay of Fundy.

Bus Station

Edmundston
Victoria Street, near Hébert Boulevard
☎*739-8309*

Woodstock Bus Stop
☎*328-2245*

Practical Information

Area code: *502*

Tourist Information Offices

New Brunswick Tourist Information Centre
☎*800-561-0123*

Saint-Jacques
Trans-Canada Highway
☎*735-2747*

Exploring

Saint-Jacques

This is the first village that many travellers (or at least those arriving from Québec) will encounter on their tour of New Brunswick. It is therefore no coincidence that Saint-

Jacques is home to one of the province's largest tourist-information centres, as well as a provincial park, **Les Jardins de la République**, which has campsites, a pool and play area for children, as well as hiking and cycling trails. There are also two major attractions nearby.

The **New Brunswick Botanical Garden ★★** *($3; Jun to Sep; Hwy. 2, Exit 8,* ☎*735-2699 or 735-2525),* destined to become one of the region's greatest draws, is worth visiting for a number of reasons. Some 75,000 plants have been distributed over a well laid-out area of 7ha that offers a lovely panoramic view of the region's gentle, wooded valleys. The garden's designers had the clever idea of installing an unobtrusive sound system, enabling visitors to explore the garden with the music of Bach, Chopin or Mozart in the background.

The **Antique Automobile Museum ★** *($2.50; late May to mid-Sep; right beside the Garden,* ☎*735-2525)* grew up around the private collection of Edmundston resident Melvin Louden. It displays a lovely selection of antique cars, some of which are very rare nowadays, including the Bricklin – the only automobile made in New Brunswick – and the 1933 Rolls Royce Phantom.

Edmundston

The region's largest urban area, Edmundston is naturally the heart of northwestern New Brunswick's French-speaking community, which refers to it affectionately as the capital of the mystical République de Madawaska. The driving force behind the city's prosperity is immediately evident in the urban landscape – the pulp and paper industry, which has flourished due to the richness of the neighbouring forests and the city's highly advantageous location at the confluence of the Madawaska and St. John Rivers. While Edmundston's industrial character is unmistakable, the city is also very proud of its festive spirit and cultural life, which is at its peak during the **Foire Breyonne** (☎*739-6608),* the largest French-speaking event in the country to be held outside of Québec. It is during this period, at the end of each July, that visitors can best discover the richness and generosity of the local population.

The impressive **Cathedral of the Immaculate Conception ★** *(145 Rice St.)* towers over the city of Edmundston. It was built during the dark years of the Great Depression with materi-

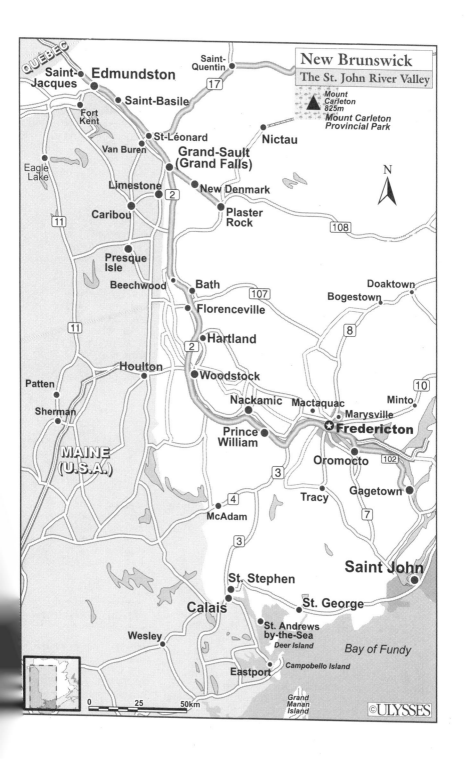

New Brunswick
The St. John River Valley

als from all over the world, including Africa, India, Italy and France. The stained-glass windows are superb.

Visitors interested in learning about the history of the area and its inhabitants can stop by the **Madawaska Historical Museum** *($1; mid-Jun to Sep; 338 Main St., ☎263-1300)*, which houses a permanent collection of artifacts linked to the region's development. The museum also includes a gallery devoted to the work of contemporary Madawaskan artists.

The **Petit-Témis Interprovincial Linear Park** *(☎739-1992)* stretches some 130km and connects Edmunston and Rivière-du-Loup (Québec). This green space includes a network of hiking and cycling trails, some of which offer breathtaking views along the Madawaska River.

Saint-Basile

For many years, colonists from Québec and Acadians who came here seeking refuge formed only a small community, served for more than four decades by a single parish, Saint-Basile. Founded in 1792, the parish originally stretched from the Saint-François River to the present-day city of Grand Falls. Saint-Basile has therefore been dubbed the "Cradle of Madawaska."

The République de Madawaska

The origins of the mythical République de Madawaska date back to the region's early colonization, a time when the British and the Americans were continuously redefining the border between Maine and New Brunswick after skirmishes and tortuous political negotiations. Tired of being mere pawns in all of this, the people of Madawaska, scorning the authorities, eventually decided to "found" their own republic, which had the very vaguest of borders, but more or less encompassed the French-speaking population in this part of the country. Pushing the fantasy even further, they decided that the republic would have its own president, namely, the mayor of Edmundston. Behind this peculiar historical legacy lies a very strong cultural bond between French-speakers on both sides of the border, which can best be appreciated during Edmundston's Foire Brayonne, a festival held each year at the end of July.

Saint-Basile has recently become known for an entirely different reason as well: popular singer Roch Voisine was born here.

Saint Leonard

Without a doubt, Saint-Léonard offers the clearest possible illustration of the arbitrary nature of Canada-U.S. border, which has separated the town from Van Buren (on the U.S. side) since 1842. In any case, these two communities, linked by both history and language, still bear allegiance to the same republic: Madawaska!

From Saint-Léonard, visitors can either go to Mount Carleton Provincial Park or head to the northeastern part of the province on Rte. 17.

Mount Carleton

Mount Carleton Provincial Park ★ *(Take Rte. 180 from Saint-Quentin, ☎235-2025 or 735-2525)* is in the heart of New Brunswick, in the wildest part of the province.

The Brayons

Inhabitants of the République are known as "Brayons", a term whose origins remain obscure. The word might come from *brayer*, meaning "crush," since crushing flax was a common chore for Madawaskan women.

The Brayons are descendants of both Quebecers and Acadians. The former came to New Brunswick in the 18th and 19th centuries seeking new land to settle, while the latter were driven from the lower St. John River area by an influx of Loyalist colonists at the end of the 18th century.

At 820 m-high, Mount Carleton is the tallest peak in the Atlantic provinces. This park is mostly frequented by hikers and has campsites.

From Saint-Léonard, you can continue on Hwy. 2 along the St. John River up to Grand Falls.

Grand Falls (Grand-Sault)

A charming little town on the banks of the St. John, at the point where the river plunges 23m, Grand Falls is a dynamic, engaging community whose mostly French-speaking population has Québécois and Acadian roots. This pretty spot was frequented by the Malecite First Nations for many years before becoming a British military post in 1791. The city was finally established in 1896. In addition to its attractive location, Grand Falls has a charming town centre. Its wide boulevard, flanked by low houses facing right onto the street, gives it a slightly midwestern character. It is worth noting that Grand Falls is the only town in Canada with an officially bilingual name–Grand Falls-Grand Sault. With its green valleys, the surrounding region, known for its potatoes, makes for a lovely outing.

The magnificent **waterfall ★★** that inspired the town's name is the largest and most impressive in Atlantic Canada. The waters of the St. John plunge 23m, then rush for about 2km through a gorge whose sides reach as high as 70m.

At the far end of the gorge, the turbulent water has eroded the rock, creating cavities known here as "wells," since water stays in them after the river rises. Visitors can start off their tour by dropping by the **Malobiannah Centre** *(on Chemin Madawaska, alongside the falls)*, which is both an interpretive centre and a regional tourist information centre. From here, there is a splendid view of the falls and the hydroelectric dam. A footpath heading out from the centre makes it possible to observe the falls and the gorge from all different angles. At the **Centre La Rochelle** *($1; Centennial Park)*, on the opposite bank, right in the centre of town, there is a staircase that leads down to the river bed, offering a better view of the gorge, the wells and the waterfall.

To learn more about Grand Falls and its surrounding area, visitors can head to the little **Grand Falls Museum** *(free admission; Jun to Aug; Rue Church, ☎473-5265)*, which displays a diverse assortment of objects linked to the region's history.

Rte. 108 leads to New Denmark, Plaster Rock and finally the Miramichi River, which flows into the Atlantic.

New Brunswick

New Denmark

New Denmark is a small rural community similar in every way to other towns in the region, except that it also happens to be the hub of the largest Danish colony in North America. Its origins date back to 1872, when the provincial government invited a handful of Danes to settle at the confluence of the Salmon and St. John Rivers. These people were promised good, arable land, but instead inherited uneven, rocky soil. The provincial authorities apparently chose this precise spot along the river so that the Danes would act as a buffer between the French-speakers in the north and the English-speakers in the south. The settlers ended up staying anyway, and their descendants, who now number just under 2,000, hold an annual festival on June 19 to commemorate their ancestors' experience.

Beechwood

Visitors can stop in this tiny hamlet to examine its **hydroelectric power station** or enjoy a picnic in the park by the river.

Bath

The pretty, peaceful village of Bath, located on the east bank of the St. John River, has no sights per se, but it is graced with a few lovely white residences, which are owned by local notables. Visiting here is like stepping back into another era, far from the hustle and bustle of modern cities.

Florenceville

This little village witnessed the humble origins of the McCain company, now an international frozen food empire known especially for its potatoes and French fries. The family is the second wealthiest in New Brunswick, after the Irvings. At the edge of Florenceville stands an imposing factory, which still processes tonnes of locally-grown potatoes each year. In the centre of the village, visitors can stop at the **Andrew & Laura McCain Gallery ★** *(free admission; open all year, Tue noon to 5pm, Wed 10am to 5pm, Thu noon to 8pm, Fri 10am to 5pm; McCain Street; ☎392-6769).*

This gallery displays works by New Brunswick artists, artisans and photographers, and also presents the occasional international exhibit.

Hartland

Home town of Richard Hatfield, the province's eccentric former prime minister, Hartland is an adorable village typical of the St. John River Valley. It is known for its remarkable **covered bridge ★★**, the world's longest. Stretching 390m across the river, the structure was built in 1899, at a time when simply covering a bridge made its skeleton last up to seven times longer. Today there are more covered bridges in New Brunswick than anywhere else on Earth. Visitors who would like to stop for a picnic and admire the local scenery will find an attractive park on the west bank of the river.

Covered Bridge

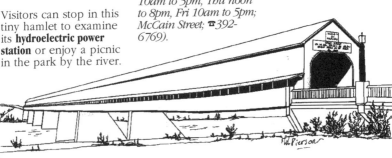

Woodstock

After the Revolutionary War, tens of thousands of U.S. citizens who had fought on the British side took refuge in Canada, a territory Great Britain had wrested from France two decades earlier. In 1784, one of these Loyalists, Captain Jacob Smith, sailed up the St. John to the mouth of the Meduxnekeak River, where British authorities had granted him a piece of land. A few decades later, Woodstock was founded on that spot. Now a medium-sized town, it is the seat of Carleton County. Although known for being somewhat conservative, Woodstock takes pride in living up to its nickname, "Hospitality Town." At the end of July, the town holds an annual festival known as **Old Home Week**, which celebrates family and tradition.

Woodstock's Main and Connell Streets are graced with several pretty historic buildings, including **Connell House** *(free admission; Jul and Aug, 7am to 5:30pm; 128 Connell St., ☎328-9706)*, an impressive upper-class residence. Neoclassical in style, it belonged to the honorable Charles Connell, a local politician who also served as New Brunswick's postmaster until he had to resign in the wake of a controversy that erupted when he issued a stamp in his own honour.

Built in 1833, the **Old Carleton County Courthouse** ★ *(free admission; Jul and Aug; Rte. 560, Upper Woodstock, north of the town centre, ☎328-9706)* is a two-storey wooden building whose modest facade conceals an interior adorned with lovely, sober woodwork. The building served as the Courthouse for over 75 years, until a new Courthouse was inaugurated in the centre of town. A local farmer then used the building as a barn for nearly half a century before the Carleton County Historical Society finally purchased and renovated it in 1960.

Nackawic

Visitors can make a brief stop in Nackawic to see its **giant axe**. A tribute to the region's lumberjacks, it is the largest in the world.

Prince William

A wonderful open-air museum covering 120ha on the banks of the St. John, **Kings Landing** ★★ *($10; Jun to mid-Oct, every day 10am to 5pm; along the Trans-Canada Highway in Prince-William, ☎363-4999, ≈363-4989)* is a reproduction of an early 19th-century Loyalist village. It includes more than 20 historic buildings and about 30,000 objects that help illuminate the area's past, including furniture, clothing and tools. To enliven the atmosphere, there are people dressed in period clothing, who perform the daily tasks of 19th-century villagers, as well as answering visitors' questions. There is no more pleasant and effective means of learning about Loyalist history than a visit to Kings Landing, the best museum on the subject.

Mactaquac

Mactaquac is the site of a very popular **provincial park** *(off of Rte. 2, ☎363-4747)* where visitors can enjoy activities year-round. The park features beaches, hiking trails, campgrounds, a marina, a golf course and also a trail for cross-country skiing. The park is located alongside the river, whose waters are regulated by the largest **hydroelectric dam** in the Maritimes.

Fredericton

(see p 53)

Oromocto

A somewhat dreary place, Oromocto is home to the soldiers stationed at Gagetown, a very important Cana-

New Brunswick

dian military base. It features a **military museum** *(free admission; open all year; on the Canadian base; ☎422-2530)*, which displays weapons from the 18th, 19th and 20th centuries.

Gagetown

After winding its way through the fields of a prosperous farming region, the little road heading out of Oromocto leads to Gagetown, a tiny village on the banks of the majestic St. John. Everything here —the church, the general store, the handful of houses, the very location – is so pretty that you'd think it is straight out of a fairy tale. This peaceful spot has retained the old-fashioned character of a Loyalist village, as well as an atmosphere that couldn't possibly be more Anglo-Saxon. With all that charm, it is hardly surprising that each year Gagetown attracts artists seeking inspiration, as well as vacationers looking for a place to relax. Sailors stop here, too, tying their yachts or sailboats to the village wharf. Although Gagetown is small, it nevertheless boasts several bed and breakfasts, a very good inn, an art gallery and several craft shops. There is also a free ferry service to the other side of the river.

The **Tilley House ★** *($2; mid-Jun to mid-Sep, every day 10am to 5pm; Front St., ☎488-2966)* was built in 1786, making it one of the oldest residences in New Brunswick. It now houses the Queens County Museum, which displays all sorts of objects relating to local history and the life of the house's most illustrious owner, Samuel Leonard Tilley, one of the Fathers of Canadian Confederation (1867).

At the **Loomcrofter Studio ★** *(south of the village, near the school, ☎488-2400)*, visitors will find the studios of various designers and weavers of tartan cloth. The building itself is one of the oldest in the St. John River Valley.

Outdoor Activities

Cycling

Both the St. John River Valley and the Acadian coast are very interesting regions, but the distances between villages can be quite long. One solid word of advice: avoid the roads in the middle of the province (along the Miramichi River, for example), as these are long and monot-

onous. Some parks, such as the Petit-Témis Interprovincial Linear Park, (which connects Edmunston and Rivière-du-Loup, Québec by bike, situated 130km farther), are particularly beautiful by bike.

Canoeing

Saint-Quentin

Centre de Plein Air du Vieux Moulin
☎235-1110

Cruises

Grand-Sault (Grand Falls)

To admire the gorge a little closer, 45min cruises aboard pontoons are organized by the Falls and Gorge Commission. *($15, ☎475-7769 or 475-7766 www.grandfalls.com)*

Accommodations

Edmundston

Hostelling International
$20 non-members
88 beds
10647 81st Ave., T6E 1X1
☎*988-6836*
≈*988-8698*
Edmunston has its own youth hostel, which offers 88 beds, two fully equipped kitchenettes and a game room. Centrally located, it is a great choice for those on a tight budget. Mountain-bike rentals on site.

Auberge Le Fief
$80
ℜ, *tv*
8 rooms
87 Church St., E3V 1J6
☎*735-0400*
Edmunston has very few charming establishments, but Le Fief, a beautiful historic home, is an exception. Its decor is meticulous, and the rooms, all of which have private bathrooms, are lovely. Perfect location in the centre of town.

Howard Johnson Hotel
$90
tv, ℜ, ≈
103 rooms
100 Rice St., E3V 1T4
☎*739-7321 or 800-654-2000*
≈*735-9101*
The convention centre of the "capital" of Madawaska, the province's second largest, is located right downtown. Adjoining it is the Howard Johnson Hotel, which offers the most comfortable lodging in Edmunston. Designed for both business people and vacationers, the hotel features a wide range of services, two restaurants and a bar.

Grand Falls (Grand-Sault)

Hill Top Motel
$63
tv, ℜ
28 rooms
131 Madawaska Rd., E3Y 1A7
☎*473-2684 or 800-496-1244*
≈*473-4567*
The Hill Top Motel is the only motel located in the heart of Grand Falls, just a few hundred metres from the Interpretive Centre. As its name implies, the Hill Top is located atop a promontory offering a view of the city's hydroelectric dam. The rooms are clean but decorated with little imagination.

Maple Tourist Home
$55
tv
3 rooms
142 Main St., E3Z 2V9
☎*473-1763*
An excellent bed and breakfast located in downtown Grand Falls, the Maple Tourist Home has three spotless rooms. Guests can also relax in a comfortable common room.

Lakeside Lodge & Resort
$69
K, tv, ◌, ℜ, ⊛, ℜ, ≡
15 rooms
590 Gillespie Rd., Lake Pirie
E0J 1M0
☎*473-6252*
Not far from Lake Pirie, about 5km south of Grand Falls, the Lakeside Lodge & Resort offers nature-lovers an excellent alternative to the local motels. Seven cottages with fireplaces and kitchenettes are available, as well as eight rooms, two of which have a fireplace and a sauna.

Motel Léo
$66
tv, ℜ
44 rooms
2.5km north of Grand Falls, E0J 1M0
☎*473-2090 or 800-661-0077*
Along the Trans-Canada Highway, 2.5km north of Grand Falls, the Motel Léo rents inexpensive, well-appointed rooms. This is a fairly typical motel, where most guests only stop for one night to take a break on a long trip. The staff is very friendly.

Auberge Près du Lac
$81
tv, ℜ, ≈
100 rooms
2.5km north of Grand Falls
E0J 1M0
☎*471-1300*
for reservations:
☎*888-473-1300*
≈*473-5501*
Right next door to the Motel Léo is the Auberge Près du Lac, offering quality lodging. The complex includes motel rooms as well as

cottages on the shores of an artificial lake. Guests can choose a standard room or a wedding suite. Activities, ranging from pedal-boating on the lake, to mini-golf, basketball, working out and swimming in the indoor pool, make this a popular spot for families.

Plaster Rock

Tobique View Motel & Restaurant
$60
tv, K, ℜ
15 rooms
a few kilometres before Plaster Rock
70 Main St., E0J 3A8
☎*356-2684 or 356-2683*
⇌*356-7583*
Set back from the road, the Tobique View Motel & Restaurant is beautifully located on the shores of the peaceful Tobique River. Due to its ideal location and the tranquillity of the surroundings, this motel is popular with travellers out to explore the wilderness around Plaster Rock.

Hartland

Campbell's Bed & Breakfast
$35
tv, K
3 rooms
1km north of Hartland, E0J 1N0
☎*375-4775*
⇌*375-4014*
It is hard to imagine a more peaceful spot than Campbell's Bed & Breakfast, a farmhouse built along the St. John River near the town of Hartland. Sitting on the large porch, it is easy to appreciate the tranquillity of Richard Hatfield country. The rooms are comfortable, although a bit over-decorated, and guests have use of a fully-equipped kitchen at all times. Mrs. Campbell doesn't actually live in the B&B, but rather in a little house about 200m away on the same property.

Woodstock

John Gyles Motor Inn
$52
tv, ℜ, ⊗
20 rooms
on the Trans-Canada 8km south of Woodstock, E0J 6B7
☎*328-6622*
⇌*328-2468*
Just like the numerous other motels along the Trans-Canada on the outskirts of Woodstock, the John Gyles Motor Inn offers rooms at a good price. The quality of its restaurant, which serves various German specialties, distinguishes the John Gyles from the others.

Down House B&B
$60 bkfst incl.
ℜ, tv
4 rooms
698 Main St.
☎*328-1819*
⇌*325-1881*
A magnificent Victorian home dating from 1881, the Down House boasts a unique and attractive decor. Its rooms, which have living rooms filled with antique furniture, are simply delightful. What's more, it has a lovely terrace, where breakfast is served, and the owners greet guests with a warm welcome. One of the most highly recommended establishments in the region.

Stiles Motel Hill View
$70
tv, ℜ, ≡
30 rooms
827 Main St., E7M 6B7
☎*328-6671*
⇌*328-3737*
The only motel located inside the city limits of Woodstock, the Stiles Motel Hill View gives visitors who stop here the opportunity to discover a small Anglophone community typical of the St. John River Valley. The rooms were recently renovated; this isn't luxury, but it's still very comfortable and clean. The motel includes a small restaurant serving family-style cuisine.

Auberge Wandlyn Inn
$85
tv, ℜ, ≈
52 rooms
Houlton Exit off the Trans-Canada, E0J 6B5
☎*328-8876*
☎*800-561-0000 from Canada*
☎*800-561-0006 from the U.S.*
⇌*328-4828*
The nicest accommodations in the immediate area of Woodstock are at the Auberge Wandlyn Inn. There are 50 well-appointed rooms as well as a heated indoor pool and a dining room. For those in a hurry this motel is ideally located along the Trans-Canada and Route 95 towards the United States.

Kingsclear

Mactaquac Holiday Inn
$109
tv, ℜ, ≈, ◔, ⊛
82 rooms
Exit 274 off the Trans-Canada Hwy.
☎363-5111 or 800-561-5111
✆363-3000
The Mactaquac Holiday Inn is a large hotel complex overlooking Lake Mactaquac, a widening of the St. John River caused by a dam downstream. Besides 74 rooms, the luxurious complex includes six cottages, each equipped with a kitchenette and a dining room. Several activities are organized for vacationers, including various types of fishing. Extensive facilities make this is a prized spot for conferences and business meetings in a relaxed setting.

Gagetown

 **Steamers Stop Inn**
$75
tv, ℜ
6 rooms
74 Front St., E0G 1V0
☎488-2903
✆488-1116
A rather austere-looking house in the heart of town along the shore of the St. John River, the Steamers Stop Inn fits right in with the pastoral charm that characterizes Gagetown. There is definitely no better place to get a real feel for this little vacation spot, since everything is close by. Rooms are

well appointed, and five of them provide a view of the river. The inn also has a decent restaurant.

Restaurants

Grand Falls (Grand-Sault)

Hill Top Motel Restaurant
$-$$
131 Madawaska Rd.
☎473-2684
The best thing about this restaurant is its incredible view of the waterfall. It serves up decent family-style cuisine.

La Renaissance
$$
Motel Léo
The Grand Falls region is a big potato producer, so much so that the house specialty of the La Renaissance restaurant is the "stuffed potato": half a baked potato stuffed with ham, chicken, cheese, etc. Whatever the variation, the "stuffed potato" is quite filling and makes an economical meal. The rest of the menu includes typical home-style cooking. The decor is simple and the service is courteous.

La Violette
$$
Motel Près du Lac
La Violette is also a family restaurant, but with a more elaborate menu than its competi-

tor's at the Motel Léo. The layout of the dining room is more open and elegant. They menu includes meat, chicken, seafood... basically, a bit of everything!

Karl's German Cuisine
$$$
Lake Side Lodge & Resort
Gillipsie Rd.
☎473-6252
Grills, sausages, sauerkraut and other German dishes are among the specialities offered at this restaurant, which serves up hearty fare. Situated in the middle of the countryside, the setting is enchanting. The country-style decor, with a fireplace in the dining room and large bay windows, is charming.

Woodstock

J.R.
$-$$
Main St.
500m after the community college
☎328-9326
Both a bar and a restaurant serving home-style cooking, the J.R. is somewhat of an institution in Woodstock. This spot is quite popular on weekends when young college students and locals come here for drinks, dinner or dancing.

Heino's
$$
8km south of Woodstock
Heino's restaurant in the John Gyles Motor Inn is famous throughout the region for its

New Brunswick

excellent German family cuisine. Of course several varieties of sausage figure on the menu, as well as the great classics of that country's cuisine.

Down House B&B
$$-$$$
698 Main St.
☎*328-1819*
The Down House B&B also has a restaurant that prepares innovative cuisine using fresh, healthy ingredients – something not seen too often in this region. From dawn to dusk, guests file into this place to enjoy delicious dishes in the dining room, which has a cozy fireplace, or on the adjoining terrace.

Gagetown

Steamers Stop Inn
$$-$$$
Front St.
The menu of the Steamers Stop Inn is rich in traditional regional specialties, with particular attention paid to the choice of fresh ingredients in the preparation of the meals. Diners can enjoy a lovely view of the river from the back veranda.

Entertainment

Grand Falls (Grand-Sault)

Grits Bar and Grill
456 Broadway
☎*473-3311*
Grits is one of the favourite meeting places for youth in the region. Beer on tap as well as typical pub fare is served. Friendly, festive atmosphere.

Shopping

Saint-Jacques

The Visitor Information Centre Boutique
Hwy. 2
The Visitor Information Centre Boutique is a great place to pick up a few souvenirs. This shop sells beautiful creations by local artists,

as well as CDs and books by Acadian and New Brunswick artists and authors.

King's Landing

Kings Landing Museum Shop
Kings Landing
☎*363-5805*
The Kings Landing Museum Shop sells not only a good selection of souvenirs of the site, but also a wide selection of books on the history of the region and Atlantic Canada.

Gagetown

Acadia Gallery of Canadian Art
late Jun to late Sep, everyday 11am to 4pm
1948 Lakeview Rd.
☎*488-1119*
The charming contemporary Acadia Gallery of Canadian Art, located in the centre of Gagetown, exhibits a particularly interesting selection of works by artists using a variety of media. Since the gallery also serves as a workshop, it is often possible to meet some of the artists inspired by this enchanting site along the St. John River.

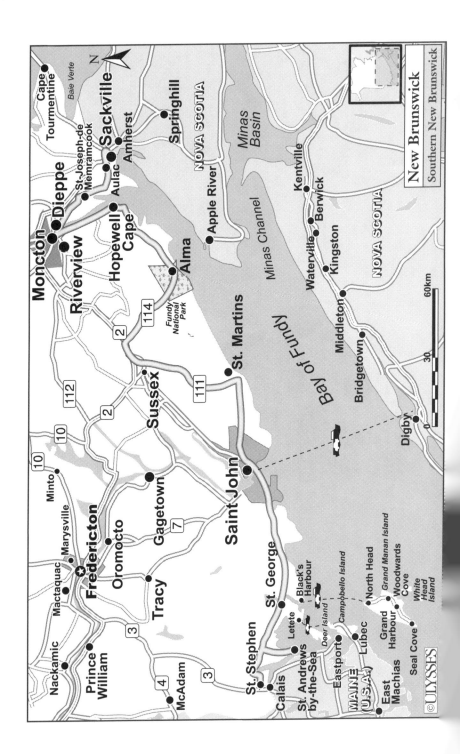

New Brunswick
Southern New Brunswick

© ULYSSES

Southern New Brunswick

All along the coastal road that leads from the border of the United States to that of Nova Scotia, the landscape, villages and towns are marked by one of the most incredible natural phenomena on Earth: the tides of the Bay of Fundy.

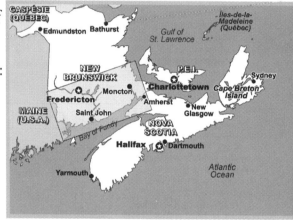

Twice a day, these tides, the highest in the world, storm the shores of the bay at lightning speed. In some places, the water can reach as high as 16m (the equivalent of a four-storey building) in just a few hours, transforming the landscape in remarkable ways over the years. The tides are so powerful that they actually reverse the flow of a waterfall in Saint John and create a tidal bore (a small tidal wave) on the Petitcodiac River.

Then, receding just as rapidly, they leave behind endless beaches perfect for clam-digging, which may be explored until the next massive rise in the water level. Adding to the pleasure of visiting this magnificent coastal region, the shores of the Bay of Fundy are studded with picturesque villages boasting a rich architectural heritage.

Saint John, the province's largest city, and Moncton, its most dynamic, are also located here. Finally, the bay is one of the best places in the world for whale-watching, since more than 20 different species come here to feed in the summer.

Finding Your Way Around

By Car

From St. Stephen to Saint John, and then on to Sussex, the major road is Highway 1. In Sussex, Highway 1 connects with Highway 2, which leads to Moncton and Aulac, at the border of Nova Scotia, where the tour ends. To reach Deer Island, take the exit for St. George from Highway 2, then follow the signs to the tiny village of Letete. A ferry crosses from there to Deer Island. It is possible to reach Campobello Island from the state of Maine by taking the road from Calais to Lubec. To reach Grand Manan Island, visitors must take the ferry from Blacks Harbour.

By Plane

St. John Airport: About 10km east of the city. A shuttle carries passengers from the large downtown hotels to the airport several times a day. The airport is served mainly by Air Canada (☎632-1517) and its partner, Air Nova, and Canadian Airlines (☎698-2630) and its partner, Air Atlantic.

Moncton Airport: Located on Champlain Street, in Dieppe. The downtown area may be reached by taxi. The airport is served mainly by Air Canada (☎857-1044) and its partner Air Nova, and Canadian Airlines (☎857-0620) and its partner, Air Atlantic.

Bus Stations

Saint John
300 Union St., at the corner of Carmarthen St.
☎658-4700

Moncton
downtown, at 961 Main St.
☎859-5060

Train Stations

Saint John
Station St.
☎800-561-3952

Moncton
Downtown, on the west side, near Main St.
☎859-3917

By Ferry

St. John: A ferry makes the crossing from Saint John to Digby, Nova Scotia three times a day except for Sunday, setting out from a dock on the west bank of the St. John River;
☎636-4048.

Grand Manan Island: A ferry makes its way five or six times a day from Blacks Harbour,
☎662-3724.

Practical Information

Area code: **506**

Tourist Information Offices

New Brunswick Tourist Information Centre
☎800-561-0123

St. Stephen
King St.
☎466-7390

St. Andrew
Hwy. 1
☎466-4858

Saint John
Hwy. 1
☎658-2940
near the Reversing Falls
☎658-2937
downtown, in the market
☎658-2855

Moncton
Main St., close to Boreview Park
☎856-4399
City Hall, 665 Main St.
☎853-3590
www.greater.moncton.nb.ca

Exploring

St. Stephen

The most important border town in Atlantic Canada, St. Stephen is a small, lively community that was founded in 1784 by American colonists wishing to remain loyal to the British crown after the Revolutionary War. Today, ironically, St. Stephen and Calais, its twin town in the state of Maine, could easily be mistaken for a single

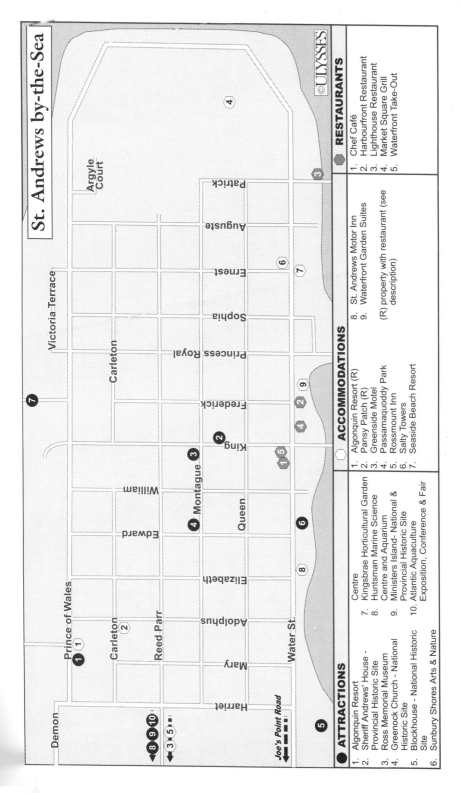

St. Andrews by-the-Sea

Victoria Terrace

Argyle Court

Joe's Point Road

©ULYSSES

● ATTRACTIONS

1. Algonquin Resort
2. Sheriff Andrews' House - Provincial Historic Site
3. Ross Memorial Museum
4. Greenock Church - National Historic Site
5. Blockhouse - National Historic Site
6. Sunbury Shores Arts & Nature Centre
7. Kingsbrae Horticultural Garden
8. Huntsman Marine Science Centre and Aquarium
9. Ministers Island- National & Provincial Historic Site
10. Atlantic Aquaculture Exposition, Conference & Fair

◇ ACCOMMODATIONS

1. Algonquin Resort (R)
2. Pansy Patch (R)
3. Greenside Motel
4. Passamaquoddy Park
5. Rossmount Inn
6. Salty Towers
7. Seaside Beach Resort
8. St. Andrews Motor Inn
9. Waterfront Garden Suites

(R) property with restaurant (see description)

⬡ RESTAURANTS

1. Chef Café
2. Harbourfront Restaurant
3. Lighthouse Restaurant
4. Market Square Grill
5. Waterfront Take-Out

town if it weren't for the St. Croix River, which forms a natural border. This lively community is celebrated on both sides of the border each year during the **International Festival**, which takes place at the end of August. In early August, another festival, this time dedicated to **chocolate**, is held only in St. Stephen, which has the distinction of being the birthplace of the chocolate bar, invented here in 1910 by the Ganong company. The ever successful **Ganong Chocolatier** *(73 Milltown Blvd.,* ☎*465-5611)* shop is a must for anyone with a sweet tooth.

The **Charlotte County Museum** *(free admission; Jun to Aug, Mon to Sat 9:30am to 4:30pm; 443 Milltown Blvd.,* ☎*466-3295)* is set up inside a Second Empire style residence built in 1864 by a prosperous local businessman. It now houses a collection of objects related to local history, especially the period when St. Stephen and the small neighbouring villages were known for shipbuilding.

The **Crocker Hill Garden & Studio** *(by reservation only; 2.4km east of St. Stephen, on Ledge Rd.,* ☎*466-4251)* is a magnificent garden looking out on the St. Croix River.

St. Andrews by-the-Sea

The most famous vacation spot in Southern New Brunswick, St. Andrews is a lovely village facing the bay. It has managed to benefit from its popularity by highlighting its astonishingly rich architectural heritage. Like many other communities in the area, St. Andrews was founded by Loyalists in 1783, and then enjoyed a period of great prosperity during the 19th century as a centre for shipbuilding and the exportation of billets. A number of the opulent houses flanking its streets, particularly **Water Street ★**, date back to that golden era. At the end of the century, St. Andrews's began welcoming affluent visitors, who came here to drink in the invigorating sea air.

St. Andrews' new vocation was clearly established in 1889 with the construction of the magnificent **Algonquin ★★** hotel on a hill overlooking the village. In addition to the picturesque charm of its many historic buildings and its location alongside the bay, with its giant tides, St. Andrews now boasts a wide selection of accommodations and fine restaurants, numerous shops and a famous golf-course. All of this

makes St. Andrews by-the-Sea a perfect place to stay during a tour of the region and its islands.

Erected in 1820, **Sheriff Andrews's House ★** *(free admission; late Jun to early Sep 9:30am to 4:30pm; 63 King St.,* ☎*453-2324)* is one of the town's best-preserved homes from that era. It was built by Elusha Shelton Andrews, sheriff of Charlotte County and son of distinguished Loyalist Reverend Samuel Andrews. Since 1986, it has belonged to the provincial government, which has turned it into a museum. Guides in period costume explain the sheriff's life and times.

A sumptuous 19th century neoclassical residence, the **Ross Memorial Museum ★** *(free admission, late May to early Oct, Tue to Sat 10am to 4:30pm, Sun 1:30pm to 4:30pm; 188 Montague St.,* ☎*529-1824)* contains an antique collection, which Henry Phipps Ross and Sarah Juliette Ross, an American couple who lived in St. Andrews from 1902 until they died, assembled over their lifetime. The Rosses had a passion for travelling and antiques, and acquired some magnificent pieces of Chinese porcelain and other now priceless imported objects, as well as some lovely furniture made in New Brunswick.

There are several remarkable churches in St. Andrews. The most flamboyant is **Greenock Church** ★★ *(at the corner of Montague and*

The centre is better known, however, for its summer courses on art, crafts and nature, for groups of children and adults.

large estate, Van Horne erected an immense 50-room summer home. Minister's Island is only accessible at low tide. To arrange a visit, con-

Algonquin Resort

Edward Sts.), a Presbyterian church completed in 1824. Its most interesting feature is its pulpit, a good part of which is made of Honduran mahogany.

Until very recently, the **St. Andrews Blockhouse** *(on the west end of Water St.),* a national historic site, was the last surviving blockhouse from the War of 1812. It was unfortunately damaged by fire, but necessary repairs are being made. Pretty **Centennial Park** lies opposite.

The attractively landscaped **Kingsbrae Horticultural Garden** *(220 King St.,* ☎*529-3335,* ⌨*529-4875)* is an 11ha garden with several species of rare flowers and shrubs.

The **Sunbury Shores Arts & Nature Centre** *(139 Water St.,* ☎*529-3386)* houses a small art gallery where visitors can admire the work of New Brunswick artists.

At the **Huntsman Marine Science Centre and Aquarium** ★★ *($4.50; Jul to Oct, 10am to 4pm; Brandy Cove Rd.;* ☎*529-1202),* visitors can learn about the bay's natural treasures. Several animal species may be observed here, including seals, who are fed every day at 11am and 4pm. There is also a touch-tank, where visitors can touch various live species of shellfish. This is an important research centre.

At the beginning of the 19th century, the **Ministers Island Historic Site** ★ *($5 per car includes tour of house; Jun to mid-Oct; Mowat Drive Rd., take Bar Rd. only at low tide until the end)* was the property of Reverend Samuel. It was purchased in 1890 by Sir William Van Horne, a Montréal resident famous for building the Canadian Pacific Railway, the first railroad linking Montréal to Vancouver. On this

tact the tourist information office *(*☎*529-3000 or 529-5081).*

At the **Atlantic Salmon Centre** *($4; Apr to Oct 9am to 5pm; Chamcook, 8km from St. Andrews on Rte. 127,* ☎*529-4581),* visitors can learn about the life cycle of Atlantic salmon, most importantly by viewing the fish in its natural environment through a window.

St. George

St. George, nicknamed Granite Town because of the rich granite deposits found in this area, is a small town with a Loyalist heritage, located alongside a pretty **waterfall** ★ on the Magaguadavic River. A small lookout at the town entrance, beside the bridge on Brunswick Street, offers a lovely view of the waterfall, the gorge, the former dam of the St. George Pulp & Paper

New Brunswick

Company and the ladder built to help salmon swim upriver in summer.

Like many towns and villages founded on the shores of the bay in the late 18th century, St. George has its share of interesting buildings, such as the **post office** *(Brunswick St.)*, with its red granite facade, and several churches, including the **Kirk Presbyterian** *(on Brunswick St., at the east exit of the village)*, the oldest church of its denomination in Canada. From St. George, visitors can head to Letete, where a free ferry service takes passengers to Deer Island between 7am and 10pm every day.

Deer Island

After cruising through a scattering of little islands covered with birds, the free ferry from Letete lands at Deer Island, with its wooded landscape, untouched beaches and tiny fishing villages. Three hours before high tide each day, visitors can view an interesting natural phenomenon from the southern point of the island – one of the largest whirlpools in the world, known locally as

the **Old Sow** ★. In summertime, a private ferry makes the crossing between Deer Island and Campobello Island about every hour.

Campobello Island

Campobello, the beloved island of former U.S. president Franklin D. Roosevelt (1882-1945), is a good place for fans of history and the great outdoors to unwind. People come here to enjoy the lovely untouched beaches, go cycling on the quiet roads or walk along the well-maintained trails that follow the shoreline.

On the eastern tip, the picturesque lighthouse at **East Quoddy Head** ★ occupies a magnificent site on the bay, from which it is sometimes possible to spot whales and other sea mammals. In the early 19th century, Campobello's beauty began to attract the attention of wealthy families living in the northeastern cities of the United States, who

built lovely summer homes here. The most famous of these families was that of Franklin D. Roosevelt, whose father, James, purchased 1.6ha on the island in 1883. Franklin himself, and then his own family, spent most of his summers here from 1883 to 1921, the year he contracted polio.

He returned on several later occasions to visit his friends on the island while serving as President of the United States. Although Campobello lies within Canada, it is most easily accessible from the border town of Lubec, Maine. During the summer months, a private ferry also shuttles hourly between Deer Island and Campobello.

Roosevelt-Campobello International Park ★ ★ *(free admission; late May to early Oct, 10am to 6pm; Rte. 774, ☎ 752-2922)* is a joint project of the Canadian and U.S. governments, launched in 1964 with the aim of increasing public awareness of Roosevelt's special attachment to Campobello Island and his magnificent property there. The visitor's centre shows a short film on Roosevelt's sojourns on the island.

Roosevelt House

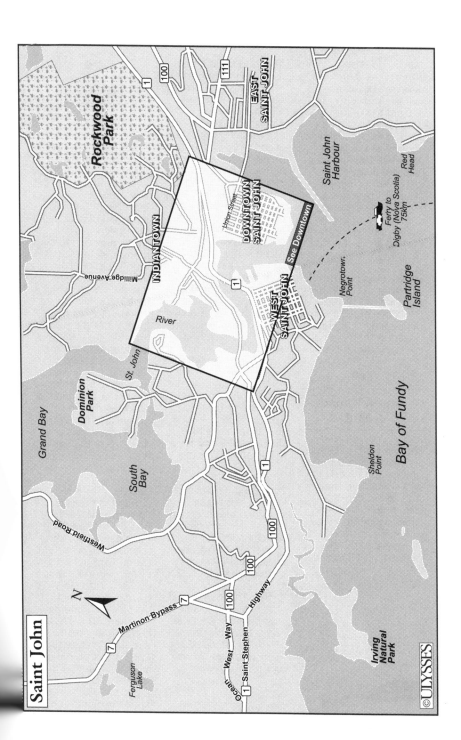

Saint John

Rockwood Park

Rockwood Park

INDIANTOWN

Millidge Avenue

St. John

River

Grand Bay

Dominion Park

South Bay

Westfield Road

Ferguson Lake

Martinon Bypass

Ocean West-Way Saint-Stephen Highway

DOWNTOWN SAINT JOHN

Union Street

WEST SAINT JOHN

EAST SAINT JOHN

Saint John Harbour

Red Head

Negrotown. Point

Partridge Island

Sheldon Point

Bay of Fundy

Irving Natural Park

See Downtown

Ferry to Digby (Nova Scotia) 75km

N

© ULYSSES

Afterward, visitors can tour the extraordinary **Roosevelt House**, most of whose furnishings belonged to the former U.S. president, then stop at the **Prince House**, the site of the **James Roosevelt House** and the **Hubbard House**. The park also includes a beautiful natural area, south of the visitor's centre, where lovely hiking trails have been cleared along the shore.

Located near Roosevelt International Park, **Herring Cove** (☎752-7000) is a lovely nature site with hiking trails, an interpretation centre, a golf course and campsites.

Grand Manan Island

For many years, Grand Manan's 275-odd bird species and unique rock formations mainly attracted scientists, including the famous James Audubon in the early 19th century. More recently, however, Grand Manan has

begun to benefit from the current ecotourism craze, since the island obviously has a lot to offer nature lovers. It is a pleasant place to explore by bicycle, and even better on foot, thanks to the excellent network of trails running alongside the jagged shoreline with its often spectacular scenery. Without question, one of the most picturesque places on the island is the lighthouse known as **Swallowtail Light ★**, which stands at the tip of a peninsula at North Head. From here, whales can regularly be seen swimming off the shores of the island. Grand Manan also features a **museum** (*Grand Harbour*, ☎662-3524) and serves as the point of departure for numerous whale-watching excursions and expeditions to **Machias Seal Island ★**, a remarkable bird sanctuary.

The island has several lighthouses, beaches and great bird-watching spots. Travellers have a choice of several B&Bs as well as an excellent **campground** (*The Anchorage*, ☎662-7022).

To reach Grand Manan Island, visitors must take the ferry from Blacks Harbour (☎662-3724), which makes five or six trips a day.

Saint John

Saint John, New Brunswick's largest city, occupies a hilly area on either side of the St. John River, at the point where it flows into the Bay of Fundy. A perfect example of the old, industrial port cities in the eastern part of North America, it has a unique, slightly mysterious charm. Lofty cranes and warehouses line the docks, which look strangely like wooden fences rising high out of the river at low tide. To add to its mysterious character, Saint John is often blanketed with a thick fog that can envelop the city at any moment, and then disappear just as quickly. The growth of the city's industries is due largely to its port, which is ice-free all year long.

The site itself was scouted out for the first time on June 24, 1604 by explorer Samuel de Champlain, who christened the river St. John (Saint-Jean) in honour of the patron saint of that day. Later, in 1631, Charles de La Tour established a trading post here. The city's history didn't really start, however, until 1783, under the English regime. From May 10 to May 18 of that year, about 2,000 Loyalists landed in Saint John, seeking a fresh start in life after the defeat of

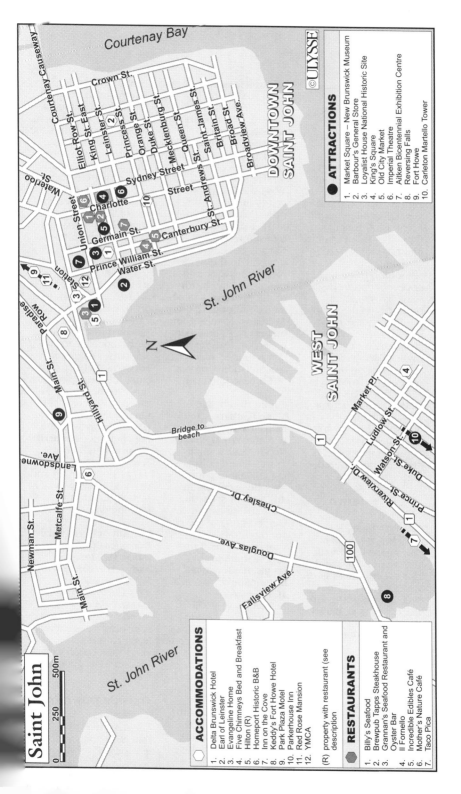

Saint John

0 — 250 — 500m

DOWNTOWN SAINT JOHN

WEST SAINT JOHN

● ATTRACTIONS

1. Market Square – New Brunswick Museum
2. Barbour's General Store
3. Loyalist House National Historic Site
4. King's Square
5. Old City Market
6. Imperial Theatre
7. Aitken Bicentennial Exhibition Centre
8. Reversing Falls
9. Fort Howe
10. Carleton Martello Tower

⬡ ACCOMMODATIONS

1. Delta Brunswick Hotel
2. Earl of Leinster
3. Evangeline Home
4. Five Chimneys Bed and Breakfast
5. Hilton (R)
6. Homeport Historic B&B
7. Inn on the Cove
8. Keddy's Fort Howe Hotel
9. Park Plaza Motel
10. Parkerhouse Inn
11. Red Rose Mansion
12. YMCA

(R) property with restaurant (see description)

⬡ RESTAURANTS

1. Billy's Seafood
2. Brewpub Tapps Steakhouse
3. Grannan's Seafood Restaurant and Oyster Bar
4. Il Fornello
5. Incredible Edibles Café
6. Mother's Nature Café
7. Taco Pica

© ULYSSE

British forces by American revolutionaries. More arrived before winter, doubling the population of Saint John.

The city then absorbed a large number of immigrants, most from the British Isles. In those years, Partridge Island, in the port, was Canada's chief point of entry and quarantine station for immigrants. Today, Saint John has a higher concentration of Irish-Canadians than any other city in the country. It is a pleasant place to visit, particularly in mid-July during **Loyalist Days**, which commemorate the arrival of the Loyalists in 1783. The excellent **By-the-Sea Festival**, in August, celebrates the performing arts, while the **Franco-Frolic**, held in June, honours Acadian culture and traditions.

Downtown

Downtown Saint John ★★, with its narrow streets lined with historic buildings and houses, lies on a hill on the east side of the river. A tour of the area usually starts at **Market Square**, laid out a little more than a decade ago as part of an effort to revitalize the city centre. The square includes a shopping mall, a convention centre, several restaurants and a hotel that combines modern construction with 19th century buildings. An excellent

tourist information office is located at the entrance to Market Square. The **New Brunswick Museum ★** (*$6; year-round, Mon to Fri 9am to 9pm, Sat 10am to 6pm, Sun noon to 5pm; Market Sq., ☎643-2300, ≈643-6081*) was recently moved and is now also located in Market Square. The oldest museum in Canada, it is devoted not only to the work of New Brunswick artists, but also to the history of the province's inhabitants – Aboriginals, Acadians, Loyalists, and others. The permanent collection features certain imported objects as well, including pieces of Chinese porcelain.

On the south side of Market Square stands **Barbour's General Store** (*$2; mid May to mid Oct; ☎658-2939*), a small brick building displaying consumer goods typically available in this type of shop during the 19th century. Guided tours of the city are offered from here. Visitors can head up Union Street to the **Loyalist House National Historic Site ★** (*$3; mid-May to mid-Sep; 120 Union St., ☎652-3590*), a very simple house built in the first decade of the 19th century, which is decorated with elegant period furniture. Union Street later intersects with Charlotte Street, where visitors can turn right to reach **King's Square ★** a pretty urban park marking the

centre of Saint John. The paths in the park are laid out in the pattern of the Union Jack; what better way for the inhabitants of Saint John to express their attachment to their mother country? Standing opposite the park on Charlotte Street is the **Old City Market ★** (*free admission; year-round, Mon to Thu 7:30am to 6pm, Fri 7:30am to 7pm, Sat 7:30am to 5pm; 47 Charlotte St., ☎658-2820*), dating back to 1876, where shoppers can still purchase fresh produce from local farms. Some merchants sell dulse, a type of seaweed that people in Saint John use generously as an accompaniment to various dishes. On another side of the park, visitors will find the sumptuous **Imperial Theatre ★** (*24 King Sq. South, ☎634-8355 or 674-4111*), built in 1913 and restored in 1994, which is dedicated to the performing arts.

The **Aitken Bicentennial Exhibition Centre** (*free admission; Jun to Sep, every day 10am to 5pm; Sep to Jun, Tue to Sun 11:30am to 4:30pm; 20 Hazen Ave., ☎633-4870*) presents exhibits specifically designed to teach children about various facets of science in a dynamic fashion.

Outside Downtown

The **Reversing Falls ★★** (*on Rte. 100, at the river*) is a unique natural phenomenon that occurs twice a day at high tide. The current of the river, which, at this point, drops 4m at low tide, is reversed at high tide when the water level of the bay is several metres higher than that of the river. This counter-current is felt as far up-river as Fredericton.

For an excellent **view** ★ of the city, head to the site of **Fort Howe** *(Main St.,* ☎*658-2090).* At the same location, there is a wooden blockhouse, which was built in Halifax and moved here in 1777 to protect the port of Saint John in the event of a U.S. attack.

The **Carleton Martello Tower National Historic Side** ★★ *($2.50; Jun to Oct 9am to 5pm; on the west bank, Whipple St.,* ☎*636-4011)* is a circular tower built during the War of 1812 to protect the port from U.S. attacks. It was also used as a command post for the Canadian army during the Second World War. Guides in 19th-century dress explain the history of both the tower and the city of Saint John. From the top, visitors can enjoy a magnificent panoramic view of the city, the port and the bay.

If Saint John were a person, **Rockwood Park** *(main entry on Mt. Pleasant Ave.)* would be its lungs. Covering 890ha, it is Canada's largest city park. All sorts of

outdoor activities may be enjoyed here, including hiking, swimming, fishing, canoeing and pedal-boating. A number of other activities are organized just for children. In the north section of the park, is the **Cherry Brook Zoo** *($3.25; open all year 10am to nightfall; Sandy Point Rd., in the north part of Rockwood Park,* ☎*634-1440),* the only zoo in the Maritimes featuring exotic animals. About 100 or so different species may be found here.

For many years, **Partridge Island** ★ *($10; May to Nov; from the port of St. John, for information* ☎*693-2598)* was the main point of entry for immigrants coming to Canada from the British Isles and the European continent. Between 1785 and 1942, it was the transition point and quarantine station for some three million immigrants who then settled in Saint John or, more commonly, elsewhere in Canada or the United States.

About 2,000 of these individuals died here; having survived the often difficult journey across the Atlantic, never had the chance to see anything beyond Partridge Island. They were buried in one of the six cemeteries located here. The island is also the site of New Brunswick's oldest lighthouse, as well as a historical museum.

The perfectly marvellous **Irving Nature Park** ★★ *(free admission; at the end of Sand Cove Rd.,* ☎*632-7777)* has a great deal to offer nature lovers. Located just a few kilometres west of the industrial city of Saint John, this magnificent park covers a 225ha peninsula trimmed with untouched beaches. The city seems a million miles away from here. Visitors can also enjoy a pleasant stroll along one of the park's trails, communing with nature and observing the plant and animal life in Southern New Brunswick.

St. Martins

St. Martins is one of New Brunswick's best-kept treasures. An idyllic fishing village looking out on the Bay of Fundy, St. Martins is adorned with numerous houses built in the 19th century, when it was known as a major producer of large wooden ships. Today, the village is very picturesque, with local fishing boats moored in its little port. It also has two covered bridges, one of which leads to the famous **echo caves** ★, cavities created in local cliffs by the action of the tides in the Bay of Fundy. Nature lovers will find long, untouched beaches in St. Martins, as well as attractive

Lions Park, which is a good place to take a walk or go swimming. As home to two of the province's best inns (see p 97), the village also has something to offer connoisseurs of fine cuisine. Finally, to enjoy a **spectacular view** ★ of the local red cliffs, head to the **Quaco Head lighthouse**, located several kilometres west of St. Martins.

Fundy National Park ★★★ *(Rte. 114, near Alma, ☎887-6000 or 887-2005)* is the ultimate place to explore the shores of the bay, observe its plant and animal life and grasp the power of its tides. It covers a densely wooded, mountainous territory of 206km², abounding in spectacular scenery, lakes and rivers and nearly 20km of shoreline. All sorts of athletic activities can be enjoyed here.

The park is a hiker's paradise, with its 120-km of trails running through the forest, near lakes and alongside the magnificent bay. Visitors can also enjoy fishing, camping on one of the many equipped or natural sites, playing a game on the excellent golf course or swimming in the heated pool. Travellers pressed for time should make sure at the very least to

visit **Pointe Wolfe** ★★, where nearby trails offer spectacular views of cliffs plunging straight into the waters of the bay. At each entrance to the park, employees offer information on the various activities available.

Alma

Alma, a small fishing village located at the entrance of the park, features a variety of accommodations and numerous

Hopewell Cap

restaurants. When the tide is at its lowest, vast stretches of the sea bed are exposed, offering an interesting place for a stroll. From Alma, Route 915 leads to a peninsula with the evocative name of **Cape Enrage** ★.

This peninsula offers beautiful views of the bay and is a great place to practice several different aquatic sports. It also has a beautiful beach off the beaten track. The route runs alongside the bay to

Mary's Point ★, a waterbird sanctuary where hundreds of thousands of semi-palmated sandpipers alight between mid-July and mid-August.

Hopewell Cape

Hopewell Cape's rock formations, nicknamed the **flower pots** ★★, are one of the province's most famous attractions. All by themselves, they symbolize the massive force of the tides in the bay. At high tide, they look like small wooded islands right off the coast. As the waters recede at low tide, they expose lofty rock formations sculpted by the endless coming and going of the tides. When the tide is at its lowest, visitors can explore the sea bed. Numerous water sports are organized from Hopewell Rock.

Moncton

Due to its location in the heart of Atlantic Canada, as well as its qualified, bilingual workforce, Moncton is now New Brunswick's rising star. Up until the

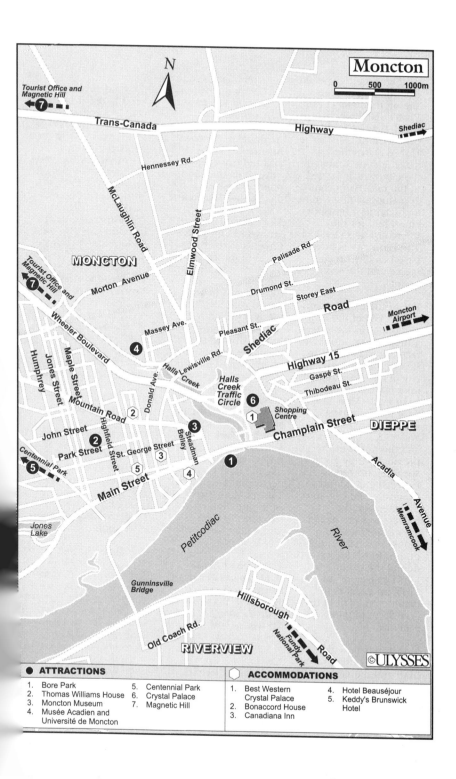

● **ATTRACTIONS**

1. Bore Park
2. Thomas Williams House
3. Moncton Museum
4. Musée Acadien and
   Université de Moncton

5. Centennial Park
6. Crystal Palace
7. Magnetic Hill

◯ **ACCOMMODATIONS**

1. Best Western
   Crystal Palace
2. Bonaccord House
3. Canadiana Inn

4. Hotel Beauséjour
5. Keddy's Brunswick
   Hotel

Acadians were expelled from the region, this site on the banks of the Petitcodiac River was a small Acadian trading post. Colonists from the United States then settled here and founded the city, which thrived in the mid-19th century as a shipbuilding centre and later as a transportation hub for the Intercolonial Railway. The economy is now based chiefly on commerce and the service sector.

For Acadians, who constitute 35% of the population, Moncton offers a unique opportunity to face the challenges and savour the pleasures of city living. Despite their minority status, they have made Moncton a base for their most important economic and social institutions and the home of the province's only French-speaking university, the Université de Moncton. Ironically, the city and by extension the university were named after officer Robert Monkton, commander of the British forces during the capture of Fort Beauséjour in 1755, an event that heralded the fall of the French Empire in North America.

Moncton is now the centre of Acadian rebirth and the vibrant energy in the air here is due in good part to the entrepreneurial spirit that characterizes today's Acadians. Moncton's immediate

surroundings include such varied communities as **Dieppe**, most of whose inhabitants are Acadian, and the very Anglophone **Riverview**. An excellent time to visit the city is in early July, when the atmosphere is enlivened by the **Moncton Jazz Festival**.

The Petitcodiac River, known locally as the Chocolate River because of the colour of its waters, empties and then fills back up again twice a day, in accordance with the tides in the Bay of Fundy. The rise in the river's water level is always preceded by an interesting phenomenon known as a **tidal bore** ★, a wave up to several dozen centimetres high that flows upriver. The best spot to watch this wave is at **Bore Park** (*downtown on Main St.*). To know what time of the day the tidal bore will occur during your stay, contact Moncton's tourist information office (*at the corner of Main St., facing Bore Park,* ☎*856-4399*).

The Second Empire style **Thomas Williams House** ★ (*free admission; May, Mon, Wed and Fri 10am to 3pm; Jun, Tue to Sat 9am to 5pm, Sun 1pm to 5pm; Jul and Aug, Mon to Sat 9am to 5pm, Sun 1pm to 5pm; Sep, Mon, Wed and Fri 10am to 5pm; 103 Park St.,* ☎*857-0590*) is a 12-room residence built in 1883 for the family of Thomas Williams, who was an accountant for the

Intercolonial Railway at the time. His heirs then lived here for nearly a century. Today, the house is a museum where visitors can learn about the lifestyle of the Moncton bourgeoisie during the Victorian era. Back in 1883, Moncton was no more than a tiny village, and the house lay outside its boundaries, in the middle of the countryside.

The **Moncton Museum** ★ (*free admission; Jul and Aug, Mon to Sat 9am to 4:30pm, Sun 1pm to 5pm; 20 Mountain Rd.,* ☎*856-4383,* ≠*856-4355*) houses a lovely collection of objects linked to the history of the city and its surrounding area. During summertime, the museum often presents large-scale temporary exhibits. The sumptuous facade was salvaged from the city's former city hall. Moncton's oldest building, dating back to 1821 and very well preserved, stands right next door.

The **Musée Acadien** ★ (*free admission; Jun to Sep, Mon to Fri 10am to 5pm, Sat and Sun 1pm to 5pm; Oct to May, Tue to Fri 1pm to 4:30pm, Sat and Sun 1pm to 4pm; Université de Moncton, Clément Cormier Bldg.,* ☎*858-4088*) displays over 30,000 objects, including a permanent collection of Acadian artifacts dating from 1604 up to the last century. The museum was founded in

Memramcook in 1886 by Père Camille Lefebvre of the Collège Saint-Joseph, and was moved to its present location in 1965. In the same building as the museum, visitors will find the **Centre d'Art de l'Université de Moncton ★★**, where works by Acadian artists are exhibited. On the west side of the city, **Centennial Park** *(St. George Blvd.)* is a place where the whole family can come to relax any time of the year. The area includes hiking trails, a small beach, tennis courts and a playground. Canoe and pedalboat rentals are also available.

The **Crystal Palace** *(499 Rue Paul, Dieppe, beside Place Champlain)* hotel complex is a family entertainment centre featuring carousels, games, miniature golf, a swimming pool, movie theatres and a science centre intended for children. Since the Crystal Palace amusement park is indoors, it is overrun with families on rainy days.

The **Magnetic Hill ★** *($2 per car; west of Moncton, Exit 88 from the Trans-Canada Hwy.)* is an intriguing optical illusion, which gives people the impression that their car is climbing a slope. The staff ask drivers to stop their engines at what seems to be the bottom of a very steep hill. Then, as if by miracle, the car seems to climb the slope. This remarkable illusion is a must for families. Other family attractions have sprung up around Magnetic Hill, including a park, a zoo, a mini-train, a go-kart track, a miniature golf course, and most of all, the superb **Magic Mountain ★** water park. Here you will also find shops, restaurants and a hotel.

Saint-Joseph-de-Memramcook

A small rural town in the pretty Memramcook valley, Saint-Joseph is of great symbolic importance to the Acadian people. This is the only region on the Bay of Fundy where Acadians still live on the farmlands they occupied before the Deportation. It thus serves as a bridge between pre- and post-Deportation Acadia. Collège Saint-Joseph, where the Acadian elite was educated for many years, was founded here in 1864.

The college hosted the first Acadian national convention in 1881. At the **Historic Site of the Lefebvre Monument ★** *($2; Jun to early Sep, everyday 9am to 5pm; Monument Lefebvre, ☎758-9783)*, visitors can learn about Acadian history by viewing an exhibition on the key factors and pivotal moments leading to the survival of the Acadian people.

Sackville

A subtle aura of affluence and a unique awareness of the past emanate from Sackville, whose beautiful residences lie hidden behind the stately trees that flank its streets. The city is home to **Mount Allison University**, a small, highly reputable institution whose lovely buildings stand on beautiful, verdant plots of land in the centre of town. On campus, visitors will find the **Owens Art Gallery** *(on campus, ☎364-2574)*, which displays a large collection of paintings by New Brunswick artists, including several works by master Alex Colville.

Waterfowl Park ★★ *(free admission; every day until nightfall; entrance on East Main St.)* is an interpretive centre focussing on the plant and animal life in saltwater marshes. Thanks to 2km of trails and wooden footbridges, visitors can enter a world of unexpected richness and diversity. In addition to being exceptionally informative, this park is a wonderful place to relax.

Aulac

After British forces captured Fort Beauséjour in 1755, the

New Brunswick

Deportation, a tragic event in Acadian history, was initiated in Aulac. Built in 1751, Fort Beauséjour occupied a strategic location on Chignecto Bay, on the border of the French and British colonial empires. The **Fort Beauséjour National Historic Site ★** *(free admission; mid-May to mid-Oct; Hwy. 2, Exit 550A,* ☎*876-2443)* includes an interpretive centre that deals with Acadian history and the Deportation. Visitors can also stroll around several of the remaining fortifications of the star-shaped structure. The view of the bay and of New Brunswick and Nova Scotia is excellent from here.

Outdoor Activities

Hiking

The **Fundy Trail Parkway** is a network of trails along the Bay of Fundy, 10km east of St. Martins. Accessible by bike or on foot, it offers panoramic viewpoints of the countryside. Some of the trails lead to beaches, and another section of the path, which heads to Fundy National Park, will soon be built.

Cycling

The islands in the Bay of Fundy, especially Campobello and Grand Manan, also feature excellent bike paths. It can also be fun to bike around the towns of St. Andrews by-the-Sea, St. John and Moncton. Several businesses offer bike rentals.

Bicycle Rentals

Danny's Bike
59 Carleton St.
St. Andrews by-the-Sea
☎**529-3834**

Freewheeling Adventure
Saint John
☎**857-3600**

Covered Bridge Bicycle Tour
Saint John
☎**849-9028**

Gary's Bicycle Rentals
239 Weldon St.
Moncton
☎**855-8754**

Whale-watching

Because of its rich feeding grounds, the **Bay of Fundy** is one of the best places in the world to observe certain species of whales. Whale-watching excursions are organized throughout the summer in the following places: **St. Andrews by-the-Sea**, **Deer Island**, **Campobello**

Island and **Grand Manan Island**, in the southwestern part of the province. Count on around $45 per 3hr excursion. Contact:

Cline Marine
Departures from St. Andrews: Deer Island and Campobello Island
☎**529-4188 or 747-2287**

Atlantic Marine Wildlife Tours
Departures from St. Andrews
☎**459-7325**

St. Andrews by-the-Sea

Outdoor Adventure
☎**755-6415**

Tide Runner
16 King
☎**529-4481**

S/V Cory
St. Andrews Wharf
☎**529-8116**
Excursions on yachts that can carry up to 40 passengers

St. George

Adventure Destination Centre
15 Adventure Lane
☎**755-2699**

Island Coast Boat Tours
Departures from Grand Manan Island
☎**662-8181**

Ocean Search
Departures from Grand Manan Island
☎**662-8488**

Seawatch
Departures from Grand Manan Island
☎*662-8552*

Starboard Tours
Departures from Grand Manan Island
☎*662-8545 or 663-7525*

Bird-watching

The forests and extensive coastline of New Brunswick are a haven for hundreds of bird species. Mary's Point, on the Bay of Fundy between Moncton and Fundy National Park, is one of the best-known observation sites in the province. Every year from mid-July to mid-August, admirers of winged wildlife and naturalists from the world over meet here to watch the flight of tens of thousands of semi-palmated sandpipers.

The islands of the Bay of Fundy are also much-lauded bird-watching sites. Grand Manan Island, as well as Machias Seal Island, permits the observation of close to 275 species of bird, including the Atlantic puffin and the Arctic tern. **Fundy National Park** spans a 206km stretch of coast, a favourite spot for many different species of birds that can easily be seen by following one of the numerous hiking trails that criss-cross the park.

Located near St. John, **Irving Nature Park** protects the penisula, which is washed by the powerful tides of the Bay of Fundy. There are sandy beaches on one side of the park and salt marshes on the other, both of which provide excellent sources of food for migratory birds. Long, wooden footbridges and trails have been built so that visitors can observe the various species of birds that come here, such as the great blue heron and the sandpiper.

Canoeing and Kayaking

Adventure High Seas Kayaking
☎*662-3563*
There's nothing like kayaking to appreciate the beauty of the island. Adventure High Seas Kayaking offers enjoyable trips.

St. Andrews by-the-Sea Seascape
☎*529-4866*
This company offers kayak trips on the Bay of Fundy, an opportunity to enjoy the great outdoors while getting to know the marine life of the bay. Half-day: $55.

St. George

Outdoor Adventure
79 Main St.
☎*755-6415*
The guided kayak and canoe trips organized by Outdoor Adventure (*$49*) offers those who are looking for adventure a chance to see the Bay of Fundy's marine life close up. Visitors may be fortunate enough to see the ocassional seal or eagle.

Piskahegan
☎*755-6269*
Piskahegan is another St. George company that brings visitors to see the natural beauty of the Bay of Fundy. Courses are also offered. Trips cost $39, $59 or $89.

Alma

Freshair Adventure
☎*887-2249*
Freshair Adventure organizes half-day trips along the coast of Fundy National Park, a wonderful opportunity to explore the flora and fauna of this vast wilderness. Half-day: $50.

Scuba Diving

Navy Island Dive Co.
15 William St.
St. Andrews by-the-Sea
☎*529-4555*
If the underwater world facinates you, go on a diving trip and explore the rich marine life.

New Brunswick

Courses and equipment rental available.

Accommodations

St. Stephen

St. Stephen Inn
$60
tv
51 rooms
99 King St., E3L 2C6
☎*466-1418 or 800-565-3088*
⇌*466-6148*
In the heart of the community, the St. Stephen Inn is a pleasant spot with typical, inexpensive motel rooms.

Blair House Bed & Breakfast
$75
tv
4 rooms
38 Prince William St. E3L 1S3
☎*466-1699*
⇌*466-2233*
A lovely period house built in the middle of the last century for an eminent Loyalist family, the Blair House Bed & Breakfast stands on a beautifully landscaped lot in the heart of St. Stephen. Comfortable rooms and a copious English breakfast are offered.

Loon Bay Lodge
$75
ℜ, =, *tv*
9 rooms
P.O. Box 101, E3L 2W9
☎*466-4213*
Situated in the middle of the countryside, Loon Bay Lodge is a good choice for those who enjoy a peaceful location. Its nine rooms with fireplaces, bathrooms and breathtaking views of the sea guarantee an enjoyable stay. The rustic charm of the facility will please those who enjoy the great outdoors but like to have comfortable accommodation. A central log cabin has a dining room and a living room where visitors can meet. Fishing and hunting trips are possible.

St. Andrews by-the-Sea

Passamaquoddy Park
$17
150 sites
☎*529-3439*
⇌*529-3246*
The best thing about this campground is its location, a stone's throw from the sea and the centre of town. It is also nicely landscaped.

Salty Towers
$45
16 rooms
340 Water St., E0G 2X0
☎*529-4585*
This large, beautiful Victorian home, which is decorated with antiques and knick-knacks in every corner, has 16 rooms, a fireplace and two kitchens to prepare meals. Its eclectic decor will please those who appreciate something a little out of the ordinary. Guests will also enjoy its laid-back atmosphere.

Greenside Motel
$70
tv, K
16 rooms
242 Mowatt Dr., E0G 2X0
☎*/⇌529-3039*
Even though St. Andrews is a rather posh vacation spot, visitors can still find inexpensive motel-style accommodations with clean, simple rooms. One option is the Greenside Motel, located just outside of St. Andrews near the golf course. Some rooms have kitchenettes.

Seaside Beach Resort
$70
May to Oct
tv, K
24 rooms + 4 chalets
339 Water St., E0G 2X0
☎*529-3039 or 800-506-8677*
⇌*529-4479*
The Seaside Beach Resort consists of 10 wood cottages ideally located on the shores of the bay. It is not the most luxurious spot, but the rooms are clean and include kitchenettes. Though this is a "resort," the mood is relaxed and ideal for families.

Waterfront Garden Suites
$75
K, tv
10 rooms
22 Douglas St., E0G 2X0
☎*529-8844*
Equipped with kitchenettes, the Waterfront is a good choice for those who want to stay a while in St. Andrews by-the-Sea but want to cut down on restaurant expenses. The property has a wonderful loca-

tion near the centre of town, facing the bay.

Rossmount Inn
$95
tv, ≈, ℜ, ⊗, ⊛
17 rooms
a few km from St. Andrews on Hwy. 127 heading east, E0G 2X0
☎ *529-3351*
≈ *529-1920*
Set in the middle of a large property overlooking the surrounding countryside, the Rossmount Inn is a magnificent inn with antique furniture in each room. The Rossmount Inn also offers an excellent dining room.

St. Andrews Motor Inn
$125
tv, ℜ
33 rooms
111 Water St., E0G 2X0
☎ *529-4571*
St. Andrews Motor Inn, right on the bay, offers comfortable, modern rooms with balconies or terraces. Some rooms even have a kitchenette. The outdoor pool behind the building looks out over the bay.

Pansy Patch
$135 bkfst incl.
ℜ, =, ≈, tv
9 rooms
59 Carleton St., E0G 2X0
☎ *529-3834*
St. Andrews's excellent reputation is partly due to quality establishments like Pansy Patch. It offers nine brand new rooms in a wonderful home built in 1912 and an equally charming cottage. Each of its tastefully decorated rooms offers a view of St. Andrews's harbour. A magnificent garden surrounds the building. Guests can also use the facilities next door at the Algonquin Hotel, which has a spa and tennis courts.

Algonquin Resort
$149
May to Oct
tv, ℜ, K, ≈, ≡, ⊘, △
238 rooms
Hwy. 127, 184 Adolphus St. E0G 2X0
☎ *529-8823 or 800-441-1414*
≈ *529-7162*
Dominating the quaint setting of St. Andrews by-the-Sea is the best and most reputed hotel in the Maritimes, the Algonquin Resort. A majestic neo-Tudor grouping in the centre of a large property, this dream hotel has withstood the test of time by carefully preserving the aristocratic refinement and Anglo-Saxon character of an elite resort of the late 1800s.

Built in 1889, the Algonquin was completely devastated by fire in 1914. Most of it was rebuilt the next year. Then, in 1991, a new convention centre was added, followed by a new wing with 54 rooms and suites in 1993.

The Algonquin offers superb, modern and very comfortable rooms and suites, excellent food at the Passamaquoddy Veranda dining room, flawless service and a whole slew of activities. If the nightly rate is beyond your budget, do at least visit the hotel and treat yourself to Sunday brunch, lunch or supper, a drink in the Library Bar or stop at the gift shop.

St. George

Granite Town Hotel
$69
tv, ℜ, K
32 rooms
79 Main St. E., E0G 2Y0
☎ *755-6415*
≈ *755-6009*
The Granite Town Hotel provides a conventional level of comfort. It is a good address to remember mainly because it is clean and ideally located for guests wanting to visit the islands in the bay.

Campobello Island

Lupin Lodge
$50
Jun to Oct
tv, ℜ
11 rooms
E0G 3H0
☎ *752-2555*
Well situated near the park, the Lupin Lodge offers relatively comfortable accommodation. The neighbouring restaurant is busy during the summer season, all day long until evening falls.

New Brunswick

Grand Manan Island

Compass Rose
$79
ℜ
7 rooms
North Head, E0G 2M0
☎*662-8570*
Grand Manan has many bed and breakfasts and several little inns. The Compass Rose, one of these friendly inns, houses rooms that are charming and comfortable, but by no means luxurious. The inn's dining room serves up fare that is perfectly satisfactory.

Fisherman's Haven Cottages
$80
5 rooms
Grand Harbour, E0G 1X0
☎*662-8919 or 662-3389*
⇄*662-6246*
Lots of families spend at least a few days of their vacation on Grand Manan Island. A popular option for such vacationers is to rent a cottage like the ones offered by Fisherman's Haven Cottages, which have two or three bedrooms. Weekly rates are available.

Saint John

YMCA
25 Hazen Ave.
☎*634-7720*
Saint John unfortunately has no youth hostel. Those in search of accommodations under $30 per person can stay at the YMCA.

Earl of Leinster
$40
K, tv
7 rooms
96 Leinster Ave., E2L 1J3
☎*652-3275*
Another low-cost alternative for accommodation is the Earl of Leinster. It offers simply decorated, comfortable rooms, and a few little extras, such as a pool table and a kitchen.

Park Plaza Motel
$58
tv, ℜ
96 rooms
607 Rothesay Ave., E2H 2G9
☎*633-4100 or 800-561-9022*
⇄*648-9494*
In the immediate surroundings of Saint John, numerous motels offer reasonably-priced accommodation in simple but clean rooms. The Park Plaza Motel is one of these. To get there take Exit 117 off of Route 1.

Five Chimneys Bed and Breakfast
$69 bkfst incl.
tv
3 rooms
238 Charlotte W., E2M 1Y3
☎*635-1888*
⇄*672-2534*
In Saint John West, just a short distance from the pier where the ferry for Digby, Nova Scotia docks, is the Five Chimneys Bed and Breakfast. The establishment is set up in an upper-class house dating from the middle of the 19th century and offers quality accommodation for the price.

Red Rose Mansion
$70 bkfst incl.
⇄, K, tv
5 rooms
☎*649-0913*
⇄*693-3233*
Located in the historic area of Saint John, the Red Rose Mansion is a towering red-brick house dating from 1904, which used to belong to the owner of the Red Rose Tea company. It's now a comfortable inn, and neither its exterior nor interior has lost any of its original old-world charm. Its five luxurious rooms have gorgeous Victorian-style decor. It also has a magnificent garden.

Homeport Historic B&B
$70 bkfst incl
tv
5 rooms
80 Douglas Ave., E2K 1E4
☎*672-7255*
The Homeport is another magnificent house in the area has been converted into a pleasant B&B. An effort has been made to keep its original charm, and every one of its large rooms is filled with antiques. The rooms are all tastefully decorated and have private bathrooms.

Parkerhouse Inn
$89 bkfst incl.
ℜ, pb, tv
9 rooms
71 Sydney St., E2L 1L5
☎*652-5054 or 888-457-2520*
⇄*636-8076*
The Parkerhouse Inn occupies a pretty, turn-of-the-century house that has preserved all of its original splen-

dour. A magnificent dining room, richly ornamented with woodwork, occupies almost the entire ground floor. A beautiful staircase leads to the upper floors, where the antique-furnished guestrooms are located. Each room has its own special charm and all have private washrooms. The Parkerhouse Inn is set right in the heart of Saint John, just behind the Imperial Theatre. The inn's restaurant has an outstanding reputation.

Keddy's Fort Howe Hotel
$87
tv, ℜ, ≈
135 rooms
corner of Portland and Main Sts., E2K 4H8
☎*657-7320 or 800-561-7666*
≈*693-1146*
For an inexpensive hotel with clean but no-nonsense rooms, located within a short distance from downtown Saint John and the major highways, Keddy's Fort Howe Hotel is your best bet. The staff is courteous, and as an added bonus, there is a bar and restaurant on the top floor.

Inn on the Cove
$95 bkfst incl.
tv, ⊛, ℑ
5 rooms
1371 Sand Cove Rd., E2M 4X7
☎*672-7799*
≈*635-5455*
If you don't see Saint John as an idyllic spot to take a relaxing and revitalizing vacation it must be because you've never come across the

Inn on the Cove, probably one of the best inns in the province. Located in a quiet setting with a spectacular view of the Bay of Fundy, the inn is actually only 5min by car from downtown.

Nature-lovers will find beautiful, wild beaches to explore close by and trails leading to Irving Nature Park. The house is furnished with taste and a particular attention to detail, and the comfortable rooms are decorated with antiques. All of the rooms are lovely, but the two located on the second floor and facing the back of the house are even better: they are larger, have their own bathrooms and offer a stunning view of the bay. The owners are friendly but discreet, and prepare excellent breakfasts.

Delta Brunswick Hotel
$95
tv, ℜ, ≈
225 rooms
39 King St., E2L 4W3
☎*648-1981 or 800-268-1133*
≈*658-0914*
In the heart of downtown on the busiest street, the Delta Brunswick Hotel is the largest hotel in Saint John, with 255 deluxe rooms and suites. Attached to a shopping mall, the building itself lacks a bit of charm. The hotel is best known for the gamut of services for vacationers and business people.

Hilton
$154
tv, ℜ, ≈, ☺, ⊛
197 rooms
1 Market Sq., E2L 4Z6
☎*693-8484 or 800-561-8282*
≈*657-6610*
The Saint John Hilton, offering high quality accommodation, lies in a beautiful setting at the end of the pier close to the market. It is a great spot to enjoy the singular beauty of this sea port whose activity is dictated by the continuous ebb and flow of the tides. Its rooms are spacious and decorated with furniture that is both modern and inviting.

Obviously, the rooms at the back of the building, which look out over the port of Saint John, are most desirable. The Hilton also has a good restaurant, Turn of the Tide (see p 102) and a pleasant bar, Brigandine Lounge (see p 103), with a view of the piers.

St. Martins

Quaco Inn
$80
tv, ℜ
6 rooms
6 Beach St., E0G 2Z0
☎*833-4772*
≈*833-2531*
The tiny coastal town of St. Martins offers a wide choice of quality accommodation. One of these is the reputed Quaco Inn, which provides comfortable lodging in the refined atmosphere of a Victorian house. Beautifully-

New Brunswick

furnished and including a dining room with a well-established reputation, this inn is among the best in the province.

St. Martins Country Inn
$95
tv
16 rooms
Hwy 111, EOG 2Z0
☎*833-4534 or 800-565-5257*
⇋*833-4725*

The divine St. Martins Country Inn is situated in the enchanting setting of a large property overlooking the town. Built in 1857 for the most important shipbuilder in St. Martins, it has maintained the serene and perhaps slightly snobby atmosphere befitting the residence of a highly-visible member of the Anglo-Saxon upper class of that era. Everything to satisfy the discerning tastes of the epicurean traveller is in place: beautifully decorated rooms filled with period furniture, a highly reputed kitchen, three splendid dining rooms and impeccable service. Reserve in advance.

Fundy National Park

Fundy Park Chalets
$73
tv, K, ℜ, ≈
29 rooms
EOA 1B0
☎*887-2808*

Visitors to Fundy National Park can choose between campsites and Fundy Park Chalets. These rather rustic-looking cottages are located near the park administration office and the golf course, not far from the coast. Each one is equipped with a room with two beds, a bathroom and a kitchenette. Provisions are available just a few kilometres away in Alma.

Alma

Parkland Village Inn
$65
ℜ
EOA 1B0
☎*887-2313*

The Parkland Village Inn, in the heart of Alma, offers a few modest rooms above the establishment's very busy ground floor restaurant.

Alpine Motor Inn
$65
EOA 1B0
☎*887-2052*
⇋*853-8090*

The Alpine Motor Inn, right in the centre of the village, is the largest hotel in Alma. Its motel-style rooms are clean and spacious. Guests here enjoy a beautiful view of the Bay of Fundy.

Captain's Inn
$70
tv
10 rooms
Main St., EOA 1B0
☎*887-2017*
⇋*887-2074*

The Captain's Inn occupies a charming wooden house in the heart of Alma. This family hotel is not especially luxurious, but the rooms are comfortable, pretty and well laid out. The owners offer an always – friendly welcome.

Moncton

Bonaccord House
$50 bkfst incl.
5 rooms
250 Bonaccord St., E1C 5M6
☎*388-1535*
⇋*853-7191*

In the heart of Moncton's historic area, the turn-of-the-century Bonaccord House today functions as a lovely bed and breakfast. The elegantly decorated, tastefully furnished guestrooms occupy the building's upper floors. Both the ground-floor living room and the veranda are perfect for reading, sipping afternoon tea or just relaxing. The Bonaccord House is ideal for those in search of an especially tranquil atmosphere.

Colonial Inn
$71
tv, ℜ, ≈
61 rooms
42 Highfield, E1C 8T6
☎*382-3395 or 800-561-4667*
⇋*858-8991*

The Colonial Inn offers motel-style accommodation right in the heart of Moncton. The rooms are well kept, the service is excellent and guests have use of a pool. This is a good spot for families.

Keddy's Brunswick Hotel
$88
tv, ℜ, ≈, ☺, ◠, ☀
191 rooms
1005 Main St., E1C 8N6
☎ *854-6340 or 800-561-7666*
⇌ *382-8923*
The years have taken their toll on the grandeur that once was Keddy's Brunswick Hotel. This is particularly evident in the outdated furniture and decor, not to mention the unpredictable elevator service. There remain, however, several good reasons to stay here, namely the affordable price and the central location.

Canadiana Inn
$90
open Mar to Nov
tv
20 rooms
46 Archibald St., E1C 5H9
☎ *382-1054*
Set in a quiet neighbourhood not far from the city's liveliest streets, the Canadiana Inn occupies a large, lovely Victorian house built at the end of the 19th century. Its rooms, equipped with comfortable furnishings, are handsomely decorated and inviting. The establishment has a pleasant upstairs terrace, as well as two dining rooms where generous breakfasts are served. The service here is very congenial.

Hotel Beauséjour
$109
tv, ℜ, ≈, ◠, ☺, ≡
310 rooms
750 Main St., E1C 1E6
☎ *854-4344 or 800-441-1414*
⇌ *858-0957*
For those travellers in search of some pampering, elegance and comfort, there is Hotel Beauséjour, Moncton's finest establishment and a member of the Canadian Pacific hotel chain.

The quality of service that has made the reputation of this chain is here, as well as beautifully-decorated and spacious rooms, an excellent restaurant and piano bar and a lovely indoor swimming pool, where it is easy to put the bustle of urban life behind, or perhaps below you. Right in the heart of Moncton, the hotel could not be more suitably located for business people and travellers hoping to take advantage of the nearby restaurants and bars.

Best Western Crystal Palace
$110
ℜ, ≈
115 rooms
499 Paul St., E1A 6S5
☎ *858-8584*
⇌ *858-5486*
Families are particularly fond of the Best Western Crystal Palace, a comfortable hotel equipped with a lovely swimming pool that is right next door to a large indoor amusement park. Its rooms are modern, airy and

standard. The Best Western appeals to business travellers as well, with its many meeting and conference rooms.

Sackville

Mount Allison University
$46 double room
☎ *364-2252*
⇌ *364-2688*
The cheapest accommodation in Sackville is in the residences of Mount Allison University, but only during the summer. The campus lies right in the middle of this small town.

Borden's Restaurant & Motel
$52
tv
8 rooms
southern end of town
146 Bridge St., E4L 3P7
☎ *536-1066*
⇌ *364-1306*
Borden's Restaurant & Motel, a small red brick building at the edge of town, has a few inexpensive, clean rooms.

Different Drummer
$65
tv
8 rooms
7 Main St., E4L 4A4
☎ *536-1291*
⇌ *536-8116*
The Different Drummer, an excellent bed and breakfast, is set up in a spacious Victorian house. All of the rooms are comfortable and furnished with real antiques. The healthy breakfast is generous and delicious.

New Brunswick

Marshlands Inn
$89
tv, ℜ
18 rooms
55 Bridge St., E4L 3N8
☎*536-0170 or 800-561-1266*
≈*536-0721*

The charm of Sackville is due in good part to the multitude of large, beautiful houses from the 1800s. One of these has been converted into the outstanding Marshlands Inn, once a sumptuous residence offered as a wedding gift by William Crane, an important man of that era, to his daughter. The inn has more than 20 rooms, each one impeccably furnished; several have private bathrooms.

Restaurants

St. Andrews by-the-Sea

Chef Café
$
180 Water St.
☎*529-8888*

Imagine America in the '50s and you've got the decor of the Chef Café, a popular but rinky-dink restaurant that clashes with the inherent chic that is St. Andrews. The menu includes simple dishes like fish and chips and lobster rolls, as well as several inexpensive breakfasts. For a more sophisticated menu, pick a spot at the back of the restaurant, in the cozier dining room known as the Captain's Table.

Waterfront Take-Out
$
40 King St.
☎*529-4228*

There's nothing refined about Waterfront Take-Out, but the place is the perfect spot to have a quick snack of fried clams. There are tables at the back or you can, as the name suggests, take out.

Market Square Grill
$$
211 Water St.
☎*529-8241*

The perfect place for an afternoon snack, the Market Square Grill is a charming café whose menu offers simply prepared, but delicious dishes. Among the choice of soups, sandwiches and fish, the chowder is a must. The evening menu, which is a little bit more refined, offers an excellent selection of fish and seafood dishes. Relaxed ambiance.

The Lighthouse Restaurant
$$-$$$
Patrick St.
☎*529-3082*

For many visitors, fresh lobster at a reasonable price is in itself enough of a reason to visit Atlantic Canada. When passing through St. Andrews, these seafood fanatics converge on The Lighthouse Restaurant. This pretty spot looking out over Passamaquoddy Bay is on the last street at the eastern edge of St. Andrews.

Pansy Patch
$$-$$$
59 Carleton St.
☎*529-3834*

Those who enjoy the pleasant setting of a restaurant as much as its food will love Pansy Patch. The tastefully decorated dining room opens onto the garden and offers a wonderful view. While enjoying this country-style atmosphere, guests can sample some delicious fish dishes, such as the *coulibiac de saumon*, as well as seafood specialities, like *paella*. A reasonably priced lunch menu is also offered.

Harbourfront Restaurant
$$-$$$
225 Water St.
☎*529-4887*

The Harbourfront has a wonderful location facing the bay, offering a beautiful view of the waves. A terrace, which faces the sea, is the perfect place to enjoy this picturesque setting. The attractively decorated interior gives the impression that you're inside an old boat. Its fish and seafood specialities, such as the lobster, are all deliciously prepared.

Passamaquoddy Veranda
$$$
Algonquin Hotel
☎*529-8823*

The Passamaquoddy Veranda offers an outstanding dining experience, as much for the elegance of its decor as for the exceptional quality of its international and regional cuisine. A meal at the Veranda is not within everyone's budget, but fortunately there is a much less expensive lunch menu and a Sunday brunch, which starts at $18.50.

Saint John

Mother's Nature Café
$
20 Charlotte St.
For a change from the traditional bacon and eggs served in most of Saint John's breakfast joints, take a morning stroll over to Mother's Nature Café. Muffins, pastries and rich coffees are the essential elements of the morning menu. The rest of the day they prepare salads, sandwiches and other light dishes.

Brigantine Lounge
$-$$
At noontime or in late afternoon, the Hilton's (see p 97) friendly Brigantine Lounge is the place to go, thanks to its breathtaking view of the port and its lunch special – an excellent deal at under $10.

Grannan's Seafood Restaurant and Oyster Bar
$$
Market Sq.
☎634-1555
Grannan's Seafood Restaurant and Oyster Bar has become an institution in Saint John. The restaurant, whose decor is a hodgepodge

of eccentric maritime-related relics and photos, a real fishmonger's paradise, opens onto an outdoor terrace, perfect for those warm summer evenings. The menu of this restaurant, which is often very crowded in the evening, is predictably composed mainly of fish and seafood dishes.

Il Fornello
$$
33 Canterbury
☎648-2377
Fans of Italian fare will love Il Fornello. This soberly decorated but welcoming bistro offers a great selection of fresh pasta and pizza from a wood-burning oven. Il Fornello is one of the most popular restaurants in Saint John.

Incredible Edibles Café
$$
42 Princess St.
Without question one of the trendiest spots in Saint John, the Incredible Edibles Café serves excellent continental cuisine and superb desserts. Feasters can sit out in the garden or in the delightful interior dining room. The menu includes excellent pasta with mussels as well as a succulent filet of salmon, among other dishes. To top off a delectable meal, or simply to satisfy a mid-afternoon craving, the raspberry cheesecake hits the spot. This café also has a reasonably priced lunch menu.

Brewpub Tapps Steakhouse
$$
78 King St.
☎634-1957
The Brewpub is particularly well known for its home-brew and convivial atmosphere. It also has a menu that offers hearty dishes, such as hamburgers and grilled chicken, for those with an insatiable appetite.

Taco Pica
$$
96 Germain St.
☎633-8492
Mexican and Guatemalan family cooking is featured at Taco Pica, a friendly little neighbourhood restaurant. Simple, nourishing dishes such as enchiladas, tacos and burritos are the main elements of the menu.

Billy's Seafood
$$-$$$
49-51 Charlotte St.
☎672-3474
Billy's Seafood, located just next to the Saint John market, facing King Square, offers a splendid menu of fresh fish, seafood and steaks. The very well-prepared Atlantic salmon and the lobster are especially recommended. The catch of the day is served as part of a full meal for about $15. All of these ocean delights are offered up in a warm, understated atmosphere.

New Brunswick

Turn of the Tide
$$$
Hilton Hotel
☎632-8564

The Turn of the Tide *(see p 97)* offers a varied menu, typical of a hotel of this calibre, with a vast choice of meat, game, and of course the requisite fresh seafood and fish. The menu is a bit pricey, but the food is sure to please, and the view of the port makes it all the more worthwhile. The decor is classic, airy and tasteful.

St. Martins

Quaco Inn
$$-$$$
☎833-4772

To top off a romantic stay in the quiet village of St. Martins, the delicious pleasure of a candlelit supper in the dining room of the Quaco Inn, one of the best restaurants on the coast, is a must. International and local specialties figure on the menu, the staples of which are of course fish and seafood.

Moncton

Grabbajabba
$
735 Main St.
☎854-7210

This friendly café is popular with students and business people, who come here to enjoy good coffee, desserts and sandwiches.

Café Robinson
$
187 Robinson St.
☎383-4600

A stroll along Main Street is all it takes to experience Moncton's North American atmosphere, but a Latin spirit does lurk nearby at Café Robinson, which serves a wide selection of coffees, pastries and sandwiches. Patrons come to this charming little café to chat with friends or simply to bury themselves in a good book or the newspaper. In the summer the tables are set outside making this the best possible place to people-watch from.

Café Joe Moka
$
corner Robinson and Main Sts.

Practically facing the Café Robinson, the Café Joe Moka offers a similar menu and an equally pleasant patio.

Fat Tuesday's Eatery & Pub
$
720 Main St.

Either you'll love it or you'll hate it, but one thing is for sure: you won't remain neutral when it comes to Fat Tuesday's Eatery & Pub, especially on weekend nights when the place is overrun by a young, noisy crowd with partying on their minds and often a drink too many under their belts. The basic formula is quite simple: serve inexpensive simple food more important, lots of beer. The menu: burgers, sand-

wiches, fries and the like.

Café Archibald
$-$$
221 Mountain Rd.
☎853-8819

A little set back from the Main, the Café Archibald is worth the trip for its well-prepared, inexpensive light meals. Salads, sandwiches, pizzas and succulent crepes are offered. The establishment has an especially pleasant terrace for summertime dining.

Degenhardts
$$
120 West Monaco St.
☎382-7777

The speciality at this unpretentious restaurant is sausage – and delicious sausage it is. Made on the restaurant-owner's farm (who opened this restaurant just to promote his sausage), it is always fresh and delicious. A sausage-lover's delight.

Trovato's Marketplace
$$
644 Main St.
☎857-4140

If you can't decide what you feel like eating, head on down to Trovato's Marketplace. Based on the Mövenpick market concept, it presents a vast selection of stalls that prepare different dishes: salads, wood-oven-baked pizza, Mexican dishes and grills. Guests can choose among its range of freshly prepared, quality food.

Fisherman's Paradise
$$
375 Dieppe Blvd.
☎*859-4388*
Fisherman's Paradise, where seafood and fish dishes share the menu with steaks, is a contender for the title of best seafood restaurant in the area.

Pastali
$$
61 Main St.
☎*383-1050*
Pastali is a good place to keep in mind if you are a fan of Italian food. Patrons enjoy the restaurant's inviting decor, warm atmosphere and delicious pasta dishes.

Windjammer
$$$
750 Main St., Hôtel Beauséjour
☎*854-4344*
In Moncton, gourmets meet at the Windjammer, one of the best restaurants in the province. Its dining room has the seductive elegance of a 19th-century trans-Atlantic liner. The menu has a few pleasant surprises in store, including caribou tournedos and many other game dishes, although obviously fish and seafood are its main highlights. In addition, the Windjammer offers a reasonably priced set menu.

Sackville

Marshlands Inn
$$$
59 Bridge St.
☎*536-0170*
The Marshlands Inn offers fine dining to satisfy the most discerning of palates. The menu is quite extensive and features mostly continental specialties as well as several regional dishes. The atmosphere is quite formal, but also very friendly.

Entertainment

Saint John

Bars and Pubs

O'Leary's
46 Princess St.
The Irish influence is known to be very strong in Saint John. It is therefore no surprise to find O'Leary's, an excellent Irish pub. The clientele is generally young, and musicians are often presented.

Brigandine Lounge
Hilton Hotel
The Brigandine Lounge is charming, with an unimpeded view of the port and its busy piers across the St. John River. Guests of this rather chic hotel make up most of the clientele of this quiet bar, which has an interesting selection of liqueurs. Evenings are usually enhanced by a pianist.

Cultural Activities

Imperial Theatre
King Sq.
☎*683-9494*
The spectacular auditorium of the Imperial Theatre, which was renovated in 1994, has been the home of the performing arts in Saint John since the beginning of this century. Concerts, plays and dance performances are presented here year-round.

Moncton

Bars and Pubs

Au Deuxième
837 Main St.
☎*383-6192*
Au Deuxième, one of the most pleasant bars in Moncton, regularly hosts excellent jazz and pop-music shows. When there is no band, this is the ideal place to have a drink among friends or to get acquainted with local people. The clientele is mainly French-speaking.

Caesar's Piano Bar
Hotel Beausejour, 750 Main St.
☎*854-4344*
Bar-hopping and pub-crawling does not appeal to everyone. Luckily there is an alternative, Caesar's Piano Bar, which serves excellent liqueurs in a relaxing, soothing atmosphere

New Brunswick

that is actually conducive to conversation.

Student bar
University of Moncton
The student bar at the University of Moncton presents concerts in the summer, providing visitors an excellent opportunity to experience the culture and music of modern-day Acadians.

Triangles
234 St. George St.
☎857-8779
Triangles is the main gathering place of the Moncton area's gay community, and although its atmosphere is rather low-key, it does have a dance floor.

Cultural Activities and Festivals

Capitol Theatre
811 Main St.
☎856-4377
The sumptuous Capitol Theatre is the main performing arts centre in Moncton. Since its reopening in 1993, after renovations restored the panache of days gone by, the theatre has presented a variety of quality productions.

July is jazz-time in the city during the **Moncton Jazz Festival**.

Shopping

St. Stephen

Ganong Chocolatier
73 Milltown Blvd.
☎465-5611
The oldest candy maker in Canada (1873), Ganong Chocolatier was also the first to produce the chocolate bar. Today, the shop sells about 75 different varieties of chocolate; just try to choose...

Oven Head Salmon
Hwy. 1, intersection Hwy. 760
Those who are fond of smoked salmon should head to Oven Head Salmon. The salmon here is smoked on the premises. Its high-quality products are wrapped to go.

Sugarsand
73 Mitown St.
This large shop is crammed with local crafts, some of which are quite beautiful.

St. Andrews by-the-Sea

North of Sixty Art
238 Water St.
☎529-4148
North of Sixty Art is an Inuit art gallery that can be visited like a museum. Works exhibited include uniquely diverse and beautiful sculptures. Among the dozens of boutiques along Water Street, this one is probably the most interesting.

Boutique La Baleine
173 Water St.
☎529-3926
✍529-3088
The Boutique La Baleine is known mostly for its quality crafts; however, it also sells books, trinkets and some clothing. There is another Boutique La Baleine inside the Algonquin Hotel.

Serendipin Art
168 Water St.
☎529-3327
Serendipin Art is a charming boutique filled with beautiful crafts, jewellery, sweaters and sculptures. Great gift ideas.

Tom Smith Gallery
136 Water St.
☎529-4234
If you didn't find what you want at Serendipin Art, head on down to Tom Smith Gallery where you will find beautiful decorations and blown glass.

Cottage Craft
200 Water St.
☎*529-3190*
Cottage Craft is worth visiting for its interesting selection of tweed clothing and items knitted with 100% pure wool as well as the array of coloured yarn for sale.

Garden By the Sea
17 Walter St.
☎*529-8905*
To stock up on essential-oil soaps made on the premises, stop by this pretty boutique.

Saint John

Saint John Market
47 Charlotte St.
There's nothing like a walk in the market, where stalls overflow with fresh produce from the region's farms. There is also a lovely selection of local crafts.

Handworks
12 King St.
☎*652-9787*
Art lovers will enjoy this gallery, where a variety of works by Atlantic artists are on display.

Moncton

Librairie Acadienne
ÉdificeTaillon, Université de Moncton
☎*858-4140*
Located on the Université de Moncton campus, Librairie Acadienne offers an excellent selection of works by Acadian authors and books on Acadian history and culture. Acadia numbers many talented writers, among whom Herménégilde Chiasson and Antonine Maillet are two of the best known.

Chapters
499 Paul St.
☎*855-8075*
If you love to read, go to the huge Chapters bookstore situated in the Crystal Palace. In addition to a vast selection of books on a range of topics, there is also a café and a restaurant.

La Différence
881A Main St.
☎*861-1800*
This shop sells a variety of crafts from the Atlantic provinces.

Wharf Village
Hwy. 2
☎*868-8841*
This hamlet, a reconstructed fishing village, is a pleasant spot to have a stroll. You can also stumble upon some great finds here in the shops that sell crafts, a variety of souvenirs, antiques and other decorative objects.

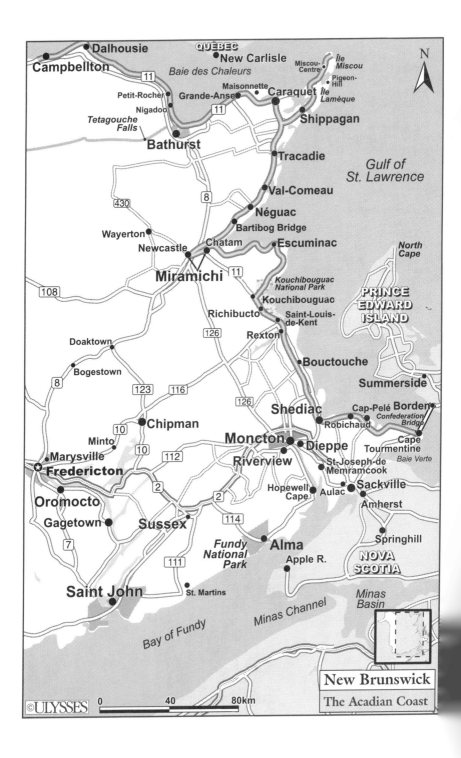

New Brunswick
The Acadian Coast

Acadian Coast

M odern Acadia lies

mainly here, all along the east coast of New Brunswick, which is studded with a string of villages and towns whose inhabitants are mostly of Acadian descent.

It was here that the majority of Acadians fleeing deportation or returning from exile sought refuge two centuries ago, to build a new Acadia. This lovely region is known chiefly for the simple beauty of its landscape and the candid hospitality of its inhabitants, but also also evokes all sorts of other images – long, white sand beaches washed by incredibly warm waters, fresh lobster to be enjoyed at any time of the day, fishing ports bustling with activity and a population with an inherently festive spirit.

In short, the Acadian coast offers visitors a wealth of delightful activities, as well as an opportunity to discover not only the legacy of 18th- and 19th-century Acadia, but also mod-

ern Acadia, which is marching resolutely forward, more confident than ever.

Thanks to its beaches, which are blessed with surprisingly warm water, Shediac has been the largest vacation spot on the coast for a long time. Over the past few years, however, a few other places have sprung up, so it is now possible to explore the diversity that the Acadian coast has to offer.

Finding Your Way Around

By Car

Except for a small section between Cape Tourmentine and Shediac, Highway 11 is the main road used on this tour. The highway passes through most of the towns and villages on the coast, skirts around the peninsula, then runs alongside Baie des Chaleurs to the Québec border.

From Newcastle, visitors can cross New Brunswick from east to west on Highway 8, which runs through the Miramichi River valley.

Highway 180 also leads from Bathurst to Saint-Quentin, passing near Mont Carleton, and Highway 17 heads from Campbellton to Saint-Leonard (on the St. John River). These two highways also cross the mountainous Appalachian countryside.

Practical Information

Area code: *506*

Tourist Information Offices

New Brunswick Tourist Information Centre
☎*800-561-0123*

Caraquet
51H St. Pierre Blvd. East
☎*726-2676*

Campbellton
Hwy. 11
☎*789-2367*

Shediac
229 Main St
☎*532-7788*

Shippagan
close to the Marine Centre in the lighthouse
☎*336-3197*

Exploring

Cap-Pelé

Cap-Pelé offers visitors a wonderful opportunity to discover the fascinating world of fishing. Founded at the end of the 18th century, this Acadian community still depends on the riches of the sea for its survival. The village is also home to *boucanières* (smokehouses), barn-like buildings where fish is smoked before being exported. The 30-odd *boucanières* in the Cap-Pelé region provide 95% of the world's smoked herring.

Beautiful **Plage de l'Aboiteau** ★★ is not far from Cap-Pelé. This splendid beach, located near a fishing port, is ideal for swimming and much less crowded than Parlee Beach Provincial Park.

Shédiac

It is hidden from the road by an embankment of boulder and rock for which the beach was named. *Aboiteau* refers to a type of seawall that extends and protects coastal farmland and is a word primarily used in Acadia.) There are also two other beautiful beaches in the Cap-Pelé area: Gagnon Beach and Sandy Beach.

The region occupies a little plateau that is almost completely denuded of vegetation and offers lovely views of the ocean. Farther along the same road, visitors will reach **Barachois**. In the centre of the village stands the oldest wooden Acadian church in the Maritimes, the **historic church of Saint-Henri-de-Barachois** ★ *(free admission; Jul and Aug, 11am to 5pm; Rte. 133, ☎532-2976)*, built in 1824.

Shediac

The town of Shediac is the best-known vacation spot on the east coast of New Brunswick. Its popularity is due largely to the magnificent beach in **Parlee Beach Provincial Park** ★★ *(Rte. 15)*, whose surprisingly warm waters are perfect for swimming. Because of this popularity, a number of recreational facilities

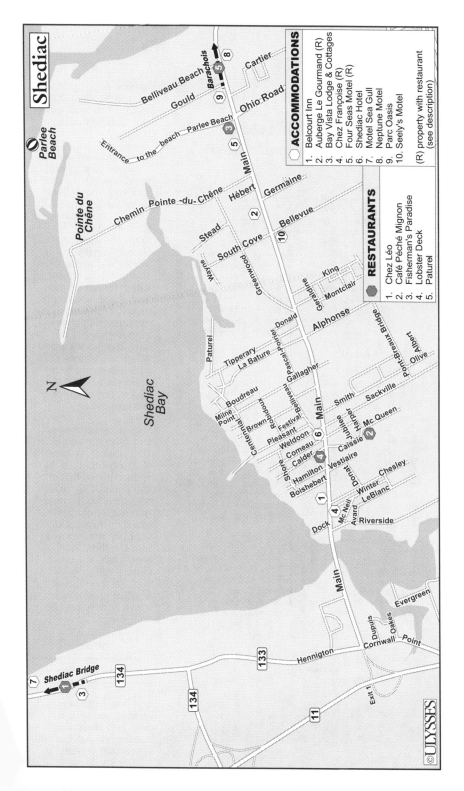

The American Lobster
(*Homarus Americanus*)

The American lobster, also known as the "northern lobster" lives along the eastern coast of North America, from Nova Scotia to North Carolina. Long before the arrival of Europeans in the Americas, Aboriginal people knew this crustacean well and used it mainly as fertilizer. It is said that in those days, lobster was so abundant you could handpick it along the coast.

Things have changed quite a bit, and lobster is now considered to be one of the most delicious and sought-after dishes. It is in high demand in markets all over the world. Its popularity has spawned local fishing industries in many coastal communities of Canada and the United States. To avoid overexploitation, both the Canadian and U.S. governments have imposed norms detailing the minimal length of the lobsters fished.

The renewal of the lobster supply is a long and perilous process. Of the 10,000 eggs laid by the female, only 1% survives past four weeks and even fewer reach maturity. It takes approximately five years for a lobster to reach its adult size and, to do so, it must moult at least 25 times. As it ages, it continues to grow slowly and moults less and less frequently. Although necrophagous, lobsters never-theless prefer live food and feed on cockles, mussels, sea urchins, crabs and, occasionally, aquatic plants.

Their characteristic colour is due to the presence of three pigments in their carapace: blue, red and yellow. Sometimes, one or more of these pigments are missing at birth, and the shell will be either red, blue, white (albinos) or black with yellow spots. It is estimated that one in 3 or 4 million lobsters has a blue carapace and one in 10 million, a red one.

Moreover, they can grow to an impressive size. Apparently, it is in Nova Scotia that the largest lobster was spotted; it measured 1.5m, weighed 20kg and had lived to the noble age of 100.

have sprung up in and around Shediac, including a lovely golf course and some amusement parks.

The town's reputation, however, is also due in good measure to the abundance of lobster found off its shores, which can be savoured fresh any time. The town has even proclaimed itself the lobster capital of the world and holds an annual **lobster festival** in mid-July. Right next to the tourist information centre, there's a gigantic lobster, that is 11m long and 5m wide and weighs 90 tonnes, which is meant to remind visitors of the regional importance of this crustacean.

Shediac was founded as a fishing port in the 19th century. A handful of lovely buildings have endured from that era and contrast sharply with the chaotic atmosphere that characterizes the town during the busy summer season. Heading northward along the coast, visitors will pass through several tiny Acadian communities, which survive mainly on fishing.

Bouctouche

A pleasant little town looking out on a large, calm bay, Bouctouche was founded at the end of the 18th century by

Acadians driven from the Memramcook valley. It has the distinction of being the birthplace of two celebrated New Brunswickers, Antonine Maillet and K.C. Irving. Winner of the 1979 Prix Goncourt for her novel *Pélagie-la-Charrette*, Antonine Maillet has gained more international recognition than any other Acadian author.

She first came into the public eye in the 1960s with *La Sagouine*, a remarkable play that evokes the lives and spirit of Acadians at the turn of the 20th century. K.C. Irving, who died recently, built a colossal financial empire involved in widely diversified operations, most importantly in the oil industry. He started out with nothing and died one of the wealthiest individuals in the world.

The relatively new **Pays de la Sagouine** ★★ *($10; mid-Jun to early Sep, everyday 10am to 6pm; at the southern entrance of the village on Rte. 134; ☎743-1400, ≈743-1414)* a re-creation of early 20th-century Acadia, drawing inspiration from Antonine Maillet's highly successful play, *La Sagouine*. Its creators cleverly decided to enliven the atmosphere with characters from the famous play, who perform theatrical and musical pieces. The highlight is Île-aux-Puces, in the centre of the bay. It is here that

the Pays de la Sagouine is the liveliest, and visitors can learn about the lifestyle of early-20th-century Acadians by talking with the characters on site. The restaurant l'Ordre du Bon Temps, located at the entrance, serves tasty, traditional Acadian cuisine. In the evenings, guests can enjoy theatre productions and musical performances.

The **Kent County Museum** ★ *($3; late Jun to early Sep, Mon to Sat 9am to 5:30pm, Sun noon to 6pm; on the east side of the village, 150 Convent St., ☎743-5005)* is one of the most interesting regional museums in the province. The building itself was used as a convent until 1969. Its various rooms contain period furniture and pieces of sacred art that evoke the history of the convent and the daily life of the nuns and their students. The museum's friendly guides give interesting tours.

Irving Eco-Centre La Dune de Bouctouche ★★ *(Rte. 475, about 5km north of Bouctouche)*. The Bouctouche dune, which extends over 12km into Bouctouche

Harbour, is the habitat of a great variety of aquatic plants and animals, as well as of migratory birds and waterfowl including great blue herons, piping plovers and long-winged terns. The dune, which protects the calm waters and salt marshes of the bay, was formed over the course of centuries by the ceaseless action of winds, tides and ocean currents.

The twofold goal of the Irving Eco-Centre is to preserve this fragile ecosystem and to educate the public about it. A 2km-long boardwalk has been built to facilitate wildlife viewing, and guides give interpretive tours of the dune. For many years now, the spectacular fine-sand beach that borders the entire perimeter of the dune has been a very popular destination for summer outings; surrounded by particularly warm waters, this is one of the

New Brunswick

best spots for swimming on the coast. The dune is located a few kilometres north of Bouctouche and can be reached by bicycle or on foot by trail through the forest.

Rexton

The English-speaking village of Rexton is the birthplace of Bonar Law (1858-1923), the only prime minister of Great Britain born outside of the United Kingdom. The **Bonar Law Historic Site** *(free admission; Jul to end of Sep, 9:30am to 4:30pm;*

Great Heron

Rte. 11 or 116, in the centre of Rexton, ☎523-7615) pays homage to that famous New Brunswicker, while offering visitors an idea of how people lived at the time of his birth. The site includes the farm and house where Bonar Law spent his early years.

Blanketed by a forest of cedars and other conifers and studded with

peat bogs, magnificent **Kouchibouguac National Park ★ ★** *(Rte. 11 or 134, ☎876-2443)*, boasts over 26 km of spectacular coastline made up of saltwater marshes, lagoons, dunes and golden, sandy beaches. It is the natural habitat of several hundred animals, including the extremely rare piping plover. The park is laced with hiking trails and bicycle paths and may also be explored by canoe or rowboat.

All equipment necessary for these sports is available on site, along with a campground. The park is a perfect place for saltwater swimming, especially at Lagoon Beach, which is washed by the warmest saltwater in the province, and excellent Kelly's Beach and Collanders Beach.

Escuminac

Visitors with a taste for pretty, isolated beaches will find several in **Escuminac Provincial Park** *(5km east of Escuminac).* Those who stop in the village can see a **monument** dedicated to

35 fishers who lost their lives at sea during a storm in 1959.

Miramichi

Situated at the mouth of the river of the same name, Miramichi is the largest town in the region, and, unlike other coastal communities, its population is mostly anglophone. Each year at the beginning of July, this community celebrates the annual **Irish Festival of Canada**. This region owes its existence to the forest industry, which has been the main economic activity in the region for decades.

The town has few attractions, but the **Ritchie Wharf Park**, which runs along the Miramichi River, is a fun place for the entire family, as a variety of activities are offered.

The 200km-long **Miramichi River ★** is renowned for its exceptional Atlantic-salmon fishing. From Miramichi, you can follow the river right up to Fredericton, thanks to Highway 8. This highway offers scenic views of a countryside, dominated by majestic evergreens. Also along Highway 8 is the **Miramichi Salmon Museum** (see below).

The Miramichi flows through a lovely landscape whose dense vegetation consists mainly of conifers. On the way to Fredericton, visitors can stop at the **Miramichi Salmon Museum** ★ *($4; Jun to late Sep; Rte. 8, in Doaktown,* ☎*365-7787),* which showcases both fishing and the life cycle of the salmon itself. Farther along in the same direction, visitors will reach the **Central New Brunswick Woodmen's Museum** *($3, late May to Sep; Hwy. 8, in Boiestown,* ☎*369-7214),* which stands on the site of a lumber camp and examines the lives of its inhabitants and the arduous line of work they pursued.

Bartibog Bridge

From Miramichi, Highway 11 West leads to the Acadian Peninsula. Bartibog Bridge is the first town on this highway.

In addition to offering an excellent view at the mouth of the Miramichi River, this tiny community is home to the very interesting **MacDonald Farm Historic Site** *($2.25; end of Jun to end of Sep; Rte. 11,* ☎*778-6085).* Born in Scotland in 1762, Alexander MacDonald served as a private in the British army during the American Revolution. In 1784, after the war had ended, MacDonald took up residence on the banks of the Miramichi River.

MacDonald Farm, now open to the public

includes a lovely Georgian-style stone house and several other buildings dating back to the early 19th century.

Tracadie-Sheila

After passing through the villages of **Néguac** and **Val-Comeau**, each of which has beaches and a provincial park, Route 11 leads to Tracadie-Sheila, a little town with numerous restaurants and hotels, as well as an attractive wharf. As the institutional buildings attest, the town's history was marked for many years by the presence of the Religieuses Hospitalières de Saint-Joseph (Sisters of Mercy), who nursed the sick – especially lepers – here from 1868 to 1965. Every year in late June and early July, Tracadie-Sheila hosts the **Festival International de la Francophonie**, which highlights French-language music and arts.

The **Tracadie Historical Museum** ★ *(free admission; Jun to mid-Aug; on the 3rd floor of the Académie Sainte-Famille, Rue du Couvent,* ☎*395-6366)* houses an exhibit on the various stages in the history of Tracadie and its surroundings. Visitors will find a selection of Micmac artifacts, religious objects and 19th-century tools. Not far from the museum lies the **leper cemetery**, where about

60 identical crosses stand in rows.

Shippagan

Protected by the strait that separates it from Île Lamèque, the site now occupied by Shippagan was originally a trading post, which gave way to a sea port at the end of the 18th century. Now a bustling little community, Shippagan boasts several industries and, more importantly, a port that accommodates one of the largest fishing fleets on the Acadian peninsula.

Its charm lies not only in its seaside location, but also in the unique atmosphere created by its port. Anyone interested in learning more about the fishing industry – the mainspring of the Acadian economy for over 200 years now – should stop in Shippagan, explore the town, stroll along the wharf and visit the marine centre. In addition, each year around the third week of July, the town holds a **Fishing and Aquatic Culture Festival** (☎*336-8726),* made up of a number of fishing related activities, including the blessing of the boats.

Most Acadians who succeeded in avoiding deportation fled from the fertile shores of the Bay of Fundy through the woods to the prov-

New Brunswick

ince's east coast. Since the soil there was much poorer, they turned to the sea for survival, taking up fishing, an economic activity that has long been an integral part of Acadian culture.

To discover the fascinating world of modern fishing in Acadia and the Gulf of St. Lawrence, especially the rich animal life inhabiting the sea bed in this region, visitors can head to the **Marine Centre and Aquarium** ★★ *($5; mid-May to Sep, every day 10am to 6pm; near the Shippagan wharf, ☎336-3013)*. A visit to the Aquarium offers a chance to view tanks with a variety of fish species from the Gulf of St. Lawrence and from the lakes and rivers of the province, as well as lobster and notably, blue lobster. The fish and crustaceans swim about the viewing tanks, which recreate their natural environment. This makes the visit particularly interesting. But the most fascinating exhibit has to be the seal tank, especially during feeding time (11am to 4pm).

There's also a video for those who would like to learn more about the history of fishing in the region. The complex also is a scientific research centre.

Île Lamèque

A ramp connects Shippagan to Île Lamèque. With its flat landscape and handful of tiny hamlets made up of pretty white or coloured houses, this island is a haven of peace where time seems to stand still. A visit to the **Église Sainte-Cécile** ★ in Petite-Rivière-de-l'île is a must. This charming, colourful wooden church provides an enchanting setting for the **International Baroque Music Festival**, a wonderful event held each year during the last week of July.

Île Miscou

Just a short ferry ride from Île Lamèque lies Île Miscou, another sparsely populated peaceful place renowned for its lovely, often deserted beaches. At the far end of the island stands the **Île Miscou Lighthouse** ★ *(at the end of Rte. 133)*, one of the oldest in New Brunswick and a marvellous spot from which to view the ocean.

A few kilometres before the lighthouse, on the same road, visitors will find an **interpretive site** ★ *(Rte. 133)* with a path and footbridges

leading through a peat bog.

Caraquet

Caraquet's charm lies mainly in the warmth and vitality of its inhabitants. The largest town on the peninsula, it is equipped with a number of hotels and restaurants. Caraquet is also considered the cultural hub of Acadia and with good reason. It is probably this town and its residents' lifestyle that best illustrate modern Acadian culture, which draws on a variety of influences without, however, renouncing its rich past.

August is by far the best time to visit Caraquet, since August 15 is the Acadian national holiday. The Tintamarre and Frolic (August 15) alone make for a memorable experience. The **Acadian Festival** *(☎727-6515 or 727-6540)* also takes place in August. At other times, visitors can attend performances by the excellent theatre company of the **Théâtre Populaire d'Acadie** *(276 Blvd. Saint-Pierre O., ☎727-0920)*, relax on one of the town's little beaches or set off on a cruise from the **Carrefour de la Mer** *(51 Blvd. Saint-Pierre Est)*.

The **Acadian Museum** ★ *($3; mid Jun to mid Sep;*

15 Blvd. Saint-Pierre Est, ☎727-1713) houses a small collection of everyday objects from the past two centuries.

An important place of pilgrimage in a lovely natural setting, the **Sanctuaire Sainte-Anne-du-Bocage ★** (free admission; everyday, all year round; Blvd. Saint-Pierre O.) includes a small wooden chapel, the Stations of the Cross and a monument to Alexis Landry, ancestor of most of the Landrys in Acadia.

No history book on Acadia could ever be as an effective an educational tool as the **Village Historique Acadien ★★★** ($10; mid-Jun to early Sep; on Rte. 11, about 10km west of Caraquet, ☎726-2600). Here, on a vast piece of land, visitors will find a reconstructed village, including about 40 houses and other buildings, most of which are authentic, dating from 1770 to the beginning of the 20th century. The atmosphere is enlivened by performers in period costume, who carry out everyday tasks using traditional methods and gladly inform visitors about customs of the past. A film at the interpretive centre presents a brief history of the Acadian people. You can now stay in town at the Hôtel Château Albert, a replica of an establishment from the early 1900s.

The **Musée de Cire d'Acadie ★** ($6; Jun to Sep, 9am to 6pm; Jul and Aug, every day 9am to 7pm; Rte. 11, near the Village Historique Acadien, ☎727-6424) is a wax museum that re-creates the main historical events that marked Acadia from its foundation to the Deportation and illustrates the daily life activities of Acadians of that era. In all, 23 scenes, eight of which are animated, present 86 figures. The reconstructions are skilfully accomplished and the tour is instructive. Each visitor is allotted a cassette guide.

Caraquet has been the oyster capital for ages. As far back as 1758, the first Acadians fished for oysters, which grow in the Bay of Caraquet. Oyster harvesting eventually became oyster farming, thanks to the creation of ostreicultural farms. You can now find out more about oyster production by going to the **Ferme Ostréicole Dugas** (free admission; beginning of May to mid-Nov, Mon to Sat, 9:30am to 5:30pm; 675 Blvd. Saint-Pierre O., ☎727-3226), which has been converted into an economuseum.

The Dugas family presents traditional know-how, which they have developed over many years. Visitors can look at a variety of exhibits, such as the oysters and old oyster-farming implements. Workshops on oyster-box making

are also offered. The visit ends with an oyster-tasting session.

Maisonnette

This hamlet, known for its oysters, is graced with one of the most beautiful beaches on the Acadian peninsula: the beach at **Maisonnette Provincial Park** (take Rte. 11 to Rte. 303).

Grande-Anse

At Grande-Anse, another tiny coastal village, visitors will find pretty **Ferguson Beach**, which lies at the foot of a cliff, and the unique **Pope Museum ★** ($5; mid-Jun to early Sep; 184 Rue Acadie, ☎732-3003). The museum's exhibit includes a model of Saint Peter's in Rome, clothing and pieces of sacred art, as well as a collection of papal iconography. A number of these objects are both rare and interesting. The museum serves as a reminder of the important role religion has played in Acadian history.

A few kilometres past Grande-Anse, Highway 135 heads south to Paquetville, the hometown of famous singer Édith Butler. Paquetville is a quaint, peaceful community that has one of the largest churches in the province, the **Église Saint-Augustin** (Parc St.).

New Brunswick

Bathurst

An industrial town situated at the mouth of the Nepisiquit River, Bathurst is the largest urban centre in the northeastern part of the province. Accordingly, all sorts of services are available here. For visitors, however, Bathurst's interest lies mainly in the numerous natural sites located nearby. Right after the port, northeast of town, visitors can observe plant and animal life in the salt marshes, wooded areas and fields encompassed by the **Pointe Daly Reserve** *(Rte. 11, toward the Acadian peninsula)*, a haven of peace stretching 40 ha. Nature lovers can also admire nearby **Papineau Falls** *(several kilometres from town on Rte. 430)*.

Sugarloaf Provincial Park *(off Hwy. 11)*, a vast garden stretching more than 1,200ha, welcomes outdoor-sports enthusiasts all year round. In winter, it's popular for downhill skiing, since the park has a 305m-mountain, with eight runs. It also has snowmobile trails and 30km of cross-country-ski trails that turn into hiking paths in the summer. Many people also come here during summer to climb the mountain and enjoy the panoramic view. There is also a campground.

Dalhousie

Dalhousie, like Campbellton, was founded by Scottish settlers at the beginning of the 19th century, although

Atlantic Salmon

a large segment of the present population of both towns is of Acadian descent. A pleasant little community, Dalhousie has a beach and a pretty marina that serves as the boarding point for cruises on Baie des Chaleurs. A visit here also offers an interesting opportunity to learn more about local history, from the pre-contact period to the present day, at the **Restigouche Regional Museum** *(free admission; open all year; 437 George St.)*. A ferry makes a daily crossing between Dalhousie and Misquasha, in Québec.

Campbellton

Located alongside the estuary of the Restigouche River, Campbellton is the largest town in this lovely region. It is renowned for fishing, especially salmon. In fact, salmon fishing is so closely linked to Campbellton's history

that a **giant salmon** was erected here. Furthermore, the town holds a **Salmon Festival** *(late Jun and early Jul)* each year. Visitors can discover another side of the region at the **Restigouche Gallery** *(39 Andrew St.)*. Because of its proximity to the Québec border, Campbellton is also home to a provincial tourist information centre.

From Campbellton, visitors can head to Mount Carleton Provincial Park by taking Rte. 17 to Saint-Quentin and then picking up the 180.

Beaches

Murray Corner

Murray Beach Provincial Park ★ *(Rte. 955)* has a lovely beach, a campground and various activities.

Cap Pelé

Aboiteau Beach ★ *(Rte. 15)* stretches 2.5 km and features lovely sand dunes. The beach is not only an excellent place to swim, it is also enchanting. Between Cap Pelé and Shediac, there are three more pretty beaches along the coast.

Shediac

Parlee Beach Provincial Park ★★ *(near Exit 17 on Rte. 15)* is probably New Brunswick's most famous beach. It is patrolled by life guards and stretches several kilometres.

Saint-Louis-de-Kent

Some of the most beautiful beaches in the province are to be found in **Kouchibouguac National Park** *(Rte. 134 and 11)*. Visitors can also rent a canoe or rowboat, go hiking or cycling and, in winter, enjoy cross-country skiing here. There are campsites as well.

Escuminac

Escuminac Provincial Park *(Rte. 117)* has a lovely beach with magnificent sand dunes. There are campgrounds in the neighbouring villages.

Île Miscou

Île Miscou Beach *(Rte. 113, 14km from the crossing)* is well laid-out and equipped with a campground and cottages.

Caraquet

Frolex Beach, the **Downtown Beach** *(Rte. 11, downtown)* and the **Caraquet Park Beach** *(Rte. 11, west of Caraquet)* are two spots where visitors can go swimming or enjoy other water sports. There are no lifeguards.

Maisonnette

Maisonnette Provincial Park *(8km east of Rte. 11, on the 303)* has a beautiful beach with shallow waters.

Grande-Anse

Peaceful **Ferguson Beach** *(Rte. 11)* lies tucked away in a pretty spot at the foot of a cliff.

Outdoor Activities

Cycling

Since the creation of the **Sentiers Péninsule Acadienne** (Acadian Peninsula Trails), you can now travel along the peninsula on two wheels. Connecting the towns of Grande-Anse, Caraquet, Shippagan and Lamèque, a distance of about 100km, the trails mostly use former railway lines, which have been filled in with crushed stone. The network of trails is easy to cover and is accessible to all. The Sentiers Péninsule Acadienne Cycling Card is on sale ($1) in the province.

Sentiers Péninsule Acadienne(Acadian Peninsula Trails) ☎726-2600
For those who want to explore the region by bike, Kouchibouguac National Park also has some pleasant trails. Bike rentals available on site.

Rental Centre ☎876-2571

Bird-watching

Bouctouche

The **Éco-Centre Irving de la Dune de Bouctouche** protects a 12km-long dune, a wonderful location that attracts flocks of birds, especially the great blue heron, the piping plover and the roseate tern. To allow visitors to see these winged creatures without disturbing their fragile habitat, long footbridges have been built underneath the dune. You can now come and go as you please by bike or on foot.

Kouchibouguac National Park

In addition to gorgeous beaches, Kouchibouguac National Park also has marshes and dunes, that attract thousands of birds every year, especially the

New Brunswick

piping plover. Long, wooden footbridges have been built so visitors can bird-watch.

Tabusintac

With an area of 4,100ha, the **Bassin et l'Estuaire de Tabusintac** (Tabustintac Basin and Estuary) *(Hwy. 11 North and Hwy. 460,* ☎ *779-8304)* is the centre of the action during the summer when thousands of birds are attracted here by the wetlands. The area is the home of the common eider, osprey and great blue heron, as well as the rare piping plover.

Canoeing and Kayaking

The Acadian coast is a great place for canoeing and kayaking. Several companies offer boat rentals and guided tours.

Bouctouche

You can explore the rivers of the Bouctouche region by kayak with the help of Expédition Sud-Acadie, which organizes a variety of tours.

Expédition Sud-Acadie
Bouctouche
☎ *743-1999*

In addition to guided tours, KayaBécano offers kayak rentals.

KayaBécano
R.R. 1
Bouctouche
☎ *743-6265*

Saint-Louis-de-Kent

To explore the natural beauty of Kouchibouguac National Park, take a guided tour on the sea with Kayakouch.

Kayakouch
10617 Rue Principale
Saint-Louis-de-Kent
☎ *876-1199*
⇄ *876-1918*

Canoe rentals are also available in Kouchibouguac National Park.

Rental Centre
☎ *876-2571*

Miramichi

The Miramichi River also offers some spectacular panoramic views that can be reached by paddling a short distance.

Miramichi Adventure Tours
☎ *627-1113*

Eastern Scenic Adventure
☎ *778-8573*

Kedgwick River

Centre Echo Restigouche offers trips lasting between one and several days, allowing you to enjoy the magnificent natural beauty of the Restigouche River.

Centre Echo Restigouche
1397 Hwy. 265
Kedgwick River
☎ *284-2022*
⇄ *284-2927*

Downhill Skiing

When Sugarloaf Provincial Park is covered with snow, Mount Sugarloaf becomes a haven for downhill skiing enthusiasts. With eight runs, it's one of the most popular ski centres in the province.

Accommodations

Cap Pelé

Les Chalets de L'Aboiteau
$85
K, tv
40 chalets
55 Allée des Chalets, E0A 1J1
☎ 577-2005
≈ 577-2083
If you are one of those people who never get tired of looking at the sea, then L'Aboiteau is the place for you. Its 40 wooden chalets, recently built along the magnificent L'Aboiteau beach, are an idyllic getaway for those who want to relax by the ocean, which stretches as far as the eye can see.

In addition to its wonderful location, all of the cottages are luxurious, with fireplaces, large bay windows and fully equipped kitchens. Each cottage can accommodate between six and eight people. Reservations are strongly recommended.

Robichaud

Motel Alouette
$79 bkfst incl.
K, tv
21 rooms
E0A 3G0
☎ 532-5378
≈ 855-0809
Motel Alouette, located next to a very busy campground, offers clean, basic rooms within walking distance of a sandy beach that is ideal for swimming.

Shediac

The Shediac region attracts a good number of visitors in the summer months, thanks to magnificent Parlee Beach. Various accommodations options are available to vacationers, some of them located near the park entrance, but there is no motel, inn or bed and breakfast directly on Parlee Beach.

For longer stays it is possible to rent one of the many cottages in the area; some of these look out over the ocean. Mrs. Ginette Arsenault, of the rental agency **Planning Plus** *(R.R.1, Shediac, E0A 3G0, ☎ 532-3896, ≈ 532-8914)*, is quite efficient at selecting and reserving cottages in the area that meet visitors' specific needs.

Neptune Motel
$45, summer only
tv, K
34 rooms
691 East Main St., E0A 3G0
☎ 532-4299
While the rooms at the Neptune Motel are furnished and decorated very simply, they are among the least expensive in the area. Located near the provincial park entrance.

Chez Françoise
$60
open Apr to Dec
tv
16 rooms
293 Main St., E0A 3G0
☎ 532-4233
≈ 532-8423
Located on a beautifully-maintained piece of property in the heart of Shediac, Chez Françoise is a wonderful inn. Built at the turn of the century, it was originally the residence of a wealthy family. The elegant interior, with its wood trim, sumptuous staircase and large front porch ideal for coffee or an apéritif, make for a charming little spot.

Seely's Motel
$58
tv, K
34 rooms
East Main St., E0A 3G0
☎ 532-6193
≈ 533-8089
Close to the provincial park's entrance, Seely's Motel offers plainly decorated rooms that are nonetheless comfortable and clean.

New Brunswick

Four Seas Motel
$60
tv, ℜ, K
42 rooms
762 Main St., E0A 3G0
☎*532-2585*
⊶*855-0809*
Near the entrance to the provincial park, the Four Seas Motel is a good choice for families. The service is efficient and friendly, the restaurant is very good and the rooms are clean and well furnished, mostly with modern pieces. During the summer season, it is best to reserve early in the morning if you want one of the less expensive rooms since they go fast.

Motel Sea Gull
$70
tv, ℜ
21 rooms
Shediac Bridge
Hwy. 134, E0A 3H0
☎*532-2530*
Accommodations directly on Parlee Beach are non-existent, but just a few kilometres north of Shediac, at Shediac Bridge, there is Motel Sea Gull which looks out over a pretty, placid bay. This is a very relaxing spot: lawn chairs have been set out here and there on the grassy grounds, from which guests can admire the beautiful panorama in complete, undisturbed tranquillity. Though not luxurious, the Sea Gull's rooms are clean and relatively inexpensive, and they are very much in demand; reservations are

a good idea. A few cottages are also available.

Auberge Le Gourmand
$75
tv, ℜ, K
6 rooms
562 Main St.
☎*532-4351*
⊶*532-1025*
In the summertime, Auberge Le Gourmand, located near the entrance to the provincial park, rents nine cottages spread out on a small wooded lot just behind the establishment's main building. Each of them has a modern washroom and kitchenette, two bedrooms and a living room that can be transformed into a third bedroom, all of which are appealingly laid out. In addition, Le Gourmand offers a few very well-kept rooms in the main building, which also houses an excellent restaurant.

Bay Vista Lodge & Cottages
$79
12 rooms
Rte. 134N, E0A 3G0
☎*532-1265*
At Shediac Cape, a few kilometres north of Shediac, the Bay Vista Lodge & Cottages comprises about 10 chalets spread out over a beautifully landscaped property in a peaceful setting. A wild beach, located nearby, makes for wonderful walks. Each cottage has a small front porch that is perfect for lounging and relaxing. The Bay Vista also rents rooms.

Shediac Hotel
$85
tv, =, ℜ
28 rooms
Main St., E0A 3G0
☎*532-4405*
In 1853, a large home was built to accommodate James Weldon, an entrepreneur who came to live in the region. The house was renovated, and today it is the home of the 28-room Hôtel Shediac, which is simply decorated and offers adequate comfort. Located in the middle of town.

Belcourt Inn
$109
tv
7 rooms
112 Main St., E0A 3G0
☎*532-6098*
A member of the Association des Auberges du Patrimoine du Nouveau-Brunswick, Belcourt Inn occupies a sumptuous patrician house that has belonged to such notables as former premier of New Brunswick Judge Allison Dysart. Erected in 1912, this three-storey Victorian building has preserved all of its olden-day splendour and charm, both inside and out.

The common rooms are spacious, furnished with antiques and richly ornamented with woodwork. The inn's seven individually decorated guestrooms are also decked out in period furniture. A very inviting porch provides an ideal setting for reading and relaxing. Belcourt Inn is situated in the heart of Shediac, just across from Chez Françoise.

Parc Oasis
$100
K, ℝ
☎*532-5339*
The Parc Oasis rents out about 20 cottages near the entrance to the provincial park, about 10min by foot from the beach. Each two-storey cottage can accommodate up to six people and includes two bedrooms, a small living room with a convertible sofa, a very clean bathroom and a kitchen. The cottages' natural-wood interiors are very appealing. Parc Oasis also offers six rooms in a main building.

Bouctouche

Bouctouche Bay Inn
$65
27 rooms
tv, ℜ
entrance to town, E0A 1G0
☎*743-2726*
⇌*743-2387*
Besides a terrific view of the bay, the Bouctouche Bay Inn offers clean motel-style rooms, some of which are very competitively priced. It is not far from the entrance to the Pays de la Sagouine (see p 111).

La Bergerie aux 4 Vents
$70 bkfst incl.
≈, tv
3 rooms
100 Ch. Alban-Léger, E0A 1G0
☎*525-9633*
⇌*525-2109*
Located some distance from town in the mid-

dle of the countryside, La Bergerie aux 4 Vents offers a pleasant stay on a sheep dairy farm. You won't have to sacrifice comfort, however, as the inn, located in the farm house, is quite comfortable. It has three cozy rooms, one of which has a whirlpool.

🐚 Old Presbytery of Bouctouche
$75
ℜ
22 rooms
157 Chemin du Couvent, E0A 1G0
☎*743-5568*
⇌*743-5566*
The Old Presbytery of Bouctouche actually occupies a presbytery constructed at the end of the 19th century. Today it is a superb family inn just outside the centre of Bouctouche, with beautiful views of the bay. The atmosphere is first-rate, ideal for relaxation, and the building, which has been renovated several times, is full of charm. An old chapel has been converted into a reception hall. The restaurant has an excellent reputation as well.

Bouctouche Bay Chalet
$80
Hwy. 475, E0A 1G0
☎*743-2848*
⇌*743-5349*
Not far from the beach and the dune, Bouctouche Bay Chalet consists of three cottages of different dimensions, all set in a shady glen near a campground.

Inn by the Dune
$85
ℜ, tv
3 rooms
R.R 1, E0A 1G0
☎*743-8182 or 743-8896*
This inn, which faces the Bay of Bouctouche, has three rooms with private bathrooms. It is conveniently located near the centre of Bouctouche. Domestic pets are welcome.

Richibucto

Motel Habitant
$70
⌂, ⊛, tv, ≈
29 rooms
Rte. 134, E0A 2M0
☎*523-4421*
⇌*523-0155*
The Motel Habitant is just over 10km south of the entrance to Kouchibouguac National Park (see p 108). It is a nice-looking motel with clean rooms and a pool. This is the most comfortable motel near the park.

Les Chalets du Havre
$125
tv, ℑ, K
20 chalets
P.O. Box 555, Rte. 134, York Point, E0A 2M0
☎*523-1570*
⇌*523-9770*
Les Chalets du Havre, a holiday resort of about 20 cottages, occupies a large peninsula near the village of Richibucto. The site is lovely, although the ground is practically bare here. The recently built cottages can accommodate up to six people, and each has two bedrooms, an all-

New Brunswick

equipped kitchenette, a bathroom and a den that can be converted into a bedroom if necessary. The cottages' interior decor is standard and modern. The entire peninsula is bordered by a long beach that is great for swimming but especially pleasant for seaside strolls. Many outdoor activities may be organized here. In summer, a ferry shuttles passengers to the splendid sand beaches of Kouchibouguac National Park.

Tracadie-Sheila

Motel Boudreau
$69
ℜ, ≈
79 rooms
Rte. 11, E1X 165
☎*395-6868*
The Motel Boudreau is a fine establishment that rents very comfortable, modern rooms. The clientele is made up mostly of business people.

Shippagan

Camping Shippagan
$17
135 camping spots
4km west of Shippagan
E0B 2P0
☎*336-3960*
≈*336-3961*
In Shippagan, campers can pitch their tent a short distance from the beach at Camping Shippagan, which is definitely, one of the most pleasant campgrounds in the region.

Motel Brise Marine
$60
ℜ, tv
51 rooms
centre of Shippagan, E0B 2P0
☎*336-2276*
Among the other accomodation possibilities, the clean, comfortable rooms of the Motel Brise Marine are worth mentioning.

Île Lamèque

🏖**Auberge des Compagnons**
$93 bkfst incl.
ℜ, tv
16 rooms
11 Main St., E8T 1M9
☎*344-7762*
≈*344-0813*
You will definitely have a pleasant stay at this inn – is both comfortable and ideally located facing the bay. Each of its 16 thematic rooms has a different decor (the circus, the Edwardian Era, fruit, and the like), and all of them are well kept. The lounge-bar, which has a fireplace is the ideal spot to end the day.

Caraquet

🏖 **Hôtel Paulin**
$45-$80
open May to Oct
9 rooms
tv, ℜ
143 Blvd. St-Pierre O., E1W 1B6
☎*727-9981*
≈*727-3165*
Also part of the Caraquet skyline for many years, the Hôtel Paulin is actually a pleasant inn that has been run by the Paulin

family for the last three generations. The rooms vary in quality: some have recently been nicely renovated while others are quite out of date but are still very clean; in all cases, however, the rooms are of good value. There is a very pretty suite at the back of the building with a view of the ocean. Guests can relax in the sitting room and enjoy the restaurant's excellent food.

Le Poirier
$45
4 rooms
98 Blvd. St-Pierre Ouest.
E1W 1B6
Caraquet also has a pleasant inn, Le Poirier, which was originally built in 1928 and has managed to keep its old-world charm. Its four simply decorated rooms are all cozy.

Maison Touristique Dugas
$55
tv
18 rooms
683 Blvd. St-Pierre Ouest.
E1W 1A1
☎*727-3195*
≈*722-3193*
There is truly something for all tastes and all budgets at the Maison Touristique Dugas. The main building, a beautiful, massive house built in 1926, numbers over 10 impeccable, pretty rooms of varying sizes. In addition to these rooms, campsites and fully equipped rental cottages are available on the grounds. The Maison Touristique Dugas offers a very

friendly welcome and excellent breakfasts in the morning. From the house, located a little bit west of Caraquet, a trail winds through the woods to the Dugas's private beach, just a 10min walk away.

Auberge de la Baie
$59
tv, ℜ
54 rooms
139 Blvd. St-Pierre Ouest.
E1W 1B7
☎727-3485
⇌727-3634
The Auberge de la Baie provides comfortable, modern motel-style accommodation. Strangely enough, most of the rooms open onto an interior hallway instead of outdoors. There is a good restaurant with polite, friendly and attentive service. Finally the ample grounds offer access to a small deserted beach located behind the inn.

Bathurst

Best Western Danny's Inn
$69
tv, ℜ, ≈
40 rooms
Rte. 134, E0B 1H0
☎546-6621 or 800-200-1350
⇌548-3266
Slightly on the outskirts of downtown Bathurst, the Best Western Danny's Inn offers spotless, modern rooms.

Country Inns & Suites
$74 bkfst incl
tv
78 rooms
777 St. Peter Ave., E2A 2Y9
☎548-4949 or 800-456-4000
⇌548-8595
With its spacious rooms and suites, the Country Inns is another Bathurst establishment that offers the comfort of a modern hotel. The little added touches, such as the fireplace in the hall, give this place a charming atmosphere.

Keddy's Le Château Hôtel
$85
136 rooms
ℜ, ≈, △
80 Main St., E2A 1A3
☎546-6691 or 800-561-7666
⇌546-0015
Situated in downtown Bathurst, Keddy's Le Château Hôtel is the largest hotel in the area. Its rooms are standard and comfortable but charmless.

Petit-Rocher

 Auberge d'Anjou
$85
ℜ, K
17 rooms
587 Main St., E0B 2E0
☎783-0587
⇌783-5587
Auberge d'Anjou is considered one of the best places to stay in this part of the Acadian coast. It occupies a beautiful 1917 house that was actually the first hotel in Petit-Rocher.

In those days, in addition to welcoming travellers, it served as the principal meeting place for villagers. The Auberge d'Anjou closed down in the 1960s and did not resume its vocation until 1994. The very successfully renovated main building is embellished by a large porch that greatly enhances its charm. Its rooms are inviting and tastefully decorated. To top it all off, the Auberge has an excellent restaurant.

Best Western Manoir Adelaide
$80
ℜ, ≈, K, ☺, tv
46 rooms
385 Adelaide St., E8C 1B4
☎684-5681 or 800-528-1234
⇌684-3433
The Manoir Adelaide offers adequate comfort as well as modern rooms, conference facilities, exercise room and pool with slides. Some rooms are equipped with kitchenettes.

Campbellton

Aylesford Inn
$65 bkfst incl.
tv
6 rooms
8 McMillan Ave., E3N 1E9
☎759-7672 or 759-8557
A beautiful example of Campbellton's architectural heritage, the Aylesford Inn is a magnificent, stately Victorian residence built at the turn of the 20th century. The house is set on a beautifully landscaped property.

New Brunswick

Adding to the character of the place, the rooms are all decorated in period furniture. Breakfast is served each morning.

Restaurants

Cap Pelé

Restaurant de la Plage de L'Aboiteau
$
L'Aboiteau Beach
☎577-2005
If you want to have a bite to eat but don't want to leave the beach, you can have breakfast at the Restaurant de la Plage de L'Aboiteau. It offers basic fare at reasonable prices and has a magnificent view of the sea.

Chez Camille
$
2385 Ch. Acadie, Hwy. 15
☎577-4710
Another great place to eat in Cap Pelé is the reasonably priced Chez Camille, which has become very popular with fried-chicken lovers. Patrons claim that it's one of the best restaurants of its kind in the province.

Shediac

Chez Léo
☎532-4543
Chez Léo's menu offers several simply prepared seafood dishes, sand-wiches and fries. The lunch menu is always delicious – especially the fried chicken.

Café Péché Mignon
$
15 Queen St.
☎532-6555
When the owners of the Café Péché Mignon opened for business in the summer of 1994, they did so believing there was space in Shediac for a little French café. They couldn't have been more right! Besides excellent desserts and coffees, the menu includes a good choice of simple dishes like excellent quiche and some Acadian specialties. The atmosphere is particularly friendly and reflects the bohemian spirit of the owner, who is a painter.

Four Seas Restaurant
$$
634 Main St.
☎532-2585
The Four Seas Restaurant, in the motel of the same name, is another family restaurant. This one offers a rather varied menu, including seafood. Patrons surely don't come for the relatively boring decor, but rather for the reasonable prices and the quality of the food.

Paturel
$$-$$$
Cape Bimet Rd.
☎532-4774
About 5km outside of Shediac towards Cap-Pelé, a small road leads to the famous Paturel, a simple restaurant with an ocean view that serves fresh seafood at prices that are reasonable, all things considered. Portions are generous, especially the Seafood Platter, which includes a variety of seafood from the region. To add to the maritime atmosphere, the restaurant lies right next to Paturel Seafood Ltd., a seafood-processing plant.

Fisherman's Paradise
$$-$$$
Main St.
☎532-6811
There are no surprises at the Fisherman's Paradise, which, as its name suggests, is devoted to the treasures of the sea. A special place is reserved on the menu for the king of seafood: the lobster. With its exquisite interior decor made up of numerous model ships, this place is among the most chic in Shediac. For those unfortunates who are not seafood aficionados, Fisherman's Paradise offers a good variety of steaks.

Lobster Deck
$$$
312 Main St.
☎532-8737
Located in the centre of town, the Lobster Deck has delicious, fresh fish and seafood specialities prepared in a variety of ways: grilled, fried, au gratin or coated with sauce. The dining room has an amusing decor: the tables are shaped like lobster pots, and the walls are adorned with stuffed lobsters,

one of which weighs 20kg. On beautiful sunny days, guests can dine outdoors on the adjoining terrace.

Chez Françoise
$$$
93 Main St.
☎532-4233
Undeniably one of the best restaurants in the region, Chez Françoise offers refined French cuisine and an excellent wine list. And to add to your dining pleasure, the dining room is decorated with elegance and style. On lazy summer afternoons, the establishment's front porch is the perfect place for sipping a cool drink.

Auberge Le Gourmand
$$
562 Rue Main
☎532-4351
The lovely dining room at the Auberge Le Gourmand is a pleasant setting for a hearty meal. Grilled scallops, shrimp, lobster in various preparations, filets of salmon and cod, steaks and poultry constitute the main elements on the menu. For starters, both the succulent seafood *chaudrée* (chowder) and the grilled escargots are excellent choices.

Bouctouche

La Cuisine à Yvette
$
facing the entrance to Parc des Dunes de Bouctouche
Don't be swayed by the rather modest look of

this spot. This fast-food stand does offer simple dishes, but they are well prepared and inexpensive. The menu offers some local specialties, including chicken stew and, for the more adventurous, an amazing *poutine râpée*. Succulent lobster rolls are another option.

L'Ordre du Bon Temps
$-$$
entrance to Pays de la Sagouine
☎743-1400
L'Ordre du Bon Temps the restaurant at the Pays de la Sagouine offers visitors the chance to sample traditional Acadian specialties like *fricot de poulet, poutine râpée, poutine à trou, pâté à la râpure* or *pâté aux palourdes*. The menu probably has the most extensive selection of Acadian dishes in all of Acadia, so take advantage of it.

Restaurant du Gîte de la Sagouine
$$
45 Blvd. Irving
☎743-5554
"*Chu bin fière de vous ouère*" ("I'm really proud to welcome you"). These are the first words of welcome at the Restaurant du Gîte de la Sagouine – a sure sign of the good things to come. The menu at this family restaurant offers Acadian dishes, such as *fricot de poulet* (chicken stew), *poutine râpée*, as well as expertly prepared seafood.

Tire-Bouchon
$$-$$$
Old Presbytery
☎743-5568
Acadian hospitality is at its best at Tire-Bouchon the excellent dining room in the Old Presbytery, where chef Marcelle Albert introduces diners to the most refined regional specialties. The name, which means "corkscrew," is quite fitting considering the fine bottles stocked in the wine cellar.

St. Thomas

St. Thomas Fish Market
Hwy. 535
☎743-5965
Sometimes it's nice to have some simply prepared seafood in a plain-looking restaurant. St. Thomas Fish Market is such a place. The seafood here is prepared on the premises, and the freshness is guaranteed!

Shippagan

Bistro Pirate Maboule
$$
121 16th St.
☎336-0004
The creative menu at Bistro Pirate Maboule is the first thing you notice about this bistro. Dishes have evocative names, like "Captain Haddock's Haddock," the "Seven Seas Salad" and the "Captain's Feast." Everything is scrumptious. The decor, which looks like

New Brunswick

an old pirate ship, is also quite attractive. The atmosphere is delightful and will please everyone – especially families.

Abri des Flots
$$-$$$
next to the Aquarium
☎*336-8454*
Very elegant and endowed with a splendid view of the port, the Abri des Flots is, as one might expect, an excellent fish and seafood restaurant. Lunchtime, when the lobster rolls and other small meals are available at relatively reasonable prices, is a good time to stop in for a bite. During the evening, gourmets benefit from a wide choice. Those with a big appetite can attempt to discover all the wonders of the sea in one meal with the "Sea in Your Plate."

Île Lamèque

Auberge des Compagnons
11 Main St., E8T 1M9
☎*344-7762*
The Auberge des Compagnons serves delicious meals and is considered one of the best restaurants in the region.

Betrand

La Pantrie
$$
Hwy. 325, a few kilometres south of Caraquet
☎*764-3019*
La Pantrie offers an opportunity to sample some traditional Acadian dishes, such as *poutine râpée, gallettes à la morue sèche, miche du pêcheur* and *poutine à trou*. These specialities from a bygone era are served up in an old-style home, with wood stove and antique furniture. The place is delightful. In winter, the restaurant turns into a *cabane à sucre* (sap house). Reservations recommended.

Caraquet

Café Phare
$-$$
186 Blvd. St-Pierre Ouest
☎*727-9460*
Café Phare, a recently opened, adorable café that already has a great number of devotees, is a good spot for breakfast or a light meal. It is welcoming and has a pleasant front patio that is very crowded when the weather is good. Café Phare mainly serves salads, quiches, sandwiches and pastries. There is also a choice of a few more elaborate dishes on the daily menu.

Caraquette
$-$$
89 Blvd. St-Pierre Ouest
☎*727-6009*
For dining in a friendly family atmosphere check out the Caraquette. The reasonably priced menu is varied and includes steaks, pasta, chicken and sandwiches, as well as lots of fish and seafood. Most dishes cost less than $10.

Hôtel Paulin dining room
$$
143 Blvd. St-Pierre Ouest
☎*727-9981*
The Hôtel Paulin dining room offers what has become something of a rarity in the region, a table d'hôte or set menu, instead of the usual à la carte service. Regional and French specialties make up the menu. On nice summer days there is service on a beautiful terrace.

Auberge de la Baie dining room
$$
139 Blvd. St-Pierre Ouest.
☎*727-3485*
Airy and modern, but at the same time friendly and inviting, the Auberge de la Baie dining room offers a good variety of dishes, including seafood and steaks. The service is very attentive. Some of this restaurant's specialties are baked scallops, *Coquilles St. Jacques au gratin* and Provençale frogs' legs.

Poisson d'Or
$$-$$$
Carrefour de la Mer
☎*727-0004*
Come nightfall, Poisson d'Or, a pretty restaurant with the atmosphere of a French bistro, becomes a popular meeting place for locals and visitors alike. The menu offers seafood and fish, in addition to succulent, charcoal-broiled steaks.

Paquetville

La Crêpe Bretonne
$-$$
1085 Rue Du Parc
☎764-5344
If your tummy starts to grumble as you pass through the little town of Paquetville, silence it with a stop at La Crêpe Bretonne, a small restaurant whose specialties are crepes and seafood. These two are sometimes combined in scallops and béchamel crepes, lobster and béchamel crepes, crab and béchamel crepes, etc. A good place for an inexpensive lunch or a good evening meal.

Nigadoo

 Fine Grobe-sur-Mer
$$-$$$
☎783-3138
A short side trip from Bathurst or Caraquet to fine Grobe-sur-Mer is a must for aficionados of fine cuisine. This little restaurant offers an original menu of local and international specialties prepared with ingredients that are always fresh. The bread that accompanies meals is baked fresh on the premises.

Petit-Rocher

Auberge d'Anjou
$$
587 Rue Principale
☎783-0587
Auberge d'Anjou has a pretty dining room and a splendid terrace that is very enjoyable on sunny summer days. The menu lists a great variety of seafood, fish and meat dishes. Auberge d'Anjou is reputed to be one of the best restaurants on the coast.

Entertainment

Bars

Caraquet

Le Vieux Sage
Blvd. St-Pierre
☎727-7243
Le Vieux Sage, which occupies all three stories of a large, beautiful house, is the main bar in the Caraquet region. It has two dance floors as well as a terrace.

Festivals and Cultural Events

Shediac

Lobster Festival

Tracadie-Sheila

Festival International de la Francophonie

Shippagan

Festival des Pêches et de L'Aquaculture

Lamèque Island

International Baroque Music Festival

Caraquet

Festival Acadien

Théâtre Populaire d'Acadie

Campbellton

Salmon Festival

Shopping

Shediac

Le P'tit Cadeau
336 Main St.
☎532-3348
Le P'tit Cadeau offers an interesting selection of arts and crafts.

St. Thomas

St. Thomas Fish Market
☎743-5965
Located not far from Bouctouche, this market is a must for those who want to stock up on seafood or just sample some on the premises.

Nan's Clay Studio
Hwy. 535
☎743-6480
On your way to the market you'll pass the Stella Anne Daigle studio, a local artist. Day after day, she creates beautiful pottery inspired by the

New Brunswick

local natural environment.

Caraquet

Les Blanc d'Arcadie
340 Blvd. Saint-Pierre Est.
☎ 727-5952
Les Blanc d'Arcadie is an experimental farm that breeds goats and produces high-quality milk. To do this, the animals' diets and hygiene are given special attention. After the milk is produced, it is prepared for con

sumption or turned into delicious cheese, which can bought on the premises. Visitors can explore the farm, sample its products, as well as pet some of the goats and their young.

Bathurst

Nipisigut
96 Main St.
☎ 548-5575
To stock up on equipment for all expeditions, stop by Nipisigut, the largest outdoor supply store in New Brunswick.

Atholville

Poissonneire Ouellette
156 Notre Dame St.
☎ 753-7166
Before leaving New Brunswick, take a jaunt to Poissonnerie Ouellette in Atholville, only a few kilometres from Campbellton. You can buy some lobster here and have it packed to go.

The Acadian coast is well-known for its charming little villages scattered about along the coast. Located on the shores of the Northumberland Strait, Cap-Lumière is certainly no exception to this rule.
- *Roger Michel*

Vhen visited at the right time, the peaceful lighthouse at Cap Fourchu, Nova Scotia, ll allow you to ee Yarmouth's impressive fishing fleet passing by.
- *B. Terry*

Built in 1750, St. Paul's Anglican Church, Nova Scotia, is Canada's oldest Protestant church. - *Tibor Bognár*

Nova Scotia

T he magnificent province of Nova Scotia looks like a long peninsula, connected to the continent by nothing more than a narrow strip of land known as the Isthmus of Chignecto.

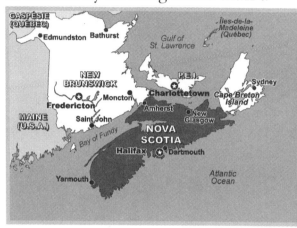

In "Canada's Ocean Playground," the sea is never far away. In fact, no part of the territory of Nova Scotia is more than 49 km from the water, be it the Atlantic Ocean, the Northumberland Strait or the Bay of Fundy.

The proximity of the coast has shaped the character and lives of Nova Scotians as much as it has the splendid maritime landscape.

The coastline, stretching hundreds of kilometres, is punctuated with harbours and bays, their shores dotted with fishing villages and towns.

What is most striking about Nova Scotia is the way its architectural heritage blends so harmoniously with the natural setting.

From the tiniest fishing village to Halifax, the capital, there are few places where the architecture of the houses and buildings, often dating back to the 19 th century, does not fit in beautifully with the surrounding landscape.

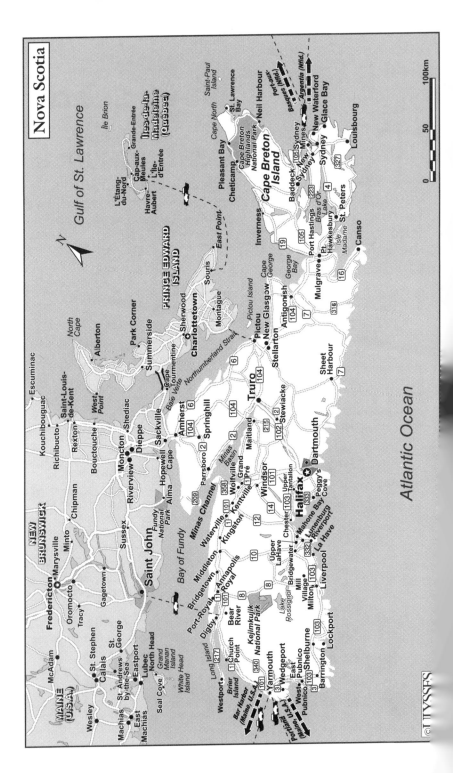

Nova Scotia

Gulf of St. Lawrence

Atlantic Ocean

©ULYSSES

0   50   100km

Halifax ★★★

is the beautiful, vibrant and delightful capital of Nova Scotia and the largest city in the Atlantic provinces.

A city with a rich architectural heritage, built at the foot of a fortified hill overlooking one of the longest natural harbours in the world, Halifax is a delightful place to visit. The city's location, which is outstanding from both a navigational and a strategic point of view, has been the deciding factor in its growth.

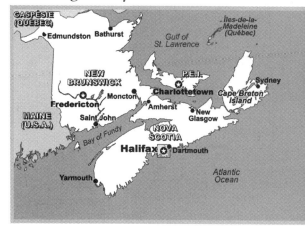

In 1749, the British began developing the site, which had long been frequented by the Micmac First Nation. That year, 2,500 British soldiers and colonists led by Governor Edward Cornwallis settled here with the aim of securing Britain's claim to the territory of Nova Scotia.

At the time, France and its North American colonies were the enemy. Over the following decades, Halifax served as a stronghold for British troops during the American Revolution and the War of 1812 against the United States. A military past is evident in the city's present-day urban landscape, its most striking legacy being, of course, the Citadel, whose silhouette looms over the downtown area.

Not only a military city, Halifax has always been a commercial centre as well. Its access to the Atlantic, its excellent port and, starting in the late 19th century, its connection to the Canadian rail network have all favoured trade. Historic Properties, made up of warehouses built on the pier, is the oldest architectural grouping of its kind in the country, bearing witness to the city's long-established commercial tradition.

Halifax is now the largest urban centre in the Atlantic provinces, with a population of over 330,000 (including the inhabitants of its twin city,

Dartmouth). It has a more varied, even cosmopolitan appearance than the rest of Atlantic Canada, and boasts several superb museums and a whole slew of other attractions. Visitors are sure to enjoy strolling around Halifax and scouting out its restaurants, bustling streets and wide assortment of shops.

Finding Your Way Around

By Car

Entering Halifax and reaching the downtown area is generally very easy by car; many road signs clearly indicate the way. If in doubt, remember that Halifax lies on the southwest side of the harbour (Dartmouth is on the other side), and the downtown area faces right onto the port. Visitors will have little trouble finding their bearings downtown, since Citadel Hill and the port serve as landmarks. The most important downtown artery is Barrington Street.

By Plane

Halifax International Airport is served by planes from Europe and the United States. Air Canada and Canadian Airlines offer flights from major Canadian cities. For more information, please refer to the "Practical Information" chapter, see p 31. There is shuttle service from the airport to the big hotels downtown.

By Train

VIA, the Canadian railway, ends at Halifax. The station is near downtown. To find out the passenger train schedule, call ☎*800-561-3952*

Practical Information

Area code: *902*

Tourist Information Office

Visitor Centre
1595 Barrington St.
☎*490-5946*
⌐*490-5973*

The provincial government operates a reservation service for hotels, bed & breakfasts, campgrounds and car rentals. Information on festivals, ferry service and weather forecasts is also available. Dial ☎*800-565-0000* in North America or ☎*(902) 425-5781*.

Historic Properties
Loner Water St.
☎*424-4247*

Exploring

The Citadel and Its Surrounding Area

The **Halifax Citadel National Historic Site** ★ ★ ★ *($6; early May to late Oct, 9am to 5pm; Jul and Aug until 6pm; Citadel Hill;* ☎*426-5080)* is the most striking legacy of the military history of Halifax, a city that has played an important strategic role in the defence of the East Coast ever since it was founded in 1749. The fourth British fort to occupy this site, this imposing star-shaped structure overlooking the city was built between 1828 and 1856. It was the heart of an impressive network of defences intended to protect the port in the event of an attack.

Visitors can explore the Citadel alone or take part in an interesting guided tour, which traces the history of the various fortifications that have marked the city's landscape since 1749, and explains their strategic value. All of the rooms used to accommodate soldiers and store arms and munitions are open to the public, and visitors can move about

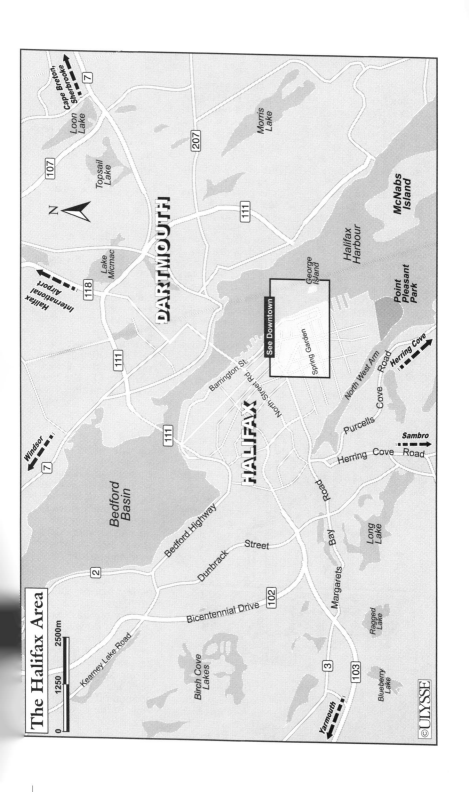

The Halifax Area

0   1250   2500m

N

Kearney Lake Road

Birch Cove Lakes

Bicentennial Drive

[102]

Dunbrack   Street

Bedford Highway

Bedford Basin

[2]

[7] Windsor

[107]

[118] Halifax International Airport

Lake Micmac

[111]

Topsail Lake

Loon Lake

[7] Cape Breton, Sherbrooke

DARTMOUTH

[207]

Morris Lake

[111]

HALIFAX

Margarets

Bay   Road

Long Lake

Herring   Cove   Road

Purcells   Cove

North West Arm

Spring Garden

See Downtown

George Island

Barrington St.

North Street Rd.

[111]

Halifax Harbour

McNabs Island

Point Pleasant Park

Herring Cove

Sambro

Ragged Lake

Blueberry Lake

[103]

[3] Yarmouth

© ULYSSE

through the corridors leading from one room or level to another. It is also possible to walk along the ramparts, which offer an incomparable view of the city and its port. In summer, students dressed and armed like soldiers of the 78th Highlanders and the Royal Artillery perform manoeuvres within these walls. The site also includes a **military museum** (☎427-5979) that houses an extensive collection of British and Nova Scotian arms and uniforms. A fascinating, 15min audio-visual presentation on the history of Halifax may be viewed as well.

Right in front of the Citadel, towards the port, stands one of the most famous symbols of Halifax, the **Old Town Clock** ★ *(Citadel Hill, opposite the main entrance of the Citadel)*, with its four dials.

the Halifax garrison from 1794 to 1800. It serves as a reminder that the prince was a great believer in punctuality.

Northwest of the Citadel, visitors will find the **Nova Scotia Museum of Natural History** ★ *($3.50; Jun to mid-Oct, Mon, Tue, Thu and Fri 9:30am to 5:30pm, Wed 9:30am to 8pm, Sun 1pm to 5:30pm; mid-Oct to late May, Tue, Thu, Fri and Sat 9:30am to 5pm, Wed 9:30am to 8pm, Sun 1pm to 5pm; 1747 Summer St.,* ☎424-6099*)*, whose mission is to collect, preserve and study the objects and specimens most representative of Nova Scotia's geology, plant and animal life and archaeology.

The museum features exhibits on subjects such as botany, fossils, insects, reptiles and marine life. One of the most noteworthy items on display is a whale skeleton.

Old Town Clock

The clock was presented to the city in 1803 by Prince Edward, son of George III of Britain, who served as commander in chief of

Visitors can also view a film on the birds living along the province's coast. The archaeology exhibit is particularly

interesting, presenting the lifestyle and material possessions of the various peoples who have inhabited the province's territory over the centuries. The exhibit is organized in chronological order, starting with the Palaeolithic age, then moving on to the Micmacs, the Acadians and finally the British.

Stretching southwest of the Citadel are the lovely, verdant **Public Gardens** ★★ *(main entrance on South Park St.)*, a Victorian garden covering an area of 7 m, which dates back to 1753. Originally a private garden, it was purchased by the Nova Scotia Horticultural Society in 1836. The present layout, completed in 1875, is the work of Richard Power. A fine example of British know-how, the Public Gardens are adorned with stately trees concealing fountains, statues, charming flowerbeds, a pavilion and little lakes where ducks and swans can be seen swimming about.

This is an absolutely perfect place to take a stroll, far from the occasionally turbulent atmosphere of downtown Halifax. During summer, concerts are held here on Sunday afternoons, and the Friends of Public Gardens organization offers guided tours of the garden *(*☎422-9407*)*.

South of the Public Gardens, near Victoria Park, stands the **Cathedral Church of All Saints** ★ *(free admission; mid-Jun to mid-Sep, 1:30pm to 4:30pm; 1320 Tower Rd.; ☎424-6002)*, whose remarkable stained-glass windows and exquisite woodwork will take your breath away.

The structure was completed in 1910, two centuries after the first Anglican service was held in Canada. It is located in a pretty part of the city, where the streets are flanked by stately trees. Some of Halifax's most prominent educational establishments can be found nearby.

Downtown Halifax and the Port

As early as a decade after Halifax was founded, **Grand Parade** *(between Harrington and Argyle Sts.)* had become a trading and gathering place for city residents. It is now a garden in the heart of the downtown area, flanked by tall buildings on all sides.

At the south end of Grand Parade, visitors will find **St. Paul Anglican Church** ★ *(free admission; Jun to Sep, Mon to Sat 9:30am to 5pm; Oct to May, Mon to Fri 9am to 4:30pm; 1749 Argyle St., Grand Parade)*, the oldest Protestant church in Canada, built in 1750 after the model of St.

Peter's Church in London, England. Despite the wearing effects of time and the addition of several extensions, the original structure has been preserved.

Inside, visitors can examine a piece of metal from

the *Mont Blanc*, one of the ships that caused a terrible explosion in Halifax in 1917. On the north side of Grand Parade stands **City Hall** *(free admission)*, an elegant Victorian-style building dating back more than a century.

Children of all ages can come face-to-face with scientific phenomena at **Discovery Centre** *($5; Mon to Sat 10am to 5pm, Sun 1pm to 5pm; 1593 Barrington St., ☎492-4422)*. Several interactive exhibits teach through scientific experiments.

In the Dominion Building, a fine example of the city's rich architectural heritage erected at the end of the last century, is the **Art Gallery of Nova Scotia** ★★★ *($5; Tue to Fri 10am to 6pm, Sat and Sun noon to 5pm; 1741 Hollis St., op-*

posite Province House; ☎424-7542), four flours of modern exhibition space containing the most remarkable art collection in Nova Scotia.

Province House

The permanent collection, consisting of nearly 3,000 pieces, is devoted to both popular and contemporary art. Although many works are by painters and sculptors from Nova Scotia and the Atlantic provinces in general, artists from other Canadian provinces, the United States and Europe are also represented. The Art Gallery presents the occasional touring exhibition as well. Finally, there is a wonderful boutique selling local crafts.

Seat of the government of Nova Scotia, **Province House** ★ *(free admission; Jul and Aug, Mon to Fri 9am to 5pm, Sat and Sun 10am to 4pm; Sep to Jun, Mon to Fri 9am to 4pm; Hollis St.; ☎424-4661)*, an elegant Georgian style

Nova Scotia

edifice dating from 1819, is the oldest provincial legislature building in Canada. Visitors can take a guided tour through the Red Chamber, the library and the legislative assembly chamber.

The buildings and old warehouses along the Halifax pier, the oldest of their kind in Canada, have been renovated and now form an attractive and harmonious architectural grouping known as **Historic Properties** ★★★ *(bordered by Duke and Lower Water Sts., ☎429-0530)*. Numerous shops, restaurants and cafés have set up business here, along with an excellent provincial tourist information office.

This is a very popular, pleasant place, whose narrow streets lead to a promenade along the pier. The ***Bluenose II*** is

often moored here during the summer. Built in Lunenberg in 1963, the *Bluenose II* is a replica of the most beloved ship in Canadian history, the *Bluenose*, which sailed the seas from 1921 to 1946 and is depicted on the Canadian ten-cent piece. When it is moored here, the *Bluenose II* offers two-hour cruises around the Halifax harbour.

A tour of Halifax's impressive port aboard this or any other ship offering similar excursions is a marvellous way to get to know the city *(for more information, contact the tourist information office, Historic Properties; ☎424-4247)*.

Looking right out onto the harbour, the **Maritime Museum of the Atlantic** ★★ *($6; Jun to mid-Oct, Mon to Sat 9:30am to 5:30pm, Tue until 8pm; mid-Oct to May, Wed to Sat 9:30am to 5pm, Tue until 8pm, Sun 1pm to 5pm; 1675 Lower Water St., near the port; ☎424-7490)* presents a wonderful exhibition that offers a comprehensive overview of the city's naval history.

On the ground floor, there is a reconstruction of William Robertson and Son, a store that furnished shipowners, shipbuilders and captains with materials for a century. On the same floor, visitors will find an assortment of historical artifacts related to Halifax's military arsenal and a varied collection of small craft, particularly lifeboats. The second floor features an absolutely extraordinary assortment of boat models, from sailboats to steamships.

Visitors can also tour the ***Acadia***, which is moored at the pier behind the museum. This ship first sailed out of Newcastle-on-Tyne, England back in 1913 and spent most of the following 57 years gathering information for charts of the Atlantic coast and the shores of Hudson Bay. Close to the museum is the ***HMCS Sackville*** is a convoy ship that was used in World War II and has now been converted into a museum dedicated to the sailors who served in that war. At the **interpretive centre**, located in an adjacent building, visitors can view a 15-min film on the Battle of the Atlantic.

Canada has given refuge to thousands of people. For more than 40 years, from 1928 to 1971, many of the men and women who came to the country stopped

Historic Properties

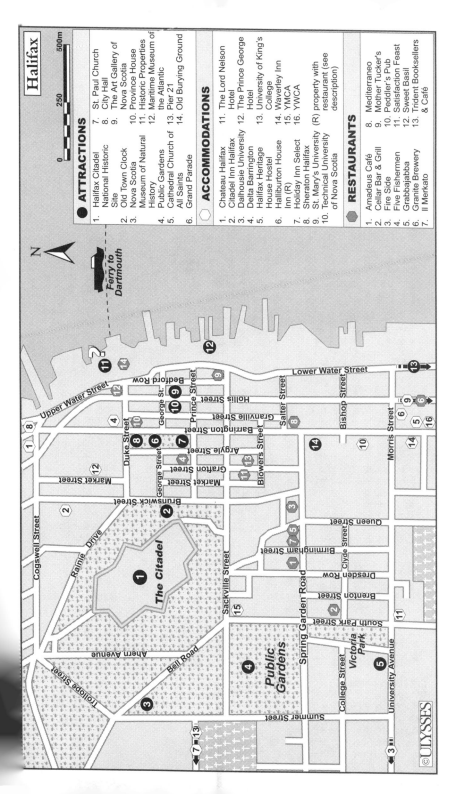

Halifax

0 250 500m

N

Ferry to Dartmouth

© ULYSSES

● ATTRACTIONS

1. Halifax Citadel National Historic Site
2. Old Town Clock
3. Nova Scotia Museum of Natural History
4. Public Gardens
5. Cathedral Church of All Saints
6. Grand Parade
7. St. Paul Church
8. City Hall
9. The Art Gallery of Nova Scotia
10. Province House
11. Historic Properties
12. Maritime Museum of the Atlantic
13. Pier 21
14. Old Burying Ground

◇ ACCOMMODATIONS

1. Chateau Halifax
2. Citadel Inn Halifax
3. Dalhousie University
4. Delta Barrington
5. Halifax Heritage House Hostel
6. Haliburton House Inn (R)
7. Holiday Inn Select
8. Sheraton Halifax
9. St. Mary's University
10. Technical University of Nova Scotia
11. The Lord Nelson Hotel
12. The Prince George Hotel
13. University of King's College
14. Waverley Inn
15. YMCA
16. YWCA

(R) property with restaurant (see description)

⬡ RESTAURANTS

1. Amadeus Café
2. Cellar Bar & Grill
3. Fire Side
4. Five Fishermen
5. Grabbajabba
6. Granite Brewery
7. Il Merkato
8. Mediterraneo
9. Mother Tucker's
10. Peddler's Pub
11. Satisfaction Feast
12. Sweet Basil
13. Trident Booksellers & Café

Map labels

The Citadel

Public Gardens

Victoria Park

Cogswell Street
Rainie Drive
Ahern Avenue
Trollope Street
Bell Road
Sackville Street
Summer Street
College Street
University Avenue
Spring Garden Road
South Park Street
Brenton Street
Dresden Row
Birmingham Street
Clyde Street
Queen Street
Morris Street
Bishop Street
Salter Street
Hollis Street
Granville Street
Barrington Street
Argyle Street
Grafton Street
Market Street
Blowers Street
Brunswick Street
George Street
Duke Street
Prince Street
George St.
Bedford Row
Upper Water Street
Lower Water Street
Market Street

Blockhouses and Martello Towers

Besides the fortifications built in strategic spots throughout the colony, notably in Halifax and in Kingston (Ontario), the English defense system consisted of blockhouses and Martello Towers dispersed in various parts of the territory.

A "blockhouse" is a two-storey square tower made with squared wooden beams laid horizontally. It is topped with a shingle roof to protect the structure during bad weather. During attacks, soldiers would settle on the second floor whence they could look down on their assailants. The landing was built wider than the base so that the soldiers could shoot their muskets from holes judiciously pierced in the floor, thus preventing the enemy from approaching the tower. Blockhouses, autonomous little defensive outposts, could also be used as barracks or reserves. The Fort Edward Blockhouse (see p 161), in Windsor, Nova Scotia is a good example.

The Martello tower, on the other hand, is built of stone and can reach a height of 10m. The ground floor was used primarily as a reserve and the one above it, as barracks. Its thick walls were intended to ensure the protection of the soldiers, and its round form, to allow soldiers to fire cannons full circle.

Sixteen of these towers were built in Canada: five in Halifax, one in Saint John (New Brunswick), four in Québec City, and six in Kingston. They were popular because of their low construction costs and their robust appearance. None of these towers was ever attacked, however, so we do not know how effective they might have been.

transformed into a museum in memory of these people. Interactive exhibits attempt to bring these memorable moments back to life, and a slide show tells about the lives of the people in transit. There's also a café, a tourist information centre and a store.

Farther south, on Barrington Street, at the corner of Spring Garden Road, lies the **Old Burying Ground** ★ *(free admission; Jun to Sep, 9am to 5pm; Barrington St. and Spring Garden Rd.)*, Halifax's first cemetery, which is now considered a national historic site. Some of the old tombstones are veritable works of art. The oldest, marking the grave of John Connor, was erected in 1754. A map containing information on the cemetery is available at St. Paul Church *(Grand Parade)*.

While visiting Halifax, make sure to stroll along **Spring Garden Road** ★, the busiest and most pleasant commercial street in Atlantic Canada. Lined with all sorts of interesting shops, restaurants and cafés, it looks like the local Latin Quarter. Parallel to Spring Garden Road, but farther north, **Blowers Street** is another attractive artery, flanked by somewhat less conventional shops and businesses.

in Halifax at **Pier 21** *($6; 9am to 8pm; 1055 Marginal Rd.,* ☎*425-7770).* The pier also welcomed thousands of refugees during the Second World War and was the departure point for Canadian soldiers heading off to battle in foreign lands.

A former transit point, this pier has since been

On the Outskirts of Halifax

Point Pleasant Park ★ *(at the end of Young Ave.)* covers an area of 75ha on Halifax's south point. Here, visitors will find kilometres of hiking trails along the coast, offering lovely views through the forest. Due to its location at the entrance of the harbour, Point Pleasant was of great strategic importance to the city for many years.

The first Martello tower in North America, now the **Prince of Wales Tower National Historic Site** ★ *(free admission; Jul to Sep, 10am to 6pm; Point Pleasant Park; ☎426-5080)*, was erected here in 1796-97. Drawing inspiration from a supposedly impregnable tower on Corsica's Martello Point, the British erected this type of structure in many places along the shores of their Empire. The Prince of Wales Tower was part of Halifax's extensive network of defences. It now houses a museum on its history.

McNabs Island, measuring 4.8 km by 1.2 km and located right at the entrance of the harbour, was also part of the city's defenses. The British erected Fort McNab here between 1888 and 1892, equipping it with what were then the most powerful batteries in all of the city's fortifications.

Visitors can examine the vestiges of the structure at the **Fort McNab Historic Site** ★ *(☎426-5080)*, while enjoying a stroll around this peaceful, pretty island, which features a number of hiking trails.The ferry to McNabs Island leaves from Cable Wharf. For the schedule, contact the tourist information office *(Historic Properties, ☎424-4247)*.

Just outside town (about 12km), there's another attraction worth a visit: **York Redoubt National Historic Site** *(free entry; mid-Jun to end Oct 9am until nightfall; Purcell's Cove Rd., ☎426-5080)*. The redoubt was built in 1793 on a site where the military could easily watch the comings and goings of boats in the town harbour, thereby insuring adequate defence. It also included a battery, a Martello tower and a stockade. It was used throughout the 19th century and even during the Second World War. A visit to this historic site offers a unique view of Halifax harbour.

The road continues to **Sir Sandford Fleming Park**, a vast 95ha garden, which was bequeathed to the town by Sir Fleming. This scientist developed the idea of standard time zones, today in use throughout the world.

Farther south, there's Sambro, a fishing town where you can take a boat to Sambro Island to see the **Sambro Lighthouse**. Built between 1758 and 1760, it's the oldest operating lighthouse in North America.

Dartmouth

From the pier in front of Historic Properties in Halifax, visitors can take a **ferry** *(about $1)* to Dartmouth, on the opposite shore, which offers a splendid view of both the port and McNabs Island. The town of Dartmouth boasts an attractive waterfront, beautiful residences, a variety of shops and restaurants and several tourist attractions, including the **Historic Quaker House** ★ *(free admission; early Jun to early Sep; 57-59 Ochterlaney St., ☎464-2300)*. This is the only remaining example among some 22 similar houses built around

1785 by Quakers who came to Dartmouth from New England. Guides in period dress tell visitors about the Quaker lifestyle.

Outdoor Activities

Cycling

Many visitors decide to tour Nova Scotia by bicycle, either bringing their own or renting one in Halifax or Sydney. Here are a few places that offer rentals:

Bike Rental

Atlantic Canada Bicycle Rally
Box 1555, B3J 2Y3
☎ *423-2453*

Several roads in the Halifax area make wonderful bike trips. Among these, the trails that meander through Point Pleasant Park (39km in total) will especially delight those who enjoy rides in the forest and along the ocean. However, note that the paths are not open to cyclists on weekends or on holidays.

Hiking

Visitors to Nova Scotia can enjoy the use of many trails leading into the heart of superb natural settings or offering lovely views of the coast. The government publishes a book on these trails entitled *Hiking Trails of Nova Scotia*, which is available by contacting:

Nova Scotia Government Bookstore
Box 367, 1700 Granville St.
Halifax, B3J 2T3
☎ *424-7580*

Visitors can also obtain a copy of a pamphlet entitled *Walking in Nova Scotia* by calling ☎ *800-448-3400*.

The tours in the towns of Halifax (Historic Downtown Walk – duration 2hrs) and Dartmouth (Dartmouth Heritage Walk – duration 1hr 30min) have been planned out so visitors can explore the main attractions of these towns on foot. Another pleasant trail to walk on during beautiful summer days is the Halifax Boardwalk, which is situated by the sea alongside the piers of the town.

In Halifax, **Point Pleasant Park** is a great getaway, with 39km of hiking trails, some of which lead into the forest, while others run along

the seashore, with magnificent views.

Cruises

In Halifax, Harbour Hopper Tours offers exceptional trips. Comfortably seated in this unusual vehicle, you first ride through the streets of town to discover its historic buildings. Then you head to Halifax harbour for a boat ride – aboard the same amphibious craft – which offers a different view of the Nova Scotian capital.

Harbour Hopper Tours
Cable Wharf
☎ *490-8687*

Accommodations

Halifax Heritage House Hostel
$18 for members
$22 for non-members
15 rooms
1253 Barrington St., B3J 1Y3
☎ *422-3863*
Several hundred metres from the train station and about 15min by foot from the city's main attractions, the Halifax Heritage House Hostel is part of the International Youth Hostel Federation. A pretty, historic building, it can accommodate about 50 people and is equipped with a kitchenette.

A number of other institutions offer inexpensive accommodation. During summer, rooms are available in the residence halls at **Dalhousie University** *($37 for a single room, $53 for a double room; front desk Howe Hall, 6136 University Ave., B3H 4J2,* ☎*494-2108, 494-3831 or 494-8840,* ✆*496-1219)*, **St. Mary's University** *($23 for a single room, $33 for a double room; open May to Oct; 923 Robie St., B3H 3C3,* ☎*420-5591,* ✆*496-8107)*, **University of King's College** *($16 for a single room, $22 for a double room; 6350 Coburg Rd., B3H 2A1,* ☎*422-1271, ext. 115,* ✆*423-3357)* and the **Technical University of Nova Scotia** *($23 for a single room, $40 for a double room; 527 Morris St.,* ✆*420-2628)*. Students are usually offered a discount.

Rooms are also available at the **YMCA** *($28 for a single room, $38 for a double room; 1565 South Park St.,* ✆*425-0155)* and the **YWCA** *($32 for a single room, $47 for a double room; 1239 Barrington St.,* ✆*423-7761)*. The latter accepts women only.

Waverley Inn
$79 bkfst incl.
32 rooms
tv, ℜ
1266 Barrington St., B3J 1Y5
☎*423-9346*
✆*425-0167*
The Waverley Inn boasts a rich tradition of hospitality dating back more than a century. This sumptuous house, built in 1865-66, was the personal residence of wealthy Halifax merchant Edward W. Chipman until 1870, when a reversal of fortune plunged him into bankruptcy.

A few years later, sisters Sarah and Jane Romans purchased the house for $14,200. In October 1876, the Waverley Inn threw open its doors and was considered the most prestigious hotel in the city for several decades to follow. It has welcomed many famous individuals, including English author Oscar Wilde, who stayed here in 1882.

Despite the passing of time, the Waverley Inn has managed to preserve most of its original grandeur. Of course, it is no longer as luxurious, since its rooms, decorated in a rather heavy style, are now outmoded according to modern standards of comfort. However, this inn is sure to interest visitors seeking a truly authentic Victorian atmosphere. The Waverley Inn is located near the train station, about 15min walk from the city's major attractions.

Holiday Inn Select
$89
232 rooms
ℜ, ≈, ⊛, ⌂, ☉
1980 Robie St., B3H 3G5
☎*423-1161*
✆*423-9069*
The Holiday Inn Select possesses rooms that are very comfortable, spacious and functional, in addition to an excellent dining room. A common room on the executive floor permits guests to prepare their own breakfasts in the morning, which, for frequent travellers, makes for a pleasant change of atmosphere from hotel restaurants.

The only inconvenience of the Holiday Inn Select is its location at least 15min by foot from downtown and from the main activities of interest there, but this drawback is compensated by the hotel's relatively reasonable rates.

Prince George Hotel
$95
200 rooms
tv, ℜ, ≈, ☉, ⊛, ⌂
1725 Market St., B3J 3N9
☎*425-1986 or 800-565-1567*
✆*429-6048*
The Prince George Hotel offers excellent accommodation in rooms that are quite attractively furnished and luxurious. Located right near the World Trade and Convention Centre, this place is particularly popular among business people, and features a conference room that can accommodate up to 200 people. The hotel terrace offers a splendid view of the city.

Nova Scotia

Lord Nelson Hotel
$109
200 rooms
tv, ℜ
1515 South Park St. B3J 2L2
☎*423-633 or 800-565-2020*
⇆*491-6148*

The newly renovated Lord Nelson Hotel offers many advantages. Located in an extremely lively section of Halifax, it stands opposite the magnificent Public Gardens, just steps away from Spring Garden Road, the city's busiest commercial artery, and a short distance from several colleges and universities. The smallest rooms rank among the least expensive in Halifax. Although modestly furnished and a bit outdated in appearance, they nevertheless offer an acceptable level of comfort. The Lord Nelson's impressive entrance hall, with its coffered ceiling, is a vestige of the *belle époque*. This is a good option for travellers on a limited budget.

Delta Barrington
$120
201 rooms
tv, △, ℜ, ≈
1875 Barrington St., B3J 3L6
☎*429-7410*
☎*800-268-1133 in North America*
⇆*420-6524*

An elegant building located just steps away from Historic Properties, the Delta Barrington looks out on a lively neighbourhood full of shops, restaurants and outdoor terraces. The rooms are a bit old-fashioned but nevertheless decently furnished and comfortable.

Halliburton House Inn
$120 bkfst incl.
30 rooms
tv, ℜ
5184 Morris St., B3J 1B3
☎*420-0658*
⇆*423-2324*

The Halliburton House Inn lies tucked away on a quiet residential street near the train station, just a short distance from Halifax's main attractions. A pleasant, elegant place, it offers an interesting alternative to the large downtown hotels. In terms of comfort, Halliburton House Inn has all angles covered.

The pleasant rooms are well-decorated and adorned with period furniture, giving them a lot of character. There are also several lovely common rooms, including a small living room to the left of the entrance, a library and an elegant dining room where guests can enjoy excellent cuisine.

The inn's three buildings look out on a peaceful, pretty garden full of flowers, where guests can sit at a table beneath a parasol. Halliburton House Inn, erected in 1809, was originally the home of Sir Brenton Halliburton, chief justice of the Supreme Court of Nova Scotia.

Citadel Inn Halifax
$125
270 rooms
tv, ℜ, ≈, ☉
1960 Brunswick St., B3J 2G7
☎*422-1391 or 800-565-7162*
⇆*429-6672*

Comfortable but somewhat lacking in charm, the Citadel Inn Halifax is attractively located just a stone's throw away from the Citadel. Guests have access to an indoor pool and a gym, as well as to a dining room and a bar. Furthermore, parking is free, which is a real bonus in Halifax.

Chateau Halifax
$135
300 rooms
tv, ℜ, △, ⊛, ≈
1990 Barrington St., B3J 1P2
☎*425-6700 or 800-268-1133*
⇆*425-6214*

The Chateau Halifax offers superior accommodation in spacious, sober and very comfortably furnished rooms. The friendly, pleasant hotel bar, Sam Slick's

Lounge, is a perfect spot to enjoy a drink with friends or hold an informal meeting.

The Chateau features an indoor pool and numerous sports facilities. It allows access to a shopping centre containing stores and restaurants, and lies just minutes away from the city's main sights and the World Trade and Convention Centre.

 **Sheraton Halifax**
$139
353 rooms
tv, ℜ, ⌂, ≈
1919 Upper Water St., B3J 3J5
☎*421-1700 or 800-325-3535*
⤝*422-5805*
Halifax is home to a good number of luxury hotels. None of these, however, boasts a more spectacular or enchanting site than the Sheraton Halifax, located right on the pier, next to Historic Properties. Furthermore, particular care was taken to ensure that the building would blend harmoniously with its surroundings, which make up the oldest part of the city.

The rooms are spacious, well-decorated and inviting. There hotel has two restaurants as well as, conference rooms, an indoor pool and several other athletic facilities. In addition to all this, the Sheraton houses the only casino in Halifax, which is very busy evenings and weekends.

Restaurants

The largest city in the Atlantic provinces, Halifax is also the most cosmopolitan; by their diversity, its restaurants eloquently bear witness to its status as the region's first city. A bit of everything may be found in Halifax, including, notably, great restaurants, the quality and refinement of which rival the best dining rooms of larger North American cities.

Fish and seafood, of course, are favoured in local gastronomy. Nonetheless, delights of French, Italian, Chinese and Indian cuisine may also be enjoyed, to mention but a few. This said, what is most surprising is the number of cafés and terraces that line arteries like Spring Garden Road, Blowers Street and Argyle Street and which, in the summertime, lend Halifax an almost European air.

Amadeus Café
$
5675 Spring Garden Rd.
☎*423-0032*
The nearby Amadeus Café has a selection of coffees, teas, hot chocolates, cold drinks during the summer and a small assortment of pastries. It has a beautiful street-front terrace. Among other treats, it offers mouth-watering cinnamon rolls.

Grabbajabba
$
5475 Spring Garden Rd.
☎*423-1651*
A good place to stop for a snack or continental breakfast during a stroll along Spring Garden Road, Grabbajabba is a small café that serves excellent cappuccino, espresso and other types of coffee. The menu also includes a small assortment of breads, buns, muffins and sandwiches priced at less than $5.

Granite Brewery
$
1222 Barrington St.
☎*422-4954*
There is no better spot at which to take the pulse of daily life than the Granite Brewery. A little away from the main tourist attractions of the city and, more remarkably, miles away in attitude from the fashionable atmosphere of trendier restaurants, this pub offers simple dishes that are inexpensive and always generously dished out. Checkered tablecloths, an interior decor dominated by wood tones and a few subtle lamps create a convivial, unpretentious atmosphere. The kitchen closes at 12:30am every night.

Peddler's Pub
$
Granville St., Barrington Place
Sunny late afternoons are very enjoyable here: a glass of wine in hand, seated at a table on the patio near the historic district of town. The rather limited menu

Nova Scotia

offers appetizers and simple dishes. Popular music shows are sometimes presented here at night.

Mediterraneo
$
1571 Barrington St.
☎423-4403
If you feel like some Lebanese cuisine, head to Mediterraneo for excellent food at reasonable prices (the daily specials are less than $5.50). With its relaxed atmosphere, the restaurant is popular with students, who come here to satiate their appetite while respecting their budget. The place is also renowned for its breakfasts.

Satisfaction Feast
$
1581 Grafton St.
☎422-3540
Vegetarians and other fans of vegetarian cuisine will be in their element at the Satisfaction Feast, where the aromas wafting through the air will make your mouth water with expectation. You won't be disappointed, since the chef seems to have an unlimited imagination when it comes to preparing meals that are balanced, appetizing and inexpensive. Breakfast is served here. The interior is bright and airy.

Trident Booksellers & Café
$
1570 Argyle St.
☎423-7100
What a pleasure it is to enjoy an excellent cup of coffee while poring over a book! That's the concept behind the Trident Booksellers & Café, an extremely friendly, airy place located a few steps away from Blowers Street. The menu is similar to that of Amadeus Café (see above). Newspapers are always available for customers, and books (often secondhand), are sold at modest prices.

Fire Side
$-$$
1500 Brunswick St.
☎423-5995
The Fire Side is a typical pub with cozy wood panelling and a warm atmosphere. People usually come here for drinks (especially martinis), but it also offers light fare, such as the classic salmon sandwich, shrimp dishes and quesadillas.

Il Merkato
$$
5475 Spring Garden Rd.
☎422-2846
For inspired Italian cuisine, Il Mekato – a little bistro with a modern, inviting decor, located on the liveliest street in the city – is the place. Fresh pasta, pizza and some original meat dishes are featured on the menu, as are Italian ices and other delectable desserts. In just a short time Il Mekato has become one of the most popular spots in Halifax.

Mother Tucker's
$$
1668 Lower Water St.
☎422-4436
A well-known Canadian institution, Mother Tucker's restaurant has a branch in Halifax, right near Historic Properties. Mother Tucker's is known mainly for its excellent roast beef, but the menu also lists steak and, on rare occasions, lobster. Brunch is served on Sundays.

Sweet Basil
$$
1866 Upper Water St.
☎425-2133
Just a few steps away from Historic Properties, Sweet Basil is a good restaurant that serves bistro-style cuisine. The chef outdoes himself concocting delicious dishes prepared and presented in an original manner. Top billing goes to pasta, which is served with fresh, quality ingredients. Both the cuisine and the decor evoke a subtle blend of Latin and modern styles. There is seating outside on the little terrace at the back. This place offers good value.

La Maison
$$-$$$
1541 Birmingham St.
☎492-4339
Much more than a simple French restaurant, La Maison offers a whirlwind tour of the flavours of French-speaking America and Europe. There are many appetizers to choose from, including

steak tartar, warm goat-cheese salad, and an excellent bouillabaisse of mussels, scallops and shrimp. Mouth-watering lamb chops, seafood papillote, duck in Grand Marnier sauce and a variety of steaks are some of the main dishes prepared at La Maison. The food is served either in the relaxing atmosphere of the dining room, which has a classic decor, or, when the weather is fair, on the peaceful terrace.

Upper Deck Restaurant
$$-$$$
Privateer's Warehouse
Historic Properties
☎422-1289
A Halifax classic, the Upper Deck Restaurant occupies the top floor of the Privateer's Warehouse. The dining room's pretty maritime decor, accented by miniature models of great old sailing vessels, leaves no doubt as to the specialties of the house: fish and seafood. Always fresh, these delights from the deep are particularly well prepared and attractively presented here. Poultry and meat are also served. In addition to its excellent cuisine, courteous service and a pleasant ambience make the Upper Deck one the best options in the Historic Properties neighbourhood.

Halliburton House Inn
$$$
5184 Morris St.
☎420-0658
The dining room at the elegant Halliburton House Inn is a perfect place to enjoy a long, intimate dinner for two or linger over a meal among friends. Furnished in a tasteful, elegant manner, the place has a lot of style and emanates an atmosphere of opulence. Aside from a few exceptions, like the alligator appetizer, the menu is made up of classics, including an excellent *steak au poivre* flambéd with brandy, lamb *à la Provençale*, Atlantic salmon and *coquilles Saint-Jacques*.

Cellar Bar & Grill
$$$
5677 Brenton Pl.
☎492-4412
Located downstairs in an inviting cellar, this lovely establishment has two dining rooms decorated with brick, stone and wood. The cuisine here is also delightful. The menu includes gazpacho and lobster bisque, calamari, tzatziki and mussels, pasta with wild mushrooms and grilled Atlantic salmon – there's something here for everyone. Excellent wine list.

Five Fishermen
$$$
1740 Argyle St.
☎422-4421
Set up inside one of the oldest buildings in town, an old renovated school, the Five Fisher-men is a great favourite with fish and seafood lovers. Lobster obviously gets top billing on the menu. Other dishes include Atlantic salmon and trout, as well as a variety of steaks. It is worth noting that the kitchen closes later than most others in town, around 11pm on Sundays and at midnight during the rest of the week. The wine list, furthermore, is very extensive.

Entertainment

Bars and Danceclubs

The city of Halifax is home to an impressive number of pubs, bars and danceclubs, most of them concentrated in the downtown area.

Lower Deck Pub
Privateer's Warehouse
In the historic district, there is the Lower Deck Pub, which presents performances of traditional music from Atlantic Canada some evenings.

Peddler's Pub
Granville St., Barrington Place
For a drink on a sunny terrace in late afternoon, opt for Peddler's Pub, where popular music shows are sometimes presented.

Nova Scotia

Fire Side
1500 Brunswick St.
☎423-5995
The Fire Side is a cozy English pub decorated with attractive woodwork. It's renowned in the capital for its martinis – apparently, the best around. For those who prefer hopped beverages, it also offers an excellent selection of local beers.

Granite Brewery
1222 Barrington St.
The Granite Brewery has all the atmosphere of a local pub.

Diamond Pub
1663 Argyle St.
A rather eccentric decor and a wide selection of beers make the Diamond the preferred spot of a young, hip clientele.

Economy Shoe Shop, Café & Bar
1661-1663 Argyle St.
☎452-6077
If you and your friends can't agree on where to go for a night out, check out this bar. It has several rooms, each with its own unique decor, bar and different music. Live jazz on Monday evenings.

Velvet Olive
1770 Market St.
☎492-2233
Among the many bars that have sprung up in Halifax, the Velvet Olive is famous because of its Art Deco decor, its martinis and its pool tables – not to mention the fact that it serves food until midnight on Fridays and Saturdays.

Bearly's
1269 Barrington St.
☎423-2526
Bearly's has live blues from Thursday to Sunday. The atmosphere is friendly and lively.

Reflexions Cabaret
5184 Sackville St.
More sophisticated music sets the rhythm at Reflexions Cabaret, a nightclub that caters primarily to the Halifax region's gay and lesbian communities although it welcomes a mixed clientele.

Theatres

Halifax's most renowned theatre company, the **Neptune Theatre** *(5216 Sackville St.,* ☎429-7070) is devoted to presenting classic plays.

The latest American movies are presented at **Famous Players Cinemas** *(5657 Spring Garden Rd.,* ☎423-5866). Other theatres show popular films, but they are all located outside the downtown area. To see what's playing and when, check the listings in the local newspaper. For less recent movies, head to **Wormwood's Dog & Monkey Cinema** *(2015 Gottingen St.,* ☎422-3700), a repertory theatre.

Large-scale rock concerts are held at the **Halifax Metro Centre** *(1284 Duke St.,* ☎451-1221). For that matter, when artists of interna-

tional renown come to the Maritimes, they usually choose to play in Halifax.

Fans of classical music can attend concerts given by the **Symphony Nova Scotia** *(1646 Barrington St.,* ☎421-7311).

Casinos

A recent addition, the only casino in Halifax is in the **Sheraton** *(Upper Water St.,* ☎425-7777). It is very large, includes a great many slot machines and gaming tables, and is open without interruption from noon on Thursdays to 4am Monday mornings. On Tuesdays and Wednesdays the casino also closes at 4am.

Shopping

Without a doubt, the most pleasant place to shop is **Historic Properties** *(bordered by Duke and Lower Water Sts.),* the historic neighbourhood alongside the Halifax wharves. Shops selling crafts and clothing take up a large portion of the space in this harmonious architectural grouping built in the 19th century.

Another enjoyable place to shop is **Granville Promenade** and **Barrington Place Shops** *(on Barrington St., near*

Historic Properties), two complexes located right near one another. Both are renovated historic buildings. Shoppers can stop for a refreshment on one of the many terraces of the nearby cafés and pubs.

For a pleasant stroll in a lively part of town that looks like the local Latin Quarter, take **Spring Garden Road** *(between Barrington and South Park Sts.)*, a large commercial artery lined with cafés, restaurants and numerous shops.

A Selection of Shops

The **Gallery Shop** *(Art Gallery of Nova Scotia, 1741 Hollis, ☎424-2836)* offers an excellent

selection of local crafts, as well as works by painters, sculptors and other artists from Nova Scotia. Pieces by Micmac artists are also available.

The **Micmac Heritage Gallery** *(Barrington Place Shops, Granville Level, ☎422-9509)* is the most impressive gallery dedicated to Micmac arts and crafts in the Atlantic provinces. Articles on display include leather mittens and moccasins, woven baskets, jewelry and paintings.

The **Houston North Gallery** *(Sheraton Hotel, 1919 Upper Water St.)* presents a remarkable collection of First Nations and Inuit sculptures and paintings.

The **Government Bookstore** *(1700 Granville St.)* sells all of the books and publications put out by the government of Nova Scotia. Many of these deal with plant and animal life, geology, history– in short, all sorts of subjects that might interest travellers who want to know more about Nova Scotia.

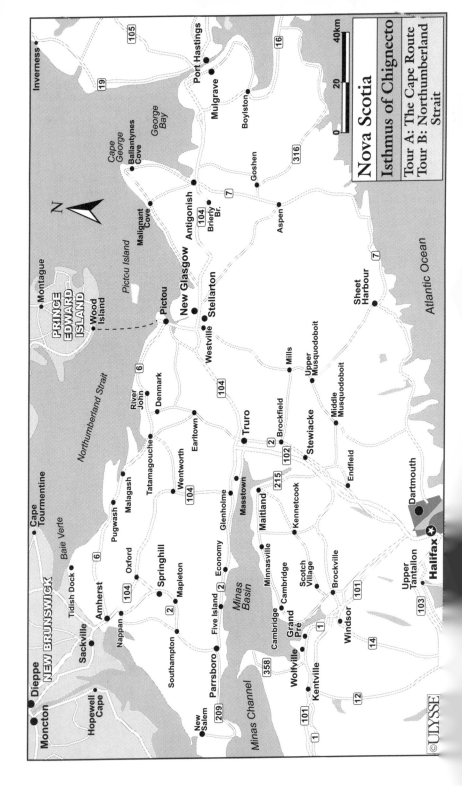

Nova Scotia

Isthmus of Chignecto

Tour A: The Cape Route
Tour B: Northumberland
Strait

© ULYSSE

Isthmus of Chignecto

The Isthmus of Chignecto, the narrow strip of land that connects Nova Scotia and New Brunswick, offers a variety of changing landscape, bordered by the Northumberland Strait on one side, and the Bay of Fundy on the other.

There are a number of spectacular and relatively unexplored areas, especially along the Bay of Fundy. The tides in this bay, which are the highest and strongest in the world, have carved the unique landscape. The Northumberland Strait side is renowned for its lovely beaches washed by warm water – a great place for a swim. This coast is also famous as the place where the first Scottish colonists settled during the 1770s. Today, a variety of cultural events celebrate this Scottish heritage.

A few average-sized towns line the Isthmus of Chignecto, such as Amherst, which is the gateway to Nova Scotia.

Finding Your Way Around

The Isthmus of Chignecto includes two tours. **Tour A: The Northumberland Strait ★**, which runs along the strait from Cape Breton Island to the town of Amherst. **Tour B: The Cape-Road ★**, which heads from Amherst to Maitland and the old town of Acadie (see p 157).

By Bus

Visitors can reach a variety of destinations within Nova Scotia, as there are buses running from Halifax to Yarmouth, Amherst and Sydney *(Acadian Lines,* ☎*454-9321)* and along the southern coast of the province.

By Ferry

From Saint John (New Brunswick) to Digby (Nova Scotia):
MV Princess of Acadia
Departure: three times daily during summer
☎*888-249-7245*
☎*(902) 566-3838*

From Portland (Maine) to Yarmouth (Nova Scotia):

Prince of Fundy Cruise
Box 4216, Station A, Portland
Maine, 04101
☎ *800-341-7540 from Canada and the United States*
www.princeoffundy.com
Departure: daily from May to October

From Bar Harbor (Maine) to Yarmouth (Nova Scotia):
Marine Atlantic
☎ *888-249-7245*
Departure: once daily, mid-May to mid-September

Tour A: Northumberland Strait

The ferry linking Caribou (Nova Scotia) to Wood Islands (Prince Edward Island) provides daily service from May to December:

Northumberland Ferry
Box 634, Charlottetown, P.E.I.
C1A 7L3
☎ *888-249-7245*

A ferry links North Sydney with Argentia, Newfoundland three times a week in summer.

Practical Information

Area code: **902**

Tourist Information Offices

The provincial government operates a reservation service for hotels, bed & breakfasts, campsites and car rentals. Information on festivals, ferry service and weather forecasts is also available:
☎ *800-565-0000 in North America*
☎ *425-5781*

Tour A: The Northumberland Strait

By mail:
Antigonish-Eastern Shore Tourist Association,
Musquodoboit Harbour, B0J 2L0
☎ / ≈ *889-2362*

On site:
Pictou
open from mid-May to mid-Oct
intersection of Hwy. 106 and Rte. 6

Exploring

Tour A: The Northumberland Strait

A few historic villages and towns lie tucked along the coast of the Northumberland Strait between Cape Breton and the New Bruns-

wick border. The first Scottish settlers arrived here at the end of the 18th century. There are also several charming beaches, blessed with the warmest waters in the province. In fact, because of the Gulf Stream, the Northumberland Strait has the warmest waters north of the Carolinas in the United States.

Antigonish

Antigonish is a small town, home to the lovely buildings of **St. Francis Xavier University**, founded in 1853. Like Pictou, Antigonish welcomed many Scottish colonists from the 1770s onwards. The Highland Games, a huge celebration of traditional Scottish music, dance and sports, have been held here since 1861. Since Antigonish lies at the intersection of several major thoroughfares, it does have a few places to spend the night, as well as a number of restaurants and shops.

Melmerby Beach

Near New Glasgow, Route 289 leads to **Melmerby Beach Provincial Park**, which has some picnic areas and a pleasant beach.

Pictou

Pictou holds symbolic importance in Nova Scotia's history. This is the *Hector*, a ship

carrying the first Scottish settlers to Nova Scotia, dropped anchor. Many Scots later followed, seduced by a climate and geography reminiscent of home. They colonized other parts of the coast and Cape Breton Island. Pictou's lively downtown streets are lined with handsome buildings dating back to those early years of settlement.

A ferry service runs between Caribou, just beside Pictou, to Wood Islands, on Prince Edward Island. Close by, **Caribou Provincial Park** has a beautiful beach that is perfect for swimming.

Hector Heritage Quay ★★ *($3.50; mid-May to mid-Oct, every day 10am to 8pm; downtown, at the port,* ☎*485-6057)* is an interpretive centre devoted to the history of the *Hector,* the schooner that carried the first Scottish settlers

to Pictou in 1773. The exhibition is very thorough. Behind the building, visitors can watch artisans reconstruct an exact replica of the *Hector.*

The **McCulloch House** ★ *($1; early Jun to mid-Oct, Mon to Sat 9:30am to 5:30pm, Sun 1pm to 5:30pm; Old Haliburton Rd.,* ☎*485-4563)* is a modest house built in 1806 for Reverend Thomas McCulloch, one of the most influential people in the Pictou area at the time. The house is furnished with original pieces.

Housed in the old railway station, the **Northumberland Fisheries Museum** ★ *($3; late Jun to early Sep, every day 9:30am to 5:30pm; Front St.)* contains a collection of items related to the history of fishing in this region, and features an authentic fishing hut.

Tatamagouche

Less than 2km east of this little community lies **Tatamagouche Provincial Park**, where the inviting waters of the Northumberland Strait are great for swimming.

Malagash

Malagash is home to one of Nova Scotia's two vineyards. Make sure to stop at **Jost Vineyards** *(free admission; mid-Jun to mid-Sep, Mon to Sat 9am to 6pm, Sun noon to 6pm; Rte. 2,* ☎*257-2636)* for some

wine-tasting. The Jost family, originally from the Rhine Valley in Germany, came to Canada in 1970.

Pugwash

Pugwash is a popular vacation spot. **Gulf Shore Provincial Park**, located about 5km north of the village, has a long beach ideal for swimming.

Tour B:
The Cape Route

This tour joins Amherst to Maitland by way of the Minas Basin, with many capes jutting out onto the Bay of Fundy and revealing splendid natural landscapes.

In addition to the magnificent coastal landscape, shaped by the largest tides in the world, the Cape Route covers several quaint towns and picturesque villages.

Amherst

Gateway to Nova Scotia, Amherst is home to several hotels and a large provincial tourist information centre. This site, on the Chignecto Isthmus, first attracted Acadians, who founded a settlement here named Beaubassin in 1672.

Controlled by the British since 1713, the Acadians abandoned Beaubassin in 1750 by order of the French army and Fort Beauséjour was erected (New Brunswick) on French territory, several kilometres to the north, the following year. The British responded by building Fort Lawrence on the former site of Beaubassin.

This fort was abandoned in 1755, after the British captured Fort Beauséjour, an event that heralded the deportation of the Acadians. In 1764, one year after the signing of the Treaty of Paris, under which France ceded all its North American possessions to Great Britain, colonists from the British Isles began flooding into the region, and there founded Amherst. This community flourished in the 1880s, when it was integrated into the Canadian rail network. It is now a quiet town with about 10,000 inhabitants.

The centre of Amherst boasts several magnificent public buildings made of stone. Visitors will also find the **Cumberland County Museum** *($1; Jun to early Sep, Mon to Sat 9am to 5pm, Sun 2pm to 5pm; Jun to early Dec, Tue to Sat 10am to 4pm; Dec to early Mar, Tue to Sat 10am to 4pm; Mar to early Jun, Tue to Sat 10am to 4pm; 150 Church St.; ☎667-2561),* which exhibits an assortment of ob-

jects related to local history.

From Amherst, visitors can take Route 242 along the banks of Cumberland Basin and Chignecto Bay. Those who want to can stop at the **Joggins Fossil Centre** *($3.50 for the centre, $10 for a guided tour of the Fossil Cliff; Jun to Sep, 9am to 6:30pm; Main St.; ☎251-2727),* which features the world's largest collection of fossils. Visitors can also take a guided tour of a site containing a large number of fossils.

Rte. 2 and Hwy. 104 both lead from Amherst to Springhill. You can also take Rte. 209 to Advocate Harbour, at the tip of the Isthmus of Chignecto.

Springhill

Springhill was founded in 1790 by Loyalist colonists who intended to support themselves by farming. The area did not actually develop, however, until 1871, when the Springhill Mining Company coal mine opened. For nearly a century after, Springhill was one of the largest coal producers in Nova Scotia. The difficulties and dangers of coal mining were not without consequence. In 1891, 125 men and boys lost their lives in an accident in one of the galleries. Two more catastrophes, in 1956 and 1958, claimed the lives of 39 and 75 men respectively. After that,

several mines remained in operation, but large-scale coal mining came to an end in Springhill. To add to this string of bad luck, the city was also the victim of two devastating fires (1957 and 1975).

To find out everything there is to know about popular singer Anne Murray, a Springhill native, head to the **Anne Murray Centre** *($5.50; mid-May to early Oct, 9am to 5pm; Main St.; ☎597-8614).* Her fans will be delighted by the exhaustive collection of objects that either belonged to Murray at one time or summon up key moments in her life and career. Audiovisual aids frequently complement the presentation. Few details have been neglected; the exhibit starts off with a family tree tracing Murray's family origins back two centuries.

The **Springhill Miners' Museum** ★★ *($4.50; mid-May to early Oct, 9am to 5pm; on Rte. 2, take Black River Rd.; ☎597-3449)* offers an excellent opportunity to discover what life was like for Springhill's miners. A visit here starts out with a stop at the museum, which explains the evolution of coal mining techniques and tells the often dramatic history of Springhill's mining industry. Visitors are then invited to tour an old gallery.

Situated near Parrsboro, the **Ottawa House Museum By-the Sea** *($1; mid-Jun to mid-Sep, every day 10am to 6pm; 3km from Parrsboro)* is also worth a visit. Erected at the end of the 18th century, this building was an inn before it became the summer home of Sir Charles Tupper, the former Prime Minister of Canada and one of the fathers of Confederation. The exhibit includes objects dating from the beginning of colonization in this region. Some of the rooms are decorated with period furniture.

Parrsboro also offers summer theatre at the **Ship's Company Theatre** *($18; 38 Main St.; ☎254-2003 or 800-565-7469)*, which presents plays by Canadian, especially Maritime, playwrights. The plays are staged aboard an old restored ferryboat, from which the theatre gets its name.

Continue along Rte. 2 to Parrsboro.

Parrsboro

At the edge of the Minas Basin, marking the farthest end of the Bay of Fundy, Parrsboro is a small community graced with several pretty buildings dating back to the 19th century. The region's tide-sculpted shoreline is a treasure-trove for geologists. It is therefore no surprise that Parrsboro was chosen as the location for

the **Fundy Geological Museum** ★ *($3; early Jun to mid-Oct, every day 9:30am to 5:30pm; Two Island Rd., near the centre of Parrsboro; ☎254-3814)*, a provincial museum devoted to the geological history of Nova Scotia and other regions. Various types of fossils, rocks and stones are on display. The exhibit is lively and interesting, created with the lay person in mind. There is also a fun video, designed to teach children about geography.

Continue on Rte. 2 then Hwy. 104 to Truro. You can go in the opposite direction, on Rte. 209, to reach Advocate Harbour, at the tip of the Isthmus of Chignecto.

Advocate Harbour

The **Chignecto Cape Provincial Park** *($2; Hwy. 209, ☎424-5937)* is a wonderful place for a hike, since it has 20km of trails with some breathtaking views of the region. This park also has some campgrounds.

Also close to Advocate Harbour, **Cape D'Or Lighthouse** *(6km from Hwy. 209)* is a lighthouse that overlooks the Bay of Fundy at the place where it meets the Minas canal. The buildings that belonged to the former lighthouse keeper now house an interpretation centre, as well as a café.

Truro

Served by the railway since 1858, and now located at the heart of the province's road network, Truro is the region's chief industrial and commercial centre. The town, which has a population of about 12,000, features several historic buildings and numerous shops, restaurants and accommodations. The downtown area lies on either side of the Salmon River, which empties into the Minas Basin further on. The **tidal bore** ★, a wave that flows upriver twice a day, is a rather strange natural phenomenon caused by the Bay of Fundy's powerful tides, that can be observed here. In the centre of town, visitors can relax or go for a walk in **Victoria Park** ★ *(entrance on Brunswick St.)*, a 400ha natural park with a stream running through it. There are several waterfalls along the stream.

To get to know the history of the region, head to the **Colchester Historical Society Museum** *($2; Jun to Sep, Tue to Fri 10am to 5pm and Sat and Sun 2pm to 5pm; Oct to May, Tue to Fri 10am to noon and 2pm to 5pm; 29 Young St., ☎895-6284, ≈895-9530)*. In addition to its exhibits, mostly devoted to history and genealogy, the museum also displays temporary expositions on a range of different themes.

Nova Scotia

*From Truro, continue
along Rte. 2, then take the
215 towards Maitland.
Visitors who don't want to
go to Maitland can reach
Windsor quickly by taking
Hwy. 102 and then
Hwy. 101.*

Maitland

A major shipbuilding centre in the 19th century, Maitland is now a tiny hamlet with a few lovely residences. It was here that a prosperous local entrepreneur named William D. Lawrence built the largest wooden ship in Canadian history. The *William D. Lawrence*, a magnificent vessel with three 80m masts, nearly ruined its creator. Completed in 1874, the boat nevertheless enjoyed a very successful career, sailing on oceans around the world.

Today, visitors can tour the **Lawrence House** ★ *(free admission; early Jun to mid-Oct, Mon to Sat 9:30am to 5:30pm, Sun 1pm to 5:30pm; Rte. 215,* ☎*261-2628)*, the entrepreneur's principal residence, built in 1870 at the top of a valley overlooking the bay. Most of the furniture that adorns this beautiful house belonged to Lawrence. In one of the rooms, visitors will find a 2m model of the *William D. Lawrence*.

*Continue along the 215 to
reach Windsor.*

Beaches

Tour A: The Northumberland Strait

There are some beautiful beaches along the Sunrise Trail, including those in **Amherst Shore** *(Rte. 366, west of Northport)*, **Gulf Shore** *(5km north of Pugwash)*, **Heather** *(Port Howe)*, **Caribou** *(near Pictou)* and **Pomquit Beach** *(on*

the road north of Pomquet) Provincial Parks.

Outdoor Activities

Hiking

Tour B: The Cape-Road

Situated at the tip of the Isthmus of Chignecto near Advocate Harbour, **Chignecto Cape Provincial Park** *($2; Hwy. 209,* ☎*424-5937)* offers great views of the coastal landscape along its 20km of hiking paths. Some of the trails lead to beaches and spectacular cliffs.

Accommodations

Tour A: The Northumberland Strait

Antigonish

Maritime Inn Antigonish
$88
tv, ℜ
34 rooms
Hwy. 104 exit 33, B26 2B7
☎*863-4001 or 888-662-7484*
≈*863-2672*
Well-located in the heart of town, the newly renovated and named Maritime Inn Antigonish offers comfortable accommodation in spacious modern rooms. The Library Lounge is reminiscent of an English pub.

Pictou

Consulate Inn
$59
⊛, ℜ
5 rooms
157 Water St., B0K 1H0
☎*485-4554 or 800-424-8283*
≈*485-1532*
Constructed in 1810, this beautiful stone house stands in the heart of Pictou, facing the bay. At different times during the 19th century, it was home the Bank of British North America and then to the American Consulate in Pictou,

from which it drew inspiration for its name.

On the ground floor there is a cozy dining room that serves some of the best food in Pictou. The guestrooms are prettily decorated and comfortable. Some of them have whirlpool baths and balconies overlooking the bay. Behind the house, there is a lovely pavilion that is ideal for reading or for simply whiling away the long days of summer.

🏠 Walker Inn
$75 bkfst incl.
ℜ, *tv*
10 rooms
34 Coleraine St., B0K 1H0
☎*485-1433 or 800-370-5553 for reservations*
Located in the heart of Pictou, the Walker Inn is a pretty brick building dating back to 1865. This place is charming, and its rooms have been renovated in order to furnish each with a private bath. The Walker Inn is kept by a friendly French Canadian couple. By reservation only, evening meals may be enjoyed in the inn's beautiful dining room.

Pictou Lodge Resort
$95
ℂ, ℜ, ≈
50 rooms
Braeshore Rd., B0K 1H0
☎*485-4322 or 888-662-7484*
≠*485-4945*
Just outside the town of Pictou, along a little stretch of beach washed by Northumberland Strait's pleasant

waters, is the Pictou Lodge Resort, a group of cottages built on a large, grassy lawn. The log cottages are very appealing, and each of them has a bedroom, a modern washroom, a little living room, a kitchen and a porch. The Pictou Lodge Resort restaurant, in elegant and inviting wooden building, serves refined cuisine in a dining room set around a central stone fireplace.

Tatamagouche

Train Station Inn
$59
tv
4 rooms
21 Station Rd., B0K 1V0
☎*657-3222 or 888-724-5233*
≠*657-9091*
The pretty Train Station Inn is a former railway station dating back more than a century. Its four rooms, each with a private bath, are adorned with period furniture. Guests have access to a terrace on the second floor.

Tour B: The Cape Route

Amherst

Victorian Motel
$50
tv
20 rooms
150 East Victoria St., B4H 1Y3
☎*667-7211*
If you are driving in from New Brunswick, Amherst is the first town you will pass through. It is a good

place to stay overnight, since there are several motels here, most situated alongside the big access roads. The inexpensive Victorian Motel is located downtown and a good option for travellers on a limited budget. Rooms are clean and quiet, if not particularly charming.

Comfort Inn by Journey's End
$98
pb, tv
60 rooms
143 South Albion St., B4H 2X2
☎*667-0404 or 800-228-5150*
≠*667-2522*
The Comfort Inn by Journey's End, located near the downtown area, shopping malls and fast food restaurants, offers a standard level of comfort, perfect for businesspeople or travellers stopping for the night.

Springhill

Rollways Motel
$57
tv, ℜ
12 rooms
9 Church St., B0M 1X0
☎*597-3713*
Although Springhill has little to offer in terms of accommodation, visitors can stay at the Rollways Motel, whose rooms are decent, but no more than that.

Truro

Howard Johnson
$60
ℂ, ℜ, *tv*
40 rooms
165 Willow St., B2N 4Z9
☎*893-9413*
≠*897-9937*

Nova Scotia

Located at the heart of Nova Scotia's road network, Truro has several hotels and motels belonging to big North American chains that are known for providing decent rooms at reasonable rates. One of these is the Howard Johnson, which offers comfortable rooms, some equipped with kitchenettes.

Comfort Inn by Journey's End
$90
tv
81 rooms
12 Meadow Dr., B2N 5V4
☎*893-0330 or 800-228-5150*
In the same category is the Comfort Inn by Journey's End, whose modern rooms are well-suited to the needs of business people.

Restaurants

Tour A: The Northumberland Strait

Antigonish

Sunshine on Main Café & Bistro
$-$$
332 Main St.
☎*863-5851*
The menu at this pleasant restaurant lists a wide selection of dishes, including Italian pasta, excellent pizza, seafood, meat and many vegetarian options. Tasty desserts and various types of

coffee are also served. The Sunshine opens early in the morning for breakfast.

Pictou

Stone House Café and Pizzeria
$-$$
11 Water St.
☎*485-6885*
Established in a lovely house in Pictou's historic district, the Stone House Café and Pizzeria is a very appealing family restaurant that serves simple, well-prepared food that will please fans of American-style pizza. In nice weather it is possible to sit on the restaurant's terrace facing the port.

 ### Salt Water Café
$$
on the dock, next to Hector's
☎*485-2558*
The Salt Water Café is an enchanting spot for lunch. Its menu consists of a few light seafood and meat dishes, sandwiches and salads. The café has a pretty patio overlooking the waters of the port.

Consulate Inn
$$-$$$
157 Water St.
☎*485-4554*
The elegant and convivial dining room at the Consulate Inn is perfect for long, luxurious suppers. A good selection of seafood and meat dishes is featured on the menu,

including *coquilles Saint-Jacques*, Porto steak and an interesting seafood-curry recipe. The dessert list, although short, features excellent chocolate cake.

Shopping

Tour A: The Northumberland Strait

Pictou

Grohmann Knives
1168 Water St.
☎*485-4224*
Grohmann Knives is a family business founded in the 1950s. Their high-quality knives are now sold in many countries around the world.

Green Thumb Farmer's Market
exit 20
The Green Thumb Farmer's Market is a great place to buy fresh fruits and vegetables, as well as numerous local products.

Old Acadia

A t one time, the magnificent land of Nova Scotia was the focus of the rivalry between the French and British empires. Originally inhabited by the Micmac First Nation, it was the site of the first European colony in America north of Florida.

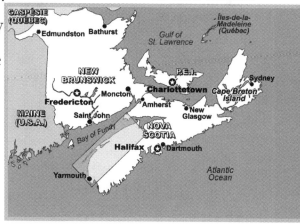

In 1605, one year after a failed attempt to settle Île Sainte-Croix, a French expedition led by De Monts founded Port-Royal at the mouth of the river now known as the Annapolis. The founding of this permanent settlement marked the birth of Acadia.

Port-Royal continued to grow over the following decades, and the Acadians even founded new settlements on the shores of the Bay of Fundy. The many wars between the French and the British proved fatal for Acadia, however.

In 1713, with the signing of the Treaty of Utrecht, France ceded Acadia to Great Britain, and the territory was renamed Nova Scotia. British citizens of French origin, the Acadians declared themselves neutral in the conflict between France and Great Britain. British authorities, however, were not reassured.

In 1755, when war was imminent, the British decided to take a drastic step and deport 14,000 Acadians over the next eight years. In the following decades, various immigrants settled in Nova Scotia, including Planters seeking new land to farm, Loyalists after the American Revolution, and citizens of the British Isles, especially Scots.

Visitors will discover many fascinating sites bearing witness to Nova Scotia's turbulent history, such as the Fortress of Louisbourg on Cape Breton Island, Citadel Hill in Halifax, the Grand-Pré National Historic Site, commemorating the deportation of the Acadians, and the Abitation de Port-Royal, a replica of the first permanent French settlement in North America (1605).

Finding Your Way Around

By Ferry

From Saint John (New Brunswick) to Digby (Nova Scotia):
MV Princess of Acadia
Departure: three times daily during summer
☎*888-249-7245*
☎*(902) 566-3838*

From Portland (Maine) to Yarmouth (Nova Scotia):
Prince of Fundy Cruise
Box 4216, Station A, Portland Maine, 04101
☎*800-341-7540 from Canada and the United States*
www.princeoffundy.com
Departure: daily from May to October

From Bar Harbor (Maine) to Yarmouth (Nova Scotia):
Marine Atlantic
☎*888-249-7245*
Departure: once daily, mid-May to mid-September

By Bus

Visitors can reach a variety of destinations within Nova Scotia, since there are buses running from Halifax to Yarmouth, Amherst and Sydney *(Acadian Lines,* ☎*454-9321)* and along the southern coast of the province.

Practical Information

Area code: *902*

The provincial government operates a reservation service for hotels, bed & breakfasts, campgrounds and car rentals. Information on festivals, ferry service and weather forecasts is also available:
☎*800-565-0000 in North America*
☎*425-5781*

Tourist Information Offices

By mail

Central Nova Tourist Association
Box 1761, Truro, B2N 5Z5
☎*893-8782*
⇒*897-6641*

Yarmouth County Tourist Association
Box 477, Yarmouth, B5A 4B4
☎*742-5355*
⇒*742-8391*

On site

Highway 104, Amherst, at the New Brunswick border
open year-round

Annapolis Royal
Annapolis Tidal Project, Rte. 1
mid-May to mid-Oct

Digby
Shore Road, towards the ferry landing
mid-May to mid-Oct

Yarmouth
228 Main St.
early May to late Oct

Exploring

Windsor

The site now occupied by Windsor, at the confluence of the Avon and Sainte-Croix Rivers, was frequented by Micmacs (Mi'qmaq) for many years before being colonized. They referred to it as Pisiquid, meaning "meeting place." Acadians began settling here in 1685 and succeeded in cultivating the land by creating a network of dykes.

Although this part of Acadia was ceded to Great Britain under the terms of the Treaty of Utrecht in 1713, the British presence was not felt in the area until Charles Lawrence erected Fort Edward here in 1750. By building the fort, Lawrence was attempting to strengthen Britain's authority over the

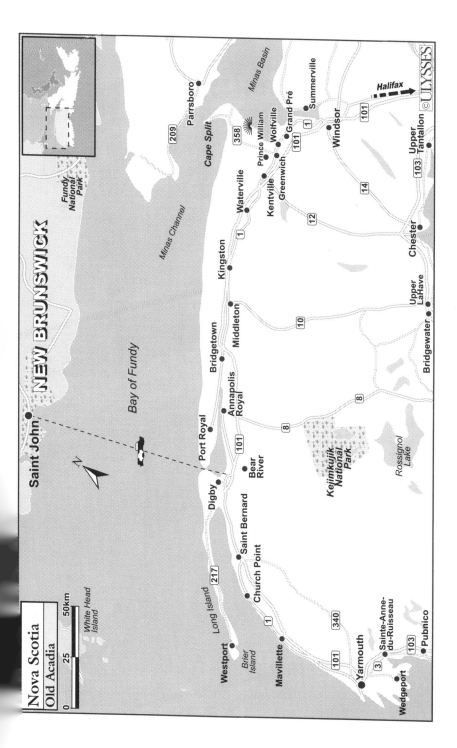

Nova Scotia
Old Acadia

© ULYSSES

The Deportation

In the 1670s, a small group of Acadians moved from the region of Port-Royal, the first Acadian settlement, founded in 1605, to the fertile land along Minas Basin. These industrious farmers managed to free up excellent grazing land alongside the basin by developing a complex system of dykes and aboiteaux. The area became relatively prosperous, and its population grew steadily over the following decades.

Not even the signing of the Treaty of Utrecht in 1713, under which France ceded Acadia to Great Britain, could hinder the region's development. Relations between the Acadian colonists and British authorities remained somewhat ambiguous, however. When France and Great Britain were preparing for the final battle for control of North America, the Acadians declared themselves neutral, refusing to swear allegiance to the British crown. The British accepted this compromise at first. However, as the tension mounted between the two colonial powers, the British began to find the Acadians' neutrality more and more irritating.

Various events, such as the surprise attack on the British garrison at Grand-Pré by troops from Québec – with the help, it was suspected, of Acadian collaborators – increased British doubts about the Acadians' sincerity. In 1755, Charles Lawrence, the governor of Nova Scotia, decided to take an extraordinary step, ordering the expulsion of all Acadians. With 5,000 inhabitants, the region along Minas Basin was the most populated part of Acadia, and Grand-Pré the largest community. That year, British troops hastily rounded up the Acadians, confiscated their land and livestock and burned their houses and churches. The Acadians were put on boats, often separated from their families, and deported. Of the approximately 14,000 colonists living in Acadia at the time, about half were sent away. Some of the ships went down at sea, while others transported their passengers to ports in North Ameri-ca, Europe and elsewhere. After years of wandering, some of these Acadians, ancestors of today's Cajuns, found refuge in Louisiana. Those who escaped deportation had to hide, fleeing through the woods to the northeast coast of present-day New Brunswick, all the way to Québec or elsewhere. One thing is for sure: the deportation order issued by Charles Lawrence succeeded in wiping Acadia from the map. In the following years, the land was offered to Planters from New En-gland, who were joi-ned by Loyalists at the end of the American Revolution, in 1783.

territory and protect the British from the Acadians. In 1755, about 1,000 of the region's Acadians were rounded up here before being deported. During the 19th century, Windsor was an important centre for shipbuilding and the exportation of wood and gypsum.

Despite major fires in 1897 and 1924, the town has managed to preserve some lovely residences. It is the starting point of the Evangeline Route.

The **Fort Edward National Historic Site** ★ *(free admission; early Jun to early Sep, 10am to 6pm; in the centre of Windsor; ☎542-3631)* consists only of a blockhouse, the oldest fortification of its kind in Canada. This structure is all that remains of Fort Edward, erected in 1750. An interpretive centre provides information on the history of the fort. The site also offers a gorgeous view of the Avon River.

Erected in 1835, **Haliburton House** ★ *(free admission; early Jun to mid-Oct, Mon to Sat 9:30am to 5:30pm, Sun 1pm to 5:30pm; 414 Clifton Ave.; ☎798-2915)*, also known as **Clifton House**, was the residence of Thomas Chandler Haliburton (1796-1865), judge, politician, businessman, humorist and successful author. This plain-looking wooden house is adorned with magnificent Victorian furniture. It stands on a large, attractively landscaped 10ha property. Haliburt

on made a name for himself in Canada and elsewhere by writing novels featuring the character Sam Slick, an American merchant who comes to Nova Scotia to sell clocks. Through this colourful character, Haliburton offered a harsh but humorous critique of his fellow Nova Scotians' lack of enterprise. A number of the expressions Haliburton created for his character such as "Truth is stranger than fiction" are commonly used today in both French and English.

Shand House *(free admission; early Jun to mid-Oct, Mon to Sat 9:30am to 5:30pm, Sun 1pm to 5:30pm; 389 Avon St.; ☎798-8213)*, a fine example of Victorian architecture, was built between 1890 and 1891. The furniture inside belonged to the family of Clifford Shand, the house's original owner.

From Windsor, Route 1 leads to Grand-Pré, then passes through the communities of the Annapolis valley.

Grand-Pré National Historic Site

Grand-Pré

Before the Deportation of 1755, Grand Pré was one of the largest Acadian communities on the Bay of Fundy. The dikes built by Acadians in that period, which still protect the region's fertile land, are visible nearby.

The **Grand-Pré National Historic Site** ★★ *($2.50; site year-round, church mid-May to mid-Oct, 9am to 6pm; Route 1 or Rte. 101, Exit 10; ☎542-3631)* commemorates the tragic deportation of the Acadians. Here, visitors will find Église Saint-Charles, a replica of the Acadian church that occupied this site before the Deportation, which houses a museum. The walls are hung with six large and extremely moving paintings by Robert Picard, depicting life in colonial Acadia and the Deportation.

The stained-glass windows, designed by Halifax artist T.E. Smith-Lamothe, show the Acadians being deported at Grand-Pré. Visitors will also find a bust of American author Henry Wadsworth Longfellow and a statue of Evangeline. In 1847, Longfellow wrote a long poem entitled *Evangeline: A Tale of Acadie*, which told the story of two lovers separated by the Deportation. The site also

Nova Scotia

includes a smithy and a placard explaining the principal behind the dykes and aboiteaux (sluice gates) developed by the Acadians before they were expelled from the region.

Wolfville

Wolfville is a charming little university town. Its lovely streets are lined with stately elms concealing sumptuous Victorian residences. The city has about 3,500 permanent residents, while the university, **Acadia University**, founded in 1838, welcomes about 4,000 students a year. With its Victorian atmosphere, excellent cafés and restaurants and magnificent inns, this beautiful town is a perfect place to stay during a tour of the region.

Wolfville was founded in 1760, several years after the deportation of the Acadians, by Planters from New England who were attracted by the excellent farmlands available here. The community was known as Upper Horton and then Mud Creek before being christened Wolfville in honour of local judge Eilsha DeWolf in 1830. Twice a day, from the shores of the small, natural harbour, visitors can observe the effects of the high tides in the Bay of Fundy.

Aboiteaux constructed by the Acadians in the 17th century can be seen nearby. Dikes that were constructed in the port by Acadians in the 17th century still mark the landscape. Today, interesting walking trails run along the tops of them for many kilometres; the opportunity to see them up close should not be missed.

While touring the pretty university campus, take the time to stop in at the **Acadia University Art Gallery** *(free admission; early Jun to Aug, every day noon to 5pm; Sep to May, Mon to Fri 11am to 5pm, Sat and Sun 1pm to 4pm; Beveridge Art Centre, at the corner of Main St. and Highland Ave.; ☎585-1373)*, which often presents interesting exhibitions of contemporary art, as well as works from other periods.

The **Randall House Historical Museum** *(free admission; mid-Jun to mid-Sep, 10am to 5pm, Sun 2pm to 5pm; 171 Main St.; ☎542-9775)* displays objects, furniture, paintings and photographs from the region dating from 1760 to the present day.

Continue along Route 1 to Greenwich, then take Route 358 to Port Williams. Once there, turn right and continue until you reach Starrs Point.

Starrs Point

This prosperous rural region is home to the **Prescott House Museum ★** *(free admission; early Jun to mid-Oct, Mon to Sat 9:30am to 5:30pm, Sun 1pm to 5:30pm; near Rte. 358; ☎542-3984)*, a remarkable Georgian style residence erected around 1814. Its first owner was Charles Ramage Prescott, a local businessman and eminent horticulturist, who introduced a variety of new plant species into the province. The interior, decorated with period furniture, is magnificent. Most delightful of all, however, is the little garden, where visitors can stroll about.

Continue along Route 358 towards Cape Split.

The Route to Cape Split

After passing through some of the region's magnificent rolling landscape and picturesque little villages, take a few moments to stop at the **Lookoff ★** *(Rte. 358)*, which offers an extraordinary view of Minas Basin and the Annapolis valley. Then go to the end of Route 358, where a trail (13km return) leads to the rocky points of **Cape Split ★★**.

At Cape Split, get back onto Route 1, heading to

the right. This road runs along the Annapolis Valley to Annapolis Royal, passing through a number of lovely communities founded in the late 18th century along the way. Before reaching Annapolis Royal, turn right.

Port-Royal

In 1604, one year after the king of France granted him a monopoly on the fur trade in Acadia, Pierre du Gua, Sieur de Monts, accompanied by Samuel de Champlain and 80 men, launched the first European attempt to colonize North America north of Florida. In the spring of 1605, after a difficult winter on Île Sainte-Croix, De Monts and his men settled at the mouth of the waterway known today as the Annapolis River, where they founded Port-Royal.

From 1605 to 1613, the settlement of Port-Royal occupied the area now known as the Port-Royal National Historic Site. After efforts to colonize this region were abandoned, the capital of Acadia was moved first to La Have (on the Atlantic coast) for several years, and then to the present site of Annapolis Royal.

The **Port-Royal National Historic Site** ★ ★ *($2; mid-May to mid-Oct, 9am to 6pm; from Rte. 1, take the road leading to Granville Ferry; ☎532-*

2898) is an excellent reconstruction of the small wooden fortification known as "Abitation" as it appeared in 1605. It was here that fruitful, cordial relations were established between the French and the Micmacs.

This site also witnessed the first performance of the Neptune Theatre and the founding of the first social club in North America, known as "L'Ordre du Bon Temps." Today, visitors can see the various facilities that enabled the French to survive in North America. Staff in period costume take visitors back to those long-lost days. One of the guides is of Micmac origin and can explain the relationship between the French and the Micmacs, who were always allies. Acadian visitors can ask to see a map of the region, which shows where each Acadian family resided in the mid-17th century.

The **Annapolis Tidal Project** *(Upper St. George St.; Rte. 1, ☎532-7018)* is an experimental project where visitors can discover how the powerful tides in the Bay of Fundy can be used to produce electricity. There is a tourist information office here as well.

Annapolis Royal

It was here that Port-Royal, the capital of Acadia, was established in 1635. Because of its advantageous location, the settlement was able to control maritime traffic. In 1710, the British took over the site and renamed the town Annapolis Royal in honour of Queen Anne. Until Halifax was founded in 1749, Annapolis Royal was the capital of the British colony of Nova Scotia. Today, Annapolis Royal is a peaceful village with a rich architectural heritage, graced with residences dating back to the early 18th century. Wandering along its streets is a real pleasure. It is also possible to stay in some of the lovely houses here.

At the **Fort Anne National Historic Site** ★ ★ *($2.75; mid-May to mid-Oct, 9am to 6pm, until 5pm the rest of the year; St.George St.; ☎532-2397)*, visitors will find an old fort, in the heart of which lie the former officers' quarters, now converted into a historical museum. The exhibition provides a detailed description of all the different stages in the history of the fort, which was French before being taken over by the British. Visitors can enjoy a pleasant stroll around the verdant grounds, which

Nova Scotia

Fort Anne National Historic Site

offer lovely views of the surrounding area.

While in the area, make sure to take a walk in the **Annapolis Royal Historic Gardens** ★★ *($5; late May to mid-Oct, 8am until dark;* ☎*532-7018)*, which have been carefully laid out according to British and Acadian horticultural traditions.

Digby

A charming town with a picturesque fishing port, Digby lies alongside Annapolis Basin and the Digby Strait, which opens onto the Bay of Fundy. It is known for its scallop-fishing fleet, the world's largest. Its port is therefore a very lively place, where visitors will be tempted to linger, fascinated by the comings and goings of the boats. From Digby, visitors can also head over to Saint John, New

Brunswick aboard the ferryboat *MV Princess of Acadia*, which sets out from the port.

From Digby, Route 217 leads to Brier Island.

Long Island and Brier Island

Veritable havens of peace, Long Island and Brier Island attract thousands of visitors each year because the waters off their shores are frequented by sea mammals, especially whales who come to the Bay of Fundy to feed during summertime. Whale-watching cruises set out from Westport (Brier Island) and Tiverton (Long Island) every day during summer. Many walking trails on Brier Island allow for pleasant strolls along the island's rocky shore and offer very lovely views of the bay.

From Brier Island, visitors have no other option but to head back towards Digby.

Saint-Bernard

Heading out of the very Anglo-Saxon Annapolis Valley, visitors will be surprised by the sudden change in the architecture. Case in point, an imposing Catholic church stands in the centre of the little Acadian village of Saint-Bernard.

The **Église Saint-Bernard** is not only a symbol of the fervour of the local Catholics, but also of the courage and perseverance of the Acadian people. It was built over a period of 32 years, from 1910 to 1942, by villagers who volunteered their time and effort. From Saint-Bernard to the outskirts of Yarmouth, the coast is studded with more than a dozen Acadian villages. These communities were founded after the Deportation by Acadians who, upon finding their former land around Grand-Pré and Port-Royal occupied by Planters, began settling along this barren coast in 1767.

Pointe-de-l'Église (Church Point)

Farther along the coast, the road passes through another little Acadian village, Pointe-de-l'Église (Church Point), which is home to the splendid **Église Sainte-Marie ★**. Built between 1903 and 1905, it is the largest and tallest wooden church in North America. The interior has a very harmonious appearance.

Right next door stands **Université Sainte-Anne**, Nova Scotia's only French-language university, which plays an important cultural role in the province's Acadian community. The university houses a museum containing objects related to the history of the local Acadians.

A visit to Pointe-de-l'Église and its surroundings would not be complete without taking the time to eat a *pâté de râpure*, a local dish available at the university snack-bar, among other places. The Acadian flag is flown in front of many residences along the road to Yarmouth. In Meteghan, travellers can stop a spell at **La Vieille Maison** *(free; mid-Jun to early Sep, every day 9am to 7pm; Meteghan, ☎645-2389),* a 19th-century house in which the lifestyle of Acadians of the period is exhibited.

Yarmouth

Yarmouth was founded in 1761 by colonists from Massachusetts. Life here has always revolved around the town's bustling seaport, which is the largest in western Nova Scotia. Now a major port of entry for visitors from the United States, Yarmouth has a large selection of hotels and restaurants, as well as an excellent **tourist information office** *(288 Main St.).* Two ferries link Yarmouth to the state of Maine: the **Bluenose** *(☎800-341-7981),* which shuttles between Yarmouth and Bar Harbor all year round, and the *MS Scotia Prince (☎800-341-7540),* which offers service between Yarmouth and Portland from the beginning of May to the end of October.

A good way to learn about Maritime history and the town's heritage is to view the extraordinarily rich collection on display at the **Yarmouth Country Museum ★** *($2.50, 22 Collins St., ☎742-5539),* a small regional museum set up inside a former Presbyterian church. This vast jumble of objects includes miniature replicas of ships, furniture, old paintings and dishes. The museum's most important piece, however, is an octagonal lamp formerly used in the Cape Fourchu lighthouse.

Equally remarkable is the **Firefighters Museum ★** *($2; Jun, Sep and mid-Oct, Mon to Sat 9am to 5pm; Jul and Aug, Mon to Sat 9am to 9pm, Sun 10am to 5pm; mid-Oct to Jun, Mon to Fri 9am to 4pm, Sat 1pm to 4pm; 451 Main St.; ☎742-5525),* which displays two full floors of fire engines. The oldest vehicle, which the firefighters had to pull, dates back to the early 19th century.

Cape Fourchu ★ *(turn left after the hospital and continue for 15km)* is undeniably less spectacular than Peggy's Cove, but much more peaceful. Its lighthouse, erected in 1839, stands on a rocky promontory. Visitors who arrive at the right time will be able to see Yarmouth's impressive fishing fleet pass by just off shore.

From Yarmouth, head east on Route 3 to begin the Lighthouse Route.

Nova Scotia

The Whales of the Bay of Fundy

The Bay of Fundy is one of the best places in North America for whale-watching. Every summer, various species travel to the bay, which is rich in plankton and krill, to feed. During the season, there are four predominant species.

The humpback whale *(Megaptera Novaeangliœ)* can be found in many of the world's waters. There are presently about 10,000 of them. Easily identifiable by their large fins, they can reach a length of 15m and live up to 80 years.

The fin whale *(Balaenoptera Physalus)* distinguishes itself by its large nose. The estimated population of the fin whale is about 123,000, and a small group of them swims in Atlantic waters. With a length that can reach 25m and a weight of 80 tonnes, it is the second largest mammal after the blue whale.

The minke whale *(Balaenoptera Acutorostrata)*, with a maximum length of 10m, is a fast swimmer. It prefers shallow coastal waters and estuaries and is, therefore, frequently spotted. It can be recognized by a white spot in the middle of its fin. This fin-back can live up to 50 years.

The right whale hasn't been hunted since 1935, but its worldwide population is not more than 2,000, 300 of which are found on the coast of the Americas. They can reach a length of up to 18m and live 40 years. They have whalebones up to 2m long and can be recognized with their particularly large heads.

Boat trips are offered at many ports on the Bay of Fundy, whether they be in New Brunswick or Nova Scotia.

Outdoor Activities

Hiking

Several provincial parks with hiking paths have been created so that visitors can enjoy the natural beauty of the Bay of Fundy. This is a wonderful opportunity to disappear into the woods or walk along the coast and admire the beautiful flora and fauna of this region. The **Blomidon Provincial Park** (Canning) offers 16km of hiking paths as well as a picnic area at the summit of Cape Blomidon.

Hiking trails run the length of **Digby Neck**, near Tiverton. Hikers can go to a spot where they can see the Balancing Rock, a basalt formation.

Whale-watching

Every year, whales come to the Gulf of St. Lawrence and the waters south of the island, in the Atlantic Ocean. During this period, visitors can take part in one of the 3hr whale-watching expeditions organized by various local companies.

**Brier Island Whale &
Seabird Cruises**
$37
*two to five departures
daily, May to mid-Oct*
Westport
☎*839-2995*

Pirate's Cove
$35
*three departures per day,
Jun to Oct*
Tiverton
☎*839-2242*

Bird-watching

The Bay of Fundy is a
haven for birds, espe-
cially during spring and
fall when they stop
here during their sea-
sonal migration. Brier
Island, surrounded by
the waters of the Bay of
Fundy and St. Mary's
Bay, is one of the best
bird-watching spots in
the province. The rich
waters here attract
more than 243 species.

Accommodations

Windsor

Clockmaker's Inn
$60
3 rooms
1399 King St.
☎/⇋*798-5265*
Windsor is home to
many glorious turn-of-
the-century Victorian
residences. The
Clockmaker's Inn, laid
out in one of these
gems, displays all of the

charm of that era with
its interior decor and
choice of antiques
adorning its guestrooms
and common areas.
This is an especially
quiet and relaxing spot.

Hampshire Court Motel
$80
tv
open mid-May to mid-Oct
1080 King St., B0N 2T0
☎*798-3133*
⇋*798-4668*
Not far from the centre
of town, visitors will
find the Hampshire
Court Motel, a rather
charming place set in
the midst of a pretty,
peaceful garden. The
Hampshire Court offers
several different types
of accommodations,
including clean, com-
fortable motel rooms,
cottages, and charming,
antique-furnished
rooms in the historic
main building.

Wolfville

Roselawn Lodging
$55
≈
32 Main St., B0P 1X0
☎*542-3420*
⇋*542-0576*
Located just at the
entrance to Wolfville,
Roselawn Lodging
offers motel rooms and
10 cottages, all of them
very well maintained
and of excellent value.
It occupies vast
grounds that include a
swimming pool and a
playground. The
Roselawn is especially
suitable for families.
Special rates are avail-
able for stays of one
week or longer.

Blomidon Inn
$89
26 rooms
ℜ, *tv*
127 Main St., B0P 1X0
☎*542-2291 or 800-565-2291*
⇋*542-7461*
At the elegant
Blomidon Inn, visitors
can stay in a sumptu-
ous manor built in
1877. At the time, costly
materials were used to
embellish the resi-
dence, which still fea-
tures marble fireplaces
and a superb, carved
wooden staircase. This
place has all the ingre-
dients of a top-notch
establishment: a splen-
did dining room where
guests can enjoy re-
fined cuisine, impecca-
ble, friendly service and
richly decorated sitting
rooms. This majestic
building stands in the
centre of a large prop-
erty bordered by stately
elms. The Blomindon
Inn is a veritable sym-
bol of Nova Scotian
hospitality. All of the
rooms are adorned with
antique furniture and
include private baths.

Tattingstone Inn
$89
tv, ≈, ◌, ℜ, pb
10 rooms
434 Main St., B0P 1X0
☎*542-7696 or 800-565-7696*
⇋*542-4427*
The superb Tatting-
stone Inn offers taste-
fully decorated rooms,
some containing 18th-
century furniture. The
accent here is on com-
fort and elegance.
Guests can stay in one
of two buildings; the
main residence has the
most luxurious rooms.

Nova Scotia

Victoria's Historic Inn
$98
15 rooms
tv
416 Main St., B0P 1X0
☎*542-5744 or 800-556-5744*
The charming village of Wolfville boasts several high-quality, luxurious establishments, most of which are located along Main Street. One of these, Victoria's Historic Inn, harks back to another era. A lovely residence dating from 1893, it has been renovated in order to make the rooms more comfortable and improve the decor. Furthermore, all of the rooms include private baths. The inn is adjoined by a motel with several rooms.

Canning

The Farmhouse Inn
$79 bkfst incl.
9757 Main St., B0P 1H0
☎/⇌ *582-7900*
The Farmhouse Inn goes a little overboard with the country-style ambiance in each of its rooms, which are decorated with wallpaper, flowery quilts, dolls, artificial fireplaces (in some rooms) and wooden furniture. Nevertheless, this kitsch decor makes the rooms cozy enough. Guests appreciate the little added touches, such as coffee and tea served in the rooms every morning. Located in town, this establishment also boasts a lovely garden with maple trees, which gives the property a certain charm.

Annapolis Royal

Auberge Wandlyn Inn
$65
30 rooms
⌂
Rte. 1, B0S 1A0
☎*532-2323*
⇌*532-7277*
Slightly west of Annapolis Royal on the road to Digby, this motel rents about 30 well-tended, functional rooms. The Wandlyn is particularly appropriate for families.

🌴 Garrison House Inn
$90
ℜ, *pb/sb*
open Apr to Dec
7 rooms
350 George St., B0S 1A0
☎*532-5730*
⇌*532-5501*
Several bed & breakfasts and excellent inns offer visitors the pleasure of staying in the heart of Annapolis Royal, one of the oldest towns in North America. One of these is the Garrison House Inn, is a magnificent hotel located in the heart of Annapolis Royal, just facing Fort Anne. Its antique-filled rooms are simply gorgeous. The room on the top floor with a view out the back is definitely the most stunning with its large windows and many skylights; reservations are a good idea for this room in particular. Very inviting common areas, including a delightful library and a restaurant on the ground floor, contribute to the pleasure of a stay here.

Smith's Cove

🌴Mountain Gap Resort
$75
108 rooms
ℜ, ≈
Rte. 101, B0V 1A0
☎*245-5841 or 800-565-5020*
The Mountain Gap Resort is the oldest resort in the province (1915) and has an irresistible old-fashioned charm reminiscent of 19th-century New England. Its wooden cottages and other buildings occupy expansive grounds strewn with wildflowers on the shores of Digby Bay. Rooms, suites and cottages, not overly luxurious but always comfortable, are available. Each cottage has a porch – the perfect place for gazing out at sunsets over the bay; cottage number 23 is especially well situated. There is a staircase that leads down to the beach at low tide, and the grounds also include a swimming pool, a playground for children, a tennis court and a pleasant restaurant.

Digby

Digby is a sizeable vacation spot with a number of impressive hotel complexes. Visitors can, however, find inexpensive rooms here. Two options are the **Siesta Motel** (*$65; 15 rooms, pb, tv;*
81 Montague Row,
B0V 1A0, ☎245-2568,
⇌245-2560) and the nearby **Seawind Motel**

($60; 7 rooms, tv, pb; 90 Montague Row, BOV 1A0, ☎245-2573). Both are well located alongside Digby's natural harbour, just a few minutes' walk from most of the local restaurants.

Admiral Digby Inn
$79
44 rooms
≈
Shore Rd., BOV 1A0
☎245-2531 or 800-465-6262
Lodging is also available at the Admiral Digby Inn, a very well-maintained two-storey motel near the home port of the ferry to Saint John, New Brunswick.

The impressive Pines Resort Hotel
$140
87 rooms
≈, ☺, ℜ, K, tv
Shore Rd., BOV 1A0
☎245-2511 or 800-667-4637
⇔245-6133
The impressive Pines Resort Hotel stands on a hill overlooking the bay in a lovely natural setting. Every part of this hotel was conceived to ensure an excellent stay, from the superb interior design and pretty, comfortable rooms to the excellent restaurant and inviting bar. Guests also have access to a wide range of athletic facilities, including tennis courts, a swimming pool and a gym; there is also a golf course nearby.

Westport

Brier Island Lodge
$109
pb/sb, K, ℜ, tv
P.O. Box 1197, BOV 1H0
☎839-2300 or 800-662-8355
⇔839-2006
On Brier Island, the most comfortable place to stay is the Brier Island Lodge. This two-storey motel occupies an auspicious site at the top of a small valley and overlooks the village of Westport and St. Mary's Bay. The rooms are modern and spacious; most of them are enhanced by large windows facing the bay. The restaurant, which serves tasty local cuisine, also contributes to the quality of a stay here.

Mavilette Beach Park

Cape View Motel and Cottages
$63
tv, K
open May to Oct
20 rooms
Salmon River, BOW 2Y0
☎645-2258
⇔645-3999
Driving along the coast between Digby and Yarmouth, visitors will pass through several Acadian communities. The Cape View Motel and Cottages lies alongside a beach near one of these villages. This is not a very luxurious place, but the rooms are well-kept and decently furnished. The region itself is conducive to relaxation, and visitors can enjoy pleasant strolls along the beach.

Yarmouth

Manor Inn
$55
53 rooms
≈, ℜ
P.O. Box 56, B0W 1X0
☎742-2487
⇔742-8094
The Manor Inn stands isolated a few kilometres east of Yarmouth, on a large lot on Doctors Lake. This four-building establishment encompasses about 50 rooms with varying levels of comfort. Some prettily decorated rooms occupy the main building, a house that dates to the middle of the 19th century and the old coach house just next to it. A few of these are adorned with fireplaces. Most of the rooms, located in the other two buildings, set back a little from the main one, are modern and motel-style and equipped with porches or patios. The fare in the dining room is more than adequate.

Harbour's Edge B&B
$75
3 rooms
12 Vancouver St., B5A 2N8
☎742-2387
⇔742-4471
This B&B is a great choice for those who love old houses. Meticulously renovated, it successfully recaptures the charm of yesteryear. It offers three cozy rooms, all of which are

Nova Scotia

attractively decorated and include private bathrooms. In addition to the beauty of this home, guests can enjoy the veranda, which opens onto a large garden facing the town harbour. The garden is an ideal spot for bird-watching.

Rodd Colony Harbour Inn
$100
65 rooms
tv, ℜ
6 Forest St., B5A 3K7
☎ *742-9194 or 800-565-7633*
⇌ *742-6291*
The Rodd Colony Harbour Inn lies directly opposite the boarding point for the ferry to Maine. Since it is located on the side of a hill, there is a lovely view from the back. The rooms are spacious and well-designed. The bar is a pleasant place for a drink.

Best Western Mermaid Motel
$100
tv, ℜ, ≈
45 rooms
545 Main St., B5A 1J6
☎ *742-7821 or 800-772-2774*
⇌ *742-2966*
Best Western Mermaid Motel occupies a two-storey building at the west entrance to Yarmouth. Its rooms are modern and immaculate. There is no dining room on the premises, but coffee is served in the morning and Captain Kelly's, located nearby, is reputed to be among the best restaurants in Yarmouth.

Restaurants

Wolfville

Coffee Merchant
$
at the corner of Main and Elm Sts.
☎ *542-4315*
If you're craving a good cup of coffee, head over to the Coffee Merchant, which serves good cappuccino and espresso. This is a pleasant place, where it is tempting to linger, read a newspaper or gaze out the window at the comings and goings of the people on the street. The menu is fairly limited, but nevertheless lists a few sandwiches and muffins.

Acton's Grill and Café
$$
268 Main St.
☎ *542-7525*
Despite its size, Wolfville numbers many impressive dining rooms, Acton's Grill and Café being a case in point. This little restaurant, with its rather subdued ambience, offers regional nouvelle cuisine that is both savoury and original. In addition, the menu posts a fine wine list.

Blomidon Inn
$$-$$$
127 Main St.
☎ *542-229*
The Blomidon Inn has two dining rooms – a small, very cozy one in the library and a larger one richly decorated with mahogany chairs. The latter is embellished by a picture window that looks out onto a beautiful landscape. The menu is equally exceptional, featuring such delicious dishes as poached salmon and scallops and salmon Florentine.

Chez La Vigne
$$-$$$
117 Front St.
☎ *542-5077*
Chez La Vigne, renowned for excellence for many years now, offers fine regional cuisine made with fresh products from the valley. Every evening, an interesting and reasonably priced, table d'hôte menu is set; the wine and beer selection is also impressive. Weather permitting, it is possible to dine al fresco on a prettily landscaped back terrace.

Kentville

Paddy & Rosie's Pub, Brewery and Restaurant
$-$$
42 Aberdeen St.
☎ *678-3199*
One of the friendliest places in Kentville, Paddy & Rosie's is both a pub, where you can sample a home-brewed beer while nibbling on

nachos or chicken wings and a restaurant that creates some refined dishes, such as mussels, shrimp and other seafood. Relaxed atmosphere and courteous service.

Annapolis Royal

Sunshine Café
$
274 St. George
☎*532-5596*
After visiting Fort Anne, it is pleasant to sit down and enjoy a refreshment or a light meal at the Sunshine Café. Big windows make this place bright and cheerful. The coffee is good, and the menu consists of simple, inexpensive and well-prepared dishes including an excellent choice of meats and desserts.

Leo's
$$
222 St. George St.
☎*532-7424*
Leo's occupies the oldest house in the Maritimes (1712). It is the place to keep in mind for breakfast, a light lunch or a more elaborate evening meal. It is a friendly, unpretentious spot that offers a menu of seafood, meat and pasta.

The Fat Pheasant
$$-$$$
200 St. George St.
☎*526-0042*
The former town post office has a new tenant: The Fat Pheasant, an exceptional establishment with a great res-

taurant, a cozy lounge and an Irish pub. You can start your evening off in the comfortable lounge on the main floor, which is decorated with woodwork and bookcases – the perfect spot to enjoy a beer. Then, you can go upstairs to the dining room, which is adorned with a beautiful brick wall and woodwork. The menu offers Italian and French specialities, including seafood and beef. In the basement, there's an Irish pub, where musicians perform on weekends.

Digby

Digby's famous scallops are of course *the* local specialty, and most of the town's restaurants are in proximity to the port. The **Red Raven Pub** (*$-$$; Water St.,* ☎*245-5533*), a family restaurant, dishes up simple, inexpensive fare. Just nearby, the **Fundy Restaurant** (*$-$$; Water St.,* ☎*245-4950*), just a shade more elegant than the Rod Raven, presents a slightly more varied menu. Scallops are the stars on both menus.

Pines Resort Hotel
$$$
Shore Rd.
☎*245-2511*
At the dining room in the Pines Resort Hotel visitors will find classic cuisine served in a refined atmosphere. The menu features an excellent Bras d'Or salmon. In addition, an

excellent wine list and an interesting selection of desserts are offered. This dining room is the undisputed favourite of local gourmets.

Westport (Brier Island)

Brier Island Lodge
$$
☎*839-2300*
For an intimate dinner or a light lunch, the best place on the island is the dining room at the Brier Island Lodge where a beautiful, large window provides a splendid view of the bay. The restaurant's menu lists a great variety of seafood and meat dishes.

Belliveau Cove

Roadside Grill
$
☎*837-5047*
Just west of Church Point, travellers can break bread at the Local Roadside Grill. French Canadians gather at this unpretentious little restaurant to share the latest local news. The menu offers a few Acadian specialties, including *râpure* dishes of beef, chicken or shellfish for less than $4.

Nova Scotia

Mavilette Beach Park

Cape View Motel
$-$$
Salmon River
☎645-2258
The restaurant at the Cape View Motel offers a lovely view over St. Mary's Bay. Some Acadian specialties are featured on the menu, including *râpure*, as are many seafood, chicken and meat dishes. The service here is very friendly.

Yarmouth

Ceilidh Café
$
276 Main St.
☎742-0031
The Ceilidh Café is a great place to snack on a sandwich, soup, quiche or simply enjoy a good cup of coffee.

Captain Kelly's Kitchen
$$
577 Main St.
☎742-9191
This beautiful dining room, decorated with woodwork, is laid out in a large, turn-of-the-century residence that also houses an English pub. The captain's cuisine varies greatly, from hamburgers to seafood by way of Acadian *râpure* and beef stew. Dishes are generally well prepared.

Queen Molly Brew Pub & Restaurant
$$
96 Water St.
☎742-6008
The first things you notice here are the brewery vats, which hint at what you can expect to find inside: five different kinds of home-brewed beer and a menu typical of this kind of establishment, including hamburgers and chicken. However, the design of the dining room, a huge timber – frame room, is less typical of pubs. For those who prefer the outdoors, there's a terrace with a lovely view (open seasonally).

Entertainment

Wolfville

Atlantic Theatre Festival
356 Main St.
☎542-4242 or 800-337-6661
Excellent classic plays are presented

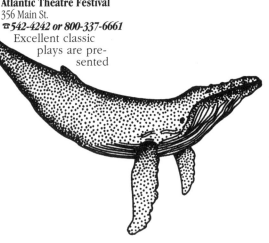

from mid-June to early September in the city's 500-seat amphitheatre. Ticket prices vary between $22 and $34 per person.

Annapolis Royal

The Fat Pheasant
200 St. George St.
☎526-0042
The main floor of the Fat Pheasant is delightful. This cozy room has a bookcase and beautiful woodwork – the perfect place to sip a drink. There's a friendly Irish pub in the basement, where you can have a beer and light snack (typical pub fare). The place gets hopping on weekends with a variety of live entertainment.

Lighthouse Route

This route, which runs along the southwest coast of Nova Scotia, boasts some of the most picturesque scenes in the province. Here, a string of charming villages blends harmoniously into the beautiful, unspoiled natural setting.

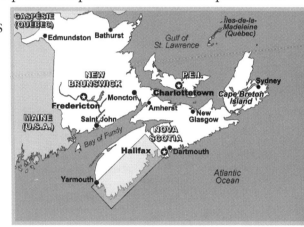

While exploring the area, visitors will pass through hamlets and fishing ports with wooden houses dating back to the 19th century, when the region enjoyed an era of prosperity due to the local construction of fishing schooners. The tips of rocky capes all along the coast are crowned by silhouettes of lighthouses, the most famous being the one at Peggy's Cove.

Practical Information

Area code: **902**

Tourist Information Offices

On site:
11 Blockhouse Hill Rd.
Lunenberg
☎*634-8100*
≈*634-3194*

South Shore Toursim Association
P.O. Box 149
Mahone Bay, B0J 2E0
☎*624-6466*
≈*624-9734*
www.ssta.com

The provincial government operates a reservation service for hotels, bed & breakfasts, campgrounds and car rentals. Information on festivals, ferry service and weather forecasts is also available:
☎*800-565-0000 in North America*
☎*425-5781*

Exploring

The road from Wedgeport to Pubnico West links a series of little Acadian fishing villages. The Acadian presence in this part of the province has persisted since 1653, a rare feat of continuity in Nova Scotia. Many people in the area have the surname Entremont and are direct descendants of Sieur d'Entremont, the first French colonist to settle the region. Interestingly, Acadians from this part of the province have preserved various old terms and expressions that are no longer current among other French Canadians. A nice example is that instead of *soixante-dix*, *quatre-vingt* and *quatre-vingt-dix* ("seventy," "eighty" and "ninety," respectively), people here say, *septante*, *octante* and *nonante*.

Wedgeport is still a very active fishing harbour; it's home to the **Wedgeport Sport Tuna Fishing Museum** *($2; mid-Jun to mid-Sep; Rte. 344, ☎663-4345)*, a little museum dedicated to sport tuna fishing. Farther along, a stop at the **Argyle Township Court House & Goal ★** *($2; Jun to Oct, every day 9am to 5pm; ☎648-2493)* is an absolute must when in **Tusket**, a pretty village bordered by expanses of clam water. Erected in 1805, this is the oldest building of its kind in Canada. The courtroom, the cells and the jailor's quarters are all open to the public.

Continuing along Route 3, **Sainte-Anne-du-Ruisseau Church ★** *(Rte. 3; Sainte-Anne-du-Ruisseau)*, exquisite with its splendid ceilings and stained-glass windows, is impossible to miss. Built in 1900, it is the oldest Catholic parish in the region (1699).

Contine westward – Route 3 intersects Route 335, which leads to **West Pubnico**.

West Pubnico

West Pubnico is an Acadian fishing village that offers picturesque views of the ocean. **Le Musée Acadien** *($2; mid-Jun to mid-Sep, Mon to Sat, 9am to 5pm, Sun 12:30pm to 4:30pm; ☎762-3380)*, in West Pubnico, exhibits antique objects, some of which date back as far as the 18th century. There is a gift shop on the premises.

Continue heading east on Route 3.

Barrington

Barrington was founded in 1761 by about a dozen Quaker families from Cape Cod, in the United States. Four years later, the community began building a **Meeting House ★** *(early Jun to end of Sep, Mon to Sat 9:30am to 5:30pm, Sun 1pm to 5:30pm; Rte. 3)*, today, a national historic site known as the Old Meeting House Museum.

The Meeting House serves both as a place for the church services of various denominations and a meeting place. This New England-style building is the oldest Nonconformist site in Canada, and the only remaining

building among the five that were built during this period of Nova Scotia's history. The museum recounts the history of the building and the region.

Barrington features another interesting historic site, the **Woolen Mill ★** *(free admission; early Jun to late Sep, Mon to Sat 9:30am to 5:30pm, Sun 1pm to 5:30pm; Rte. 3, ☎637-2185)*, a mill built in 1884 and originally powered by a waterfall. The Woolen Mill is an interpretive centre where visitors can learn how mills revolutionized the process of weaving wool.

Shelburne

Shelburne was founded in 1783, the final year of the American Revolution, when about 30 ships carrying thousands of Loyalists arrived in Nova Scotia. By the following year, the town already had over 10,000 inhabitants, making it one of the most densely populated communities in North America. Today, Shelburne is a peaceful village. **Dock Street ★**, which runs alongside the natural harbour, is flanked by lovely old buildings that form a harmonious architectural ensemble.

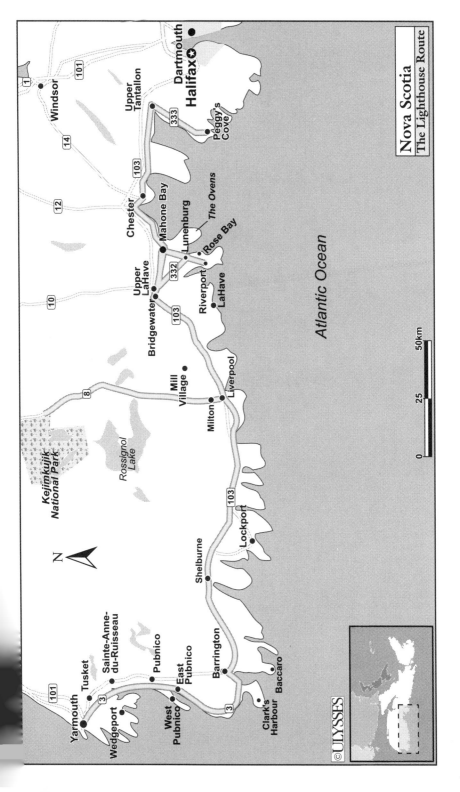

Nova Scotia
The Lighthouse Route

Atlantic Ocean

0   25   50km

© ULYSSES

This historic section features several points of interest, including the **Ross Thomson House** ★ *($2; early Jun to mid-Oct, every day 9:30am to 5:30pm; 9 Charlotte Lane; ☎875-3141)*, whose general store dates back to the late 19th

Ross Thomson House

century. It is furnished in a manner typical of that type of business in those years.

In the same neighbourhood, visitors can stop in at the **Dory Shop** ★ *($2; mid-Jun to Sep, every day 9:30am to 5:30pm; Dock St.; ☎875-3219)*, a workshop where fishing vessels were built in the last century.

Also noteworthy is the **Shelburne County Museum** *($2; mid-May to mid-Oct, every day 9:30am to 5:30pm; Dock St.; ☎875-3219)*, whose collection deals with the arrival of the Loyalists and the history of shipbuilding in this area, among other subjects.

A $4 pass grants admission to all three of these museums.

Lockeport

This pretty town a few kilometres past Shelburne has some of the most beautiful white-sand beaches in the province. There are five of these in the immediate vicinity of Lockeport, including spectacular **Crescent Beach** ★, which extends over 1.5km and which was once depicted on the Canadian 50-dollar bill. It is possible to stay in Lockeport, at bed and breakfasts or in cottages along the beach. On the way to Liverpool, a few other exquisite sand beaches make up part of the landscape, notably in **Summerville Centre**, **Hunts Point** and **White Point**. Accommodation is also possible near these beaches.

Liverpool

In the late 19th and early 20th centuries, the port of Liverpool was commonly frequented by privateers recruited by Great Britain. Privateers differed from pirates in that they were working in the name of a government, which gave them an official status of some sort, thereby protecting them. After pillaging villages or attacking enemy ships, they had to hand over a part of the booty to their protector.

The **Perkins House** ★ *(Jun to mid-Oct, Mon to Sat 9:30am to 5:30pm; Sun 1pm to 5:30pm; 105 Main St.; ☎354-4058)* was the home of writer Simeon Perkins, famous for his journal describing life in the colony between 1766 and 1812. The Perkins House, now open to the public, is an example of the Connecticut style and dates back to 1876.

From Liverpool, visitors can set off on an excursion to **Kejimkujik National Park** ★★ *($5 per day; mid-Jun to mid-Oct; P.O. Box 236, Maitland Bridge, B0T 1B0; ☎682-2772)* by taking Route 8. The park covers 381km² in the heart of Nova Scotia. Crisscrossed by peaceful rivers teeming with fish, this territory was once inhabited by Micmacs who established their hunting and fishing camp here. It is still considered a prime location for canoeing. The park also features camping sites, a pleasant beach (Merrymakedge) and various trails leading into the forest.

A part of the park, **Kejimkujik Seaside Adjunct National Park ★**, stretches 22km along the shoreline, near Port Mouton. The landscape here is more rugged than in the rest of the park. Although the area is bordered by steep, glacier-sculpted cliffs there are a few coves nestled here and there, with sandy beaches tucked inside. Trails have been cleared to enable visitors to explore the park and observe the local plant and animal life; seals can sometimes be seen along the shore.

Those who don't wish to go to Kejimkujik National Park can take Route 3 east to Exit 17, near Mill Village, to get back onto Route 331.

La Have

Christened La Have by Champlain and de Monts, who stayed here for a while in 1604, this little cape was chosen by Isaac de Razilly to be the site of the capital of Acadia from 1632 to 1636. Visitors will now find a monument marking the location of the former Fort Sainte-Marie-de-Grâce, built to protect the little colony. Right nearby, the **Fort**

Point Museum *(free admission; Jun to Aug, every day 10am to 6pm; Sep, Sat and Sun 1pm to 5pm; Rte. 331, ☎688-2696)* presents an exhibition on local history and the early days of the colony.

Bridgewater

Located on either side of the La Have River, Bridgewater is a bustling little town with several restaurants and hotels. Visitors can stop at the **DesBrisay Museum** *($2; mid-May to end of Sep, Mon to Sat 9am to 5pm, Sun 1pm to 5pm; Oct to mid-May, Tue 1pm to 5pm, Wed 1pm to 9pm, Thu to Sun 1pm to 5pm; 130 Jubilee Rd.; ☎543-4033)*, which houses a collection of objects related to local history and regularly hosts touring exhibitions in a modern space.

To learn all there is to know about how the mill revolutionized the wool-weaving industry, head to the **Wile Carding Mill ★** *(free admission; early Jun to end of Sep, Mon to Sat 9:30am to 5:30pm, Sun 1pm to 5:30pm; Rte. 325, at the corner of Pearl St. and Victoria Rd.; ☎543-8233)*. Guides in period dress offer interesting tours of

the mill and explain the various steps involved in weaving wool.

At Upper La Have, take Route 332 towards Riverport and Rose Bay.

Rose Bay

In 1861, gold diggers came to try their luck at **The Ovens Natural Park ★** *($5; mid-May to mid-Oct, 9am to sunset; Rte. 332; ☎766-4621)*. Little by little, these prospectors abandoned the area, only to be replaced by other inquisitive individuals who were more attracted by the beauty of the setting than anything else. For many years, the sea has been sculpting the rock of the cliffs here, hollowing out caves that the water surges into with great force. Paths have been cleared alongside the precipices, affording some magnificent views. Boating excursions make it possible to view the cliffs from the water as well.

Get back on Route 3 near Lunenberg.

Lunenburg

Lunenburg is definitely one of the most picturesque fishing ports in the Maritimes. Founded

The Bluenose

The *Bluenose* has a special place in Canadian maritime history. Built in Lunenburg in 1921, this extraordinary schooner won every race it participated in throughout its career.

In October 1921, after a summer of fishing, the *Bluenose* received, to everyone's surprise, the International Fisherman's Trophy for winning a race involving Canadian and American sailors. From then on, and until 1938, the *Bluenose* did not lose a race, despite the many Canadians and Americans who built ships for the sole purpose of defeating it.

Equipped with eight sails, the *Bluenose* was a superb, 49m schooner. Its hull was made of red oak, spruce and pinewood, its deck, of Douglas fir, and its structure, of mahogany. The *Bluenose* needed a crew of 18 and could reach speeds of up to 16 knots.

The glory of the *Bluenose* and other fishing schooners ended in the early 1940s with the arrival of massive modern trawlers with steel hulls. In 1942, despite the effort of its captain, Angus Walters, the *Bluenose* was sold in the West Indies.

The *Bluenose* was immortalized, however, and its image now appears on the Canadian 10-cent coin. In addition, a copy of the *Bluenose* was built in Lunenburg in 1963, the *Bluenose II*, which now travels the seas. In summer, the *Bluenose II* is moored at Lunenburg or Halifax harbour, and offers pleasant cruises. More about the *Bluenose* and its history can be found on the Internet at *www.Bluenose2.ns.ca*.

have survived to the present day. The village occupies a magnificent site on the steep shores of a peninsula with a natural harbour. A number of the colourful houses and buildings here date back to the late 18th and early 19th centuries. In fact, because of the architecture, parts of Lunenburg are somewhat reminiscent of the Old World. Lunenburg was recently named a Unesco world heritage site, a title awarded to the village because of its architecture.

A very busy fishing port, Lunenburg also has a long tradition of shipbuilding. The celebrated *Bluenose*, a remarkable schooner never efeated in 18 years of racing, was built here in 1921. Lunenburg is an extremely pleasant place to visit in the summertime. Its streets are lined with shops selling quality products. The art galleries are particularly interesting.

The atmosphere here is also enlivened by all sorts of activities, including the **Nova Scotia Fisheries Exhibition and Fisherman Reunion**, a celebration of the world of fishing, which has been held each year at the end of August since 1916.

The **Fisheries Museum of the Atlantic** ★ ★ *($7; mid-May to mid-Oct, every day 9:30am to 5:30pm, mid-Oct to mid-*

in 1753, it was the second British settlement in Nova Scotia, Halifax being the first. Its original population consisted mainly of "foreign Protestants" from Germany, Montbelliard and Switzerland. German was commonly spoken in Lunenburg up until the end of the 19th century, and various culinary traditions

May, Mon to Fri 8:30am to 4:30pm; on the waterfront; ☎634-4794), set up inside an old fish-processing plant, commemorates the heritage of the fishers of the Atlantic provinces. Visitors will find an exhaustive, three-floor introduction to the world of fishing, including an aquarium, an exhibit on the 400-year history of fishing in the Grand Banks of Newfoundland, a workshop where an artisan can be observed building a small fishing boat, an exhibit on whaling and another on the history of the *Bluenose,* and more.

Three ships are tied to the pier behind the building, including the *Theresa E. Connor,* a schooner built in Lunenburg in 1938 and used for fishing on the Banks for a quarter of a century. Expect to spend at least 3hrs for a full tour of the museum.

The ***Bluenose II*** *($20; ☎641-1963)* is moored in Lunenburg harbour when it is not in Halifax. Built in 1963, it's a 43.5m schooner, a replica of the famous *Bluenose* that is portrayed on the Canadian 10-cent coin. Enjoy cruises on this historic ship.

Wandering the streets of Lunenburg, visitors are invariably seduced by the town's pretty houses and beautiful buildings, especially **St. John's Anglican Church** and **St. Andrew's Presbyterian Church**.

Make sure to take the opportunity to visit the little fishing hamlet of **Blue Rock ★**, located a short distance from Lunenburg. Peaceful and picturesque, this handful of houses lies on a rocky cape overlooking the ocean.

Continue heading east on Route 3.

Mahone Bay

Mahone Bay is easily recognizable by its three churches, each more than a century old, built side by side facing the bay. Like Lunenburg, it was first settled by "Protestant foreigners" in 1754, and like a number of other communities on the Atlantic coast, its port served as a refuge for privateers. Until 1812, these individuals pillaged enemy ships and villages, while paying British authorities to protect them.

Later, until the end of the 19th century, Mahone Bay enjoyed a period of great prosperity due to fishing and

Mahone Bay

Peggy's Cove

large farms in the 19th century.

At Upper Tantallon, take Route 333.

Peggy's Cove

The picturesque appearance of the tiny coastal village of Peggy's Cove has charmed many a painter and photographer. The little port, protected from turbulent waters, is lined with warehouses standing on piles.

Farther along, visitors can stroll across the blocks of granite that serve as a base for the famous lighthouse of Peggy's Cove, which houses a post office during summertime. It is best to be careful when walking here, especially when the water is rough. On the way out of Peggy's Cove, visitors can stop at the **William F. de Garthe Memorial Provincial Park** ★ to see a sculpture of 32 fishers, along with their wives and children, carved into a rock face 30m-long. William de Garthe, who spent five years creating this sculpture, was fascinated by the beauty of Peggy's Cove, where he lived from 1955 until his death in 1983, and by the lifestyle and courage of the local fishers.

shipbuilding. The lovely old houses lining the streets of the village bear witness to this golden era. Mahone Bay has a pretty sailing harbour and several good inns and bed & breakfasts.

Visitors can also go to the **Settlers Museum** *(free admission; mid-May to early Sep, Tue to Sat 10am to 5pm, Sun 1pm to 5pm; 578 Main St.; ☎624-6263)*, which features a collection of antique furniture, dishes and other old objects from the area. The house itself dates back to 1850.

Continue along Route 3.

Chester

Chester was founded in the 1760s by New England families. It has been a popular vacation spot since the

beginning of the 19th century. Many well-heeled residents of Halifax have second homes here, and visitors will find a number of quality hotels and restaurants, an 18-hole golf course, three sailing harbours, several craft shops and a theatre, the **Chester Playhouse** *(22 Pleasant St.).* Perched atop a promontory overlooking Monroe Bay, Chester cuts a fine figure with its lovely residences and magnificent trees.

From Chester, Route 12 leads to the **Ross Farm Living Museum of Agriculture** ★ *($5; early Jun to mid-Oct, every day 9:30am to 5:30pm; New Ross; ☎689-2210)*, a 23ha farm inhabited by five successive generations of the Ross family from 1916 onwards. Guides in period dress liven up the museum, which has about 10 buildings typical of those found on

Beaches

Along the Atlantic coast
of this route there are
gorgeous beaches of
fine sand in the area of
Lockeport, close to
Shelburne and near Liverpool at **Summerville
Centre**, **Hunts Point** and
White Point. Spectacular
Crescent Beach ★, in
Lockeport, is 1.5km
long and is but one of
five beautiful beaches
in that area.

Outdoor
Activities

Whale-watching

The southwest coast
has a variety of marine
animal life. Seals,
humpback whales and
Atlantic puffins are just
a few of the numerous
species that you can
see by taking one of
the boat trips departing
from different towns in
the region.

**Lunenburg Whale Watch-
ing Tour**
Jun to Oct
P.O. Box 475
Lunenburg, B0J 2C0
☎*527-7175*

Peggy's Cove Water Tours
Jun to mid-Oct
Peggy's Cove, B0J 2N0
☎*823-1060*

Diving

There are many ship-
wrecks along the south-
west coast of Nova
Scotia because of the
heavy sea traffic
through these waters
over the years. A few of
these wrecks have
turned into incredible
artificial reefs for ma-
rine life that attract
divers. Along Port
Mouton, the Spectacle
Marine Park has 16 dive
sites, some of which
abound with marine
fauna, while others are
shipwrecks. Among
these, Matthew Atlantic
is one of the artificial
reefs that can be ex-
plored by divers of all
levels.

**Queens County Marine
Park Society**
Port Mouton
☎*683-2188*

Lunenburg offers a
unique dive site. In
1994, the *HMCS
Saguenay*, a Canadian
destroyer, was inten-
tionally sunk off
Lunenburg to become
the figurehead of
Lunenburg Marine Park.
This wreck has also
become a unique ref-
uge for thousands of
marine animals, making
this spot a magnificent
place to go diving in
Nova Scotia. Dive trips
for experienced divers
are organized by:

Jo's Dive Shop
296 Lincoln St.
Lunenburg
☎*634-3443*

Hiking

Kejimkujik National
Park has lovely trails
for those who enjoy
hiking in the forest.
There are 14 paths
covering several kilo-
metres, offering breath-
taking natural beauty.
Whether you prefer to
hike along Roger's
Creek, Mill Falls or
Merrymakedge beach,
or to bird-watch at
Peter's Peak, each trip
is a chance to discover
some of the many
treasures of this vast
wilderness.

Canoeing and
Kayaking

The southwest coast is
sprinkled with many
little islands and coves,
which makes it the
perfect spot for canoe-
ing and sea-kayaking.
For those who get
excited about the idea
of paddling alone on
the waves, several
companies rent boats
and organize trips.

Nova Scotia

Seaclusion Kayak Adventures
kayak rentals: $35/half-day, $45/day
1270 Argyle Sound Rd.
West Pubnico
☎762-2191

Mahone Bay Kayak Adventures
kayak rentals: $30/half-day, $45/day
canoe rentals: $20/half-day $35/day
618 Main St.
Mahone Bay
☎624-6632

Rossignol Surf Shop
216 Main St.
Liverpool
☎354-3733

The best place to go canoeing in Nova Scotia is undoubtedly **Kejimkujik National Park** (☎682-2772), which is crisscrossed by scores of rivers that are easily accessible with these vessels. From amateurs interested in short excursions to more experienced canoeists, everyone can enjoy this thrilling activity here. Canoes may be rented at **Jakes Landing** (*$3/hr, $15/day*).

Accommodations

Barrington Passage

Old School House Hotel
$45
ℜ
12 rooms
Hwy. 3, B0W 1G0
☎637-3770
≈637-3867
This old village school, which served its original function from 1889 to 1969, was transformed a few years ago into a hotel establishment. Its rather modestly decorated rooms occupy the two upper floors of the building. On the ground floor, a restaurant and a bar attract local clientele. A little set back from the school are adequately comfortable cottages that are also available for rental.

Clyde River

Clyde River Inn
$60 bkfst incl.
3 rooms
Hwy. 103
☎637-3267
Absolute calm reigns over Clyde River, a tiny hamlet located in the middle of the countryside, a few kilometres from Barrington. Just next to Clyde River's little white church stands a beautiful house painted brilliant red that is home to the Clyde River Inn. This bed and breakfast offers three comfortable

and inviting upstairs rooms. Patricia and Mike, the owners of the establishment, are always welcoming.

Shelburne

Cape Cod Colony Motel
$50
tv
23 rooms
234 Water St., B0T 1W0
☎875-3411
For inexpensive accommodation, opt for the peaceful Cape Cod Colony Motel, which has clean, modern rooms and lies just a short walk from Dock Street.

Cooper's Inn
$75
ℜ
7 rooms
875 Dock St., B0T 1W0
☎/≈875-4656
☎800-688-2011
Located in the very heart of Shelburne's historic section, looking out on the harbour, lovely Cooper's Inn is one of the best hotels in the province. It occupies a magnificently renovated old house that was built for a wealthy Loyalist merchant in 1785.

The decor of each room and the choice of furniture for the house were carried out with such minute attention to detail that a simple visit to Cooper's Inn is a pleasure in itself. All of the rooms are comfortable and equipped with private bathrooms. A splendid, very bright suite has been laid out on the top floor; it is well worth the $135 rate. In addition, one of the rooms is easily accessible to travellers with disabilities. Each room is named for one of the house's former owners. To top it all off, the inn's dining room serves up cuisine that pleases the most distinguishing palates.

Lockeport

To fully profit from the fine-sand beach in Lockeport, visitors can stay at **Seaside Cottages** (*$110; 8 rooms; Rte. 3; Crescent Beach, B0T 1L0, ☎/≈656-2089*) or at **Ocean Mist Cottages** (*$110; 5 rooms; Crescent Beach, B0T 1L0, ☎656-3200, ≈656-2203*). These closely bunched, comfortable houses, each of which has two bedrooms, directly overlook Crescent Beach.

Summerville Beach

⛵ Quarterdeck Beachside Villas & Cabins
$125
ℜ, tv
16 rooms
Rte. 3, Exit 20 off of Hwy. 103
B0T 1T0
☎*683-2998 or 800-565-1119*
≈*683-2457*
Cottages equipped with all the comforts, a long fine-sand beach, a relaxed atmosphere and an excellent restaurant are the foundations of the Quarterdeck's reputation. Its villas, built directly on the beach, each have two bed-

rooms, a living room with a fireplace, a very well-equipped kitchenette and a modern bathroom. The largest room in each house is on the second floor and is splendidly laid out with a whirlpool bath and a superb terrace overlooking the ocean. The Quarterdeck leaves nothing to be desired, either as the setting for a restful family vacation or as an intimate lovers' retreat.

White Point

White Point Beach Resort
$110
tv, ℜ, ≈
71 rooms
43 cottages
Rte. 3, Exit 20A or 21 off of Hwy. 103, B0T 1G0
☎*354-2711 or 800-565-5068*
≈*354-7278*
The White Point Beach Resort offers luxurious modern accommodation in small cottages or in a large building facing directly onto a beach that stretches 1.5km.

The complex is attractive and has been carefully and tastefully laid out in order to make the most of its beautiful surroundings. In addition to swimming at the beach or in the pool, visitors can play golf or tennis or go fishing. The bar, which offers a magnificent view of the ocean, is particularly pleasant.

Liverpool

Lanes Privateer Inn
$60 bkfst incl.
ℜ, tv
27 rooms
33 Bristol Ave., B0T 1K0
☎*354-3456 or 800-794-3332*
≈*354-7220*
Lanes Privateer Inn offers clean, modestly decorated rooms at reasonable rates. It is well located alongside the Mersey River, on the shore opposite the centre of town. After the local B&B, this is one of the least expensive places to stay in the area.

Bridgewater

Auberge Wandlyn Inn
$59
ℜ, tv, ≈, ⌂
71 rooms
50 North St., B4V 2V6
☎*543-7131 or 800-561-0000*
≈*543-7170*
Bridgewater has several modern motels, including the Auberge Wandlyn Inn, whose rooms have little charm but are clean and well laid-out. The Wandlyn Inn, like other establishments in Bridgewater, has the advantage of being a half-hour drive from Lunenburg, where the choice of accommodations is sometimes limited during the summer.

Nova Scotia

Lunenburg

1826 Maplebird House B&B
$55 bkfst incl

≈

4 rooms
36 Pelham St., B0J 2C0
☎/≈*634-3863*

Built more than 150 years ago, this home witnessed the first years of Lunenburg's history. All these years left their mark on the house, so it was completely renovated to restore some of its original charm. It now exudes the atmosphere of a bygone era and offers comfortable accommodation. Its many amenities include a pool in the garden as well as a veranda facing the harbour.

Blue Rocks Road
$55 bkfst incl.

3 rooms
579 Blue Rocks Rd., B0J 2C0
☎*634-8033*

The gently rolling hills of Lunenburg make wonderful bike trips, and one establishment has been built to respond to the needs of cycling enthusiasts: the Blue Rocks Road. Situated in the middle of the countryside, this place is a good departure point for excursions in the region. It offers three attractively decorated, well-kept rooms, as well as various services, such as bike rentals, repairs, accessories and clothing. Travel information is also available here.

Bluenose Lodge
$60 bkfst incl.

ℜ, *tv*
9 rooms
corner Falkland Ave. and Dufferin St., B0J 2C0
☎/≈*634-8851*
☎*800-565-8851*

The Bluenose Lodge is a splendid Victorian house located a few minutes' walk from the centre of Lunenburg. Furnished with antiques, the rooms are full of character, and all include a private shower.

Marinee King Inn
$60 bkfst incl.
open mid-Feb to Dec
4 rooms
15 King St., B0J 2C0
☎*800-565-8509*

A visit to Lunenburg offers an opportunity to discover the old-fashioned charm of the town's numerous 19th-century residences, many of which have been converted into pleasant inns. One good, relatively inexpensive option is the Marinee King Inn, a lovely Victorian house built around 1825. The decor remains quite typical of that era, when tastes leaned towards heavily furnished rooms. In the evening, guests can enjoy a delicious meal in the dining room.

Hillcroft Café & Guest House
$65 bkfst incl.

ℜ
3 rooms
53 Montague St., B0J 2C0
☎/≈*634-8031*

Hillcroft, which is also home to a restaurant, is a pretty little house dating from the 1850s. The establishment offers three decent rooms with sloping ceilings and shared bathrooms.

Brigantine Inn
$65 bkfst incl.

ℜ, *tv*
7 rooms
82 Montague St., B0J 2C0
☎*634-3300 or 800-360-1181*

The Brigantine Inn is extremely well-located facing the port. Most of the spotless, attractively decorated rooms feature large windows and balconies with splendid views.

Rum Runner's Inn
$65

ℜ
9 rooms
66 Montague St., B0J 2C0
☎*634-9200 or 888-778-6786*
≈*634-4822*

Located right near the Brigantine Inn, the Rum Runner's Inn offers similar lodgings: motel rooms with views of the port.

Arbor View Inn
$75 bkfst incl.

ℜ
6 rooms
216 Dufferin, B0J 2C0
☎*634-3658*

The magnificent view on the harbour distinguishes this establishment from the others in town. Situated on a hill close to the centre of town, it has a peaceful location and its large, well-kept garden is lovely. The interior decor is also attractive: each room has beautiful antiques, wallpaper, paintings and a cozy ambience. There's also one another draw: it offers some of the best cuisine in the region (see p 188).

Pelham House B&B
$90 bkfst incl
224 Pelham St., B0J 2C0
☎*634-7113*
≈*634-7114*
For those who appreciate impeccably run B&Bs, Pelham House is the place to stay. The four bedrooms are creatively decorated and offer some little extras (one of them has access to a veranda that faces the harbour). Guests are pampered here and nothing is left to chance: the breakfast is delectable, the dining room is gorgeous and the living room, where you can read or watch television, is large and cozy. However, the place is not suitable for young children.

The Old Hammett Hotel
$90
K
4 rooms
120 Montague St., B0J 2C0
☎*634-8165*
This hotel, which occupies a building that dates back to 1790, directly overlooks the port. It offers adequately furnished suites, each equipped with a kitchenette, a living room, one bedroom and a bathroom. The living-room couch folds out into a bed, so each suite can accommodate up to four people.

Boscawen Inn
$90 bkfst incl.
open mid-Apr to Dec
ℜ
20 rooms
150 Cumberland, B0J 2C0
☎*634-3325 or 800-354-5009*
A superb Victorian house dating from 1888, Boscawen Inn lies in the heart of Lunenburg, on the side of the hill overlooking the port. The location is spectacular, and the pleasant terrace offers an unimpeded view of the town's historic section. Guests can also relax in one of three sitting rooms, which, like all the other rooms in the house, are adorned with period furniture.

Mahone Bay

Coan Trail Retreat
$75
≈, *tv*
11 rooms, 2 cottages
1 penthouse
R.R. 1, B0J 2E0
☎*624-8824*
≈*624-8899*
The recently built Ocean Trail Retreat presents different accommodation options to meet the varying needs of travellers: there are rooms, a penthouse and a cottage. All of them have modern, but rather cold interiors. Nevertheless, they offer several advantages, such as kitchenettes in the cottages and balconies with barbecues.

Sou'Wester Inn
$75
4 rooms
788 Main St., B0J 2E0
☎*624-9296*
The village of Mahone Bay is sure to please visitors with a taste for large 19th-century houses. Some of these residences are now high-quality B&Bs. One of the best is the Sou'-Wester Inn, a magnificent Victorian residence originally owned by a shipbuilder. The entire house is furnished in the style of the period. Guests are invited to relax on the terrace overlooking the bay.

Amber Rose Inn
$80
tv, ℝ
3 rooms
319 Main St., B0J 2E0
☎/≈*624-2060*
Formerly a general store, the Amber Rose Inn is now a well-kept inn, adorned with antique furniture that gives it an old-world charm. Built in 1875, it offers two rooms with private bathrooms and televisions. Guests have access to a living room where they can relax and read a book.

Manse Country Inn
$95 bkfst incl.
4 rooms
88 Orchard St., B0J 2E0
☎*624-1121*
≈*624-1182*
This magnificent inn stands on a hillside just off the main road, behind the three churches of Mahone Bay. This house was originally the residence of the United Church pastor.

The recently opened Manse Country Inn offers four superb rooms, all of them decorated and furnished in flawless taste. The common rooms, including a living room with a fireplace, are all equally ravishing and offer breathtaking views of the bay. The rooms, each of which has a private washroom, are distributed in the main building and in the adjoining Carriage House; one of them has a pleasant balcony. In Mahone Bay, more charming lodgings than these are hard to find indeed!

Chester

Windjammer Motel
$50
ℜ, *tv*
18 rooms
Rte. 3, B0J 1J0
☎275-3567
Chester has always been a favourite with wealthy families. However, the relatively low prices of the rooms at the Windjammer Motel help make the local tourist industry a bit more diversified. The rooms, fairly standard for this type of accommodation, have recently been renovated. The Windjammer lies at the entrance to town on Route 3, on the way in from Mahone Bay.

Mecklenburg Inn
$65 bkfst incl.
open late May to late Oct
4 rooms
78 Queen St., B0J 1J0
☎275-4638
A charming residence built at the end of the 19th century, the Mecklenburg Inn has adorable rooms, a terrace and a charming, relaxing sitting room. The dining room is open in the evening.

Captain's House Inn
$95 bkfst incl.
ℜ
9 rooms
29 Central St., B0J 1J0
☎275-3501
⇌275-3502
Visitors who opt for the Captain's House Inn will stay in a superb house dating back to the early 19th century. The top-notch rooms have been tastefully furnished and decorated. In addition to this elegant setting, guests enjoy an outstanding view of the bay.

Haddon Hall Inn
$150
ℜ, ≈
9 rooms
67 Haddon Hill Rd., B0J 1J0
☎275-3577
⇌275-5159
Chester is home to numerous excellent hotel establishments. Unlike the Mecklen-burgh Inn and the Captain's Inn, two distinguished hotels in the heart of Chester, the Haddon Hall Inn is slightly set back from the centre of town and perched on a hill. This magnificent house built in 1905

belonged successively to many important personalities in the province's history before being transformed into an inn a few years ago. Nothing was overlooked in the process of making Haddon Hall, the most luxurious hotel in the area: each of its uniquely decorated rooms is splendid; exquisite cuisine is served in its elegant, ground-floor dining room; a lounge area has been set up around a pleasant swimming pool and the grounds are resplendent with flowers, just to mention a few examples.

Blandford

Century House
$70 bkfst incl.
3 rooms
5206 Hwy. 329, B0J 1C0
☎228-2041
⇌228-2827
Located on the road between Chester and Peggy's Cove, this charming B&B is nestled by the sea in a 19th-century home. The lovely Century House is adorned with works by local artists – a great way to get to know the regional art. Guests receive royal treatment here, with well-kept rooms and a courteous welcome.

Hubbards

 Dauphinee Inn
$125 bkfst incl.
ℜ, ⊛, tv
6 rooms
167 Shore Club Rd., B0J 1T0
☎*857-1790 or 800-567-1790*
⇄*857-9555*
Built high up on the shores of Hubbards' Cove, the Dauphinee Inn is an extremely peaceful place that offers an opportunity to relax in an enchanting setting. Each room has a wide balcony where guests can sit comfortably and gaze at the boats sailing in and out of the bay. Equipped with a whirlpool, the suites, located on the top floor, are particularly beautiful. In the evening, guests can savour excellent cuisine in the dining room or on the terrace, which is very pleasant at sunset.

Restaurants

West Pubnico

Red Cap Restaurant
$-$$
☎*762-2112*
Travelling through the Acadian villages of this part of the province, the urge is strong to stop a spell and chat with the area's friendly residents. Lunch at the Red Cap presents an excellent opportunity for just such an encounter. This unpretentious restaurant proposes a menu of a few Acadian dishes, regional specialties and affordable seafood dishes.

Shelburne

Claudia's Diner
$
149 Water St.
☎*875-3110*
Claudia's Diner is a picturesque place with a decor that will take you back a quarter of a century. The food is fairly simple: fish and fried chicken, grilled liver, hamburgers, seafood *chaudrée*, lobster rolls and similar light dishes are listed on the menu.

Loyalist Inn
$
160 Water St.
☎*975-2343*
For family-style cuisine with a Maritime flavour, head to the Loyalist Inn, which, in spite of its nondescript dining room, features a good menu. The food is simple – seafood chowders, lobster rolls, poached fish and all sorts of other dishes, especially meat and chicken. This is a good place to enjoy a satisfying meal with the family.

⚘ Charlotte Lane Café
$$
13 Charlotte Lane
☎*875-3314*
The very charming Charlotte Lane Café prepares original, refreshing cuisine that includes such diverse items as Gorgonzola spaghetti, filet of Atlantic salmon, Camembert chicken, Porto cutlets, vegetable curry, in addition to 20 or so other delicious, always beautifully presented dishes. The appetizers are just as mouth-watering. Behind the establishment there is a small patio, with just a few tables which, in good weather, is the most delightful spot in all of Shelburne.

Cooper's Restaurant
$$$
Cooper's Inn
36 Dock St.
☎*875-4656*
Cooper's Restaurant offers the elegance and ambiance of a historic house built in 1785 and the flavours of refined regional cuisine. For starters there is a choice of dishes such as smoked salmon wrapped in a spinach crepe. About 10 main dishes are offered, including succulent sauteed scallops and excellent pasta topped with lobster. A selection of about 20 wines, including some excellent vintages, as well as a great variety of aperitifs and digestifs, rounds out the menu.

Summerville Beach

Quarterdeck Restaurant
$$
Rte. 3, Exit 20 off of Hwy. 103
☎*683-2998*
The Quarterdeck Restaurant, located almost right on Summerville Beach, is an excellent

spot for fish and sea-
food. The restaurant,
whose large back ter-
race stands on piles,
looks out on the ocean.
It is particularly pleas-
ant to sit outside for
breakfast. In the eve-
ning, guests can eat
either on the terrace or
in the warm, inviting
dining room. The food
is succulent and the
service, friendly and
attentive. The Quarter-
deck also rents out
rooms and cottages
looking out onto the
beach (see p 183).

Lunenburg

Historic Grounds Coffee House
$
100 Montague St.
☎634-9995
For a muffin or a sand-
wich, a quick stop at
this little café, which
has a patio overlooking
the docks, is called for.
It is a modest-looking
spot, but serves good
cappuccinos, espressos
and cafés au lait, as
well as a variety of teas.

Knot Pub
$
4 Dufferin St.
☎634-3334
A traditional pub, the
Knot Pub has darts, a
selection of beer and a
menu that offers typical
fare, such as hamburg-
ers, steak, fried fish and
chicken wings – and a
friendly, unpretentious
ambience to boot.

Hillcroft Café & Guest House
$$-$$$
53 Montague St., B0J 2C0
☎634-8031
Hillcroft Café is a great
find for those feel like
something a little out of
the ordinary. The menu
is inspired by an eclec-
tic array of culinary
traditions, and its sea-
sonings are influenced
by French, Middle-East-
ern and Asian cuisine.
Babaghanouj, clam
chowder, Thai chicken
(curry and coconut
sauce) and Dijon
chicken are just a few
of the many innovative
dishes on this interna-
tional menu.

Arbor View Inn
$$$
216 Dufferin St.
☎634-3658
Outside of town, but
with a beautiful view of
the harbour, Arbor
View will delight those
who enjoy a good meal
in a peaceful setting.
Although you have to
walk a ways from town
to get there, it's worth
the trip. The artistically
inspired, original
dishes, such as steamed
fillet of salmon in a
banana leaf, fresh sea-
food linguini with curry
sauce, as well as steak
with Cape Breton Is-
land chanterelle mush-
rooms, are all delicious.

Magnolia's Grill
$-$$
Montague St.
☎634-3287
With walls covered in
photographs from dif-
ferent eras, high booths
and bouquets of fresh

flowers adorning its
tables, this restaurant is
very attractive indeed.
Simple but delicious
cuisine, perfect for
lunch, is served here.
The menu is based on
excellent soups, sand-
wiches and salads, as
well as a few more
elaborate dishes. The
fish cake, a local rec-
ipe, is one of the better
selections. Desserts,
black and herbal teas,
and coffees complete
the menu.

Boscawen Inn
$$
150 Cumberland St.
☎634-3325
Lunenburg boasts a
magnificent location
overlooking a natural
harbour. The Boscawen
Inn, a Victorian house
standing on the side of
a hill, is a good place
to appreciate the natu-
ral beauty of the sur-
roundings and the har-
mony of the local
architecture. The dining
room menu consists
mainly of excellent fish
and seafood dishes.

Grand Banker Seafood Grill
$$
82 Montague St.
☎634-3300
Some evenings it is
difficult to find a free
table at the Grand
Banker Seafood Grill. It
has become this popu-
lar thanks to its location
and its very inviting
dining room. The menu
is composed mainly of
simple, well-prepared
dishes, including grilled
scallops or shrimp, crab
cakes, seafood, pasta

dishes and steaks. There is a small patio.

Lunenburg Dinner Theatre
$$
116 Montague St.
☎634-4814
Every summer evening of the week except Monday, the Lunenburg Dinner Theatre combines dining with entertainment by presenting a musical. The atmosphere is friendly, and guests are sure to have a good laugh.

Mahone Bay

Saltspray
$
621 S. Main St.
☎624-9902
Those who enjoy savouring their meal while taking in a beautiful view will appreciate the terrace at Saltspray, which overhangs the bay. There's nothing too fancy on the menu, but the offerings, consisting mostly of sandwiches, are more than adequate.

Innlet Café Seafood House & Grill
$$
east end of the bay
249 Edgewater St.
☎624-6363
This pleasant, pretty restaurant equipped with a small terrace presents an astonishing variety of meat, poultry, seafood and fish dishes. Some lighter meals, such as quiches, pasta, salads and sandwiches, also figure on the menu

and are just right for lunch.

Mimi's Ocean Grill
$$
662 Main St.
☎624-1342
A small restaurant with a very attractive interior, Mimi's is a top choice for either lunch or dinner. Lamb chops, excellent grilled fish, Cajun shrimp and sauteed scallops are some of the dishes on the evening menu. At noon, tasty light meals may be savoured for under $10. The menu also lists a variety of desserts including Italian ices, lemon pie and cheesecake.

Chester

Foc'sle
$
42 Queen St., corner of Pleasant
A well-known local institution, the Foc'sle serves family-style cuisine that is hardly original, but nonetheless satisfying and inexpensive. Since this is one of the oldest taverns in Nova Scotia, people also come here to enjoy a night out.

The Rope Loft
$$
marina
☎275-3430
With its interior decked out like a warm Irish pub and its terrace facing the marina, this restaurant has everything going for it, morning, noon and night, fair weather or foul. Its menu is reliable, although not

especially original. It mainly features fish and seafood dishes, steak and poultry, all of it well prepared.

Entertainment

Chester

During July and August, the **Chester Playhouse** (*about $18; 22 Pleasant St.,* ☎275-3933) presents plays and concerts in the evening.

Shopping

Shelburne

Charlotte Lane Café & Craft
13 Charlotte Lane
☎875-3314
Not only is it one of the best places to eat in town, Charlotte Lane Café also sells a variety of beautiful crafts created by Nova Scotian artists.

Lunenburg

Houston North Gallery
110 Montague St.
☎634-8869
Visitors interested in First Nations and Inuit art should make sure to stop in at the Houston North Gallery, which displays a remarkable assortment of sculptures and paintings.

Bluenose II Company Store
121 Bluenose Dr.
☎*634-1963*
The famous *Bluenose* is honoured at the Bluenose II Company Store. Those looking for a memento of this schooner will have an endless selection to choose from. The profits go to a good cause: keeping the *Bluenose II* in operation.

Carriage House Gallery
290 Lincoln St.
☎*634-4010*
The Carriage House Gallery exhibits and sells works by a variety of Scottish artists.

Chester

The Warp & Woof Gifts & Gallery
81 Walter St.
☎*275-4795*
The Warp & Woof Gifts & Gallery sells carvings, pottery, woolen sweaters and other beautiful crafts made by Maritime artists.

Cape Breton Island

Northeast of Nova Scotia,
lie the charming villages, untouched forests and rugged cliffs of Cape Breton Island. The meeting of land and sea will take your breath away.

The island, it seems, was discovered in 1497 by John Cabot, and colonized quite early by the French, who settled here in the 17th century.

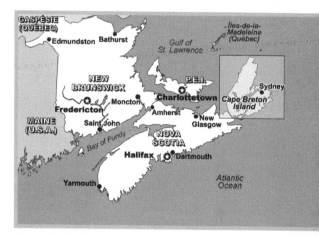

They called the island "Île Royale". In 1713, Acadia was ceded to Great Britain under the Treaty of Utrecht. France compensated for this loss by accelerating development on Île Royale, most importantly by building the Fortress of Louisbourg in 1719. Acadian villages therefore also sprang up along the north shore of Île Royale.

The island did not remain under French rule, however, and finally ended up in the hands of the English in 1758. Louisbourg was destroyed two years later, in 1760.

Since rebuilt, the fortress ranks among the most impressive historic sites in Eastern Canada.

In addition to its vivid history, Cape Breton boasts marvellous stretches of wilderness, delighting of countless nature lovers each year. Cape Breton Highlands National Park is a perfect exemple, with its hiking trails and spectacular views.

The Cabot Trail is the best way to enjoy and appreciate the beauty of Cape Breton Island. This steep, winding road makes a full circle around the island, passing through dense forests and charming villages along the way. No visit to Nova Scotia would be complete without seeing Cape Breton Island.

Finding Your Way Around

This chapter is composed of one tour:
Cape Breton

Island ★★★, that covers all of the island.

By Plane

Yarmouth International Airport
☎*(902) 742-6484*

Sydney Airport
☎*(902) 564-7720*
≈*(902) 564-2726*

By Car

The quickest way to get to Cape Breton Island from Halifax is via Highway 102, and then the Trans-Canada to Port Hastings. The island is also accessible by taking Highway 7 which follows the Atlantic Ocean.

The route passes through peaceful rural communities and a few fishing ports, such as Musquodoboit Harbour with its superb stretches of sand at **Martinique Beach**.

Either of these routes will take you to Cape Breton Island. Once there, you can go either to Sydney, Louisbourg or near Baddeck, which marks the beginning of the Cabot Trail.

By Bus

From Halifax, visitors can take the bus as far as Sydney. It is worth noting, however, that no bus goes all the way around the island (aside from private tour buses). There is no way

to get around easily, except in Sydney, so it is best either to rent a car or rely on your own resources (hitchhiking, cycling).

Acadian Lines
Halifax to Sydney
☎*(902) 454-9321*

Transit Cap Breton
around Sydney
☎*(902) 539-8124*

By Ferry

From Port-aux-Basques (Newfoundland) to North Sydney (Nova Scotia)
Marine Atlantic
Box 355 Purvers Street, North Sydney, B2A 3V2
☎*800-341-7981*
Departure: once daily year-round

Practical Information

Area code: *902*

Tourist Information Offices

By mail:
Tourism Cape Breton
20 Keltic Drive, Sydney River
☎*539-9876*
≈*539-8340*

On site:
Port Hastings
on the way onto the island, along the Canso Causeway
mid-May to mid-Oct

There are also booths in Louisbourg, Baddeck and Margaree Forks.

The provincial government operates a reservation service for hotels, bed & breakfasts, campsites and car rentals. Information on festivals, ferry service and weather forecasts is also available:
☎*800-565-0000 in North America*
☎*425-5781*

Exploring

Sherbrooke

A handful of quaint little houses make up this tiny hamlet of 397 people. What attracts most travellers, however, is the fishing in St. Mary's River that flows nearby. Take time as well to visit **Sherbrooke Village** (*$7.25; early Jun to mid-Oct, 9:30am to 5:30pm;* ☎*522-2400,* ≈*522-2974*), a reconstruction of a 1860-1880 village. Guides in period costume lead tours of the thirty buildings.

Continue on Route 211, then Route 316 until it intersects with Highway 16. Continue towards Canso.

Canso

The post of Canso was established on this site as of 1605 because it

Confederation Bridge measures 13km and connects Canada's smallest province, Prince Edward Island, to New Brunswick, on the continent. - *P. Quittemelle*

Despite its small size, Prince Edward Island is covered from coast to coast by imposing fields that tickle the eye with their striking colours.
- *P. Quittemelle*

Thanks to their red sand, blazing-green dunes and lapis-blue sea, the beaches of Prince Edward Island are among the most beautiful in Canada.
- *Perry Mastrovito*

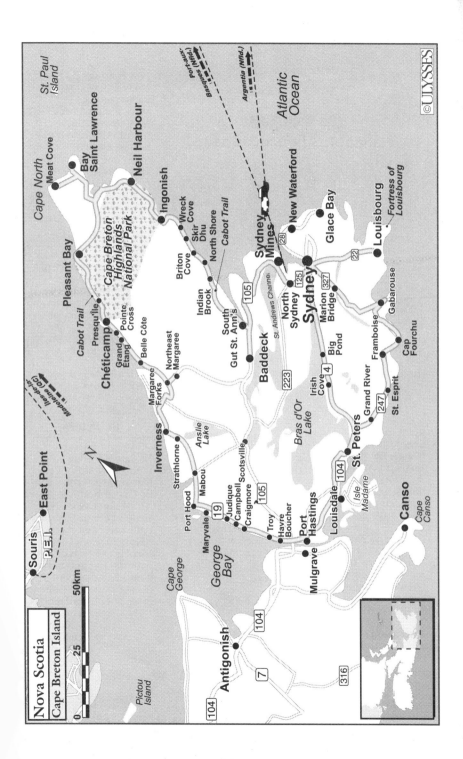

The Bald Eagle
(Haliaeetus Leucocephalus)

The bald eagle, the emblem of the United States, is the only eagle to be found solely in North America. Bald eagles are seen in various areas of Canada, such as on Cape Breton Island, near large stretches of water where they draw their basic diet of fish. This imposing bird has a wingspan of up to 2.5m, a weight of up to 7kg and can live 40 years. It is mono-gamous and stays faithful to its partner until death.

was protected by Grassy Island from strong ocean currents, and because of its location at the entrance to Chedabucto Bay. The town is a departure point for visits to the **Grassy Island National Historic Site** *(early Jun to mid-Sep, 10am to 6pm, departure at 11am; Jul and Aug, departure at 2pm; Box 159, Baddeck, B0E 1B0, ☎295-2069).*

An integral part of the fishery during the 18th century, the Canso region was coveted by many and the object of dispute between the English and the French. At the Canso **Visitor Reception Centre**, you can view a short film on the colonization of Grassy Island and its eventual destruction in 1744. Visitors can then take a boat to the island, where an inter

pretive trail leads to more interesting attractions.

Get back onto the Trans-Canada by Highway 16.

Port Hastings

The small town of Port Hastings is the gateway to Cape Breton Island. Although not a particularly pretty town, it is a major crossroads for travellers, with highways leading to both Baddeck and Sydney.

Bald Eagle

Port Hastings does offer many practical facilities, including restaurants, service stations and most importantly, a tourist information office (see p 192).

Head towards Sydney via Highway 4 at Louisdale, or take Route 320 to get to Isle Madame.

Isle Madame

This tranquil peninsula covers an area of 42.5km² and has several pleasant picnic areas. Isle Madame was settled by the Acadians and a Francophones still live here today.

From Isle Madame, go back to Highway 4 and continue towards Sydney.

St. Peters

St. Peters is situated on the narrow strip of land that separates the Atlantic Ocean from Bras d'Or Lake. Colonists settled here in 1630 and built Fort Saint-Pierre. About 20 years later, Nicolas Denys took over the fort and turned it into a trading and fishing post. To learn more about this French pioneer, visit the **Nicolas Denys Museum** *($0.50; Jun to Sep, every day 9am to 5pm; 46 Denys St.).*

The trading post developed gradually, but really took off 140 years ago, when a canal was dug between Bras d'Or Lake and the ocean to provide passage for boats. Every year, from the park on either side, many ships (maximum 4.88 t) can be observed passing through the canal. An outdoor display shows how the locks work.

Bras d'Or Lake

Bras d'Or Lake is an inland sea with 960km of shoreline. It thus occupies a good part of the island, dividing it into two areas, the Cape Breton Lowlands and Highlands. This vast salt-water expanse attracts many animal species, including the magnificent bald eagle. For those who like to fish, trout and salmon abound in the lake and its many channels (St. Andrews Channel, St. Patrick Channel).

Aboriginal peoples have long been attracted to the shores of this lake with its abundance of fish. The Micmacs established themselves here permanently. Their presence remains constant to this day on the four reserves that have been created – the Whycocomagh, Eskasoni, Wagmatcook and Chapel Island. Besides the reserves, there are several villages around

the lake. The **Bras d'Or Scenic Drive** ★ *(follow the signs marked with a bald eagle)* goes all the way around the lake.

From St. Peters to Sydney

The fastest way to Sydney is along Highway 4.

The road to Sydney passes through small towns along the shores of Bras d'Or Lake, as well as through some Aboriginal reserves.

Another option from St. Peters is to take Route 247 along the ocean. At Marion Bridge take Route 327 that leads to Sydney.

This road winds along the coast and passes through several charming fishing villages, including l'Archevêque. Unfortunately, the road is in poor condition.

Sydney

With a population of 25,000, Sydney is the largest town in the area. J.F.W. DesBarres, a Loyalist from the United States, founded the town in 1785. A few years later, Scottish immigrants settled here. Sydney grew quickly at the beginning of the century, when coal mining industries were established here. Coal-mining is still Sydney's primary industry. The town has all the services necessary to accommodate visitors

and is a good place to stop for a rest before going on to Louisbourg. Otherwise, Sydney offers few attractions.

Cossit House *(free admission; Jun to mid-Oct, 9:30am to 5:30pm; 75 Charlotte St.,* ☎539-7973*)* is the oldest house in town. Restored and decorated with period furniture, it looks just as it did long ago. Guides dressed in period costume lead tours through the house and are available to answer any questions.

Nearby, on Charlotte Street is the **Jost House** *(free admission; Jul and Aug, Mon to Sat 9:30am to 5:30pm; Sep and Oct, Mon to Sat 10am to 4pm ; 54 Charlotte St.,* ☎539-0366*)*, which was the home of a rich merchant.

To find out more about Sydney's history, visit **St. Patrick's Church Museum** *(87 Esplanade)*. Built in 1828, this Catholic church is the oldest in Cape Breton. It features an exhibit on the town's past.

Take Highway 22 to Louisbourg.

Louisbourg

Visitors are drawn to Louisbourg because of the nearby Fortress of Louisbourg, which is the area's main attraction. Many of the local businesses, including hotels, motels and restaurants, are geared

Nova Scotia

towards tourists. It takes a full day to see the fortress, while the town itself offers few attractions.

The **Fortress of Louis-bourg** ★★★ *($11, children $5.50; Jun and Sep 9:30am to 5pm, Jul and Aug 9am to 7pm;* ☎ *733-2280)* was built strategically at the water's edge, where enemy ships could be seen and attacks could be countered. The fortress is ideally located since it was built outside of the town itself and is removed from all modern development. It been easier, therefore, to recreate the atmosphere of the fledgling French colony back in 1744. Cars are not permitted close to the fortress, and a bus provides transportation to the site.

During the 18th century, France and England fought over territory in America. The French lost Acadia, which then became Nova Scotia. It was during this turbulent period in 1719 that French authorities decided to build a fortified city on Île Royale and began constructing the Fortress of Louisbourg. As the most complex system of fortifications in New France, this undertaking presented some major challenges.

Besides being a military stronghold, Louisbourg was also a fishing port and a commercial centre. Within a short

peroid of time, its population had grown to 2,000 inhabitants. Everything was designed to enable colonists and soldiers to adjust to their new environment, and houses and garrisons were erected. Nevertheless, conditions were rough, and colonists had some difficulty adapting. Despite these hardships, the colony grew and local business flourished.

The French presence on Île Royale was a thorn in the side of the English colonies stationed further south. In 1744, when war was declared in Europe between France and England, the Louisbourg garrison attacked the English villages in the area. As a result, they took over an English outpost. This situation incensed the English in New England, and provoked William Shirley, governor of Massachusetts, to send his troops to attack the French bastion in 1745.

Four thousand New England soldiers ventured an attack on the supposedly impenetrable Fortress of Louisbourg. Despite their reputation, the French troops were underequipped and poorly organized. They had never even imagined such an attack possible, and could not defend themselves. After a six week-long siege, the Louisbourg authorities surrendered to the British troops.

A few years later, in 1748, Louisbourg was returned to France when the two nations signed a peace treaty. Life carried on in the fortress, and within a year, Louisbourg was as active as before. This renewed prosperity was short-lived, however, since the fortress was conquered once and for all by British troops in 1758, ending the French presence in the area.

Hardly 10 years after this conquest, the fortress was left to ruin, and only was it rebuilt much later. Today, almost one quarter of the fortress has been restored and, during the summer, people dressed in period costume bring it to life again, recreating the Louisbourg of long ago. There are soldiers, a baker and a fisherman with his family. The scene is most convincing, and a stroll down the streets of this old French fortress is a fascinating experience.

To get to Glace Bay, return to Sydney, and take Highway 4 from there.

Glace Bay

Glace Bay lies on the Atlantic coast and is rich in coal, which forms the base of Glace Bay's industry. The town's name is of French origin and refers to the pieces of ice *(glace)* that can be seen drifting along the coast.

This small town, which has a population of about 20,000, features two interesting attractions.

Guglielmo Marconi (1874-1937) became famous for proving that it was possible to send messages using a wireless telegraph. At the age of 22, Marconi had already developed a wireless station from which messages could be sent over a short distance. In 1902, he sent the first trans-Atlantic message from his transmitting station at Table Head. At the **Marconi National Historic Site** ★ *(free admission; Jun to mid-Sep, every day 10am to 6pm; Timmerman St., ☎295-2069)* visitors can learn about Marconi's discoveries and see his work table, as well as the radio station from which the first message was sent.

The Glace Bay area's mining industry dates back many years. As long ago as 1790, French soldiers from Louisbourg were already coming to Port Morien for coal. The industry really took off at the beginning of the 20th century when mines were dug here, most importantly at New Waterford. Today, Glace Bay produces more coal than any other town in Eastern Canada.

To learn more about this industry, visit the **Miner's Museum** ★★ *($3.50; Jun to early Sep, 10am to 6pm, Tue until 7pm; rest of the year, every day Mon to Fri 9am to 4pm; 42 Birkley St., ☎849-4522)*, which has exhibits showing the various tools and techniques used in coal mining. There is also a recreation of a typical mining town from the beginning of the century. Finally, the most fascinating part of the museum is a guided tour of a coal mine.

Fortress of Louisbourg

Go back to Sydney via Highway 4. To reach Baddeck, take Route 125, then take the Trans-Canada (Highway 105).

Baddeck

Baddeck is a charming village, perfect for taking a stroll or enjoying a bite to eat on a terrace. Whether you decide to stay for a few days to enjoy the comfortable hotels and calm atmosphere, or simply stop for a few hours before heading off on the Cabot Trail, Baddeck offers many attractions that make it worth the detour. One fascinating sight is the summer home of the inventor Alexander Graham Bell.

The **Alexander Graham Bell National Historic Site** ★★ *($4.25; every day, Jun 9am to 6pm, Jul and Aug 8:30am to 7:30pm, Sep to mid-Oct 8:30am to 6pm; town's east exit, Chebucto St., ☎295-2069)*. Many of Bell's inventions are on display here, as are the instruments he used in his research. Bell's life story is also told. Visitors will learn, for example, that after teaching sign language for many years, he created an artificial ear that recorded sounds. This experiment led to his invention of the telephone.

Nova Scotia

Alexander Graham Bell

Alexander Graham Bell was born in 1847 in Edinburgh, Scotland. He settled in Brantford, Ontario with his parents in 1870. From very early on, the brilliant inventor shared his father's interest in teaching sign language to the deaf. Bell's research led him to teach at the University of Boston, where he trained teachers to work with the deaf. He created an artificial ear that could record sounds, which led to his invention of the telephone in 1876. Bell became rich and famous and spent a number of years with his wife Mabel, herself deaf, at his summer home in Baddeck (Nova Scotia), where he continued to do research in various fields.

From Baddeck, the Cabot Trail is the only road that goes around this part of the island. Take this route north towards Ingonish.

The Cabot Trail

The Cabot Trail follows precipitous cliffs that jut out over the Atlantic Ocean, and passes through some picturesque little villages. Leaving Baddeck, the road follows the shore before climbing up to the plateau on the north end of the island. The many lookouts along this road offer magnificent panoramic views. It's worth taking the time to stop and appreciate the beauty of the landscape, where a restless sea, steep hills and a dense forest are home to a variety of animal species.

The first village after Baddeck is tiny **South Gut St. Ann's**, home to the **Gaelic College**, an institution devoted to the survival of Gaelic culture in North America. Courses are offered in Gaelic language, singing and bagpipe playing.

The road continues along the coast to **Ingonish Ferry**, where it begins to mount the vast plateau occupying the north end of the island at an elevation of 366m. The natural scenery grows more and more spectacular as you go.

Cape Breton Highlands National Park ★★★ begins here. The park, created in 1936, protects 950km² of wilderness inhabited by moose and bald eagles. A wide range of activities is offered throughout the oldest park in Eastern Canada. Just about everything is available for outdoor-enthusiasts: magnificent views, a forest inhabited by fascinating animal life, beaches, campsites, 27 hiking trails and even a golf course.

At Cape North, the road heads back south, but you can continue further north by taking the small road to Meat Cove.

This road leads first to the charming fishing village of **Bay St. Lawrence ★**. Built at the water's edge, the village has little wooden houses and a picturesque port, where cormorants can be seen gliding above the waves. The road climbs along the **cliffs ★★** and winds its way to **Meat Cove**, a perfect place to stop for a picnic and enjoy the **superb view ★** over the ocean waves.

To get back on the Cabot Trail, you will have to retrace your steps.

The road continues west. From Cape North to **Pleasant Bay**, visitors can gaze at the canyon formed by the sides of the hills. The **view ★★** is stunning. After being on the move for a while, Peasant Bay is a welcome and *pleasant* spot to rest.

The plateau ends near **Petit Étang**. The road heads back down and follows the Gulf of St. Lawrence to the Acadian region of Cape Breton. The landscape is surprising, as forests and steep cliffs give way to a barren plateau studded with Acadian villages. Among these is **Chéticamp**, a quiet village with simple houses and a fishing port. It is a departure point for seal- and whale-watching excursions. More villages with French names follow, including **Grand Étang**, **Saint-Joseph du Moine**, **Cap-Lemoine** and **Belle Côte**.

The west part of the Cabot Trail ends at Margaree Harbour. You can continue your journey by cutting across the plateau back to Baddeck. The highlight along this route is the **Margaree Salmon Museum** (*$0.50, mid-Jun to mid-Aug, 9am to 5pm; ☎248-2848*) in **Northeast Margaree**. The museum displays the various implements used for salmon fishing.

To leave Cape Breton Island from Baddeck, take the Trans-Canada (Highway 105). You can also continue along the west coast of the island.

Ceildish Trail

The road along the west coast of the island leads to the Ceildish Trail. This region was settled by Scots, and vestiges of Gaelic culture still remain. More than anywhere else on Cape Breton Island, the villages along the Ceilidh Trail offer an excellent opportunity to discover Scottish heritage. Gaelic music is heard throughout this region, and a few musicians here are now famous on the national and international music scenes. Furthermore, the warm waters here wash up against a few of the island's beautiful beaches, especially near **Mabou ★**. There are a number of modest little villages along the Gulf of St. Lawrence. In this region, Mabou is definitely the nicest place to stay. A few kilometres past Mabou is the **Glenora Distillery**, which produces a single malt whisky. There is also an inn and a pub here (see p 205).

This road leads to Port Hastings, where you can get back on the Trans-Canada again.

Beaches

On Cape Breton Island, there are also lovely beaches near **Mabou**

and in **Trout Brook Park, Inverness** and **Ingonish**.

Along the Northumberland Strait, **Lavilette Beach** is a particularly noteworthy spot on the north coast of the island. This beach is located in the park of the same name, and is a lovely ribbon of sand that stretches 1.5km.

Outdoor Activities

Bicycling

Bike Rentals

Open Horizons Cycling
Auberge Gisèle Country Inn
387 Shore Rd., Box 132
Baddeck, B0E 1B0
☎*295-2849*

Sea Spray Cycle Centre
R.R.2, Dingwall, B0C 1G0
☎*383-2732*

Hiking

Visitors can explore **Cape Breton Highlands National Park** by hiking along one of its 27 trails. There is something for everyone here, from short trails that take about 20min to long excursions leading to the top of steep hills. The tourist information centre distributes a pamphlet entitled *Walking in the Highlands.*

Those interested in joining an organized hiking expedition can contact:

Highland Hiking Expeditions
R.R.2, Dingwall, B0C 1G0
☎*383-2933*

Bird-watching

Cape Breton is another excellent location for bird-watching. From cormorants and kingfishers to impressive bald eagles, a variety of species can be spotted near the coast, around **Bras d'Or Lake** and in **Cape Breton Highlands National Park**.

It is also possible to take a trip to the coast of Bird Island where you can see the Atlantic Puffin. These small marine birds come here to nest between May and August. Some excursions offer a chance to observe other species as well, such as the black guillemot, the razorbill and the great blue heron.

Puffin Boat Tour
departure from Baddeck or Ingonish
☎*929-2563*

Whale-watching

Atlantic Whale Watch
departures at 10am, 1:30pm and 4:30pm
Ingonish Beach
☎*285-2320*

Island Whale Watch and Nature Tours
departures at 10:15am, 1:30pm and 4:30pm
St. Lawrence Bay
☎*383-2379*

Whale and Seal Cruise
departures at 9am, 1pm and 6pm
Pleasant Bay
☎*224-1316*

Seaside Whale & Nature Cruises
three departures daily
Laurie's Motor Inn, Chéticamp
☎*224-3376*
☎*800-95-WHALE*

Whale Cruisers
$25
Jul and Aug
departures at 9am, 1pm and 6pm
Cheticamp
☎*224-3376*

Kayaking

The rugged coastline of Cape Breton Island offers incredible panoramic views. Kayak trips are a particularly good way to observe the scenery from another vantage point. A few companies organize excursions.

Experience Kayaking
North River
☎*567-2322*

Golf

In **Cape Breton Highlands National Park**, visitors will find the magnificent **Highland Links** *(Ingonish,* ☎*285-2600)*, which ranks among Nova Scotia's most spectacular golf courses.

Deep-sea Fishing

Various outfits organize deep-sea fishing expeditions. Participants are provided with all necessary equipment and instruction.

Whale Island
$25
Ingonish
☎*285-2338 or 800-565-3808*
⇄*285-2338*

Deep-Sea Fishing Chéticamp
$25
P.O. Box 221, Chéticamp
B0E 1H0
☎*224-3606*

Accommodations

From Halifax

Liscomb Mills

Liscomb Lodge
$129
ℜ, *tv*
Liscomb Mills, Rte. 7, B0J 2A0
☎*779-2307 or 800-665-6343*
≈*779-2700*
The Liscomb Lodge is a true paradise for nature lovers, as it is located on the edge of the water, perfect for fishing and canoeing among other activities. The area is peaceful, the rooms comfortable, and the grounds magnificent.

Cape Breton Island

Sydney

 **Rockinghorse Inn**
$70
tv
8 rooms
259 Kings Rd., B1S 1A7
☎*539-2696 or 800-664-1010*
≈*539-2696*
For charming accommodation in a peaceful environment close to the downtown area, head to the Rockinghorse Inn. This renovated Victorian residence has eight charming rooms, each with its own private bath. Staying here makes it easy to forget that Sydney is an industrial town.

Delta Sydney
$109
≈, ℜ, *tv*, △, ☺, ✳
152 rooms
300 Esplanade, B1P 1A7
☎*562-7500*
☎*800-268-1133 from Canada*
☎*800-887-1133 from the U.S.*
≈*562-3023*
Downtown Sydney consists mainly of a few streets alongside the river, and most of the town's hotels are located here. One of these is the Delta Sydney, whose facade looks out on the Sydney River. The rooms are a bit lacking in charm, but thoroughly functional. As a bonus, the hotel features a great swimming pool with a slide – sure to be a hit with the children.

Cambridge Suites Hotel
$109 bkfst incl.
tv, ≈, *K*, ℜ, △, ☺
150 rooms
380 Esplanade, B1P 1B1
☎*562-6500 or 800-565-9466*
≈*564-6011*
Right next door is the Cambridge Suites Hotel, which is about as comfortable as the Delta, though more care has been taken with the decor. The rooms are actually small apartments equipped with kitchenettes. The hotel is also home to an excellent restaurant called Goodies.

Louisbourg

Point of View Suites
$115
ℜ, *K*, *tv*
8 rooms
5 Lower Commercial St.
B0A 1M0
☎*733-2080 or 888-374-8439*
Not far from the Louisbourg Fortress, this lovely new establishment was recently built. It has attractively designed modern rooms and a warm ambiance. Each room has a kitchenette and a balcony. There is also a restaurant that serves excellent dishes, such as snow crab (in season). As its name suggests, this place offers a magnificent view of the sea.

Baddeck

Telegraph House
$52
tv, ℜ
43 rooms
205 Chebucto St., Rte. 205
exit 9, B0E 1B0
☎*295-1100*
The Telegraph House is a fine-looking Victorian house set in the heart of town. Its 43 rooms, which have a slightly old-fashioned charm about them, are pleasant and comfortable.

Auberge Gisèle
$85
early May to late Oct
ℜ, ✳, ≈, △
19 rooms
Rte. 205 exit 8, 387 shore Rd.
B0E 1B0
☎*295-2849 or 800-304-0466*
≈*295-2033*
Also on the shores of Bras d'Or Lake, the Auberge Gisèle offers

Nova Scotia

rooms with a pleasant view, and is a good place to keep in mind. Upon arrival, visitors will be enchanted by the pine-bordered lane leading up to this lovely residence, whose rooms are all attractively decorated. There are a few more rooms in a nearby annex.

Duffus House
$95
tv
9 rooms
108 Water St., B0E 1B0
☎*295-2172*
Visitors will enjoy the particularly relaxing atmosphere at one of a handful of charming inns along the waterfront, including Duffus House, one of the oldest residences in town. Built in the 19th century, it is nicely furnished with antiques and boasts a lovely garden. Each room has its own private bath.

Inverary Inn
$95
tv, ℜ
150 rooms
Hwy. 105 exit 8, B0E 1B0
☎*295-3500 or 800-565-5660*
⇄*295-3527*
At the cozy Inverary Inn, guests can stay in either the main building or in charming little wooden cottages. The decor and the vast grounds give this place a rustic feel well-suited to the Nova Scotian countryside.

Silver Dart Lodge
$97
≈, tv, ℜ
84 rooms
Rte. 205 exit 8, B0E 1B0
☎*295-2340*
☎*888-662-7484*
⇄*295-2484*
and
MacNeil House
$160
6 rooms
These two establishments share a magnificent park covering about 38ha and look out onto beautiful Bras d'Or Lake. Given the exquisitely peaceful setting, this is the perfect place to relax. The Silver Dart has pretty, comfortable rooms and several cottages, some with fireplaces, while the McNeil offers luxurious rooms, some of which also feature fireplaces.

Ingonish Beach

There are several campsites in **Cape Breton Highlands National Park** *(no reservations; ☎285-2329)*. Average rates are about $14 for a tent and $20 for a trailer.

The Castle Rock Inn
$89
ℜ, tv
15 rooms
R.R.1, B0C 1L0
☎*285-2700 or 888-884-7625*
⇄*285-2525*
This beautiful Georgian home, which was converted into an inn, is gorgeously located with an excellent view of the surrounding area. The place is very peaceful and is ideal for nature lovers. The rooms are attractive, although the

decor is rather drab. Guests can relax on the pretty terrace.

Ingonish Chalets
$129
7 chalets, 5 rooms
B0C 1L0
☎*285-2008 or 888-505-0552*
This little establishment, which is composed of cottages and motel rooms, is right near one of the most beautiful beaches on this part of the island. The cottages and the rooms are comfortable, clean and welcoming.

Keltic Lodge
$298
open Jun to Oct and Jan to Mar
≈, K, ℜ, tv
32 rooms
Middle Head Peninsula B0C 1L0
☎*285-2880 or 800-565-0444*
⇄*285-2859*
The Keltic Lodge is very well located alongside a cliff overlooking the sea. Slightly removed from the access roads, in a tranquil environment, the Keltic Lodge offers top-notch accommodation just a short distance from the Cabot Trail. The buildings are handsome and the rooms, some of which are in cottages, are both charming and comfortable. The dining room features a gourmet menu.

Dingwall

Markland Coastal Resort
$90
K, ℜ, tv
3 km from Dingwall, B0C 1G0
☎*383-2246 or 800-872-6084*
⇄*383-2092*
An excellent place to relax, admire the sea, walk along the beach or depart from to explore the Cabot Trail, the Markland Coastal Resort offers comfortable accommodation in wooden cottages with a cozy interior.

Each cottage has several rooms equipped with a terrace. The large, grassy space opposite the cottages leads to an untouched beach. The Markland is an ideal spot for couples or families who enjoy a peaceful, secluded setting and the outdoors. The fine food served in the dining room hits the spot after a long day in the fresh air.

Chéticamp

Auberge Doucet
$60
tv
12 rooms
on the way out of Chéticamp
B0E 1H0
☎*224-3438 or 800-646-8668*
⇄*224-2792*
The Auberge Doucet, which stands on a hill at the edge of town, rents out large, comfortable rooms. Although the front garden is somewhat disappointing, the inn boasts a lovely setting and

beautiful views of the Gulf of St. Lawrence.

Laurie's Motor Inn
$85
K, ℜ, tv
61 rooms
Main St., B0E 1H0
☎*224-2400*
⇄*224-2069*
There are several places to stay in the centre of the Acadian community of Chéticamp. One of these is Laurie's Motor Inn, a motel stretching alongside the Gulf of St. Lawrence. Although the decor is not very original, the rooms are clean and comfortable. To enjoy a satisfying meal, stop in at the motel's dining room, which has a very decent menu. The seafood is especially good.

Margaree Valley

Normaway Inn
$89
May to Nov
ℜ
28 rooms
Margaree Valley, Egypt Road
B0E 2C0
☎*248-2987 or 800-565-9463*
⇄*248-2600*
The Normaway Inn has been welcoming vacationers for over 60 years. The place has a great deal of charm, due to its magnificent garden, which stretches across several hundred hectares, creating a pastoral atmosphere. Appropriately, the main building looks somewhat like a farmhouse.

The rooms are located inside this building and in a number of cottages. Some of them

include fireplaces and whirlpool baths. Guests also have access to a cozy living room.

Mabou

Mabou River Hostel
members $18 bkfst incl., non-members $20 bkfst incl.
Hwy. 19
☎*945-2356 or 888-627-9744*
The only youth hostel on Cape Breton Island is in Mabou, a quaint village renowned for its culture and Gaelic music. The hostel is well kept and offers only private or semi-private rooms. A kitchen is available for guests to use.

Dungreigan Country Inn
$95 bkfst incl.
ℜ, tv
8 rooms
Hwy. 19, B0E 1X0
☎*945-2207*
The Dungreigan Country Inn is located in an idyllic spot with a wonderful view near the harbour. The architecture of its two new buildings is 19th-century in style. The interior also has an old-world theme, as its rooms are furnished with antiques. The restaurant has established a reputation for delicious cuisine.

Restaurants

Sydney

On Charlotte Street, there are a number of little snack-bars serving hamburgers and fries.

Restaurant at the Delta Hotel
$$
300 Esplanade
☎562-7500
The Restaurant at the Delta Hotel has a very decent menu featuring a fair number of fish dishes. With its large picture windows looking out onto the water, the place boasts a lovely view. Breakfast served.

Joe's Warehouse
$$
424 Charlotte St.
☎539-6686
Don't be turned off by the Western look of Joe's Warehouse, which happens to be a local institution. Although the decor is not exactly sophisticated and the music sounds like what you'd hear in a shopping mall, the atmosphere is still very inviting. People come to Joe's for the generous portions of delicious prime rib. Seafood is also included on the menu.

Louisbourg

At the fortress, a restaurant has been set up in one of the buildings facing the water. The food is no more than decent, but at least visitors can eat lunch without leaving the site.

Grubstake
$$
1274 Main St.
☎733-2308
Another possibility is the Grubstake, whose specialty is seafood. For those who prefer grill or poultry, the menu also lists steak and chicken dishes.

Baddeck

Baddeck Lobster Suppers
$$
Ross St.
☎295-3307
If you are hungry for lobster, head over to Baddeck Lobster Suppers. The main dish includes lobster and unlimited seafood chowder, mussels, salad and dessert.

McCurdy's
$$
Silver Dart Lodge, Shore Rd.
☎295-2340
The Silver Dart Lodge (see p 202) is pleasantly located on the shores of Bras d'Or Lake. Its restaurant, McCurdy's, which looks out onto this magnificent body of water, offers an unbeatable atmosphere. In addition to the view, people come here to sample tasty seafood dishes

and savour Scottish cuisine.

Ingonish Beach

Purple Thistle Dining Room
$$$
☎285-2880
The Purple Thistle Dining Room is the restaurant at the splendid Keltic Lodge (see p 202). In a refined atmosphere, guests can taste a variety of specialties, many of which are made with seafood. The hotel has another, simpler restaurant, **Atlantic** (**$$**), which is a good place to go for lunch.

Ingonish Ferry

The Castle Rock
$$$
R.R. 1
☎285-2700
The Castle Rock Inn offers good food in a quiet, relaxing location. Its menu includes an excellent selection of delicious fish and seafood.

Cape North

Morrison's Pioneer Restaurant
$
☎383-2051
You can't miss Morrison's Pioneer Restaurant, a wooden building located right alongside the road. Despite its modest appearance, it is one of the better family-style restaurants in the area. The food is simple (seafood chow-

der, beef stew, etc.) but good.

Dingwall

Markland Hotel
$$
☎*383-2246*
The restaurant at the Markland Hotel has a pine-panelled dining room with a stylish, if not extravagant, decor. The menu is extremely interesting, and simply reading it over will whet your appetite. The offerings include grilled salmon with Mousseline sauce and grilled filet of pork with plums in a red-wine and onion sauce.

Pleasant Bay

Cabot Trail.com Internet Café
$
☎*224-1976*
There is nothing fancy here. The coffee is nothing to write home about, but if you want to hook up to the Internet, this is *the* place.

The Rusty Anchor
$$
☎*224-1313*
The terrace of this small restaurant, which faces the ocean, is a great place to be on gorgeous summer evenings. The menu includes expertly prepared fresh seafood.

Chéticamp

Harbour Restaurant and Bar
$-$$
☎*224-2042*
The Harbour Restaurant, which has a great view of the coast, is a good place to dine after an excursion on the Cabot Trail. The place has a friendly atmosphere and is decorated with old black-and-white photos of Chéticamp. The menu includes a variety of scrumptious dishes, such as the lobster on Kaiser bread, the hot chicken sandwich, the fresh Atlantic salmon and the sirloin.

Laurie's
$-$$
☎*224-2400*
At Laurie's, visitors might be surprised to discover that the menu lists both lobster and hamburgers. This restaurant has something for everyone, in terms of both taste and budget. Guests can try such succulent dishes as the fisherman's platter, which includes lobster, crab and shrimp. The Acadian staff is as friendly as can be, amiably telling their guests to "enjoy *le repas*."

Mabou

Dungreigan Country Inn
$$$
Hwy. 19
☎*945-2207*
Mabou has a few good restaurants. The Dungreigan Country Inn offers several regional and international classic gourmet dishes, which are all deliciously prepared, including fresh halibut, scallops in basil cream sauce and rosemary lamb. Its pleasant dining room, which opens onto the harbour, is accented with flowers, and, if the temperature warrants it, a cosy fire. The lunch menu offers light, healthy fare, such as salads, vegetarian dishes and sandwiches. The dining room is open year round.

Glenville

Glenora Inn & Distiller Resort
$$$
☎*258-2662*
Along the road near Mabou is one of the best-known establishments on Cape Breton Island, the Glenora Inn, which is both an inn and a distillery that makes pure malt whiskey. Here you can enjoy seafood chowder, trout, salmon or lamb, while listening to Celtic music in the dining room.

Nova Scotia

Entertainment

Mabou

Red Shoe Pub
Mabou
The Red Shoe Pub is a friendly place to go in the evening to hear performances by local musicians, some of whom are internationally renowned.

Shopping

Baddeck

In the centre of town, visitors will find the **Village Shops**, which include an attractive craft shop with articles by local artisans.

Cabot Trail

Visitors will find a number of stores selling local and Aboriginal crafts along the Cabot Trail. Quilts, wooden sculptures and pottery are among the products available.

Prince Edward Island

T hink Prince Edward Island and many people envision a rare harmony of rural and maritime landscapes, the epitome of a smooth serene life.

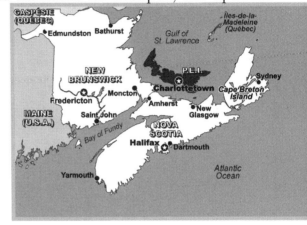

S et back from the peaceful roads and tucked away behind rolling valleys of farmland lie picturesque little fishing villages, adorable white clapboard churches, and the pulsing glow of a lighthouse towering over the sea from isolated rocky outcrops. Most striking in these charming scenes is the brilliant palette of colours: the vibrant yellow and green of the fields falling over the cliffs of deep rust red into the lapis blue of the sea.

B athed to the north by the Gulf of St. Lawrence and to the south by the Strait of Northumberland, this island is above all known for its magnificent white sand dunes and beaches, often deserted and extending between sea and land as far as the eye can

see. It goes without saying that these ribbons of sand are among the most beautiful on the east coast of the continent. They offer great spots for swimming, long walks and discoveries. The beaches may be what initially attracts most visitors, but they quickly discover the

many other treasures Prince Edward Island (P.E.I.) has to offer. For starters, the small capital city of Charlottetown, whose architecture and unique atmosphere give it an antique charm; from there the possibilities are virtually endless, the friendliest fresh lobster feasts you can imagine, the storybook world *Anne of Green Gables*, the kindness of the inhabitants, and the richness of the magnificent plants and wildlife of Prince Edward Island National Park.

Prince Edward Island is about 255km long, making it the smallest Canadian province. It was originally christened Île Saint-Jean by the explorer Jacques Cartier, who sailed along its shores in 1534. Acadians began colonizing these Micmac grounds in 1720, continuing until 1758 when the island fell into British hands, who rechristened it in honour of the son of King George III.

As in other Atlantic provinces, the shipbuilding years were a veritable golden age that ended in the second half of the 19th century. At the same time, negotiations began between the North American British colonies about the possibility of creating a confederation. It was in Charlottetown in 1864 that delegates from each of these colonies finally met, and three years later that the Dominion of Canada was born as a result of this conference. Today, islanders

are proud to remind you that their province was literally the birthplace of Canadian Confederation.

Finding Your Way Around

Prince Edward Island is divided into Four tours:
Tour A: Charlottetown ★★,
Tour B: Central P.E.I. ★★,
Tour C: Eastern P.E.I. ★ and
Tour D: Western P.E.I. ★.

By Car

Prince Edward Island has a good road network. Due to the lack of adequate public transit, the best way to tour the island is either by bike or by car.

The island is accessible from Cape Tormentine, New Brunswick, via the 13km-long **Confederation Bridge** (*$35.50/car, round-trip;* ☎437-7033 or 888-437-6565, *www.confederationbridge .com*), which spans Northumberland Strait. For islanders, the bridge's inauguration in 1997 marked a veritable revolution: crossing the strait now takes 10min by car compared to a half hour by ferry. You can pay the toll with cash, credit card or debit card.

By Plane

Visitors flying to the island arrive at Sherwood airport, about 4km north of downtown Charlottetown (☎566-7992). Air Canada (☎894-8825 or 892-1007), and its partner Air Nova, as well as Canadian Airlines (☎892-5358) and its partner Air Atlantic, are the major airline companies serving this airport. Four car-rental agencies have offices in the airport such as Budget (☎566-5525).

By Ferry

From May to December, you can reach P.E.I. by taking the **Northumberland Ferries**, which link Caribou (Nova Scotia) to the Wood Islands (*May to Nov, no reservation; car $47, passenger $10.75;* ☎888-249-7245). The trip takes 75min.

P.E.I. is also accessible by ferry from the Îles-de-la-Madeleine (Québec) aboard the **Lucy Maud Montgomery** (*car $64.25, adults $33.75; one ferry/day, reserve if possible;* ☎418-986-3278), which arrives in Souris, near the northeastern point of the island.

By Bus

Prince Edward Island has limited bus service. However, there is a bus to Cavendish from the big hotel chains in

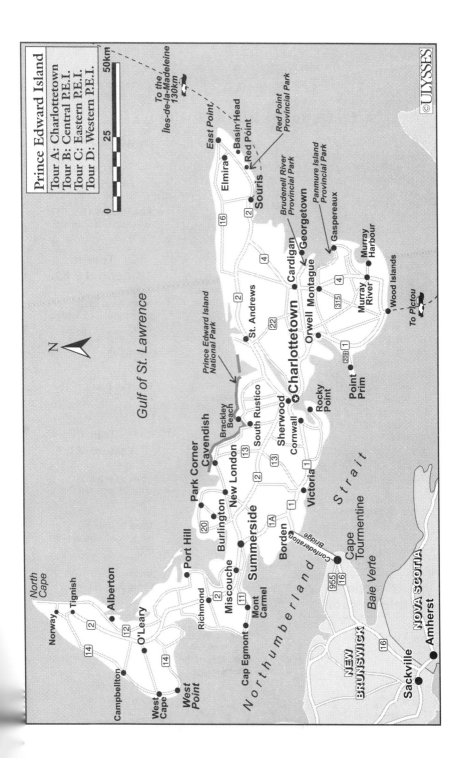

Prince Edward Island

Tour A: Charlottetown
Tour B: Central P.E.I.
Tour C: Eastern P.E.I.
Tour D: Western P.E.I.

© ULYSSES

0   25   50km

N

Gulf of St. Lawrence

To the
Îles-de-la-Madeleine
130km

East Point

Basin Head
Red Point
Red Point
Provincial Park

Elmira

Souris

16
2

Brudenell River
Provincial Park

Cardigan

Georgetown

Panmure Island
Provincial Park

Gaspereaux

4

Murray
Harbour

St. Andrews

2

4

Orwell Montague

22

Charlottetown

315

Murray
River

Wood Islands

To Pictou

1
289

Prince Edward Island
National Park

Sherwood

Cornwall

Rocky
Point

Point
Prim

Brackley Beach

South Rustico

13

Cavendish

New London

13

1

Park Corner

2

Victoria

Burlington

20

Port Hill

Summerside

Borden

1A

1

Confederation
Bridge

Strait

Cape
Tourmentine

955
16

Baie Verte

Miscouche
2

Richmond

11

Mont
Carmel

Cap Egmont

Alberton

Tignish

12

O'Leary

North
Cape

Norway

14

Campbellton

West
Cape

West
Point

14

Northumberland

NEW
BRUNSWICK

16

Sackville

NOVA SCOTIA

Amherst

A Bridge to the Island

It was discussed for years, but following an election promise of the current federal government, that old dream of a bridge linking Prince Edward Island to the mainland finally came true in 1997. The Confederation Bridge between Cape Tourmentine (N.B.) and Borden (P.E.I.) spans no less than 12.7km across the Strait of Northumberland. This bold project demanded the latest technology and the hiring of 1,000 local workers. The building of a bridge, however, did not please everyone on the island.

Throughout the construction, a good many islanders took action to condemn a project they believed would lead to the end of their unique way of life. A few years after the end of the project, however, the controversy died down quite a bit. The bridge allows for easier access to the Island and its bucolic character has remained intact; Prince Edward Island remains the most peaceful of the Canadian provinces. (www.confederationbridge.com)

downtown Charlottetown (*departure 9am, return 6pm*).

Practical Information

Area Code: **902**

Tourist Information

Provincial Tourist Information Office

The island's main provincial tourist information office is in Borden-Carleton, right at the foot of the Confederation Bridge, ☎*800-463-4734* or *629-2428*, ⇥*629-2428*,*www.peiplay.com*

For information on the province's parks: *www.gov.pe.ca*

A hotel reservation service is also available: ☎*888-268-6667*

Tour A: Charlottetown

Charlottetown
at the corner of Water and Prince Sts.

Tour B: Central P.E.I.

Borden-Carleton
at the foot of Confederation Bridge

Cavendish
on Rte. 6

Brackley Beach
on Rte. 15

Tour C: Eastern P.E.I.

Poole's Corner
at the intersection of Rtes. 3 and 4

Wood Islands
on the road that leads to the ferry

Souris
on Rte. 2

Confederation Bridge

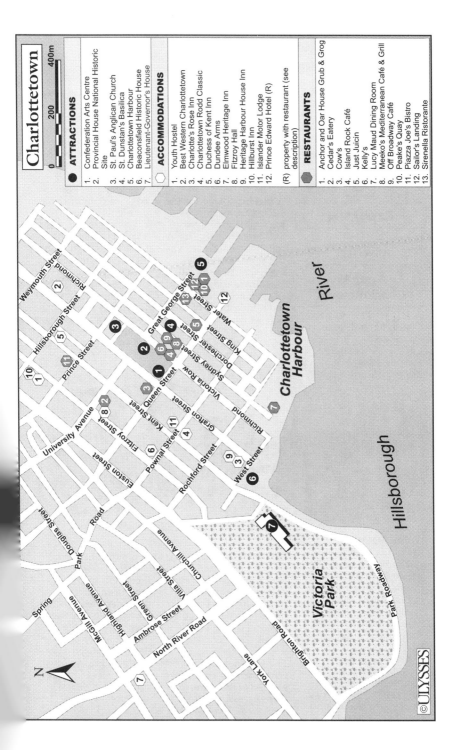

Charlottetown

0 200 400m

● **ATTRACTIONS**

1. Confederation Arts Centre
2. Provincial House National Historic Site
3. St. Paul's Anglican Church
4. St. Dunstan's Basilica
5. Charlottetown Harbour
6. Beaconsfield Historic House
7. Lieutenant-Governor's House

⬡ **ACCOMMODATIONS**

1. Youth Hostel
2. Best Western Charlottetown
3. Charlotte's Rose Inn
4. Charlottetown Rodd Classic
5. Duchess of Kent Inn
6. Dundee Arms
7. Elmwood Heritage Inn
8. Fitzroy Hall
9. Heritage Harbour House Inn
10. Hillburst Inn
11. Islander Motor Lodge
12. Prince Edward Hotel (R)

(R) property with restaurant (see description)

◆ **RESTAURANTS**

1. Anchor and Oar House Grub & Grog
2. Cedar's Eatery
3. Cow's
4. Island Rock Café
5. Just Juicin
6. Kelly's
7. Lucy Maud Dining Room
8. Meeko's Mediterranean Café & Grill
9. Off Broadway Café
10. Peake's Quay
11. Piazza Joe's Bistro
12. Sailor's Landing
13. Sirenella Ristorante

© ULYSSES

Tour D:
Western P.E.I.

Summerside
on Rte. 1A

Portage
on Rte. 2

Exploring

Tour A:
Charlottetown

Charming and quaint, Charlottetown has a unique atmosphere. Despite its size, it is more than just a small, typical Maritime town it is a provincial capital with all the prestige, elegance and institutions one would expect for its status. Though everything here seems decidedly scaled down, the capital of Prince Edward Island has its parliament buildings and sumptuous lieutenant-governor's residence, a large performance and visual-arts complex, pretty parks and rows of trees concealing beautiful Victorian residences, a prestigious hotel and several fine restaurants. Adding to its charm is its picturesque location on the shores of a bay at the confluence of the Hillsborough, North and West Rivers.

A meeting place for the Micmac, the site was known to explorers and French colonists in the 18th century. It was not until 1768, however, that British settlers actually founded the city, named Charlottetown in honour of the wife of King George III of Great Britain. Less than a century later, Charlottetown made its way into history books as the cradle of Canadian Confederation. It was in this little town, in 1864, that the delegates of the North American British colonies met to discuss the creation of the Dominion of Canada.

The **Confederation Arts Centre** ★ ★ *(free admission; Jul to Aug, 9am to 9pm; Sep to Jun, Mon to Sat 9am to 5pm, Sun 2pm to 5pm; 145 Richmond St., ☎628-1864 or 800-565-0278, ⇌566-4648, www.confederationcentre .com)* was constructed in 1964, one century after the decisive meeting of the Fathers of Confederation in Charlottetown. The complex was designed to increase public knowledge of current Canadian culture and its evolution over the last 135 years. The Arts Centre has many facets, including a museum with several impressive exhibits, an art gallery and a public library. There are also several beautiful auditoriums where visitors, during the summer, can take

Confederation Arts Centre

in a performance of *Anne of Green Gables*. Presented every summer for more than three decades now, this musical is a fun way to spend an evening in Charlottetown and become immersed in the world of Prince Edward Island's most famous author, Lucy Maud Montgomery.

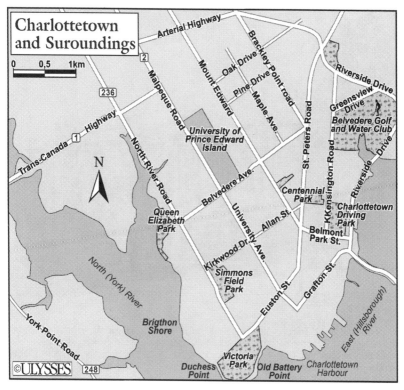

The **Province House National Historic Site ★★** *(free admission; Jul and Aug, 9am to 6pm; Sep to Jun, Mon to Fri 9am to 5pm; corner of University Ave. and Grafton St., beside the Confederation Art Centre, ☎566-7626)* can honestly be considered the cradle of Canadian Confederation. It was here that the 23 delegates from United Canada (present-day Ontario and Québec), Nova Scotia, New Brunswick and Prince Edward Island assembled in 1864 to prepare the Confederation of 1867. Ironically, the host of this decisive conference, Prince Ed-

ward Island, did not join the Dominion of Canada until a few years later, in 1873. Visitors can see the rooms where the Canadian Confederation was worked out and watch a short film explaining the significance of the event. Province House is now the seat of the Legislative Assembly of Prince Edward Island.

St. Paul's Anglican Church ★ *(free admission; corner of Grafton and Prince Sts.)* was erected in 1896 to replace several Anglican churches built in the previous century. Its interior is splendid,

especially the wooden vault and stained-glass windows.

St. Dunstan's Basilica ★ *(free admission donations accepted; corner of Great George and Sydney Sts.)*, a beautiful example of the Gothic style, is the most impressive religious building on Prince Edward Island. Its construction began in 1914, on the same site occupied successively by three Catholic churches during the previous century.

Pretty Great George Street, where you can browse through many

Province House National Historic Site

shops and second-hand stores, ends up at the small **port of Charlottetown**, a pleasant area where visitors will not only find a park and marina but also **Peake's Wharf** ★ *(at the end of Great George St.)*, a collection of shops in charming renovated old buildings. Close by stands the classy **Prince Edward Hotel** (see p 234), as well as a few restaurants.

Beaconsfield Historic House ★ *($2.50; Jul to early Sep, every day 10am to 5pm; Sep to Jun, Tue to Fri and Sun 1pm to 5pm; early Nov to mid-Jun, Tue to Fri and Sun 1pm to 5pm; 2 Kent St., ☎368-6603)* was built in 1877 for wealthy shipbuilder James Peake and his wife Edith Haviland Beaconsfield.

It is one of the most luxurious residences in the province, with 25 rooms and nine fireplaces. After James Peake declared personal bankruptcy in 1882, his creditors, the Cunall family, moved in. The family had no descendants, so Beaconsfield House served as a training school from 1916 on, and was converted into a museum in 1973.

On the other side of Kent Street, shielded behind a stately row of trees, stands the splendid **Lieutenant-Governor's residence** *(corner of Kent St. and Pond Rd.)*. It has been the official residence of the British crown's representative on Prince Edward Island since 1835. Magnificent, beautifully designed **Victoria Park** ★, which spreads out before the residence, is a lovely place for a stroll.

Tour B: Central P.E.I.

This section covers the central region of the island, including the regions known as "Anne's Land" and "Charlotte's Shore." It extends from the southern coast along the Strait of Northumberland, east of Charlottetown to the northern shores on the Gulf of St. Lawrence, and from the town of Malpeque to Tracadie. This beautiful farming region is relatively flat along the southern coast, while towards the northern coast it offers pretty landscapes of valleys and rolling farmland leading to splendid steep cliffs and some of the most beautiful fine-sand beaches on the island. A unique ecosystem makes up an important part of this coastline and is protected in Prince Edward Island National Park.

The northern coast is called "Anne's Land" because it was here, in New London, that Lucy Maud Montgomery was born and it was this idyllic corner of the island that inspired *Anne of Green Gables.* Montgomery fans from around the world can make a veritable pilgrimage to the spots that marked the childhood of the island's biggest star. The southern region, called "Charlotte's Shore" because of its biggest attraction, is dotted with little coastal villages, including the adorable town of Victoria.

Take the TransCanada from Charlottetown to Cornwall, then Rte. 19 (follow the sign for the Blue Heron Tour) south to Rocky Point.

★
Rocky Point

Rocky Point is located at the end of a point of land, at the mouth of the West River and facing the Hillsborough River, which was always a strategic point in the defense of Char-

lottetown and the back-country against a possible attack from the sea. Early on this site was of particular interest to the colonial empires who would fight battles to win control of the island.

The French were the first to establish themselves here in the 1720s, by founding Port la Joye, captured in 1758 by the British who then founded Fort Amherst. The fine-tuning of the fort came that same year when the war between France and England began in earnest. The British garrison had the important role of protecting the island from French invasion and controlling maritime traffic in the Northumberland Strait throughout the whole war.

However, as of 1763, with the end of the war, the fort's importance decreased significantly and was abandoned by the British in 1768. The **Port La Joye - Fort Amherst National Historic Site** ★ *($2.25; mid-Jun to early Sep, every day 9am to 5pm; Rte. 19; ☎566-7626)* houses a small interpretive centre presenting an exhibit on the various documents related to the French colony (Port La Joye) and the British presence at the site (Fort Amherst). There is also a short documentary film on the history of the Acadians of Prince Edward Island. Very little remains today of Fort Amherst. There is, however, a lovely view of the surrounding fields and of the city of Charlottetown from the site.

Lucy Maud Montgomery

Lucy Maud Montgomery was born on November 30th, 1874 in New London, P.E.I. But early in her childhood she had to leave New London to live with her grandparents, Alexander and Lucy MacNeill, in Cavendish, who raised her after the death of her mother. Her first novel *Anne of Green Gables*, inspired by her own orphan life, was a huge success as soon as it appeared in 1908, it has since been translated into 16 languages. L.M. Montgomery later published 23 novels up until her death in 1942. Her most famous work remained however the story of Anne, that enchanting little orphan with the red hair and freckled face.

The **Micmac Village** *($3.25; mid-Jun to early Sep, every day 9am to 5pm; Rte. 19, ☎566-7626)* is also worth a stop when visiting Rocky Point. There is a small museum, a gift shop and a reconstruction of a Micmac village, the Aboriginal that inhabited the island before the arrival of European colonists.

The road from Rocky Point to Victoria is calm and there are several great views of the strait along the way. This tranquil country region consists essentially of farms, small peaceful hamlets and provincial parks. Here and there along the road, are the small fruit and vegetable stands of farmers selling produce from their harvest.

Victoria

The beautiful residences lining the streets of this charming and peaceful coastal town attest to the opulence of another era. Founded in 1767, this seaport played a significant role in the local economy up until the end of the 19th century, when bit by bit the development of the railway on Prince Edward Island outmoded it. Fishing trawlers can still be seen, however, bobbing about just beyond the once busy harbour. Today the interest in Victoria lies mostly in its old-fashioned character and in

the friendliness of its residents. Country life on the island is best represented here. There are two inns, a few restaurants, and a famous chocolatier...

When arriving from the east you'll first come to **Victoria Provincial Park** (see p 221), which extends to the water and including a small beach and a picnic area. The **Victoria Seaport Museum** *(free admission; Jul to early Sep, Tue to Sun 10am to 5pm; Rte. 116; ☎658-2602)* is located close by in a lighthouse. Besides the several photographs of Victoria on display, you can also climb to the top of the lighthouse for a view of the village, the coast and the surroundings.

Just a few streets make up the centre of Victoria. There are several shops, restaurants, as well as **The Victorian Playhouse** *(☎658-2025),* which presents, top-notch concerts and theatre all summer long, adding to the charm of town.

Borden

This town has little to offer visitors. It is, however, one of the most visited spots on the island, since this is the starting point of Confederation Bridge, which links Prince Edward Island to New Brunswick (see p 49). There are several businesses and restaurants,

as well as a good tourist information centre.

You can also visit an **interpretation centre ★**, that has an interesting exhibit on the population, culture and history of the island. It is an excellent introduction to the life of the islanders.

If you are not be continuing west to Summerside (see Tour D: Western P.E.I.) from Victoria or Borden, we suggest taking the secondary road, Rte. 231, which joins with Rte. 2 to reach Kensington.

Kensington

Kensington is one of the larger communities on this part of the island. Situated at the junction of Routes 2 and 20, it is the entrance to "Anne Country." Information on the town and its surroundings is available at the tourist information office in the **train station** *($5; late Jun to early Sep; Rte. 20, ☎836-3031),* which happens to be one of the prettiest on the island. The main attraction in Kensington is the **Towers & Water Gardens** *($5; late Jun to early Sep; Summerside Rd., ☎836-3336),* which consists of a series of miniature reconstructions of famous buildings, all of them set in gardens.

Burlington

One of the most popular attractions as far as

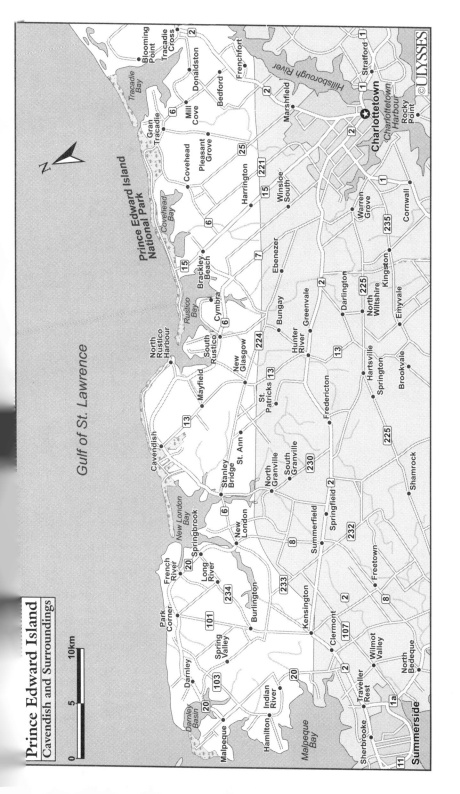

Prince Edward Island
Cavendish and Surroundings

Gulf of St. Lawrence

Prince Edward Island National Park

Tracadie Bay

Blooming Point
Tracadie Cross
Donaldston
Bedford
Frenchfort
Marshfield
Charlottetown
Charlottetown Harbour
Rocky Point
Stratford

Hillsborough River

Gran Tracadie
Mill Cove
Covehead
Pleasant Grove
Harrington
Winsloe South
Warren Grove
Cornwall

Covehead Bay
Brackley Beach
Cymbria
Rustico Bay
South Rustico
North Rustico Harbour
Mayfield
New Glasgow
St. Patricks
Ebenezer
Bungay
Greenvale
Hunter River
Darlington
North Wiltshire
Kingston
Emyvale
Springton
Hartsville
Brookvale

Cavendish
Stanley Bridge
St. Ann
North Granville
South Granville
Fredericton
Shamrock

New London Bay
New London
Springbrook
Summerfield
Springfield
Freetown

French River
Long River
Burlington
Kensington
Clermont
Wilmot Valley
North Bedeque

Park Corner
Spring Valley
Traveller Rest

Darnley
Indian River
Sherbrooke
Summerside

Darnley Basin
Hamilton
Malpeque
Malpeque Bay

N

0   5   10km

Cavendish:
The ideal family destination

The Cavendish region is the ideal family-vacation spot. First of all, Prince Edward Island National Park is located here and has sandy beaches that make a great natural playground. Also nearby, are all the tourist attractions related to the children's novel *Anne of Green Gables* as well as a whole array of activities to enliven a vacation with children.

There are amusement parks like the **Burling-** ton Amusement Park & Go-Karts *(Rte. 234, Burlington, ☎836-3098)*, the **Rainbow Valley Family Fun Park** *(Cavendish, ☎963-2221)* or the **Brackley Beach Drive-in Theatre and Fun Park** *(Rte 15, Brackley Beach, ☎672-3333)*, theme museums like the **Ripley's Believe It or Not Museum** *(Rte. 6, Cranberry Village, Cavendish, ☎963-2242)* and the **Royal Atlantic Wax Museum** *(at the intersection of Rtes 6 and 13, Cavendish, ☎963-* 2350*)*, various worthwhile attractions such as the **Woodleigh Replicas & Gardens** *(Rte 234, Burlington, ☎836-3401)* and the **Kensington Towers & Water Gardens** *(Rte 2, Kensington, ☎836-3336)*, drive-ins, minigolf, a heap of family restaurants and the list goes on. With all its attractions, more and more families are choosing the Cavendish region as a destination for summer holidays.

children are concerned, **Woodleigh** *($6.80; Jun, Sep and Oct, every day 9am to 5pm. Jul to Aug, every day 9am to 7pm; Rte. 234; ☎836-3401)* is the brain-child of Col. Ernest Johnstone, who constructed replicas of famous buildings and monuments on his property after his return from the First World War up until his death 50 years later.

The site opened in 1958 and now has more than 15 wooden and stone buildings, several of which can be visited, and a variety of other monuments dispersed across the pretty wooded property. The most impressive building is probably the replica of the Tower of London. Celtic music shows are organized, usually on Sundays.

Indian River

Indian River was a Micmac meeting place up until 1935, hence the apparent origin of the town's name. Today, Indian River is no longer a town nor even village, but it is still the site of impressive **St. Mary's Roman Catholic Church** ★ *(Rte. 104)*. Built between 1900 and 1902, St. Mary's is the most famous work of island architect William C. Harris and the largest wooden church on Prince Edward Island, with a seating capacity of up to 600 people. Its neo-Gothic altar and elegant belltower are particularly remarkable.

Malpeque

Malpeque, which means "large bay" in Micmac, is a pretty little community bordered by expanses of water. The town is world-famous thanks to the celebrated oysters that are gathered from the bay. The best place from which to admire the bay is **Cabot Beach**

Provincial Park, whose wild beaches are almost completely deserted.

Park Corner

Park Corner was granted to James Townshend in 1755 as compensation for his service in the British army, and was put on the map by one of his direct descendants, Lucy Maud Montgomery.

Anne of Green Gables Museum at Silver Bush ★

($2.50; Jun and Sep to Oct, every day 9am to 6pm; Jul and Aug, 9am to 7pm; ☎886-2807) was actually a favourite house of Lucy Maud Montgomery. It belonged to her aunt and uncle, Annie and John Campbell. She adored it and was married here in July, 1911. Today it is a historic house, decorated with period furniture and many of the author's and her family's personal effects.

New London

The small community of New London has the distinguished honour of being the birthplace of the writer who has made Prince Edward Island famous internationally. The main attraction is the house where she was born, the **Lucy Maud Montgomery Birthplace** *($2; late May and Jun, Sep to mid-Oct, every day 9am to 5pm; Jul and Aug, 9am to 7pm; intersection of Rtes. 6 and 8, ☎886-2099 or 436-7329).* Personal objects, including L.M. Montgomery's wedding dress, can be viewed in this simple house.

★
Cavendish

The Cavendish area is a sacred spot for tourists to P.E.I. Located next to some of the most beautiful beaches on the island, and several big tourist attractions, Cavendish has many lodging possibilities, restaurants and shops. It is for many a gateway to the national park, and therefore has an excellent tourist information centre.

Green Gables House ★

($6.00; mid-May to late Jun, 9am to 5pm; late Jun to late Aug, 9am to 8pm; late Aug to late Oct, 9am to 5pm; Rte. 6, west of Cavendish, ☎672-6350, ≈672-6370) is the house that Lucy Maud Montgomery used as the main setting for her famous novel *Anne of Green Gables.*

Green Gables House

Built towards the middle of the last century, the house belonged to David and Margaret MacNeil, older cousins of the author's. L.M. Montgomery used to love strolling down "lover's lane," located in the woods on her cousins' property. She was so inspired by the surroundings that it became the backdrop for her novel. In 1936, the site was included in the establishment of Prince Edward Island National Park.

A visit to the island would not be complete without at least a one-day trip to **Prince Edward Island National Park ★★★** *(three welcome centres: in Cavendish, near the intersection of Rtes. 6 and 13, ☎963-2391; opposite the Dalvay-by-the-Sea Hotel, ☎672-6350; Brackley, at the intersection of Rtes. 6 and 15, ☎672-2259),* which stretches for kilometres along the northern coast of the

Prince Edward Island

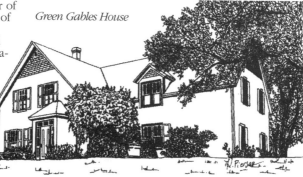

The Piping Plover

In all of Prince Edward Island National Park, there are just 25 pairs of these little birds, which measure about 19 centimetres and have sandy beige plumage, with a few black feathers on the head and neck.

The piping plover feeds on insects and tiny crustaceans, and may often be seen combing the beach in search of nourishment. It also builds its nest in the sand, a little bit above the waterline at high-tide.

During the 28-day incubation period of their eggs and until the baby birds set off on their own at the end of July, the parents watch over the nest, which is well-hidden in the sand, safe from predators.

Unfortunately, the nests are also well-hidden from people strolling along the beach, who can inadvertently cause irreparable damage to them. The number of piping plovers has diminished greatly over the past ten years, and if the population is to grow, the nests must be protected from any disturbance. While walking along the beach, therefore, it is crucial that visitors pay careful attention to all signs.

Peninsula, which extends to the east of St. Peters Bay (see p 226).

There are trails leading right into the heart of the park. On the Reeds and Rushes trail, visitors can observe the animal life in a pond from a floating footbridge. Other species of plant and animal life may be discovered on one of the four other marked trails, which are suitable for all ages and crisscross the park.

The beaches here are also terrific for families. Be careful around the neighbouring sand dunes, however, since the piping plover, a small, endangered species of bird, sometimes nests there. Footbridges have been laid out in order to protect this fragile environment; please respect the signs.

There are four **campsites** in Prince Edward Island National Park. The first, on Robinson Island (formerly know as Rustico Island), offers visitors a particulary peaceful environment, while the Cavendish campground, located near the ocean, provides a wide variety of services to its users. More campsite can also be found at the Stanhope campground. For more information or to make reservation call **800-213-7874**. The fourth site, Brackeley Group tenting is for groups only.

Island, from Blooming Point to New London Bay. The park was created in 1937 with the goal of preserving a unique natural environment, including sand dunes (with their fragile ecosystem), red sandstone cliffs, magnificent beaches and salt-water marshes.

While exploring the park, visitors will be constantly delighted by stunning views of the sheer coastline, the sudden appearance of a red fox or one of the many activities that may be enjoyed here. In February 1998, the park was expanded and now includes the Greenwich

Piping Plover

The road between Charlottetown and Victoria passes through two attractive parks, **Victoria Provincial Park** and **Argyle Shore Provincial Park**, both of which are pleasant places to relax. Visitors can stop at either one to enjoy a picnic, sit and gaze at the sea or take a swim. **Strathgartney Provincial Park** lies alongside the West River. It is an excellent spot for camping, with sites available for both tents and trailers.

★
New Glasgow

From Cavendish, the route travels through beautiful landscapes of rolling hills to New Glasgow, a picturesque little village whose handsome houses rise from either bank of the Hunter River. New Glasgow is appealing simply for its rural charm, but its pleasant restaurants, especially the **P.E.I. Preserve Co.** *(Rte.13, at the intersection of Rtes. 234 and 258, ☎964-2524)*, which houses a shop that sells various home-made provisions and an excellent dining room, are equally attractive.

★
North Rustico

North Rustico, a charming village where the main activities are fishing and, more specifically, lobster-trapping, overlooks both Rustico Bay and the Gulf of St.

Lawrence. One of the national park's beautiful sandy **beaches ★★** is directly accessible from this village. Nearby, North Rustico Harbour is an equally enticing destination that offers beautiful maritime scenery.

★
South Rustico

Once a large Micmac settlement known as Tabooetooetun, the region of Rustico Bay was one of the first parts of the island to be colonized by the French and a good number of the descendants of these early inhabitants still reside in the South Rustico region. The name Rustico derives from the gradual transformation of the name of the first French man to settle in the area, René Rassicot. **Café St-Jean** (see p 244), in Oyster Bed Bridge, is a hub of the lively culture of local Acadians.

South Rustico itself is actually a crossroads in the middle of the countryside around which stand the main institutions of the Acadian community: the church, the presbytery, the cemetery, the school and the **Farmer's Bank of Rustico ★** *($1; Jul to Aug, Tue to Sun 10am to 4pm; Rte. 243, ☎963-2304)*. This farmer's bank was founded in 1864 by Father George-Antoine Belcourt, to give Acadians the opportunity to participate in the

economy. It was the first people's bank in the country, and for a certain time, the smallest chartered bank in Canada. It is now a museum and the exhibit tells of Father Belcourt's work and the historic location. Right next door, the modest **Saint Augustine Church** *(Church St.)* is the oldest Acadian church on the island.

Brackley Beach

This small hamlet on the shores of Rustico Bay is worth a visit to see the **Baywatch Lighthouse** *($1.50. early Jun to mid-Sep, 10am to 10pm; at the intersection of Rtes. 15 and 16, ☎672-3478)* and its exhibit of photographs of island lighthouses. Another recommended stop close by is **The Dunes Art Gallery** *(free admission; May, 10am to 6pm; Jun to Sep, 9am to 10pm; Oct, 10am to 6pm; Rte. 15, ☎672-2586)* where the works of the biggest artists of the island are on display. There is also a charming little restaurant. With Prince Edward Island National Park right nearby, Brackley Beach provides plenty of accommodations.

Tour C: Eastern P.E.I.

Extending to the east of Charlottetown is a lovely rural region that will delight visitors

The Acadian Presence

Although Acadians didn't settle in the Evangeline region until 1812, their presence on Prince Edward Island dates back to the 1720s, when the island was a French colony named Île-Saint-Jean.

These first colonists, who came from the area then known as Acadia (present-day Nova Scotia), founded the settlements of Port-la-Joye, Pointe-Prime and Malpèque, among others. In the following decades, the Acadian population gradually increased, then began growing rapidly in 1755, due to the arrival of refugees fleeing deportation from Nova Scotia (the former Acadia). In 1758, however, Île-Saint-Jean also fell into the hands of the British, who deported about 3,000 of the 5,000 Acadians living on the island.

After the war, the remaining Acadians, along with those who returned to the island, lived mainly in the area around Malpèque Bay. It wasn't until 1812 that some families left this region to settle in the southwest, founding La Roche (Baie-Egmont) and Grand-Ruisseau (Mont-Carmel).

seeking the tranquillity of deserted beaches, the busy atmosphere of small fishing villages and the beauty of enchanting bays that appear around every bend in the road. Somewhat hilly to the north, this region presents a varied landscape that may not always be spectacular, but is often pretty and harmonious.

None of the communities in this part of the island have more than a few hundred inhabitants, and life here revolves mainly around fishing and agriculture. A tour of eastern Prince Edward Island thus offers visitors an opportunity to discover a lovely part of the province while experiencing a way of life that remains directly dependent on nature.

Orwell Corner

A visit to the **Orwell Corner Historic Village** ★ *($3; late Jun to early Sep, every day 9am to 5pm; Trans-Canada Hwy. 30km east of Charlottetown; ☎651-8510)* is a must for anyone interested in discovering what life was like in rural Prince Edward Island back in the 19th century. This delightful village is made up of restored buildings, including a pretty little school that looks as if it came straight out of an L.M. Montgomery novel, a church, a shingle factory, several barns, a forge and a farmhouse that doubles as a general store and a post office.

The atmosphere is enlivened by characters in period dress, who are available to answer visitors' questions. Orwell Corner may be smaller than other similar historic villages, such as Kings Landing in New Brunswick, but its size gives it a charming authenticity.

A few hundred metres from Orwell Corner, tucked away in an enchanting setting, lies the **Sir Andrew Macphail Homestead** *(free admission, suggested donation; late Jun to early Sep, every day,10am to 5pm; Jul and Aug, every day, 10am to 9pm; 30km east of Charlottetown, Rte.1, ☎651-2789)*.

A native of Prince Edward Island, Andrew Macphail (1864-1938) had an extraordinary career in the fields of research and medicine, as well as in writing and journalis.m His house, furnished as it was at the beginning of the century, is a lovely part of the local heritage. There is a small dining room where light meals are served. Visitors can also explore the vast grounds by taking a pleasant walk along a 2km trail.

Point Prim

Not far from the village of Eldon, Route 1 intersects with Route 209, a small road leading to the **Point Prim Lighthouse** *(free admission; Jul and Aug, 9am to 7pm; Rte. 209,* ☎*659-2412)*, designed and built in 1845 by Isaac Smith, architect of Charlottetown's Province House. The lighthouse is open to the public, and the surrounding area is perfect for a picnic. The **view** ★ of the sea is worth the short detour.

Wood Islands

Wood Islands, the departure point for the ferry to Pictou, Nova Scotia (see p 150), has a tourist information centre. The village's setting is very pretty and offers a beautiful **view** ★ of Northumberland Strait. Very close by there are beautiful **beaches** that are ideal for swimming and often deserted. It is also possible to swim at the **beach at Wood Islands Provincial Park**, a few kilometres further east. Keep in mind that although the beaches along the shore of Northumberland

Strait are often less spectacular than those on the Gulf of St. Lawrence, the water here is significantly warmer. The park's vegetation is mainly composed of leafy trees.

Little Sands

At Little Sands, on a small plateau overlooking the waters of Northumberland Strait, the vineyards of the **Rossignol Estate Winery** ★ (☎*962-4193)*, the only vineyard of the island, suddenly appear before your eyes. The Rossignol family produces five table wines, a cider and a few fruit liqueurs here, all of which may be savoured on the spot, and they happily provide explanations of the processes by which the fruit is cultivated and pressed and how their wines are stored. The winery shop also displays lovely crafts, as well as the canvases of Little Sands artist Nancy Perkins.

Murray Harbour

Murray Harbour, which rises on the banks of the Murray River, is home to a few pretty, period houses and a charming little

harbour. Antique lovers should stop at the **Log Cabin Museum** *($2.50; early Sep, 9am to 6pm; Rte.18A;* ☎*962-2201)*, which displays a curious collection of original objects.

Murray River

Murray River is a vibrant little community that has a few restaurants and some attractive local craft shops including **The Old General Store**. Near Murray River is the beach at King Castle Provincial Park, is a pleasant recreation area that also has a small playground. From Murray River, excursions are organized by **Captain Garry's Seal & Bird Watching Cruises** (see p 232).

★
Panmure Island

A turnoff from **Gaspereaux**, a picturesque lobster-trapping village, leads to Panmure Island. **Panmure Island Provincial Park** ★, located along the road to the island, encloses

some of the most splendid sand **beaches** ★ on Prince Edward Island. Stretching on for kilometres, these dune-bordered beaches are often practically deserted. From the lighthouse on Panmure Island there is a gorgeous panoramic view.

★
Montague

Montague might not be very big, but it is nevertheless one of the largest communities on the eastern part of the province. It is home to several businesses, shops and restaurants, as well as the interesting **Garden of the Gulf Museum** ★ *($3; Jun to late Sep, Mon to Sat 9am to 5pm; 2 Main St. S.,* ☎*838-2467)*, set up inside the former post office. The exhibit deals with both local and military history. Montague is also the point of departure for excursions organized by **Cruise Manada Seal Watching Boat Tours** (see p 232). Other excursions start at the Brudenell Marina.

Georgetown

The small fishing port of Georgetown witnessed the golden age of wooden ship-building. In that era, Georgetown's natural port, which, in addition to being well protected, is the deepest on the island, was a distinct advantage. Today, numerous boutiques and cafes can be found close to the port, making it a particularily pleasant area.

Right before Georgetown, stretching along the banks of the river for which it was named, is the superb **Brudenell River Provincial Park**. This park offers a stunning view of the water, a beach, a beautiful golf course, an interesting hiking-trail that runs along the

The Golden Era of Railway

The history of the railway is closely linked to that of Prince Edward Island and its accession to Canadian Confederation. In the 1860s and 1870s, the island's inhabitants began demanding a railway, which in those years was the most efficient means of communication and transport throughout North America, as well as a virtual guarantee of economic growth.

In August of 1871, the island's government passed the Railroad Act, and construction of the railway began two months later. By the following year, however, construction costs had led to an unprecedented crisis in the island's public finances. On the verge of bankruptcy, the government had no other option but to transfer its debt to the Canadian government and join Canadian Confederation in July 1873.

Two years later, the island's railway began operating. Its main track linked Alberton, in the west, to Georgetown, in the east, and later to Elmira. Another line linked Tignish, in the west, to Souris, in the east. For nearly a century, the railway was the backbone of the island's development.

Starting in the 1960s, however, the emergence of new and more efficient means of transportation forced Canadian National to cut back its services all over the country, including on Prince Edward Island. In 1989, the island's last line was closed, bringing the golden era of the railway to an end.

river all the way to Georgetown, a good hotel and a number of camping sites.

Cardigan

A small community looking out onto the bay of the same name, Cardigan was a ship-building centre in the 19th century. It is now home to several interesting craft shops.

Souris

The little town of Souris, with its 1,600 or so inhabitants, is the largest community on the eastern part of Prince Edward Island. Accordingly, it offers a wide range of services, several restaurants and hotels and a tourist information centre. Not far away lies **Souris Beach Provincial Park**, with a picnic area and an unsupervised beach. The town's Main Street is graced with several pretty buildings that bear witness to Souris' prominent role in this region. The most striking of these are the **Town Hall** and **St. Mary's Church**. The town port is the boarding point for the ferry (see p 208) to Québec's Îles-de-la-Madeleine, situated in the heart of the Gulf of St. Lawrence.

Red Point

Red Point Provincial Park ★ was created to protect the island's magnificent red sandstone cliffs, and some

of the views here are picture-perfect. Visitors will also be charmed by the **beach** ★, a long strip of fine sand along the Northumberland Strait. The park has lovely picnic areas, too, and campers are welcome at the excellent campground.

★
Basin Head

Ideally located on one of the island's loveliest **sandy beaches** ★★, not far from some magnificent dunes, the **Basin Head Fisheries Museum** ★★ *($3; mid-Jun and late Sep, Mon to Fri, 10am to 5pm; Jul and Aug, 10am to 7pm; Rte.16, ☎357-7233)* offers visitors an opportunity to learn about all different facets of the wonderful world of fishing around Prince Edward Island.

The museum exhibits an interesting collection of artifacts related to the lives and occupation of the fishermen of old. The building itself is flanked by sheds, in which vessels of various sizes and periods are displayed, as well as a workshop where local artisans make wooden boxes like those used in the past for packing salted fish. An old canning factory stands a little farther off. In all respects, this is one of the most interesting museums in the province. To make the most of your visit, however, take a stroll along the neighbouring

beaches and dunes, as well.

East Point

For a magnificent view of the ocean and the area's coastal landscape, head to the **East Point Lighthouse** ★ *(free admission, guided tours $2.50; Jul to mid-Aug; Rte. 16; ☎357-2106)*, which stands on the easternmost tip of the island. During summer, visitors can climb to the top of this old lighthouse, which dates back to 1867.

Elmira

A tiny rural village near the easternmost tip of the island, Elmira is home to one of the six museums of the Prince Edward Island Museum and Heritage Foundation, the **Elmira Railway Museum** ★ *($1.50; mid-Jun to early Sep, every day 10am to 6pm; Rte.16A; ☎357-7234)*. Located in a bucolic setting, it occupies the town's former train station, which has been closed since 1982.

In addition to the main building, there is a warehouse and a railway car is stationed on one of the tracks. This museum's excellent exhibit is a reminder of the glorious sense of adventure that accompanied the construction of Prince Edward Island's railway.

Prince Edward Island

★
St. Peters

St. Peters was the site of the very first French establishment on Prince Edward Island (then known as Île Saint-Jean), when two Norman mariners, Francis Douville and Charles Carpentier, arrived here after their ship ran aground at Naufrage, a little further east. The site was named

series of coastal dunes (dunes and ridges), as well as some marshes, the unique and fragile habitat of a number of plant and animal species (such as the piping plover and the pileated woodpecker). Humans have also left their mark on the peninsula, especially the Micmacs, the French and the English.

St. Andrews

After Elmira, the TransCanada Highway passes through several tiny rural communities. A brief stop in St. Andrews is a must to visit the little

★

Tour D:
Western P.E.I.

The western part of Prince Edward Island is home to the province's second largest town, Summerside, as well as its most isolated area, the northwest. Southwest of Summerside, visitors can explore the Acadian region of Prince Edward Island, the domain of the Arseneault, Gallant and Richard families, among others, who live in a string of tiny coastal villages with colourful names like Baie-Egmont, Saint-Chrysostome, Mont-Carmel, Maximeville, etc.

Here, in the Evangeline region, inhabitants proudly preserve the French language and Acadian culture passed down to them by their ancestors. A tour of the western part of the island offers visitors an opportunity to discover this Acadian legacy, as well as to visit a peaceful, picturesque region whose inhabitants live mainly on fishing and potato-farming. The scenery is pretty and sometimes even spectacular, especially near North Cape.

West Point Lighthouse

Havre Saint-Pierre; it prospered, thanks to fishing, and grew to about 400 colonists by the time of the Acadian deportation in 1755. St. Peters is now a very pretty village whose sumptuous residences stretch along the shores of the bay.

The Greenwich Peninsula, which extends to the east of St. Peters Bay, will be officially added to **Prince Edward Island National Park ★★★** in July 2000. This new part of the park protects a

chapel *(free admission; late Jun to early Sep, 10am to 7pm)*, which has been moved twice. Built in 1803 on its present site, it was transported down the frozen Hillsborough River to Charlottetown in the winter of 1964, where it was used as a girl's school. It was restored in 1988 and moved back to its original site two years later.

★
Summerside

With a population around 10,000, Summerside is Prince Edward Island's second largest town. It is presently experiencing an economic boom, due to the nearby Confederation Bridge to New Brunswick, completed in 1997. It is a pleasant town, graced with lovely Victorian residences and a pretty waterfront. As the chief urban centre on the western part of the island, Summerside also has a number of shops, restaurants and places to stay.

Spinnakers' Landing ★ *(free; Harbour Dr.)* constitutes a good place to start off a visit of Summerside. This pleasant promenade, laid out near the town's port, numbers a few beautiful shops and offers a wonderful view. Harbour cruises leave from Spinnakers' Landing.

Eptek *($2; Jul to early Sep, every day 9:30am to 6:30pm; Sep to Jun, Tue-Fri 10am to 4pm; on the waterfront, Water St., ☎888-8373)* is a national exhibition centre that presents travelling exhibits of Canadian art. The same building houses Prince Edward Island's Sports Hall of Fame.

Through a collection of photographs and other articles, the **International Fox Museum ★** *(free admission, donations accepted; May to Oct, 10am to 6pm; 286 Fitzroy St., ☎436-2400)* traces the history of fox-breeding on Prince

Edward Island. After a timid start at the end of the last century, this activity represented 17% of the province's economy by the 1920s. In those years, a pair of silver foxes could fetch as much as $35,000. Efforts are now being made to revive this once prosperous industry.

By visitting the **Cavendish Figurines factory** *(149B Industrial Crescent)* you can see how *Anne of Green Gables* dolls are manufactured. Or head to the **College of Piping** *(free; 619 Water St. E., ☎436-5377)* for an introduction to traditional Scottish music.

Miscouche

In Miscouche, barely 8km west of Summerside, the **Acadian Museum of Prince Edward Island ★** *($2,75; Jul to Aug, every day 9:30am to 7pm; Sep to Jun, Mon to Fri 9:30am to 5pm, Sun 1pm to 4pm; Rte. 2; ☎432-2880)* offers an excellent introduction to the world of the local Acadians. The museum's exhibit recounts the history of the island's Acadian community, from 1720 to the present day, with the help of artifacts, writings, numerous illustrations and an audiovisual presentation, shown on request, which lasts about 15min. The museum also houses Prince Edward Island's Centre de Recherches Acadiennes, an Acadian Research

Centre that has a library and archives that may be used for genealogical research.

Wellington

From Miscouche, you can go to the small community of Wellington, where the interesting **Ecomusée de la Courtepointe** *(Promenade Acadienne, ☎854-2614)* is located. This ecomuseum is siuated in the Promenade Acadienne, a pretty little shopping complex with arts-and-crafts boutiques, built inside replicas of 19th-century buildings.

Mont-Carmel

Mont-Carmel, known for many years as Grand-Ruisseau, was founded in 1812 by the Arseneault and Gallant families. The splendour of the **Église Notre-Dame-du-Mont-Carmel ★** *(Rte. 11)*, which lies in the heart of the parish, bears eloquent witness

to the prominent role played by Catholicism in Acadian culture.

Located on the site of the very first settlement, Grand-Ruisseau (now known as Mont-Car-mel), the **Acadian Pioneer Village** ★ *($3.50; Jun to mid-Sep, 9am to 7pm; Rte. 11; 1.5km west of the church,* ☎*800-567-3228)* recreates the rustic life-style of early 19th-cen-tury Acadians. The vil-lage includes a church and presbytery, two family homes, a smithy, a school and a barn. Most of the furniture in the buildings was do-nated by citizens of neighbouring villages. There is a comfortable hotel at the entrance of the pioneer village, as well as the restaurant Étoile de Mer, which offers visitors a unique opportunity to enjoy Acadian cuisine.

Cap-Egmont

A pretty fishing village looking out on the Northumberland Strait, Cap-Egmont, often re-ferred to locally as Grand-Cap, lies in the most peaceful setting imaginable. Visitors can stop at the **Bottle Houses** *($3.25; mid-Jun to late Jun,10am to 6pm; early Jul to late Aug, 9am to 8pm; early Sep to mid-Sep, 10am to 6pm; Rte. 11;* ☎*854-2987)*, three buildings made out of a total of 25,000 bottles, set in the midst of a park filled with flowers.

O'Leary

A village typical of this region, which produces large quantities of pota-toes, O'Leary is home to the **Prince Edward Island Potato Museum** ★ *($2.50; early Jun to mid-Oct, Mon to Sat 9am to 5pm, Sun 2pm to 5pm; 22 Parkview Dr.,* ☎*859-2039)*, the only museum in Canada devoted to the history of potato-growing. The well-designed exhibit clearly illustrates this tuber's role in the his-tory of food. Visitors will also learn the vari-ous techniques used to grow potatoes. This is an excellent and in-teresting museum re-gardless of the peculiar nature of its subject matter.

★
West Point

A stop at West Point offers an opportunity to explore one of the most peaceful, pictur-esque spots on the island, **Cedar Dunes Pro-vincial Park** ★ *(Rte. 14)*, which features endless deserted beaches and dunes and constitutes an excellent spot for observing wildlife and vegetation. Another interesting spot nearby is the **West Point Light-house** *($2.50; late Jun to late Aug, 8am to 9:30pm; May to mid-Jun and Sep, 8am to 8pm; Rte. 14;* ☎*859-3606)*, which dates back to 1875 and is one of the largest in the province. In addi-tion to housing a mu-

seum and a restaurant, it is the only lighthouse in Canada that is used as an inn.

★
North Cape

The scenery around North Cape, the north-ernmost tip of the is-land, is not only pretty, but often spectacular, with red sandstone cliffs plunging into the blue waters of the Gulf of St. Lawrence. North Cape itself occupies a lovely site along the coast. Here, visitors will find the **Atlantic Wind Test Site** *($2; Jul and Aug, 10am to 8pm; at the end of Rte. 12;* ☎*882-2746)*, where wind technology is tested and evaluated. A small exhibit explains the advantages of using this type of energy.

Alberton

In 1534, during his first trip along the coast of what would eventually be Canada, Jacques Cartier apparently stopped at the present-day site of Alberton, an attractive little village now adorned with a number of pretty build-ings. Set up inside the former courthouse, built in 1878 and now a historic site, the **Alberton Museum** ★ *($3; late Jun to mid-Sep, every day 10am to 7:30pm, Sun 10am to 5pm; Church St.,* ☎*853-4048)* offers a wonderful introduction to the history of this region. The collection on display includes

such varied objects as furniture, dishes and old farming instruments.

Located at the mouth of Mill River, where it flows into Cascumpec Bay, **Mill River Provincial Park** stretches forth like a huge garden. It also features a superb golf course.

Tyne Valley

The region of Tyne Valley, on the edge of Malpeque Bay, offers some of the most beautiful rural landscapes on the island. Passing through the village itself, the **Tyne Valley Studio** *(Rte. 12)* is a must to visit; splendid wool sweaters in original designs are made right on the premises. A few kilometres north of Tyne Valley, the **Green Park Shipbuilding Museum ★** *($2.50; Jun to early Sep, 9am to 5pm; Rte. 12, Port Hill; ☎831-7947)* reminds visitors that shipbuilding was the mainspring of Prince Edward Island's economy for the greater part of the 19th century.

The museum presents an exhibit on the various techniques used in shipbuilding and the history of the trade. The site includes a reconstructed shipyard, complete with a ship in progress. Right nearby stands the Yeo house, the lovely former home of James Yeo, Jr., who owned a shipyard in the 19th century.

Parks and Beaches

The craggy, breathtakingly beautiful landscapes, endless beaches and unique plant and animal life are among the most spectacular attractions of this red crescent-shaped island, which lies 40km east of continental Canada. A number of parks have been created to highlight the natural beauty of parts of the island.

The most renowned is Prince Edward Island National Park, but there are also 29 provincial parks. More than 40 lovely beaches with sands in countless shades of pink also help make this island a veritable paradise for vacationers.

Parks

The province's parks provide all sorts of services for vacationers (camping sites, picnic areas, supervised beaches) and feature a variety of activities intended to familiarize visitors with various natural settings; nature trails and welcome centres offer information on the local plant and animal life. These parks are an inexhaustible source of discovery for the entire family.

About 15 of the provincial parks have **camping** facilities *(☎652-2356 for reservations in the eastern part of the island, and ☎859-8790 for the western part)*. Visitors can also camp in the national park, but the conditions vary (see p 220).

Beaches

The island is fringed with a series of exquisite white and red sand beaches, especially along the north coast. Magnificent sandy **beaches ★** which are ideal for swimming and undoubtedly among the most beautiful on the Eastern Seaboard, run along the entire shoreline of **Prince Edward Island National Park**. Some have been landscaped and are supervised; they usually have showers, changing

rooms and often little restaurants. Other beaches, just as beautiful but unsupervised, stretch as far as the eye can see. The eastern part of Prince Edward Island boasts equally beautiful sandy beaches.

The splendid **beach** ★ at **Basin Head**, also accessible from **Red Point Provincial Park**, is kilometres long. Another exceptional **beach** ★ is located at **Panmure Island Provincial Park**, in the eastern section of the island. Along Northumberland Strait, where the water is considerably warmer than it is in the Gulf of St. Lawrence, there are also a few lovely beaches: **Wood Islands Provincial Park**, in the southeast, is a very pleasant place to swim.

Outdoor Activities

Hiking

The railway line of yesteryear, which used to crisscross the island, has found a new purpose: it has been filled in with crushed stone and transformed into several hiking and cycling paths. The 247km network of paths is called the **Confederation Trail**. A branch of the trail heads towards the western part of the island, from Kensington to Tignish, with beautiful scenery along the way. It also passes through a number of towns, including Summerside and Wellington.

Another section of the trail criss-crosses the eastern part of the island, from Mount Stewart to Elmira. It runs along St. Peters Bay, offers magnificent views of the dunes on Greenwich Peninsula, and crosses wooded areas and wetlands, where you can observe many different species of birds, such as the Canada goose. The trail also leads to Souris and Borden-Carleton.

The various trails in **Prince Edward Island National Park** allow hikers to learn about the plant and animal life that have developed in this part of the island.

The **Reeds and Rushes Trail** (0.5km) leads through the forest to a marsh spanned by a wooden footbridge, from which hikers can observe a wide variety of insects, plants and animals.

The **Farmlands Trail** (2km) leads into the heart of the park, passing through different types of vegetation, including a spruce forest.

The **Bubbling Springs Trail** (2 km) also passes through a spruce forest, then leads to an observation post on the banks of a pond, where visitors can observe various species of water birds.

There are three other trails to help you discover the forest: **Homestead** (5.5 to 8km), **Haunted Wood** (1.6km) and **Balsam Hollow** (1km).

There are also hiking trails in the provincial parks, particularly **Mill River, Brudenell** and **Strathgartney Parks**.

Bird Watching

Nearly 315 different species of birds may be observed along the shores of the island. From the remarkable great blue heron to the kingfisher, bluejay (the provincial emblem) and rare piping plover, the island has plenty to offer amateur ornithologists. In **Prince Edward Island National Park**, there are observation points at **Brackley Marsh, Orby Head, Covehead Pier** and all along the **Rustico Island floating bridge**. It is not necessary to go to the park to observe many of these birds; they can be spotted in many different parts of the island-just keep your eyes peeled.

Bicycling

The island is a marvellous place to go bicycling, since the traffic is never heavy and there are many quiet roads crisscrossing the fields. In **Prince Edward Island National Park**, cyclists can enjoy magnificent scenery without having to worry about cars.

Cycling enthusiasts will be delighted to learn that they can pedal the entire length of the island, thanks to the **Confederation Trail** (see p 230), which links several bike paths in the eastern and western part of the island.

For information on cycling excursions, contact **Sport PEI** (☎368-4110).

The following places also organize excursions:

Charlottetown

Smooth Cycle
172 Prince St.
☎566-5530
$16/half-day, $24/day

Cycling Prince Edward Island
☎368-4110
This company organizes cycling tours of a variety of destinations in the province.

North Rustico

Outside Expedition
☎963-3366
www.getoutside.com
Outside Expedition offers bike tours that last a few days, allowing you to explore some of the most picturesque regions in the province.

Summerside

Papa Whealies Bike Rentals
$14/half-day

Blue Jay

Souris

Venture Out Cycle & Kayak
☎687-1234
$7/half-day, $10/day

Bike rentals are available all over the island. Here are a few options:

MacQueen's Bike Shop
430 Queen St., Charlottetown
☎800-667-4583
☎368-2453

Sunset Campground Bike Rentals starting
Cavendish
☎963-2440
$10/day

North Shore Windsurfing and Bike Rentals
Brackley Beach
☎672-2022
$18/day

Golf

Prince Edward Island has a lot to offer golfers, since it features several excellent greens, laid out on sites that not only make for a good game but also offer breathtaking views of the sea and the cliffs.

The 18-hole **Green Gables Golf Course** (*$34; Cavendish,* ☎963-2488) is located in **Prince Edward Island National Park**.

In **Mill River Provincial Park** (*$40;* ☎859-8873), there is an 18-hole golf course that stretches 5,944m along the banks of the Mill River.

Built around some dunes, **Links at Crowbush Cove** (*$50,* ☎961-7300) is one of the most beautiful golf courses in the province or perhaps the entire country. It offers a breathtaking view by the sea along its 18-hole course.

The 18-hole golf course in **Brudenell River Provincial Park** (*$30; Roseneath,* ☎*652-8965 or 800-698-4653*) boasts a lovely site as well. Golfers also get to enjoy the vast, peaceful park surrounding the green.

For more information on the island's golf courses consult the brochure: *Golf Prince Edward* or write to:

GOLF PEI
P.O. Box 2653, Charlottetown
C1A 8C3
☎*368-4130*

Boating

Visitors wishing to head out to sea can take part in one of a variety of short cruises offered by these local companies.

Mill River Boat Tour
$15
☎*856-3820*

Cardigan Sailing Tours
$50
☎*583-2020*

Charlottetown Peake's Warf boat cruises
various tours/ 70min $14
☎*566-4458*

Seal-watching

Groups of seals regularly swim near the shores of the island. Visitors interested in observing these large sea mammals can take part in an excursion organized for that purpose.

Cruise Manada
$17, children under 12 $8.50
☎*838-3444 or* 800-986-3444
Departures: From the Montague Marina, mid-May to late Jun and early Sep to early Oct every day 10am and 2pm, early Jul to late Aug every day 10am, 1pm, 3:30pm and 18:30pm, Jul and Aug every day 2:30pm.

Garry's Seal Cruises
$15.50, children $7.50
☎*962-2494 or* 800-561-2494
Departures: Murray River pier, May to mid-Jun every day 1pm, 3:30pm and 6:30pm, mid-Jun to mid-Sep every day 8:30am, 10:30am, 1pm, 3:30pm and 6:30pm, mid-Sep to late Oct 10:30am, 1pm, 6:30pm.

Fishing

Several companies offer deep-sea fishing excursions, giving visitors a chance to test their fishing skills while enjoying an exciting outing on the water.

Excursions of this type set out from **Covehead Harbour**:

Richard's Deep-Sea Fishing
$15
☎*672-2376*

Salty Seas Deep-Sea Fishing
$15
☎*672-3246*

A company in **Alberton** arranges similar outings:
Andrew's Mist
$25
☎*853-2307*

North Rustico:

Aiden Poiron's
☎*963-2442*
Also offers deep-sea excursions

Kayak

Outside Expedition
☎*963-3366*
www.getoutside.com
The excursions organized by this company offer magnificent views of the island's coastal region, with its red cliffs in the north and Murray River. These trips will also delight bird lovers, since they cross through several prime bird-watching areas.

Accommodations

Tour A:
Charlottetown

Youth Hostel
$12.50 members
$15 non-members
153 Mount Edward Rd.
☎ *894-9696*
The Youth Hostel
provides the least
expensive lodging in
the provincial capital
region. It's a friendly
spot set up in a barn-
like building about 3km
west of downtown,
near the university.
During summer, rooms
are also available at the
**University of Prince Ed-
ward Island** *($26 single,
32 double;* ☎ *566-0442).*

**Heritage Harbour House
Inn**
$70 bkfst incl.
early Jun to late Sep
4 rooms
9 Grafton St., C1A 1K3
☎ *892-6633*
☎ *800-405-0066*
The Heritage Harbour
House Inn is an excel-
lent bed and breakfast
located on a residential
street, just a stone's
throw from the Arts
Centre. The rooms are
impeccably clean, as
are the shared bath-
rooms.

The house itself is
warm and inviting, and
guests have use of a
day room where they
can relax, read or
watch television. Each
morning, Bonnie, the
owner and a charming

hostess, serves a conti-
nental breakfast.

The Duchess of Kent Inn
$75
tv
4 rooms
218 Kent St., C1A 3W6
☎ *566-5826*
800-665-5826
The Duchess of Kent
Inn occupies a lovely
old house built in 1875.
A charming place.

**The Charlottetown Rodd
Classic**
$85-$135
tv, ℜ, ≈
109 rooms
corner of Kent and Pownal Sts.
C1A 1L5
☎ *894-7371*
☎ *800-565-7633*
The Charlottetown
Rodd Classic is an
excellent downtown
hotel with a rather
stately appearance,
built to meet the needs
of both businesspeople
and vacationers. Reno-
vated in 1998, the invit-
ing rooms are modern
and tastefully furnished.
The hotel also houses a
good restaurant.

Fitzroy Hall
$90 bkfst incl.
⊗, tv
14 rooms
45 Fitzroy St., C1A 1RA
☎ *368-2077*
Charlottetown has pre-
served a few beautiful
Victorian homes, many
of which have been
converted into B&Bs,
One example is Fitzroy
Hall. Originally built in
1872, this impeccably
decorated house could
very well serve as a
small museum. Each
room is filled with an-
tiques and 19th-century

photos, pleasantly re-
creating the charm of a
bygone era. The own-
ers can tell you a few
haunting stories about
this home.

Hillburst Inn
$99 bkfst incl.
pb, ℜ
181 Fitzroy St., C1A 1S3
☎ *894-8004*
≈ *892-7679*
The Hillburst Inn is one
of the most beautiful
hotels on the island.
Built in 1897, this
sumptuous residence
one belonged to a man
named George
Longworth, a local mer-
chant who amassed a
fortune through ship-
building, trade and, so
it is said, bootlegging.
Once you see how
splendid-looking this
house is there will cer-
tainly be no doubt in
your mind as to
Longworth's wealth.

The richly ornamented
dining room and en-
trance hall are particu-
larly lovely and fur-
nished, as is the rest of
the house, with an-
tiques. The rooms, lo-
cated on the upper
floors, are comfortable,
very well decorated,
equipped with private
bathrooms, and each
one is unique. Guests
are accorded a very
friendly welcome;
breakfast is copious
and delicious.

Islander Motor Lodge
$103
tv, ℜ
50 rooms
146-148 Pownal St., C1A 3W6
☎*892-1217 or 800-268-6261*
⇄*566-1623*
The Islander Motor Lodge offers motel-style accommodation, but in pleasantly-furnished, quality rooms. This is a convenient place for families since it's just a few steps from the main sites and has a small, inexpensive restaurant. If you are travelling on a low budget, reserve in advance to get the less expensive rooms.

Elmwood Heritage Inn
$115 bkfst incl.
tv
121 North River Rd.
P.O. Box 3128, C1A 7N8
☎*368-3310*
⇄*628-8457*
At the end of an elm-lined lane stands the Elmwood Heritage Inn, a lovely Victorian house built in the 1880s by celebrated architect William C. Harris. Set in tranquil surroundings, about 15min on foot from downtown Charlottetown, this inn offers a few very well-decorated, antique-furnished rooms and suites. All of them have private washrooms and balconies. Each of the two suites has a fireplace, as does the living room. Bicycles, a very pleasant means of touring the city and its outskirts, are available for guests' use.

Charlotte's Rose Inn
$115
tv
4 rooms
11 Grafton St., C1A 1K3
☎*892-3699*
894-3699
Charlotte's Rose Inn is also an elegant, 19th-century Victorian home. Originally built in 1884, it has since been meticulously renovated. In addition to its old-world charm, its rooms are furnished with antiques and private bathrooms. Great location on a peaceful street in the old part of town.

Dundee Arms
$120
tv, ℜ
18 rooms
200 Pownal St., C1A 8C2
☎*892-2496*
⇄*368-8532*
The Dundee Arms, built in 1903, is an elegant inn set up inside a large Queen-Anne style residence built at the beginning of the century. The beautifully decorated bedrooms and common rooms will take you back in time. The inn also features a highly-reputed dining room. Finally, there are comfortable, slightly less expensive motel rooms available in an adjoining building.

🌴 Prince Edward Hotel
$159
tv, ℜ, ≈
211 rooms
18 Queen St., C1A 8B9
☎*566-2222 or 800-441-1414*
⇄*566-2282*
Part of the Canadian Pacific hotel chain, The Prince Edward Hotel is without a doubt the ritziest and most comfortable hotel on the island. It is also perfectly situated, looking out over the port of Charlottetown.

The interior is modern and well designed, with four restaurants and all the facilities one would expect to find in a hotel of this calibre. Business meetings and conferences are often held at the Prince Edward. Its conference rooms can accommodate up to 650 people.

Best Western Charlottetown
$179
≈, ℜ
238 Grafton St., C1A 1L5
☎*892-2461*
⇄*566-2979*
Located in the heart of Charlottetown, the Best Western Charlottetown offers comfortable rooms and suites that were renovated just a few years ago. Amenities of note include a family restaurant and an indoor swimming pool.

Cornwall

Chez Nous B&B
$100 bkfst incl.
4 rooms
Hwy. 248, Old Ferry Rd.
C0A 1H0
☎*566-2779 or 628-3852*
Located 15min by car from Charlottetown, Chez Nous B&B is another option for those who prefer to stay in the countryside rather than in town. Well lit and warmly decorated with paintings and an-

tique furniture, this home will immediately take your breath away. The owners greet their guests with a warm welcome and do everything to ensure they have an enjoyable stay in this wonderful B&B. Delicious breakfasts.

Tour B: Central P.E.I.

Strathgartney

Strathgartney Country Inn
$55 bkfst incl. sb
$110 bkfst incl. pb
ℜ
mid-May to late Sep
10 rooms
TransCanada Hwy., C0A 1H0
☎*675-4711*
Right near Strathgartney Provincial Park, the Strathgartney Country Inn is set up inside a superb upper-class residence built in 1863 on a property covering about 10ha. The fine food served in the dining room adds to the charm of this magnificent house, which is adorned with period furniture. A good choice for anyone wishing to relive the charm of the Victorian era in a rural setting.

Orient Hotel
$89 bkfst incl.
ℜ, *tv*
mid-May to mid-Oct
6 rooms
Main St., C0A 2G0
☎*658-2503*
The Orient Hotel fits in perfectly with Victoria's historic atmosphere. Built at the beginning

of the century, it is a delightful place with decorations and furniture from days gone by. It is comfortable without being overly luxurious, and guests receive a warm welcome. The Orient also has a dining room and a pretty tea room, which looks out onto the street.

Sea View

Adams Sea View Cottages
$90
tv, ℜ, *K*
mid-May to late Sep
13 rooms
R.R.2, C0B 1M0
☎*836-5259*
During summer, scores of cottages are available for rent all along the north shore of the island. There are over a dozen of these at Adams Sea View Cottages, all lined up along a beach. Each cottage has two bedrooms, a kitchenette and a refrigerator. The rooms are sparsely furnished.

Cavendish

New Glasgow Highland Camping
$20
≈
34 camping spots, 18 huts
R.R.3, C0A 1N0
☎*964-3232*
Situated in a wooded area, this campground is quite pleasant. You can pitch your tent here or stay in one of the little cabins. Near Cavendish.

Andy's Surfside Inn
$35 bkfst incl.
8 rooms
P.O. Box 5, C1A 7K2
☎*963-2405*
At Andy's Surfside Inn, the sea is all around you: it's the backdrop for the property, as well as the theme for the decor inside the inn, which is filled with martime decorations in each of its rooms. As soon as you enter, you have the impression that you are in a sailor's hideaway. The large house is modest, but has a certain allure nevertheless.

The Country House Inn
$55
K
5 rooms
R.R. 2, C0A 1N0
☎/≈*963-2055*
The Country House Inn is conveniently located near Prince Edward Island Provincial Park, the main attraction in the region. This inn is also only 2min from a beautiful sandy beach on the coast. The rooms, which are filled with a variety of knick-knacks, are basic, but offer adequate comfort.

Anne Shirley Motel & Cottages
$63-$98
K, ≈
Rte. 13, C0A 7T2
☎*963-2224 or 800-565-2243*
The Anne Shirley Motel & Cottages is a fair-sized establishment located near the centre of Cavendish. Various types of accommodation are available here: motel rooms, one- and two-bedroom apart-

ments and one- and two-bedroom cottages with kitchenettes. This spot is very well kept, modern and welcoming.

Kindred Spirits Country Inn
$65 bkfst incl.
135 bkfst incl. suite or cottage
pb, ≈, tv
mid-May to mid-Oct
14 rooms
Rte. 6, C0A 1N0
☎/≈963-2434

Furnished with antiques and exquisitely decorated, the Kindred Spirits Country Inn offers quality accommodation less than 1km from the Cavendish beach. Guests can relax in one of several common rooms, including a superb living room. Kindred Spirits has 25 rooms, 14 of which have whirlpools. The establishment also offers suites, with more luxurious accommodation, as well as 12 fully equipped, charming cottages, more suitable for families.

Osprey Outlook
$65 bkfst incl
®, tv
3 rooms
Hwy. 242, C0A 1N0
☎963-3366
≈963-3322

Even if it's just for one night, it sometimes feels good to be welcomed by a family when you are far away from home. If this is what you seek, you will feel right at home at this B&B. The house is modest, but the rooms are comfortable. For

longer stays, a small apartment is also available. The family organizes kayak and bike trips.

Lakeview Lodges & Cottages
$70-$85
≈
20 Loridale Dr., C1E 1P1
☎963-2436 or 800-565-7550

Beach and golf lovers will be in seventh heaven at the Lakeview Lodges & Cottages, located at the edge of the national park and just a few hundred metres from the Green Gables Golf Course. The Lakeview offers a few motel-style rooms and about 20 cottages equipped with one or two bedrooms each. This establishment is well maintained and surrounded by greenery.

Shining Water Country Inn and Cottages
$75-$130
ℜ, pb, tv
May to mid-Oct
10 rooms
Rte. 13, C0A 1N0
☎963-2251

In the heart of Cavendish, the Shining Water Country Inn and Cottages is a lovely old house with spacious porches all around. This inn features comfortable rooms and friendly service. Guests can relax in a pleasant, airy living room. There are cottages behind the house, which are available for about $15 extra.

Bay Vista Motel
$78
≈
R.R.2, Hunter River, C0A 1N0
☎963-2225 or 800-846-0601

The Bay Vista Motel is a quiet establishment near the main points of interest in the region. It is equipped with a pool and surrounded by a large grassy lawn where children can play in complete safety. There is a popular family restaurant nearby. The rooms are all clean, but some are more inviting than others; take the time to choose it.

Cavendish Motel
$78
tv, ℜ
early Jun to mid-Sep
35 rooms
intersection of Rtes. 6 and 13
C0A 1M0
☎963-2244 or 800-565-2243

In the centre of what could be considered the village of Cavendish, the Cavendish Motel offers clean, pleasant, modern rooms.

Cladish Breigh
$120
K
3km west of Cavendish
C0A 1M0
☎886-3313

Slightly set back from the centre of Cavendish, the Cladish Breigh numbers about 15 cottages in a beautiful setting on the edge of New London Bay. The interior design of the cottages is cosy and very inviting. Each one is equipped with a kitchenette and can house up to four people. There is a small, wild beach nearby that is unsuitable for swimming but just right for long seaside walks.

Brackley Beach

Shaw's Hotel
$70-$125
sb, pb, ℜ
C1E 1Z3
☎*672-2022*
⇌*672-3000*
Shaw's Hotel first opened its doors in 1860; since then, four generations of the Shaw family have taken the helm of this little establishment located 15min on foot from the national park.

Although the ocean is not far off, a pastoral atmosphere predominates at this hotel surrounded by farm buildings in the open countryside. The rooms are clean and comfortable, although slightly rudimentary. Some of them have private bathrooms. It is also possible to stay in one of the nearby cottages, which are equipped with fireplaces and up to four bedrooms.

North Winds Motel
$80
≈
R.R.9, Brackley Beach, C1E 1Z3
☎*672-2245 or 800-901-2245*
The North Winds Motel is set in a peaceful environment about 2km from the entrance to the national park. Its rooms are spacious and well kept. The motel also has a lovely indoor pool.

South Rustico

The heart of South Rustico is in reality a crossroads ringed by a farmers' bank, a school, a presbytery and a church – the key institutions of the local francophone community.

Barachois Inn
$125
ℜ
May to late Oct
7 rooms
Church Rd., C1A 7M4
☎*963-2194*
The Barachois Inn, located nearby, is an additional to this pretty architectural grouping. Built in the 1870s, this lovely patrician house was renovated just a few years ago and includes two rooms and two suites, all furnished in period style and each equipped with a private washroom. With its large porches and beautiful gardens, the Barachois is very appealing. It is especially suited to those who enjoy the charms of its quiet, country setting.

Little Rock

Dalvay-by-the-Sea
$190 bkfst incl.
ℜ, ≈, *pb*
P.O. Box 8, C0A 1P0
☎*672-2048*
⇌*672-2741*
www.aco.ca/dalvay
Dalvay-by-the-Sea is an impressive Victorian house located at the eastern tip of the park, a few hundred metres from magnificent white-sand beaches. It is also

the only hotel establishment within the perimeter of the national park. Built in 1896, the Dalvay was once the summer residence of Alexander Macdonald, one of the most powerful American industrialists of his era and a business partner of John D. Rockefeller. Nowadays, the house has about 20 very elegantly decorated rooms and cottages, all of them with private bathrooms.

As much because of its unique location as for its splendid design, Dalvay-by-the-Sea is one of the best hotels on the island; advance reservations for summertime stays are strongly recommended. Visitors who lodge elsewhere should stop by for a peek at the building's splendid dining and living rooms. Tennis court.

Tour C: Eastern P.E.I.

Little Sands

Bayberry Cliff Inn Bed & Breakfast
$95 bkfst incl.
tv
mid-May to late Sep
4 rooms
Rte. 4, 8km from Wood Islands
C0A 1W0
☎*962-3395*
One of the most charming establishments of its type on the island, the Bayberry Cliff Inn Bed & Breakfast offers quality accommodation.

The warm interior, with its rich woodwork, was designed with taste and care, and the rooms, each different from the next, are very inviting. Large windows have been added to the back of the house to let the sun in and provide an excellent view of the sea. The property is bordered by a red sandstone bluff.

Montague

Windows on the Water
$70
≈, pb
106 Sackville St., C0A 1R0
☎*838-2080*
Windows on the Water is a pleasant, charming inn with a very nice atmosphere, located in the heart of Montague.

All of its rooms are carefully furnished and decorated, equipped with private bathrooms, and have splendid views of the river and the town's small harbour. In the morning, breakfast is served in the dining room on a pleasant terrace. Windows on the Water is equally renowned as one of the better restaurants in the area (see p 245).

Roseneath

Rodd Brudenell River Resort
$92
ℜ, ≈, tv
May to Oct, 88 rooms
C0A 1G0
☎*652-2332 or 800-565-7633*
⇰*652-2886*
Visitors who like to spend all day playing

golf should choose the Rodd Brudenell River Resort, erected on a pretty, verdant site along a river in Brudenell River Provincial Park, right near the fantastic golf course. There are about 50 hotel rooms and 40 cottages set on the banks of the river. The rooms are modern, comfortable, well-furnished and equipped with balconies. The Rodd also offers family activities.

Little Pond

Ark Inn
$85
ℜ, tv
mid-Jun to Sep
8 rooms
R.R.4, C0A 2B0
☎*583-2400 or 800-665-2400*
⇰*583-2176*
A haven of peace, the Ark Inn stands on a large property with access to a private beach. The comfortable rooms feature futons, modern furniture and large windows. One thing that sets the Ark Inn apart is that most of its rooms are split-level, with the upper portion affording a lovely view. Some rooms are also equipped with a whirlpool. There is a pleasant restaurant on the ground floor.

Bay Fortune

Inn at Bay Fortune
$125 bkfst incl.
ℜ, tv
late May to mid-Oct
11 rooms
Rte. 310, C0A 2B0
☎*687-3745*
⇰*687-3540*
www.innatbayfortune.com
One of the most sumptuous and charming inns on the island, the Inn at Bay Fortune offers high-quality food and accommodation. The building has a unique architectural design; it stands on a lovely, verdant site, offering a superb view of the bay after which it is named. The rooms are furnished in an elegant and original, fashion, each one different from the last. Some even have a fireplace. An excellent choice!

Souris

Hilltop Motel
$68
tv, ℜ
14 rooms
Lea Crane Dr., C0A 2B0
☎*687-3315 or 800-445-5734*
⇰*687-3003*
The Hilltop Motel has clean, comfortable rooms and the advantage of being located within a few minutes from the boarding point for the ferry to the Îles-de-la-Madeleine, Québec. Breakfast is included in the price of the room.

Bed & Breakfast By the Sea & Tourist Home
$55 bkfst incl
tv
5 rooms
Hwy. 16, P.O. Box 223, C0A 2B0
☎**687-1527**
Bed & Breakfast By the Sea & Tourist Home is a peaceful accommodation alternative. Located in a large, gorgeous home, it has a magnificent view of the sea. The rooms are comfortable and the welcome courteous.

The Matthew House Inn
$145
tv
6 rooms
15 Breakwater St., C0A 2B0
☎**687-3461**
More expensive, also more elegant, the Matthew House Inn has a magnificent view of the sea and a meticulous decor. A beautiful collection of antique furniture adorns this Victorian home. The inn offers all the comfort you could hope for, especially the charming rooms, all of which have private bathrooms. The property surrounded by a large garden with majestic trees.

King Fisher

Tour D: Western P.E.I.

Summerside

Mulberry Motel
$60
tv
37 rooms
6 Water St. E., C1N 1A1
☎**436-2520**
⇄**436-4210**
At the entrance to town, there is a series of inexpensive motels. One of these is the Mulberry Motel, whose rooms offer a fairly decent and standard level of comfort.

Silver Fox Inn
$75
ℜ
6 rooms
61 Granville St., C1N 2Z3
☎**436-4033 or 800-565-4033**
The beautiful Silver Fox Inn lies a short distance from the port in an old residential neighbourhood and is surrounded by a pretty little garden. All of the rooms are well-furnished, inviting and equipped with private bathroom. Overall, the inn is elegantly decorated and has an atmosphere reminiscent of turn-of-the-century high-society.

Loyalist Country Inn
$99
tv, ℜ
50 rooms
195 Harbour Dr., C1N 5R2
☎**436-3333**
⇄**436-4304**
The most comfortable hotel in Summerside, the Loyalist Country Inn boasts an excellent location in the heart of town, with a view of the nearby port. Although they are modern, the rooms still have character, and are tastefully furnished. This hotel is a real favourite with businesspeople. Its restaurant, called the Prince William Dining Room, is highly recommended (see p 246).

Quality Inn - Garden of the Gulf
$99
tv, ℜ, ≈
92 rooms
618 Water St. E., C1N 2V5
☎**436-2295**
⇄**436-6277**
The Quality Inn - Garden of the Gulf features several sports facilities, including a nine-hole golf course and an indoor swimming pool. This modern hotel is pleasant and well-designed, making wise use of natural lighting.

Mont-Carmel

Le Village de l'Acadie
$75
tv, ℜ, ≈
late May to late Sep
60 rooms
Rte.11, C0B 2E0
☎**854-2227**
⇄**854-2304**
There is no hotel more luxurious in the Evangeline region than the Le Village de l'Acadie, located beside the Acadian Pioneer Village (see p 228) and the famous restaurant Étoile de Mer (see p 246). The complex is actually too big for the number of tourists who

visit this region, so its clean, comfortable rooms are often empty.

West Point

West Point Lighthouse
$75
tv, ℜ
late may to late Sep
10 rooms
O'Leary, R.R.2, C0B 1V0
☎*859-3605 or 800-764-6854*
⇔*859-1510*
The only inn in Canada set up inside a lighthouse (only one room is actually inside the lighthouse; the others are in the adjoining building), the West Point Lighthouse is a good spot to stop for a day or two, long enough to explore the magnificent dunes and beaches along the nearby shore. This is a friendly place, and the rooms are decent.

Tignish

Tignish Heritage Inn
$65
tv
17 rooms
P.O. Box 398, C0B 2B0
☎*882-2491*
⇔*882-3144*
A former convent built in 1868, the Tignish Heritage Inn has an unusual but pleasant setting. The simply furnished rooms are adequate. Guests can use the kitchen.

Alberton

Traveller's Inn Motel
$59
tv, ℜ
15 rooms
Rte. 12, C0B 1B0
☎*853-2215 or 800-561-7829*
The Traveller's Inn Motel, on the edge of Alberton, is not exactly charming, but nevertheless offers acceptable accommodation for the price.

Woodstock

Rodd Mill River Resort
$67
tv, ℜ
May to Oct
90 rooms
O'Leary, R.R.2, C0B 1V0
☎*859-3555 or 800-565-7633*
⇔*859-2486*
The Rodd Mill River Resort is ideal for sports buffs. Not only is there an excellent golf-course nearby, but the resort itself has an indoor pool, tennis courts, a gym and squash courts. The rooms, furthermore, are very comfortable.

Tyne Valley

Doctor's Inn Bed & Breakfast
$55
ℜ
2 rooms
Rte. 167, C0B 2C0
☎*831-3057*
The Doctor's Inn Bed & Breakfast is a country home typical of the 1860s with a pleasant garden. Its two decent, but not very luxurious rooms are available year-round. The place is very calm, and excel-

lent evening meals are available.

Restaurants

Tour A: Charlottetown

Just Juicin
62 Queen St.
☎894-3104
This is a unique spot to quench your thirst with a variety of healthy, freshly squeezed fruit juices.

Cow's
$
In front of the Confederation Arts Centre
Those with a sweet tooth will love Cow's, which offers wonderful ice cream and waffle cones.

Anchor and Oar House Grub & Grog
$
mid-May to mid-Oct
behind the Prince Edward Hotel
Water St.
☎894-1260
Just outside the Prince Edward Hotel, on the same side as Peake's Wharf, the Anchor and Oar House Grub & Grog has a simple menu idea for lunch. Most dishes are less than $6. There is a selection of salads and sandwiches, and several fish and seafood dishes round out the offerings.

Cedar's Eatery
$
81 University St.
☎892-7377
Centrally located, Cedar's Eatery offers an inexpensive, change of pace. *Kebab, falafel, shawarma* and *shish taouk*, Lebanese cuisine's most famous exports, are the headliners. The atmosphere is young, friendly and unpretentious, and the portions are generous.

Island Rock Café
$
132 Richmond St.
☎892-2222
A fun, friendly and truly inexpensive place, the Island Rock Café is conveniently situated on the street that runs in back of the Confederation Arts Centre. It looks and feels like a pub, while the menu includes pasta, burgers, nachos, fish & chips, etc. The dishes are simple, but well prepared. In the evenings, people come as much for drinks and socializing as for a meal.

Kelly's
$-$$
136 Richmond St.
☎628-6569
Charlottetown – a pretty, quiet city full of old-fashioned charm? That is definitely not the impression Kelly's is aiming for with its unusual, modern decor composed of bright colours, high mirrors and zinc counters. A hip ambiance, occasionally enhanced by live jazz, is pretty successfully created here.

Kelly's posts a varied menu that combines seafood, hamburgers, Italian pasta, poultry and other dishes. There is a nice view of the Historic Victoria Row from the terrace.

Peake's Quay
$-$$
May to Sep
36 Water St.
☎368-1330
Peake's Quay should win the trophy for the best-situated restaurant in Charlottetown. The pleasant terrace looks directly out over the city's marina. An economical menu of simple dishes, including excellent seafood crepes, is offered at breakfast time. In the evening, the menu is more elaborate but still affordable. For less than $20, you can have, among other things, a delicious plate of lobster. Peake's Quay is also a pub where people linger over a drink or two.

Off Broadway Café
$$
125 Sydney St.
☎566-4620
Perhaps surprisingly for a city of this size, Charlottetown does hide a few gems in terms of restaurants, namely the Off Broadway Café. Its relaxing, romantic and tasteful atmosphere and its excellent, deliciously concocted menu make it the hottest restaurant in town. A variety of dishes, many with a French touch, are served. And seafood connoisseurs will not

be disappointed by the main dishes and appetizers featured. Rounding up the menu is a choice selection of desserts, including many crepes.

Piazza Joe's Bistro
$$
189 Kent St.
☎849-4291
Piazza Joe's Bistro offers pizza baked in a wood burning oven, lasagna au gratin and *bruschetta*. It's a great place for Italian cuisine lovers. The relaxed atmosphere, generous portions and reasonable prices make this place an excellent choice for families and friends.

Sailor's Landing
$$
Waterfront
☎892-8098
Sailor's Landing has a great view of the Charlottetown harbour, which you can admire from the large terrace (open seasonally). Relax at this comfortable restaurant and enjoy a good seafood dinner as you take in the beautiful view. This is the kind of place you will want to come back to time and time again.

Meeko's Mediterranean Café & Grill
$$-$$$
146 Richmond St.
☎892-9800
There's an exotic feeling in the air at Meeko's, one of the few Greek restaurants on the island. Tzatziki, souvlaki and moussaka are featured on the

menu, as well as some Italian specialities and steak for those looking for a more conventional option. The dining room decor trasports you to Greece. Children's portions available.

Sirenella Ristorante
$$-$$$
83 Water St.
☎628-2271

A little establishment that is easy to miss, Sirenella Ristorante is in fact one of the best restaurants in Charlottetown. The menu is made up of Italian specialties, of which fresh pasta and meat are the essential elements. The dessert menu includes succulent Italian ice creams. It is possible to have a satisfying lunch here for under $10, and the Sirenella also has a small patio.

Lucy Maud Dining Room
$$$
4 Sidney St.
☎894-6868

The Atlantic Tourism & Hospitality Institute offers a variety of programs for young people who want to specialize in tourism or the hotel business. Among them, the cooking program merits particular mention. It not only includes cooking courses but also food-service training, and a dining room has been opened, which now welcomes guests, so students can practice their skills. Although it is a training school, visitors can expect good service and qual-

ity food – a good opportunity to discover the talents of budding chefs while enjoying a good meal. The menu offers French and Italian specialities. Reservations required.

The Lord Selkirk Dining Room
$$$
18 Queen St., Prince Edward Hotel
☎894-1208

The Lord Selkirk Dining Room offers a varied menu featuring several seafood dishes. Among the appetizers, the lobster-garnished linguine is particularly succulent. As main dishes, the parboiled Atlantic salmon, Atlantic halibut filet and duck roasted with red pepper are excellent. The ambiance at the Lord Selkirk is, of course very chic but inviting.

Tour B: Central P.E.I.

Victoria

Landmark Café & Craft
$
Jul to Sep
Main St.
☎658-2286

In the centre of the charming little village of Victoria, near the two inns and almost directly opposite the chocolate shop, visitors will find the Landmark Café & Craft an extremely friendly, warm and simple place whose walls are

adorned with pretty handicrafts. The menu consists of light homemade dishes–quiche, *tourtière* (meat pie), pasta, salads, desserts, etc.

Mrs. Profitt's Tea Room
$$
Main St., Orient Hotel
☎658-2503

For afternoon tea or a more substantial meal, head to Mrs. Profitt's Tea Room, in the charming setting of Victoria's historic Orient Hotel. The menu is not very elaborate, but does include a variety of sandwiches and desserts, as well as fresh lobster, lobster salad and lobster quiche.

New London

Fiddles & Vittles
$-$$
Rte. 6, 2km west of Cavendish
☎963-3003

Fiddles & Vittles above all targets a family clientele: the menu is not very sophisticated, the mood is definitely on the festive side, and games are organized during meals to keep children entertained. Fiddles & Vittles is housed in a large, rustic-looking building overlooking New London Bay, not far from Cavendish.

Stanley Bridge

Spot O'Tea
$$$
R.R. 6
☎886-3346

Spot O'Tea, a pretty restaurant, offers dinner-theatre, a popu-

Lobster Supper

The Cavendish region now has a well-established reputation for its traditional lobster suppers. The idea was adopted over 30 years ago, and little has changed. In various villages in the area, large, simply-furnished restaurants serve reasonably price lobster suppers to hundreds of visitors every evening.

The pleasant, informal ambiance contributes to the suppers' reputation and helps make them events not to be missed. Saint Ann's Church (see p 243), in the village of Saint Ann, was the first to serve lobster suppers and continues doing so throughout the summer in its basement.

One can also go to the New Glasgow Lobster Suppers (see p 244) or the Fisherman Wharf Lobster Suppers (see p 244), situated respectively in the communities of Glasgow and North Rustico, two charming little villages in the Cavendish region.

lar form of entertainment on the island. In addition to a good meal, guests enjoy an entertaining show. On beautiful summer nights, those who prefer to watch nature's own spectacle can sit on the terrace facing Stanley River.

St. Ann

St. Ann's Church Lobster Supper
$$
Jun to Oct
Rte. 224
☎*621-0635*
For more than 30 years now, St. Ann's Church Lobster Supper, a non-profit organization, has been serving lobster everyday from 4pm to 9pm. The menu, like those of other similar local restaurants, consists of a salad, fish soup, mussels, lobster and dessert – all for about $20. This is the type of tradition that visitors to Prince Edward Island should definitely not miss out on.

New Glasgow

Prince Edward Island Preserve Co.
$
Rte. 13, intersection of Rtes. 234 and 258
☎*964-2524*
The Prince Edward Island Preserve Co. is actually a shop selling delicious natural products. It also has a café, which serves good sandwiches and salads, as well as other dishes, including lob-

ster quiche, a smoked fish platter and mussels *à la provençale*.

Olde Glasgow Mill
$-$$
☎*964-3313*
Some high-calibre restaurants attract evening visitors to New Glasgow, one of the most picturesque villages in this part of the island. One of these little gems is the Olde Glasgow Mill, which offers an inexpensive varied menu mainly composed of seafood and fish dishes.

Café on the Clyde
$$
Rte. 224, intersection of Rte. 258

☎*964-4305*
Café on the Clyde, on the premises of the P.E.I. Preserve Co., is a great place to linger, as much for the cuisine as for the ambience. Its pretty dining room overlooking the river makes diners feel right at home. The evening menu offers a good selection of local specialties, seafood and fish. The café is open for breakfast and light meals are served all day long. The temptation to while away some time before or after a meal at the P.E.I. Preserve Co. shop, which sells a variety of home-made victuals, is practically irresistible.

Herb Garden
$$
Rte. 224
☎*621-0765*
Hidden on the road between New Glasgow

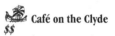

and St. Ann, there's a delicious restaurant called the Herb Garden, which offers a healthy, tempting menu. Most of the food comes from the restaurant's garden, and even the bread is baked on the premises. Always fresh and tasty, the dishes will delight travellers looking for a healthy meal.

New Glasgow Lobster Suppers
$$
Jun to mid-Oct
Rte. 258
☎*964-2870*
Looking out on the Clyde River, the New Glasgow Lobster Suppers is one of the island's classic eateries. Since opening, it has served over a million customers! During summer, hundreds of people pass through its two dining rooms every evening between 4pm and 8:30pm. The charm of this place lies in its simplicity; in the dining rooms, there are rows of plain tables covered with red-and-white-checkered tablecloths. The menu, obviously, revolves around lobster. Each meal includes an all-you-can-eat appetizer, one lobster and a home-made dessert. Prices vary depending on the size of the lobster you choose, but $20 per person is about average.

North Rustico

Blue Mussel Café
$$
☎*675-2501*
Located in an idyllic setting, the town's fishing harbour serves as a backdrop for this small family restaurant. There are only a few tables in the dining room where you can sample some of the restaurant's specialities, such as fresh fish and seafood. The owner's two daughters provide friendly, attentive service.

Fisherman Wharf Lobster Suppers
$$
mid-May to mid-Oct
Rte. 6
☎*963-2669*
A well-known local institution, Fisherman Wharf Lobster Suppers also serves traditional lobster meals, with unlimited fish and seafood soup, a vast choice of salads, bread, a lobster and a dessert for about $20. The place can seat approximately 500 people, which doesn't exactly make it intimate, but that's part of its charm.

Oyster Bed Bridge

Café St-Jean
$$
early Jun to late Sep
Rte. 6
☎*963-3133*
Both elegant and inviting, the Café St-Jean is a small restaurant set up inside a rustic-looking house looking out on the Wheatley River. In the evening, the

food is fairly elaborate, with not only seafood on the menu, but also a fair number of other well-prepared, original dishes and cajun specialities. The less expensive lunch menu consists of light dishes. The name of the café refers to the time before the British conquest, when the island was known as Île-St-Jean and the Acadian presence was very strong in this region.

Brackley Beach

Dunes Café
$$
Jun to Sep
10am to 10pm
Rte. 15
☎*672-2586*
The Dunes Café is the only place of its kind on the island. Set up in a complex with original modern architecture, which also houses a remarkable art gallery, it serves local and international cuisine in an airy decor. The lunch menu is less elaborate and easier on the pocketbook. Live music is often featured in the evening.

Tour C: Eastern P.E.I.

Orwell Corner

Sir Andrew McPhail Restaurant
$
late Jun to early Sep
Rte. 1
☎*651-2789*
Located on the historic site of the Sir Andrew

Macphail Homestead, the Sir Andrew McPhail Restaurant is a pleasant place to enjoy a good, light meal at lunchtime or take a break in the afternoon. Though the menu is simple, the food is tasty. Reservations are required for dinner *($$)*. The elegance and atmosphere of the Macphail Homestead make this a very appealing little restaurant.

Montague

 Café at Windows on the Water
$$
106 Sackville St.
☎*838-2080*
The Café at Windows on the Water is a thoroughly enjoyable spot, especially when the weather allows for dining al fresco on its pretty terrace overlooking Montague's little harbour. The main elements on the lunch menu are sandwiches, salads, soups and pasta dishes. In the evening, there is generally a selection of about 10 seafood, fish, poultry and meat dishes.

Lobster Shanty North
$$
Rte. 17
☎*838-2463*
In the purest Prince Edward Island tradition, the Lobster Shanty North offers first-rate lobster suppers consisting of a seafood appetizer, a lobster and dessert for about $20. Guests sit in a simply decorated dining room looking out on the Montague River. This restaurant has had the honour of serving Her Majesty Queen Elizabeth II and Prince Philip in 1973, as well as Prince Charles and Lady Diana in 1983. In addition to its seafood, the place is also known for its char-broiled steaks.

Cardigan

Cardigan Craft Centre and Tea Room
$
Rte. 4
☎*583-2930*
Set up inside the former railway station, the Cardigan Craft Centre and Tea Room has a simple, inexpensive menu made up of sandwiches, salads and other light dishes.

Cardigan Lobster Suppers
$$
late Jun to late Sep
Rte. 311, intersection of Rtes. 3 and 4
☎*583-2020*
Set up inside a century-old general store, Cardigan Lobster Suppers serves traditional lobster meals at reasonable prices from 4pm to 8:30pm every night. This type of supper, consisting of a seafood appetizer, a lobster and dessert, is an island tradition that is not to be missed.

Bay Fortune

Inn at Bay Fortune
$$$
Rte. 310
☎*687-3745*
Without question one of the finest restaurants in the region, the dining room of the Inn at Bay Fortune has a beautiful lay-out and offers a magnificent view of the bay. Chef Michael Smith, one of the great chefs of the province, prepares dishes using ingredients fresh from the market. The cuisine is both exquisite and original, and the service, highly professional.

Clear Spring

 The Carousel
$$
Hwy. 16
☎*687-4100*
You won't find fries or soft drinks on the menu at The Carousel. Instead, you will notice a healthy selection of foods: organic fruits and vegetables, seafood and home-made cakes and pies. The selection of fresh produce, which depends on the season, guarantees the success of this establishment. This place concocts, simply-prepared, quality dishes every day. Nestled in the middle of the forest with a magnificent view of its natural setting, this restaurant has much to offer.

Tour D:
Western P.E.I.

Summerside

 Deckhouse
$-$$
Spinnakers' Landing
Laid out in one of the buildings on Spinna-

kers' Landing, the Deckhouse is a pleasant pub that serves light meals. The upstairs terrace offers a lovely view of the port and the town.

Little Mermaid
$-$$
240 Harbour View Dr.
☎436-8722
The Little Mermaid, a modestly decorated snack bar, is located just next to Spinnakers' Landing. Simple fish, seafood and chicken dishes are served here.

Brothers Two
$-$$
618 Water St. E.
☎436-9654
With its extremely relaxed, pub atmosphere, Brothers Two is one of the liveliest and most popular spots in Summerside. People come here to eat or simply to have a drink. As in many restaurants on the island, fish and seafood are highlighted on the menu, which nevertheless lists a variety of other specialties, as well. The portions are generous here.

Prince William Dining Room
$$
195 Harbour Dr. in the Loyalist Country Inn
☎436-3333
The Prince William Dining Room offers well-prepared food and a fairly elaborate menu, including a wide choice of appetizers and main dishes. Seafood and fish make up a good part of the offerings, but various steak and

chicken dishes are also available. On some evenings, a specific dish is featured, such as the excellent surf and turf, consisting of a small steak and a lobster tail. The service is courteous, and the atmosphere, elegant but relaxed.

Tyne Valley

Seasons in Thyme
$$-$$$
Sumerside, 644 Water St. E.
☎888-3463
Seasons in Thyme is truly one of the best restaurants on the island, and its chef, Stefan Czapalay, is much celebrated throughout the Atlantic provinces for the quality and originality of his creations. He takes his inspiration from local and European recipes alike. The menu changes daily and reservations are recommended.

Mont-Carmel

Étoile de Mer
$-$$
mid-Jun to mid-Sep
Rte. 11
☎854-2227
A visit to the Evangeline region offers a good opportunity to enjoy a meal at the most famous Acadian restaurant on the island, Étoile de Mer, located at the entrance to the pioneer village. Dishes prepared according to the best-known Acadian recipes, such as *râpure, fricot au poulet, fricot aux*

palourdes and *pâté acadien* are served in a cozy dining room. None of these traditional dishes costs more than $5.25. The menu also lists a good number of other (more expensive) dishes, mostly lobster and other types of seafood and fish. This is a good place to familiarize yourself with the island's Acadian community.

West Point

West Point Lighthouse restaurant
$-$$
late May to late Sep
Rte. 14
☎859-3605
A good place to stop for a break during a tour of western Prince Edward Island, the West Point Lighthouse is an inn whose restaurant is open from daybreak to 9:30pm. The lunch menu consists of a variety of light dishes, including the usual lobster rolls, chowders and other seafood. In the evening, the cuisine is a bit more sophisticated, with more elaborate appetizers and main courses, such as a fisherman's platter, made up of five different kinds of seafood or fish for less than $20. The menu also lists steak, chicken Kiev and pasta. The restaurant is laid out in a simple fashion in the building adjoining the lighthouse. Guests can also eat on the terrace outside.

North Cape

Wind & Reef
$$
end of Rte. 12
At the same location as
the Atlantic Wind Test
Site museum, the Wind
& Reef is a perfect
place to dine on sea-
food and fish. The
menu includes other
dishes as well, but peo-
ple come here mainly
for the lobster, shrimp,
oysters, fisherman's
platter, etc. Although
the prices are not exor-
bitant, you do have to
pay a little extra for the
lovely setting. Lighter,
less expensive meals
are available at lunch
time.

Entertainment

Tour A:
Charlottetown

Buzz magazine, pub-
lished monthly, is a
good source of infor-
mation on the cultural
events in town, such as
film, theatre, music,
bars and nightclubs.

Each summer, for more
than three decades
now, the Confederation
Arts Centre has pre-
sented the musical **Anne
of Green Gables** *(Confed-
eration Arts Centre,* ☎566-
1267 *or* 800-566-1207*)*,
inspired by the work of
Prince Edward Island's
favourite daughter,
Lucy Maud Montgom-
ery. Both funny and

touching, the story of
little "Anne with an e"
is now a classic of chil-
dren's literature all over
the world. It is amazing
to see to what point
Anne has affected
young Japanese, who
now make up a signifi-
cant percentage of tour-
ists to the island. The
musical is well done
and makes for a fun
night out.

At the **Festival Dinner
Theatre** *(Charlottetown
Hotel,* ☎892-6633*)* guests
enjoy a meal while
watching (and some-
times even participating
in!) an entertaining
play. You'll laugh with,
and at, everyone. The
young actors and ac-
tresses wait the tables,
sing and play music.

For fans of Irish music,
the **Olde Dublin Pub**
(131 Sydney St.) is the
place for a Guinness
and a jig. There is often
live music, and simple
meals are also served.
Drinks can also be had
at the **Island Rock Café**
(132 Richmond St.), or
just next door, at **Kelly's**.
Also, **Cedar's Eatery** *(81
University St., 2nd floor)*
regularly showcases
popular bands on the
weekends. You can
also check out **Broadway
Café** *(125 Sydney St.)*
which hosts jazz shows.

The spacious terrace at
Sailor's Landing *(Water-
front,* ☎892-8098*)* is the
best spot in town to
have a drink and watch
the sunset over the
Charlottetown harbour.
You can also have a
meal (see p 241).

Horse-racing fans can
get their fix at the **Char-
lottetown Driving Park**
(Kensington Rd., ☎892-
6823*)*. Races are held
two to four times a
week during the sum-
mer.

Here's something for
kids of all ages: see
Charlottetown from a
London-style double-
decker bus! **Abegweit
Sightseeing Tours** *(depar-
ture from the Confeder-
ation Arts Centre,* ☎894-
9966*)* crisscross the
town several times a
day; tours of the north-
ern and southern
shores are also avail-
able.

Tour B:
Central P.E.I.

Victoria

Almost every night in
July and August, the
Victoria Playhouse *(about
$12;* ☎658-2025 *or* 800-
925-2025*)* presents en-
tertaining plays and
concerts in its little
theatre. With its quality
performances, the Vic-
toria Playhouse is as
charming as the city
itself.

Tour D:
Western P.E.I.

Summerside

The **Feast Dinner Theatre**
*(Water St., Brothers Two
restaurant,* ☎436-7674*)*,
which has been pres-
ented on summer eve-
nings (starting at
6:30pm) for the past 15

Prince Edward Island

years or so, is a dinner accompanied by a non-stop blend of music, songs and theatre that is supposed to be a laugh!

Mont-Carmel

The **Cuisine à Mémé** *(Rte. 11, the Village,* ☎*854-2228 or 800-567-3228)* brings Acadian Prince Edward Island to life through songs, music and theatre. These shows, held in the evening, are combined with a meal.

Shopping

Tour A: Charlottetown

In Charlottetown, visitors can go to **Peake's Wharf** to stroll along the pier and enjoy the seashore while doing some shopping in the pretty boutiques. There is something for everyone here – crafts, souvenirs, T-shirts, etc.

PEI Factory Shops
Trans-Canada Highway
Those who want to buy well-known brand names, such as Jones of New York, Liz Claiborne, Levi's, Island Beach Co. T-shirts with pretty island logos, or Paderno pots and pans, should head to PEI Factory Shops, where there are bargains to be had.

The large **Confederation Court Mall** *(Ken St. and University Ave.)* has 90 stores, with something for everyone.

Clothing

Both children and their parents will enjoy picking out one of the funny T-shirts and sweatshirts available at **Cow's** *(opposite the Confederation Arts Centre)*. Make sure to sample the store's excellent ice cream at the same time.

La Cache *(119 Kent St.,* ☎*368-3072)* sells comfortable clothing, as well as kitchen goods and tablecloths.

Visitors looking for warm woolens should head over to the **Wool Sweater Factory Outlet** *(Prince Edward Hotel,* ☎*566-5850)*, which offers a lovely selection of high-quality, casual sweaters.

Crafts and souvenirs

All sorts of beautiful crafts, books and souvenirs are available at **The Two Sisters** *(150 Richmond St.,* ☎*894-3407)*.

PEI has inspired many an artist. The **Island Craft Shop** *(156 Richmond St.,* ☎*892-5152)* presents some beautiful creations by members of the PEI Craft Council, an organization that promotes local artists. Sculptures, pottery, wool sweaters and

other quality crafts are sold here.

The charming **Island Poster** *(142 Richmond St.,* ☎*566-5642)* shop sells wonderful mementoes of your stay in the province; namely large, beautiful posters.

Anne of Green Gables fans can poke around in the **Anne of Green Gables Souvenirs shop** *(110 Queen St.;* ☎*368-2663)*.

The Book Emporium *(169 Queen St.,* ☎*628-2001)* has a great selection of new and used books, as well as works by regional authors.

Tour B: Central P.E.I.

Victoria

The melt-in-your-mouth home-made chocolates at **Island Chocolate** *(Main St.,* ☎*658-2320)* are an absolute delight.

Borden

Those who appreciate craft shops should check out **The Official Island Store** *(☎437-2896)*, which has, without a doubt, the loveliest crafts on the island.

Kensington

Who doesn't know Geppeto? On the island, his name is synonymous with home-made toys – wooden toys, of course. The puppets at **Geppeto's Workshop** *(Hwy. 238 ☎886-2339)* are master-pieces.

New Glasgow

The **Old Country Store** *(Rte. 13; ☎964-2769)* features a lovely selec-tion of local crafts, quilts and **Anne of Green Gables** articles – souve-nirs related to the story of that famous little redhead. Visitors are sure to find a worth-while memento here.

The **Prince Edward Island Preserve Co.** *(intersection of Rtes. 224 and 258; ☎964-2524)* sells a wide selection of excellent jams containing very little sugar.

If you didn't find the toy of your dreams at Geppeto's, you can always try another little factory that makes amusing wooden toys: **The Toy Factory** *(Hwy. 13, ☎964-2299)* in New Glasgow.

South Rustico

The pottery made on the island has become quite well known. If you are looking to buy some, **The Old Forge Factory** *(Hwy. 6, at the intersection with Hwy. 243, ☎963-2878)* is a must.

Cavendish

The **Cavendish Boardwalk** *(Rte. 6)* has all kinds of adorable little shops, some, like **Two Sisters**, specializing in T-shirts and souvenirs. Visitors will also find a branch of **Roots** (sportswear) and **Cow's**, with its cute clothing and terrific ice cream. At the front of the store, there is a selection of slightly defective Cow's cloth-ing at reduced prices.

The **Island Treasures** *(at the intersection of Rtes. 6 and 13; ☎963-2350)* shop is another good place to purchase local crafts and many other articles for the house.

Tour C:
Eastern P.E.I.

Murray River

Those who enjoy ex-ploring cute little sou-venir and craft shops should make sure to stop at Murray River, which boasts two of the loveliest craft shops in the region, if not on the entire island. **The Old General Store** *(Main St.; ☎962-2459)* features a delightful selection of housewares and quilts. **The Primrose Path** *(Rte. 3)* is a worthy competitor.

Tour D:
Western P.E.I.

Summerside

In summer, there is nothing more pleasant than strolling about **Spinnaker Landing**, with its pretty string of shops along the water-side. This complex, built on piles, also has a little outdoor theatre where a variety of ac-tivities are organized.

Tyne Valley

Shoreline Sweaters *(☎831-2950)* is a shop where visitors will find top-quality wool sweat-ers hand-knit on the premises, as well as a variety of souvenirs.

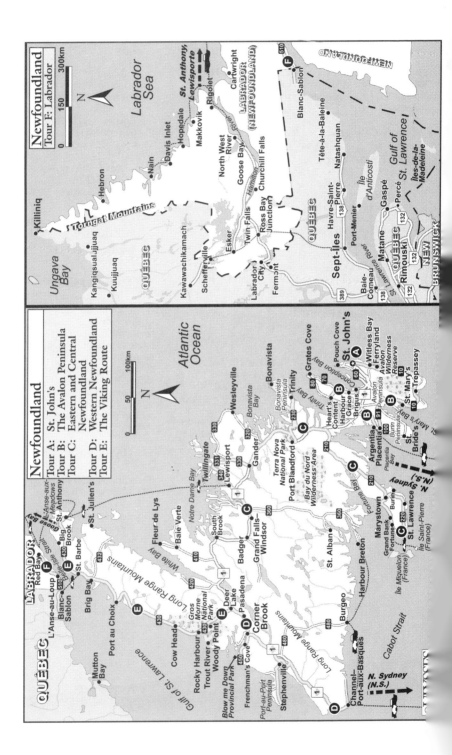

Newfoundland and Labrador

S till a little known corner of the world, Newfoundland is very different from Canada's other Atlantic provinces – not just geographically but historically and culturally, as well.

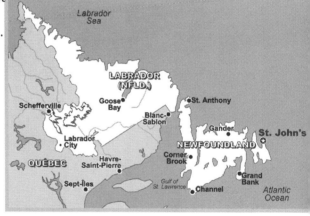

The province's geographical isolation, at the northeasternmost edge of North America, has helped forge its unique character. "The Rock," as it is aptly nicknamed, is a rocky island ill-suited to agriculture, a hostile region whose landscape, often very rugged, is so splendid that you can't help but stand back and marvel.

The west part of the island is shaped by the ancient Long Range Mountains, the tail end of the Appalachians. Gros Morne National Park, a UNESCO World Heritage Site, offers visitors a remarkable chance to explore these mountains, which in many places plunge straight into the limpid waters of deep fiords.

Farther north, toward L'Anse aux Meadows, the former site of a Viking camp, the road runs along flat and strikingly desolate coastal landscapes. Elsewhere, lofty cliffs, pebble beaches and tiny fishing villages punctuate the shore, providing scenes of picturesque enchantment.

The capital of the province, St. John's, lies in a magnificent natural setting on the shores of a long harbour rimmed with high, rocky hills. In addition to the island of Newfoundland, the province also includes Labrador covered with subarctic forests and tundra.

Labrador, sparsely populated with just

a few thousand inhabitants, covers nearly 300,000km². Both the island of Newfoundland and Labrador, far off the beaten tourist track, offer outdoor enthusiasts countless opportunities to explore a rich wilderness. Without much difficulty, visitors can observe caribou and moose, colonies of puffins and gannets, and, from the coast, whales swimming about and icebergs slowly drifting by.

The numerous traces of Aboriginal communities that have been discovered along its shores indicate that this province has been inhabited almost continuously for over 8,000 years.

The first people to settle here were natives belonging to the Maritime Archaic nation and Dorset Eskimos. The Aboriginal encountered by European explorers, however, were Beothuk, who came to Newfoundland around the year 200. Due to its relative proximity to the European continent, the island of Newfoundland was one of the very first places in the New World to be known to Europe.

Legend has it that at the end of the 5th century, St. Brendan, an Irish abbot, crossed the Atlantic in his search for new peoples to convert to Christianity and landed on this island.

The first Europeans whose presence here can actually be proved, however, were the Vikings, who, toward the year 1000, apparently used the island as a base for exploring the continent (Leif's camp), in L'Anse-aux-Meadows, the oldest European site in North America. It wasn't until several centuries later that Europeans rediscovered Newfoundland. In the 15th century, Europe learned of the teeming waters around the island through Basque fishermen. Each summer, the Basques would come to this region to fish cod in the Grand Banks and hunt whales in the Strait of Belle Isle.

Officially, however, the credit for discovering Newfoundland goes to Giovanni Caboto (John Cabot), who came here in the service of England in 1497. Over the following centuries, the French and the English competed for control of Newfoundland and the rest of North America. In 1558, the English founded their first permanent settlement in Trinity, on the Bonavista Peninsula.

Then, in 1583, Sir Humphrey Gilbert officially claimed St. John's harbour and the rest of the island of Newfoundland for Queen Elizabeth I of England. This did not, however, prevent the French from establishing their own permanent settlement, known as Plaisance (now

Placentia), on the coast of the Avalon Peninsula in 1662.

Plaisance remained the capital of the French colony of Terre-Neuve (Newfoundland) until the signing of the Treaty of Utrecht in 1713. Though the island was ceded to England under this treaty, the French continued to take an interest in it; in fact, the last battle of the Seven Years' War (or French and Indian War) took place in St. John's. The war ended with the signing of the Treaty of Paris in 1762, under which France lost its North American empire. Over the following centuries, more people, many from Ireland, settled along the coast of Newfoundland. In 1867, the year the Canadian Confederation was created, the islanders decided that Newfoundland should remain a British colony. It wasn't until 1949 that Newfoundland became the tenth and final province to join Canada.

This chapter is divided into six tours: five for Newfoundland and one for Labrador:
Tour A: St. John's ★★,
Tour B: The Avalon Peninsula ★★, Tour C: Eastern and Central Newfoundland ★, Tour D: Western-Newfoundland ★, Tour E: The Viking Route ★★★ and **Tour F: Labrador ★.**

Finding Your Way Around

By Ferry

The island of Newfoundland is accessible by ferry from North Sydney, on Cape Breton Island, Nova Scotia. These ferries, operated by the Marine Atlantic company, offer service to Port aux Basques (in southwestern Newfoundland) and Argentia (on the Avalon Peninsula, in southeastern Newfoundland). The crossing between North Sydney and Port aux Basques usually takes about 5hrs. With a few exceptions, there is at least one crossing per day, each way, between North Sydney and Port aux Basques. The one-way fare is $62 per car and $20 per adult. It takes about 14hrs to travel between North Sydney and Argentia. There is at least one crossing, each way, every Monday, Wednesday and Friday. The one-way fare is $124 per car and $55

per adult. Reservations: ☎800-563-6353.

It is also possible to take the ferry from Goose Bay, Labrador to the island of Newfoundland. This ferry, which travels to Lewisporte, in north-central Newfoundland, runs several times a week from the beginning of June to the beginning of September *(Reservations:* ☎800-341-7981). There is a good road from Goose Bay to Churchill Falls and Labrador City, then on to Baie Comeau (Québec).

Tour F: Labrador

Once a day, from June to September, a ferry travels between St. Barbe, on the Viking Highway, and Blanc Sablon (Québec), on the Strait of Belle Isle. Blanc Sablon is only 3km from the Labrador border, and there is a good road connecting it to Red Bay. The ferry schedule makes it possible to make a day trip to Labrador. Reservations: ☎931-2309.

A cargo ship sets out each week from St. Anthony, at the end of the Viking Highway, to bring supplies to some 48 communities along the coast of Labrador, as far as the village of Nain. The round trip takes about 12 days. Reservations: ☎800-563-6353.

By Plane

The province's major civilian airport is located in St. John's. There are direct flights between St. John's and a number of large Canadian cities, including Halifax, Montréal and Toronto. Air Canada also offers direct service to St. John's from London, England, while Royal Airlines offers a direct flight from Dublin, Ireland. The two main airlines that serve the island of Newfoundland are Air Canada, with its subsidiary **Air Nova** (☎1-800-463-8620) and **Canadian International** (☎1-800-426-7000). The airport is only 6km from downtown St. John's.

Tour F: Labrador

Airplanes fly into the Wabush, Churchill Falls and Goose Bay airports from outside Labrador (mostly from the island of Newfoundland). The main airlines serving Labrador are **Air Nova** (☎800-463-8620); **Canadian International**, (☎800-426-7000); Air Alliance (☎800-363-7050); Inter Provincial Airlines (☎576-1666) and Air Labrador (☎896-3387).

By Train

Tour F: Labrador

Rail service between Labrador City (Labra-

dor) and Sept-Iles (Québec) is provided by the Quebec, North Shore & Labrador Railways (☎418-968-7805 or 944-8205).

Car Rentals

The following car-rental companies have branches in St. John's and the other major towns in the province:

Avis
☎800-879-2817

Budget
☎800-268-8900

Hertz
☎800-263-0600

Thrifty
☎800-367-2277

Tilden
☎800-387-4747

Tour F: Labrador

There is an excellent road from Baie Comeau (Québec) to Labrador City, Churchill Falls and Goose Bay. From Goose Bay, motorists can take the ferry to Lewisporte, in the north-central part of the island of Newfoundland.

Practical Information

Area code: **709**

Tourist Information

Destination Newfoundland and Labrador
P.O. Box 8730
St. John's, Newfoundland
A1B 4K2
☎729-2830, 729-1965
or 800-563-6353
≈729-0057

There are about thirty tourist information centres scattered across the province, notably in St. John's and in the major ports of entry.

Exploring

Tour A: St. John's

St. John's, the provincial capital, occupies a spectacular site on the Avalon Peninsula, at the eastern tip of the island, and of Canada. The city is built like an amphitheatre around a well-protected harbour that opens onto the Atlantic Ocean by way of a narrow channel aptly known as the Narrows and is flanked on either side by tall, rocky peaks. About 1.6km long and 800m wide, St. John's harbour is an excellent inland port which is frequented by ships of all sizes flying the flags of various countries.

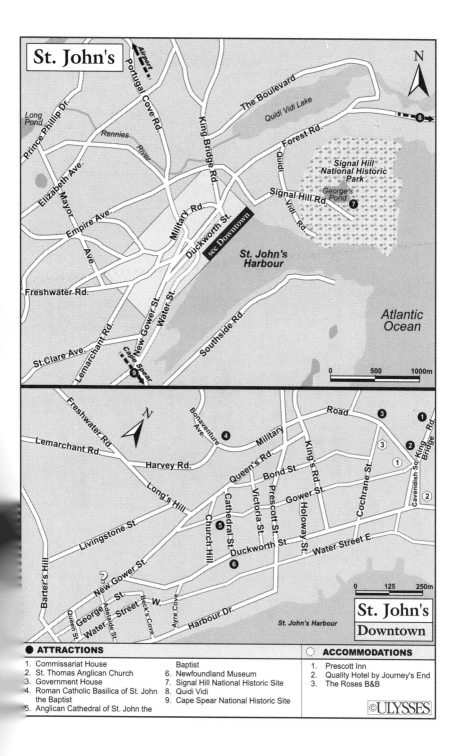

St. John's

N

The Boulevard
Quidi Vidi Lake

Airport
Portugal Cove Rd.
Prince Phillip Dr.
Long Pond
Rennies River
Elizabeth Ave.
Mayor Ave.
Empire Ave.
Ave.
Freshwater Rd.
St. Clare Ave.
Lemarchant Rd.
New Gower St.
Water St.
Military Rd.
Duckworth St.
King Bridge Rd.
Forest Rd.
Quidi Vidi Rd.
Signal Hill Rd.
Southside Rd.
Cape Spear

8

Signal Hill National Historic Park
George's Pond
7

St. John's Harbour
see Downtown

Atlantic Ocean

0   500   1000m

9

N

Freshwater Rd.
Lemarchant Rd.
Harvey Rd.
Long's Hill
Livingstone St.
Barter's Hill
New Gower St.
George St.
Adelaide St.
Beck's Cove.
Ayre Cove.
Queen St.
W. Water Street
Harbour Dr.
Bonaventure Ave.
Military
Queen's Rd.
Cathedral St.
Victoria St.
Church Hill
Duckworth St.
Bond St.
Prescott St.
Gower St.
Holloway St.
King's Rd.
Cochrane St.
Water Street E.
Cavendish Sq.
King Bridge Rd.
Road

4
5
6
3
3
2
1
2
1
2

St. John's Harbour

0   125   250m

St. John's
Downtown

● **ATTRACTIONS**

1. Commissariat House
2. St. Thomas Anglican Church
3. Government House
4. Roman Catholic Basilica of St. John the Baptist
5. Anglican Cathedral of St. John the

Baptist
6. Newfoundland Museum
7. Signal Hill National Historic Site
8. Quidi Vidi
9. Cape Spear National Historic Site

○ **ACCOMMODATIONS**

1. Prescott Inn
2. Quality Hotel by Journey's End
3. The Roses B&B

©ULYSSES

Lighthouses

Until the 19th century, trade within Canada or with the rest of the world took place mainly by boat. In some parts of the country, fishing was one of the principal means of subsistence, and many little boats sailed the coastal waters. It soon became governments' chief priority to build a network of lighthouses along the coasts and the main waterways to ensure safety.

These lighthouses were erected on rocky headlands or on islands and required ingenuity on the part of their builders. The very first ones to be built were essentially robust stone towers topped by a light.

The Sambro Island Lighthouse (see p 139), near Halifax, the oldest lighthouse in Canada still in use, is an example of this type of lighthouse. These tall towers that dominated the horizon were the most practical, but, when a lighthouse could be built on a natural headland, builders chose for a simpler model: a house (for the lighthouse keeper) on top of which a light was placed. The Cape Spear Lighthouse (see p 258), built on the coast of Newfoundland between 1834 and 1836, is a good example.

All of these lighthouses, especially those built at the extremities of Canada, were meticulously maintained and symbolized, among other things, a willingness to assure a presence *A mari usque ad mare* (from sea to sea).

Hidden behind the port installations lies a charming city whose winding streets are lined with pretty, brightly coloured wooden houses. European fishermen of various nationalities were already coming regularly to the site of modern-day St. John's as early as the fifteenth century. In 1583, Sir Humphrey Gilbert officially claimed the harbour and the rest of the island of Newfoundland for the Queen of England. Later, St. John's was often at the centre of rivalries between the French and the English, and fell into the hands of the French on three different occasions. Signal Hill was subsequently fortified to protect the city.

Commissariat House *(free admission; Jun to Sep; King's Bridge Rd., ☎729-2460)*. This Georgian-style wooden building, completed in 1821, was first used as the residence of the commissariat of the local military base and then served as the vicarage of **St. Thomas Anglican Church** *(Military Rd.)*.

This church, also known as the Old Garrison Church (1836), was the chapel of the British garrison of Fort William. Commissariat House and St. Thomas Church are among the few buildings in downtown St. John's to have survived the great fires of 1846 and 1892. Now a provincial historic site, Commissariat House was restored some time ago and furnished in the style of the 1830s.

Government House *(Military Rd., ☎729-4494)*, another building that escaped the flames, was erected in 1831 as the official residence of the governor of Newfoundland. It has served as the Lieutenant Governor's house since the province joined the Canadian Confederation. The beautifully landscaped grounds are open to the public every day, but the house itself may only be visited by appointment. The frescoes

St. John's, capital of Newfoundland and a colourful harbour town, occupies a spectacular site on the Avalon Peninsula.
- *Michel Julien*

The morning fog rising gently on Bonne Bay and the small village of Rocky Harbour, Newfoundland, on the eastern border of Canada.
- *B. Terry*

The Atlantic puffin can be found in many different places on Canada's east coast and has a distinctive beak that earned it the nickname "parakeet of the sea."
- *P. Quittemelle*

A typical picturesque scene from the coasts of Newfoundland: old rowboats washed up on the rocky shore, colourful little boats and the whitest of villages.
- *P.Couture*

adorning the ceiling were executed by Polish painter Alexander Pindikowski in 1880 and 1881. He would paint during the day then return to the local prison at night, where he was serving a sentence for counterfeiting.

Built on a promontory overlooking the city, the **Roman Catholic Basilica of St. John the Baptist** *(Military Rd.)* was designed by Irish architect John Jones in 1855. Originally a cathedral, it was converted into a basilica in 1955. Its facade is graced with two 43m-high towers. The interior is richly decorated; the left transept contains a statue of Our Lady of Fatima, a gift from some Portuguese sailors who survived a shipwreck on the Grand Banks. The front of the basilica is a splendid vantage point from which to view the city.

The elegant **Anglican Cathedral of St. John the Baptist** *(at the corner of Church Hill and Gower St.)*, with its pure Gothic lines, was designed by English architect Sir George Gilbert Scott in 1847. It was completed in 1885 but was totally destroyed by a fire in 1892. The cathedral was rebuilt a few years later under the supervision of Sir George's son. Its magnificent stained-glass windows are particularly noteworthy. Established in 1699, the parish of St. John the

Baptist is the oldest Anglican parish in Canada.

The **Newfoundland Museum** *($2.85; Tues, Wed, Fri, 9am to 5pm, Thu 9am to 9pm, Sat and Sun 10am to 6pm; Duckworth St.,* ☎ *729-0916)* houses permanent exhibitions that offer an excellent overview of the human history of Newfoundland and Labrador. The collections also examine the way of life of the six Aboriginal nations who live or once lived in these regions: the Maritime Archaic who left traces of their existence in Port au Choix, among other places; the Dorset, who lived on the shores of the island until beginning of the first century AD; the Beothuk, the predominant Aboriginal

nation in Newfoundland when the Europeans arrived, who have since been completely wiped out; the Micmac, the largest nation in Atlantic Canada; the Inuit, once called Eskimos, who still inhabit the northernmost shores of Labrador; and the Montagnais, who live in Labrador, along the shores of the Gulf of St. Lawrence. The exhibitions also explore the lives of 19th-century settlers and fishermen.

Signal Hill National Historic Site, visible from all over St. John's, is a rocky hill topped by a

Signal Hill National Historic Site

tower, which looks out over the mouth of the harbour. The hilltop commands magnificent **views** of the Atlantic, the harbour and the city

Newfoundland and Labrador

both day and night. Because of its strategic location, Signal Hill was long used as an observation and communications post. As early as 1704, flags were flown here to inform the military authorities and merchants of St. John's when ships were arriving. It was also on Signal Hill that the city's defences were erected, from the 18th century to the Second World War.

Vestiges of 19th-century military installations can still be found here. In 1762, Signal Hill was the scene of the final North American battle of the Seven Years' War (also known as the French and Indian War). The French, who had been defeated in Québec City and Louisbourg several years earlier, managed to seize St. John's for a few months, after which they were ousted by English troops led by Lieutenant Colonel William Amherst. In summer, visitors can see the **Signal Hill Tattoo**, a re-enactment of 19th-century military exercises, complete with period costumes and gun and cannon salvos.

At the Signal Hill welcome centre, there is a small **museum** *($2.50; mid-Jun to early Sep, every day 8h30am to 8pm, rest of the year 8:30am to 4:30 pm ☎772-5567)* with an exhibition on fishing and the history of St. John's and Newfoundland. **Cabot Tower**,

the main building on Signal Hill, was erected in 1897 in honour of the 400th anniversary of John Cabot's arrival in North America and Queen Victoria's diamond jubilee. The tower was a maritime signal station until 1960 and now houses an exhibition on the history of maritime signalling on this hill.

The exhibition also takes a close look at the life of Guglielmo Marconi, who, on December 12, 1901, received the first transatlantic wireless message at Signal Hill. This message, an "S" in Morse code, was sent from Cornwall, England. From the top floor of Cabot Tower, visitors can enjoy a splendid view of the ocean.

For a view of the harbour, head to the ruins of the **Queen's Battery**. From the foot of the cliff, you can see the rock to which the chain used to seal off the harbour in the eighteenth century was fastened. On the other side, you'll see the ruins of Fort Amherst, now topped by a lighthouse. Signal Hill's well laid out paths make it a pleasant place for a walk. Another trail runs along the harbour from Signal Hill to St. John's.

Standing proudly at the foot of Signal Hill, flanked by rock walls, is **Quidi Vidi**, one of the most picturesque villages in the province. It

is made up of a few dozen brightly coloured houses, a small chapel and, of course, a fishing port, which has been in use since the 17th century. Nearby, **Quidi Vidi Lake** is the scene of the annual **St. John's Regatta**, held on the first Wednesday in August. On a nearby promontory, visitors will find the remains of the **Quidi Vidi Battery** *(free admission; mid-Jun to early Sep, every day 9am to 5pm)*. Built in 1762 by the French, who occupied St. John's and its surrounding area for several months, this battery was later used by the British and was only abandoned in 1870.

The **Cape Spear National Historic Site** *(mid-May to mid-Oct, 10am to 6pm, 11km south of St. John's, on Hwy. 11, ☎772-5367)*. Cape Spear is the easternmost point on the North American continent. It was thus graced with a lighthouse (1863), which became the most important one in the province after the lighthouse in St. John's harbour.

Originally, the lighthouse was a square structure built around a tower, at the top of which were seven parabolic reflectors that reflected the light from seven lamps. The lighthouse was modernized over the years, then a new one was erected right nearby in 1955. The **old lighthouse** *($2.50; all year, every day 9am to 5pm)*, furnished the way its keeper's house was in 1939, is open to the public. Close by, visitors can see the remnants of the extensive military installations built here during the Second World War. Cape Spear is also a pleasant place to stroll along the shore. In fine weather, the view of the ocean and the coast is spectacular.

Tour B: The Avalon peninsula

Highway 10 leads south from St. John's to Witless Bay.

Witless Bay

The **Witless Bay Ecological Reserve** (see p 270) comprises three islands offshore from the villages of Witless Bay and Bauline. Each summer, these islands serve as a refuge for hundreds of thousands of seabirds, who come here to lay their eggs and raise their nestlings.

From Witless Bay, Highway 10 leads south to Ferryland.

Ferryland

A pretty fishing village that feels as if it has been left behind by time, Ferryland was the site of one of the first Eng-

lish colonies in North America (1621). The settlers were sent here by George Calvert who only stayed here for a few years then moved to present-day Maryland, thus becoming the first Lord Baltimore. Calvert's departure did not mean the end of the colony of Ferryland, however, which was taken in hand by English navigator David Kirke. At the **Colony of Avalon Archaeology Site** (*$3; late May to mid-Oct, every day 9am to 7pm; Hwy. 10; ☎432-3200*), where excavations have been carried out over the past few years, visitors can see the foundations of the colony and tour the research and analysis facilities.

To learn more about the history of Ferryland and its surrounding area, head to the **Historic Ferryland Museum** (*free admission; mid-Jun to mid-Sep, every day 9am to 5pm; Hwy. 10, ☎432-2711*), whose exhibitions deal, most notably, with the colony's earliest days.

Caribou

The 1,070km² **Avalon Wilderness Reserve ★**, located in the southeastern part of the Avalon Peninsula, attracts fishing buffs and hikers. To visit the reserve, you must obtain a permit at La Manche Provincial Park (*Hwy. 10, 11km from Cape Broyle*). The Avalon Wilderness Reserve is the natural habitat of tens of thousands of caribou. In the southernmost part of it, families of **caribou** can frequently be seen crossing Highway 10.

Cape St. Mary's is located at the southwesternmost tip of the Avalon Peninsula.

Cape St. Mary's

The **Cape St. Mary's Ecological Reserve ★★** (*May to Oct, every day 9am to 7pm; along Hwy. 100, ☎729-2424*) (see p 271) protects the most spectacular and most easily accessible colony of seabirds in North America.

From Cape St. Mary's, Highway 100 leads to Placentia, on the west coast of the Avalon Peninsula.

★ Placentia

This picturesque village on the shores of Placentia Bay became closely associated with the European presence on the island at a very early date. Basque fishermen were already stopping here by the early 16th century, as the pebble beach proved a particularly suitable spot for drying cod. Later, in 1662, the French established the first permanent settlement here.

Known as Plaisance, it was the capital of the French colony of Terre-Neuve until the signing of the Treaty of Utrecht in 1713. Under the French Regime, Plaisance's role consisted of containing English expansion in Newfoundland, defending the French fleet based in Newfoundland, and protecting Canada from invasion in times of war. France kept only limited military forces in Plaisance, which did not stop the little garrison from attacking St. John's, the English capital of Newfoundland, three times, in 1696, 1705 and 1709.

The 1705 expedition was the only one on which the French failed to seize Fort William, which overlooked St. John's, though they did burn the city. **Castle Hill National Historic Park ★** *(free admission; mid-Jun to early Sep, every day 8:30am to 8pm; early Sep to mid-Jun, every day 8:30am to 4:30pm; on Hwy 100, ☎227-2401)* protects the ruins of various 17th- and 18th-century French and

English fortifications. To defend Plaisance, the French built the Vieux Fort in 1662, Fort Louis in 1691 and Fort Royal in 1693. The English, after seizing control of the region, erected little Fort Frederick in 1721, then, during the War of the Austrian Succession (1740-1748), the New Fort. Castle Hill commands an outstanding view of Placentia and its bay.

From the Trans-Canada Highway, the 80 leads north to Heart's Content.

Heart's Content

Heart's Content is another testimony to the pivotal role long played by Newfoundland in communications between Europe and the New World. The invention of the telegraph (1837) revolutionized communications; within a few years, the main urban centres in North America, like those in Europe, were linked by telegraph lines. There was soon talk of linking the two continents by a telegraph line, but doing so presented a major technological challenge.

An American by the name of Cyrus W. Field decided to give it a try. In 1856, the Field New York, Newfoundland and London Telegraph companies succeeded in installing an underwater cable between Nova Scotia and Newfoundland, at a total cost of a million dollars. Laying out a transatlantic cable between Newfoundland and Europe was a much more formidable task, given the distance, the strong ocean currents and the depth of the water.

It took seven fruitless attempts before Field's Atlantic Telegraph Company succeeded, in 1866, in installing a cable between Heart's Content and Valentia, Ireland, which was the greatest technological feat of the day. The original **Heart's Content Cable Station ★** *($2.50; mid-Jun to early Oct, every day 10am to 5:30pm; ☎583-2160)*, now a provincial historic site, remained in operation until 1965. Today, it houses an interesting, well designed exhibition on the history of the Heart's Content transatlantic cable and, more generally, of world communications, complete with all sorts of equipment from the previous century.

From Heart's Content, take the 74 and then the 70 to Harbour Grace, on Conception Bay.

Harbour Grace

This tiny village earned a certain amount of notoriety in the 17th century, when it was the home base of English pirate Peter Easton. However, Harbour

Grace became best known not as a sea port but rather as the point of departure for some of the first transatlantic flights. Starting in 1919, a number of pilots tried to fly to Europe from Harbour Grace, the most notable being Amelia Earhart, the first woman to accomplish this feat, in 1932.

To learn more about these pilots, stop by the **Conception Bay Museum** (*$2; late Jun to early Sept, 10am to 1pm and 1:30pm to 4pm; Water St.; ☎596-5465*) its collection consists mostly of photographs and other representations of the most famous planes that stopped over at Heart's Content.

Highway 70 runs along Conception Bay to Brigus.

★
Brigus

Located on the shores of a pretty little bay, the striking village of Brigus boasts a large number of Victorian houses, whose imposing silhouettes make it look like a New England town. It was the birthplace of Captain Robert Bartlett (1875-1946), one of the great Arctic explorers. Bartlett's father and grandfather were also navigators and explorers who had ventured to the Arctic Ocean. Robert Bartlett pushed farther, becoming ship's captain for Robert Peary, who led some of the most important Arctic expeditions in history. Bartlett's former home is now the **Hawthorne Cottage National Historic Site ★** (*$2.50; mid-May to late Oct, 10am to 8pm; rest of the year 10am to 6pm; ☎523-4004*). The house has retained its original splendour and now contains an exhibition on Bartlett's life and exploits.

Tour C: Eastern and Central Newfoundland

The Burin Peninsula

On this long, isolated peninsula, flanked by Fortune and Placentia Bays, visitors can take in some rocky scenery and some lovely views of the sea. The proximity of the Grand Banks, which are teeming with fish, has led to the development of sizable local fishing and shipbuilding industries.

Marystown, the main town on the peninsula, has several restaurants, an excellent motel and other services. From Marystown, the highway leads to the pretty village of **Burin**, which occupies a very steep site on the shores of a bay strewn with tiny rock islands.

Burin was founded at the beginning of the 18th century and served as Captain James Cook's base when he was exploring the shores of Newfoundland in the 1760s. The village boasts a number of lovely homes, including the **Burin Heritage House ★** (*free admission; May to Oct, every day 10am to 4pm; ☎891-2217*), now a museum with about a dozen rooms devoted to local history, antiques and works by regional artists. To the south, the 220 runs through tiny communities of only a few houses, built on a rocky plateau. In many places, the coast is punctuated with tall cliffs.

The road continues to **Fortune**, where you can take a ferry to the French islands of Saint-Pierre and Miquelon, then continues to Grand Bank, which has a few restaurants and places to stay, a **museum** focusing on local history and an impressive **lighthouse**. A number of trails have been cleared nearby, making it possible to take in the local scenery. At the **Southern Newfoundland Seamen's Museum ★** (*early May to late Oct, every day 9am to 5pm; Marine Dr.; ☎832-1484*), visitors can learn about the history of the local fisheries through photographs, models of old ships and various other objects. Yugoslavia's pavilion for Expo '67 was moved here from Montréal to house the collection.

★
Saint-Pierre and Miquelon

The islands of Saint-Pierre and Miquelon are the last remnants of France's North American empire. In 1763, under the Treaty of Paris, France ceded all its possessions to England, except for these two islands, which are now a *département d'outremer* (DOM), or overseas department, with representation in the National Assembly in France.

The local inhabitants, who only number several thousand, are of Acadian, Basque and Breton descent. Most live in Saint-Pierre, a pretty little town made up of stone houses alongside a good natural harbour on the island of the same name. Though the islands are only 25km from the Burin Peninsula, their atmosphere and residents' way of life is far more typical of metropolitan France than of North America.

The ambiance and cuisine of its bistros and cafés are French, and many products – everything from wine and spirits to cars and motorcycles – are im-

ported directly from France. These two islands cover an area of 242km². The larger and less populous of the two, Miquelon, has some lovely beaches and powdery dunes.

On Saint-Pierre, the gateway to the archipelago, visitors can gorge themselves on French food, stroll along the narrow streets of the town, visit a small museum devoted to the history of the two islands or simply mingle with the friendly local residents. From the end of June to the beginning of September, there is ferry service from Fortune, on the Burin Peninsula (☎832-2006) to Saint-Pierre. The trip takes about 2hrs and a return adult ticket costs $65. The ferry is for passengers only.

Canadian and U.S. citizens need only show an ID card to visit Saint-Pierre, while citizens of the European Economic Community and Switzerland have to show their passport. It is also possible to reach the island by plane, as Air Saint-Pierre offers service from Halifax, Nova Scotia (☎902-873-3566). For more information on Saint-Pierre and Miquelon, contact the Agence Régionale du Tourisme in Saint-Pierre (☎508-41-22-22).

★
Trinity

A village with particularly well-preserved 19th-century architecture, Trinity sits on a promontory alongside an excellent natural harbour on the **Bonavista Peninsula ★★**. The site was named by explorer Gaspar Corte Real, who explored its bay on Trinity Sunday in the year 1501. In 1558, the English made Trinity their first permanent settlement in Newfoundland.

Thanks to its fisheries and commercial ties with London, Trinity managed to attain a certain level of prosperity. In 1615, it became the seat of the first maritime court in Canada, for a case involving a conflict between local and seasonal fishermen.

Trinity offers visitors all sorts of opportunities to step back into the past: the **Trinity Interpretation Centre** (*$2.50; mid-Jun to early Sep, every day 10am to 5:30pm; Hwy. 239, ☎464-2042*) boasts an excellent collection of maps, illustrations and period photographs; the **Green Family Forge** (*$2; mid-Jun to early Sep, every day 10am to 6pm; Church Rd., ☎464-2244*) presents an exhibition on the history of a forge dating back to the 1750s, and **Hiscock House** (*$2.50; mid-Jun to early Sep, every day 10am to 5:30pm, Hwy. 239, ☎464-2042*), open to the public, is a typical turn-of-the-century merchant's house. The most novel way to learn about Trinity's history, however, is by attending the **Trinity Pageant** ★, a series of plays about local history, presented in different places around town. The shows are held daily during summer, starting at 2pm.

From May to August, several kinds of whales come to the waters off Newfoundland. They can often be spotted from the shore. For a closer look, we recommend going on a whale-watching excursion. Trinity is a good point of departure, and a number of tour agencies organize outings.

★
Cape Bonavista

Did John Cabot really open the way to the exploration of Canada? Newfoundlanders swear that he did, and maintain that it was at Cape Bonavista that Cabot and his crew stopped for the first time in the summer of 1497, after sailing across the Atlantic from Bristol, England. In reality, no one really knows where Cabot landed in the New World. Cape Bonavista is fighting over the honour with several other sites along the Canadian coast. In any case, it was in Cape Bonavista that Newfoundlanders celebrated, with great

pomp, the 500th anniversary of Cabot's landing in 1997.

The village of Bonavista is the largest community on the peninsula. Its pretty, brightly col-

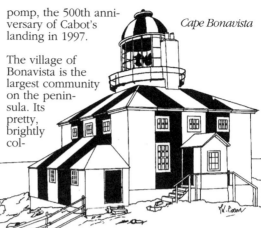

Cape Bonavista

oured houses are surrounded by a rolling landscape that unfolds onto a bustling port. Bonavista was frequented by fishermen of all different nationalities throughout the 16th century, before the English settled here around 1600.

At the beginning of the 19th century, the government of Newfoundland started building lighthouses along the shores of the island to make the waters safer for ships. In 1843, the first lighthouse on the north shore of the island was erected on Cape Bonavista. Today, you can visit the **old lighthouse** *($2.50; mid-Jun to early Oct, every day 10am to 5:30pm; Hwy. 230; ☎468-7444)*, which has been restored and furnished the way it was in the 1870s. It houses an exhibition on the history of lighthouses and the daily life of their keepers.

The point offers a magnificent **view** ★ of the sea and the rocky shoreline. Whales can often be spotted offshore in summer. If you keep your eyes peeled, you can see these giant mammals from many spots along Bonavista Bay.

Port Blandford

This little community is the gateway to **Terra Nova National Park** (see p 269).

Gander

This modern town, one of the largest in central Newfoundland, lies on the shores of Gander Lake. In 1935, the British government (the island was still a British colony at that time) chose Gander as the site of an international airport that would serve as a stopover for transatlantic flights.

As so often in its history, Newfoundland, North America's easternmost island, thus became a sort of pivot between Europe and the New World. During the Second World War, the military used the airport to defend the North Atlantic against German U-boats. Though Gander is still a hub for international air transportation, its importance diminished with the advent of long-range aircraft.

Visitors can learn about the history of aviation in Gander at the new **North Atlantic Aviation Museum** *($3; summer 9am to 9pm, winter Mon to Fri 9am to 5pm; Hwy. 1; ☎256-2923)*, which exhibits a variety of objects, including pilot's uniforms, weapons and airplane engines. About 4km east of Gander, on Highway 1, stands the **Silent Witness Memorial**, erected in memory of the 256 members of the 100th Airborne Division of the U.S. Air force who died when their plane crashed right after take-off at Gander airport in 1985.

From Gander, the 330 (North), the 331 and then the 340 will take you to **Boyd's Cove Beothuk Interpretation Centre ★** *($2.50; mid-Jun to early Oct, 10am to 5:30pm; Hwy. 340, Boyd's Cove; ☎656-3114)*. From about 1650 to 1720, Boyd's Cove was the site of a large Beothuk village. Over the past few decades, extensive archaeological excavations have been carried

out in the area. The interpretation centre presents some interesting collections of artifacts, as well as a slide show on the cultural history of the Beothuk. Interpretation trails have been laid out to reveal even more about the Beothuk way of life, and visitors can also see the site where the excavations were carried out. North of Boyd's Cove is the pretty region of **Twillingate**, a charming place during summer, when icebergs and whales can often be spotted.

Grand Falls - Windsor

Grand Falls takes its name from the spectacular **falls** on the nearby Exploits River. It has been merged with its twin, Windsor, into one town. The region's economy began to take off in 1909, when a pulp and paper mill was built here. Now owned by Abitibi-Price, the mill is still mainstay of the local economy. Earlier, the region was one of the major centres of the Beothuk, an Aboriginal group who inhabited the island of Newfoundland before the Europeans arrived, and who have since been completely wiped out. The **Mary March Regional Museum ★** *(Mon to Fri 9am to 5pm and Sat to Sun 10am to 6pm; May to Oct; 22 St. Catherine St.; ☎292-4522)* was named after one of the last members of the

Beothuk nation, who died at the beginning of the 19th century. The museum presents a short film on the Beothuk. Its collections deal with the human and natural history of central Newfoundland. Right behind the museum, visitors can tour a reconstruction of a **Beothuk village** *($2; mid-Jun to early Oct, 10am to 7pm)*.

Tour D: Western Newfoundland

Channel Port aux Basques

Located on the southwestern tip of the island, Channel Port aux Basques is the terminal for one of the two ferries from North Sydney, Nova Scotia (the other one goes to Argentia, on the Avalon Peninsula). There is nothing particularly charming about Port aux Basques, but it does have a few hotels and restaurants, as well as an excellent tourist information centre.

Port-au-Port Peninsula

From Highway 1, visitors can reach the Port-au-Port Peninsula by way of Stephenville. Dotting the shores of the peninsula, which offer lovely views of the ocean, are a few small fishing villages, home to the bulk of the French-speaking population of the island of Newfoundland. Port-au-Port was once part of what was known as the French Shore, where France had fishing and fish-processing rights until 1904. The most francophone communities on the peninsula are located near Cape St. George. The Grande Veillée festival, held in Cape St. George in August, is a wonderful opportunity to learn about the local culture.

★
Corner Brook

Newfoundland's second largest town, Corner Brook, could be termed the capital of the island's west coast. It is home to a whole slew of government services, a college affiliated with Memorial University and a number of hotels, shops and restaurants. Corner Brook occupies a magnificent site on the banks of a fiord, the Humber Arm, surrounded by big hills. Though French fishermen had probably known about this site for a long time before, it was Captain James Cook who first reported its existence, in 1767, and named it Corner Brook.

The area first started to be developed in 1864, with the construction of a sawmill. However, the local economy didn't really take off until 1923, when Corner Brook was chosen as

the site of one of the largest pulp and paper mills in the world. Be that as it may, all sorts of wonderful discoveries await nature lovers in this region. During summer, visitors can start off by taking a cruise on the Humber River. These excursions, which depart from Sandy Brook, take passengers up the river, whose shores are home to numerous species of birds. Fishing trips can also be arranged *($22; ☎634-8140)*.

Marble Mountain ★, see p 272.

About 60km west of Corner Brook, visitors can take in the splendours of **Blow Me Down Provincial Park** ★ (see p 270).

Deer Lake

Deer Lake lies at the intersection of the Trans-Canada Highway, which runs east-west across Newfoundland, and Highway 430, which leads to magnificent Gros Morne National Park and the "Viking Highway." A small, modern town, it has several restaurants and places to stay, as well as an airport for flights from Newfoundland's other urban centres and Halifax, Nova Scotia.

A number of car-rental agencies have branches here, as well. If you're

pressed for time, a flight from St. John's to Deer Lake will spare you nearly 650km of driving. Gros Morne National Park, one of Newfoundland's major attractions, is less than an hour's drive from Deer Lake.

Tour E: The Viking Highway

There is an excellent road from Deer Lake to **Gros Morne National Park** ★★★. The Viking Highway runs along the Strait of Belle Isle from the park, through strikingly desolate, rocky landscapes.

Port au Choix

Port au Choix, where fishing is still the major activity, was an important port for Basque fishermen for many years. Its name comes from "Portuchoa," which means "little port" in Basque. The Basques were not the first people to take advantage of Port au Choix's excellent location, however. The **Port au Choix National Historic Site** ★ *($2.75; mid-Jun to mid-Sep, every day 9am to 5pm; ☎861-3522)* displays traces of peoples who inhabited this region long before any Europeans arrived.

These vestiges were discovered during archaeological excavations. In the 1950s, in nearby Phillip's Gardens, archaeologists uncovered traces of a Dorset Eskimo community that occupied this site between the years 200 and 600. Dorset culture was sophisticated, as evidenced by the finely worked bone and stone carvings discovered here. In 1967, other major digs in the region led to the uncovering of a Maritime Archaic burial ground containing human bones, tools and weapons and dating back 3,200 to 4,300 years.

The Maritime Archaic survived essentially on fishing and hunting. They developed an artistic tradition and decorated their clothing with shells, seal's claws and pendants made of bone. The tools, weapons and ornaments found in the tombs indicate that these natives would prepare for a life after death not unlike their life on earth.

At the Port au Choix National Historic Site, visitors can see some of the artifacts found in this area and watch a documentary on the lifestyle of these indigenous peoples. The short walk to the Phillip's Garden's archaeological site offers a chance to contemplate the region's rugged landscape.

St. Barbe

During summer, a ferry carries passengers from St. Barbe to Blanc Sablon, Québec every day. From Blanc Sablon, an excellent road leads through several villages along the shores of the Strait of Belle Isle (see p 268), in Labrador.

L'Anse aux Meadows

The **L'Anse aux Meadows National Historic Site** ★★ *($5; mid-Jun to mid-Sep, every day 9am to 8pm; Hwy. 436, ☎623-2608)* is the only place where traces of Norwegian sailors – or Vikings, as they are sometimes called in North America – have been discovered. L'Anse-aux-Meadows is a UNESCO World Heritage Site. A group of Norwegian sailors, led by Leif Eriksson, came here from Greenland and set up a camp around the year 1000.

This camp consisted of eight buildings and was home to an estimated 80 to 100 people. The Norwegians used it as a base for their expeditions along the Atlantic coast. According to the sagas, on their expeditions from Leif's camp, Leif Eriksson and his family discovered the shores of Labrador, Newfoundland and regions farther south, on the Gulf of St. Lawrence. Eriksson named the southernmost lands Vinland, after the wild vines that grew there. The L'Anse-aux-Meadows site was discovered by Helge Ingstad and Anne Stisne Ingstad in 1960.

Visitors can see the foundations of the eight buildings uncovered by the Ingstads, and later by Parks Canada. Three buildings from Eriksson's era have been reconstructed right nearby. Excellent guided tours are available. The welcome centre presents an interesting exhibition on the vestiges found on the site and also shows a film on the captivating story of the Ingstads and Parks Canada excavations.

Viking Boat Tours ★
($25; several departures daily; Moddy Nay, about 500m from Anse-aux-Meadows; ☎623-2100) offers 2hr sea excursions aboard a superb replica of a Viking ship dating from the year 1000. The cruise is really worth the cost, especially during June and July, the best times to see whales and icebergs.

★ St. Anthony

Located on the shores of an excellent inland harbour, St. Anthony is the largest community in the northern part of the peninsula. Since 1922, it has been the headquarters of **Grenfell Mission**, which provides medical care for the isolated communities of northern Newfoundland and Labrador.

The mission was founded by Dr. Wilfred Grenfell (1865-1940), who started developing the region's first real network of hospitals, infirmaries and orphanages in 1894. To finance his projects, Grenfell created a company called Grenfell Crafts, which sold winter clothing made by local craftspeople; the profits would go to the mission. Today, you can visit the **Grenfell House Museum** (*$5; mid-Jun to mid-Sep, every day 9am to 8pm; Hwy. 430, ☎454-2281*), the Grenfell family's former home, which houses a collection of objects used by fishermen at the turn of the century. The museum's shop sells pretty winter clothing made on the premises, as well as local crafts.

From the centre of St. Anthony, visitors can go to nearby **Fishing Point**, which offers a splendid **view ★** of the ocean. Whales and icebergs can often be spotted from here during the summer. There is also a good restaurant at Fishing Point.

★ Tour F: Labrador

Labrador, separated from the island of Newfoundland by the Strait of Belle Isle, is a huge territory of nearly 300,000km². It is inhabited by only a few tens of thousands of people – Inuit, Aboriginals and English- and French-speaking Canadians – most of whom live in fishing villages along the shore or in small towns in the central and western regions.

Most of Labrador remains a vast stretch of wilderness, as yet undeveloped and still full of mystery. The south

Inuit Woman and Baby

ern part of Labrador has a gently rolling landscape strewn with lakes and rivers. Farther north, the Torngat Mountains rise to an altitude of 1,676m at their highest point. This region is covered with a subarctic forest, shrubs and scrawny trees, and, in the northernmost parts, tundra.

These infertile lands have been inhabited for over 8,000 years. The first people to live in Labrador were the Maritime Archaic. The ancestors of the Inuit, who still live in northern Labrador, arrived about 4,000 years later. Toward the year 1000, the Vikings explored the coastline of this part of the continent, but Basque whalers were the first Europeans to set up camps along the shores of Labrador, in the 16th century.

In those days, about 2,000 Basque sailors would come to the Strait of Belle Isle to hunt whales each year. Red Bay, on the shores of the Strait, was one of the Basques' most important bases. French and English fishermen and tradesmen were the next to arrive, though they did not really establish any permanent settlements along the shore until the end of the 19th century. In western Labrador, the 20th century has been marked by large-scale projects like the huge iron mine near Labrador City and the gigantic hydro-electric dam at Churchill Falls.

★ The Strait of Belle Isle

There is a road running along the Strait of Belle Isle, through the coastal villages from Blanc Sablon (Québec) to Red Bay, a distance of about 80km. Visitors can take the ferry to Blanc Sablon from St. Barbe, in the northern part of the island of Newfoundland, along the Viking Highway. The road runs through a very rugged coastal landscape, passing through tiny communities that survive mainly on fishing.

L'Anse-au-Clair, the first village along the way, was founded by the French in the 17th century, like many other communities along the coast. It has a pretty fishing port and a tourist information office, which is set up inside a church dating from the turn of the century. Farther along, at **Anse-Amour**, archaeologists have discovered the remains of a funerary monument built 7,500 years ago by the Maritime Archaic.

Nearby lies the **Point Amour Lighthouse Provincial Historic Site** *($2.50; mid-Jun to early-Oct, 10am to 5:30pm)*, which, at over 30m high, is the tallest lighthouse in eastern Canada. Right near **L'Anse Au Loup**, the

Labrador Straits Museum *($2; early Jul to mid-Sep)* recounts the history of the region with the help of various objects. Highway 510 continues to Red Bay, home of the **Red Bay National Historic Site** ★ *($5; mid-Jun to mid-Oct, 9am to 6:30)*, which was the most important fishing port for Basque whalers during the 16th century. At its peak, about 20 boats and 2,000 Basque seamen would spend the summer whale hunting in the area.

The site has an interpretation centre, which presents an excellent film on the history of whale hunting in the Strait of Belle Isle. Visitors can also take a boat out to Saddle Island, where the major archaeological excavations were carried out.

★ The Labrador Coast

The Labrador coast is still inaccessible by car, but you can get there by boat or by plane. Each week, a cargo ship sets out from the port of St. Anthony, in the northern part of the island of Newfoundland to bring supplies to some 48 tiny, isolated communities on the coast (see p 253).

The boat travels as far as Nain, in northern Labrador, offering passengers a chance to take in some remarkable scenery. This part of the coast is known as Iceberg Alley; during spring and summer, thousands of icebergs of various sizes, including some veritable mountains of ice weighing several million tons, can be seen here. There are some interesting places to visit during the stops on the trip. Nain has a **museum** devoted to Inuit culture.

Hopedale is home to the **Hopedale Mission National Historic Site** *(☎933-3777)*. The mission, established by the British government in 1782, includes a church and several other buildings that are among the oldest in the Atlantic provinces. Mary's Harbour offers access to the **Battle Harbour Resettled Fishing Community** *(free admission; early Jun to late Sep; ☎921-6216)*, where you'll find the remains of an 18th-century fishing village, including the oldest Anglican church in Labrador. Still, the coast's main appeal lies in its scenery, its isolation and its welcoming inhabitants. The round trip takes about two weeks.

Central and Western Labrador

Central and western Labrador are relatively easy to reach by car from Québec and, during summer, by ferry from the island of Newfoundland. This unspoiled expanse of wilderness, with its forests and myriad lakes and rivers, is a choice destination for fishing and hunting buffs. The subarctic forests are teeming with animal life, including a huge number of moose and the largest caribou population in the world. Together, Labrador City and Wabush form the largest community in Labrador. A number of hotels, restaurants and services can be found here. The mainspring of the local economy is an opencast iron mine, the largest in the world. A variety of outdoor activities may be enjoyed near Labrador City and Wabush, including hiking, canoeing, scuba diving, sailing and golf. The area is also home to an excellent cross-country ski centre, which maintains about 40km of trails during winter. For a lovely view of the region, head to **Crystal Falls**. The rest of Labrador is still virtually uninhabited, aside from a few small towns, such as Churchill Falls, which was built near a huge hydroelectric dam, and Goose Bay, located near a military base.

Moose

Tour C: Eastern and Central Newfoundland

Terra Nova National Park ★ (☎533-2801) covers just over 400km² of wooded, gently rolling terrain. It is bounded by the Newman Sound and the Clode Sound, which are inlets of Bonavista Bay. The park is home to numerous animal species, including moose, black bears, martens, beavers and lynxes. The waters of

Black bear

the sounds,particularly during May and August, attract various species of whales, including humpbacks. **Ocean Watch Tours** (☎533-6024) hosts cruises in the sounds for people interested in observing whales and other aquatic species. The main activities that can be enjoyed in the park are camping, hiking, fishing, canoeing and, in winter, cross-

country skiing; most organized outings start at Newman Sound. The Twin Rivers Golf Course is located at the park's south entrance. Two lookouts, both accessible by car, offer **panoramic views ★** of the park: the **Blue Hill Exhibit** *(drive 7km from the north entrance, then take a side road for 1.5km)* and the **Ochre Hill Exhibit** *(drive 23km from the north entrance, then take a side road for 3km)*.

Tour E: The Viking Highway

The internationally renowned **Gros Morne National Park ★★★** (☎458-2417) boasts 1,805km² of spectacular scenery: fiords, lakes, high plateaux, coastal dunes and boreal forests. The Long Range Mountains run the entire length of the park; Gros Morne is the highest, at 850m. In 1987, UNESCO designated Gros Morne National Park a World Heritage Site, primarily because of its geological make-up: in the southern part of the park **Tablelands** formed by the shifting of two tectonic plates give a good example of the continental drift. The park's landscape was also shaped by the retreat of the glaciers at

Newfoundland and Labrador

park's landscape was also shaped by the retreat of the glaciers at the end of the Glacial Period.

Gros Morne National Park protects numerous wild mammals, including bears, moose and caribou. It is not uncommon to see moose along the park's main roads, and various species of whales can be spotted from the shore during summer. In addition to wildlife observation, other activities to be enjoyed here are camping, hiking (over 100km of trails), swimming, boat rides, fishing and, in winter, cross-country skiing. Lodgings are available at Trout River, Woody Point, Rocky Harbour and Cow Head.

Its splendid scenery and distinctive geological characteristics make the park's **south sector** well worth exploring. From the south entrance, Highway 431 runs through a rolling landscape, then along one of the arms of **Bonne Bay ★**, a deep fiord surrounded by the Long Range Mountains. The road leads to **Woody Point**, a pretty fishing village, then on to **Trout River Pond ★★**. This 15km-long freshwater fiord lies in a glacial valley at the edge of the **Gregory Plateau** and **Tablelands ★★**, created by the shifting of the tectonic plates about 500 million years ago. Visitors can explore this part of the park by

taking a **boat ride** *(mid-Jun to mid-Sep; three departures per day from Trout River; ☎951-2101)* on Trout River.

The landscape of the **north sector** is dominated by the Long Range Mountains. The park's welcome centre, on Highway 430, a few kilometres from **Rocky Harbour**, shows an excellent documentary on the flora, fauna and geological features of Gros Morne National Park.

It also provides information on the various activities to be enjoyed in the park and hosts a number of nature talks. From Rocky Harbour, the road leads to the **Lobster Cove Head lighthouse**. The old lighthouse keeper's house now contains an exhibition on the history of the settlement of the coastline in this area. There is a trail leading from the lighthouse to a rocky beach. Much farther north in the park, a 3km trail offers access to **Western Brook Pond ★★**, a 16km-long, 165m-deep inland fiord created during the Glacial Epoch.

The rock walls that plunge into its crystalline waters reach as high as 650m in places. A **cruise** is the most pleasant way to take in the fiord's spectacular beauty. The outing lasts about 2.5hrs; for reservations, inquire at the Ocean View Motel *(☎458-2730)* in Rocky

Harbour. Trimmed with beaches and sand dunes, **Shallow Bay**, at the north end of the park, is a good place to go swimming.

Blow Me Down Provincial Park ★ *(Hwy. 450)* lies on a hilly peninsula that stretches out into the Bay of Islands, between Lark and York Harbours. The park offers a glorious view of the bay and the Blow Me Down Mountains. There is a path leading up to a lookout (about a half-hour's walk), while other trails run to the tip of the peninsula. A few campsites can be found in the park, as well.

Outdoor Activities

Bird-watching

Tour B: The Avalon Peninsula

At the **Witless Bay Ecological Reserve ★**, the main avian attraction is the Atlantic puffin, the provincial bird. Though bird colonies can be seen from the shore, you can get a much closer look by taking a cruise. A number of tour agencies, including **Bird Island Charters** *($25/ per.; ☎753-4850)* offer excursions from the villages along the coast.

The **Cape St. Mary's Ecological Reserve** ★★ *(every day 9am to 5pm; on Hwy. 100, ☎ 729-2424)*, on the southwest tip of the Avalon Peninsula and washed by the Atlantic Ocean is home to some 60,000 seabirds. The most interesting place to observe them is along Bird Rock, a tall rock a few metres from the shore, where a number of species nest.

Visitors will also find the largest gannet colony in Newfoundland, the southernmost colony of thick-billed murres in the world, and many other species of birds, including eagles. Furthermore, during July, humpback whales can be spotted offshore. The welcome centre provides fascinating information on the nature of seabirds.

Whale-watching

Nearly 20 species of whales, including about 5,000 humpbacks, visit the coast of Newfoundland and Labrador during the summer months. The whales stay in this part of the Atlantic from May to September. They can easily be observed in June and July, when their numbers are the greatest. Though many spots along the coast

are good for whale-watching, some of the best places are Gros Morne National Park and the Viking Highway as far as St. Anthony, the Twillingate area (north of Gander), the Bonavista Peninsula and the eastern shore of the Avalon Peninsula; all are points of departure for numerous sea excursions.

Iceberg-watching

The icebergs drifting off the shores of Labrador and Newfoundland are surely one of the most fascinating natural phenomena a person can witness. Every year, tens of thousands of icebergs of various sizes break off from the shores of Greenland and slowly drift southward. This phenomenon starts in March and ends in November. June and July are the best times to observe the icebergs from the shores of Newfoundland and Labrador. The Labrador coast, the Strait of Belle Isle, the northern part of the island of Newfoundland (especially Twillingate) and the eastern shore of the Avalon Peninsula are usually good vantage points during this time of year.

Hiking

Hiking buffs will be amazed by the possibilities available to them on the island of Newfoundland. Over the years, countless trails have been cleared along the island's spectacular coast, particularly on the Avalon Peninsula. There are even trails in St. John's, the capital, which make for interesting outings and offer magnificent views of the ocean. If scenic variety is what you're after, head to Gros Morne National Park, which has no fewer than 100 km of trails, some suitable for short hikes, others for four-to five-day expeditions.

Atlantic Puffin

Downhill Skiing

Tour D: Western Newfoundland

The **Marble Mountain Ski Resort** ★ *(Hwy. 1; Steady Brook, 8 km east of Corner Brook;* ☎*637-7600 or 637-7611)* is the best place for downhill skiing in the Atlantic provinces. The vertical drop is over 550m and the slopes are very steep in many places. Beginners and experts alike can enjoy the 27 trails. Aside from its excellent runs, one of Marble Mountain's major advantages is the heavy snowfall it receives – about 4m each winter, allowing for one of the longest ski seasons in the eastern part of the continent.

Accommodations

Tour A: St. John's

Memorial University of Newfoundland
☎737-7590
The student residences at Memorial University of Newfoundland are rented to the public from mid-May to mid-August. A single room goes for $18, while the double rate is $25.

The Roses B & B
$60 bkfst incl.
K, tv
4 rooms
9 Military Rd.
☎*726-3336*
≈*726-3483*
Laid out in a Victorian house typical of downtown St. John's, this bed and breakfast is a friendly and very charming spot. Its high ceilings, rich mouldings, and wood floors give it a warm atmosphere.

Its always inviting rooms are decorated with a heterogenous mix of antiques of greater or lesser value and modern furniture. Some of the rooms are equipped with fireplaces. Days at this welcoming inn always begin on the right foot with a copious breakfast served on the top floor of the house, from which there is a panoramic view of the port.

🦞 **Compton House**
$69 bkfst incl.
ॐ, ⊛, pb, tv
10 rooms
26 Waterford Bridge Rd., A1E 1C6
☎*739-5789*
≈*739-1770*
This majestic Victorian residence, converted into an inn, occupies a vast, prettily landscaped property near the Waterford River valley, about 15min by foot from the centre of the city. Guests quickly feel right at home in this lovely, elegant and inviting house brimming with period

charm. The front living room is particularly pleasant and has a fireplace, as do the little library and the dining room. The guest rooms are well furnished, very comfortable and all equipped with private bathrooms. If a little extra luxury is in order, visitors can stay in the suites, each of which is equipped with a balcony or a patio, a whirlpool and a fireplace.

Prescott Inn
$85 pb, $65 sb
K, tv
22 rooms
19 Military Rd.
☎*753-7733*
☎*888-263-3786*
≈*753-6036*
In a beautiful Victorian house just next to the Roses B & B, the Prescott Inn is a good alternative to its neighbour. Its rooms are clean and reasonably priced. The Prescott also offers a suite equipped with a kitchenette.

🦞 **Waterford Manor**
$85 bkfst incl.
⊛, ℜ, tv
7 rooms
185 Waterford Bridge Rd., A1E 1C7
☎*754-4139*
≈*754-4155*
Built at the end of the last century for the family of a local merchant, this sumptuous Queen Anne house is now one of the province's most beautiful inns. Recent renovation work has restored its former grandeur and adapted it

to meet modern expectations of comfort.

Guest rooms, each of which has its own special character, are furnished with antiques and decorated with meticulous attention to detail. They are all very pleasant, but the most beautiful of them, on the top floor, offers a fireplace and a whirlpool. Breakfast can be served either in guests' rooms or in the dining room on the ground floor. The Waterford Manor, tucked away in a pretty residential neighbourhood on the outskirts of the Waterford River Valley, is approximately a 15min walk from downtown St. John's.

Quality Hotel by Journey's End
$90
ℜ, tv
162 rooms
2 Hill O'Chips, A1C 6B1
☎*754-7788*
☎*800-228-5151*
⇄*754-5209*
Quality Hotel by Journey's End is always a sure bet. It is a welcoming, well-situated establishment near downtown that offers good value for your money. Although the rooms are comfortable, well kept and functional, there is nothing especially original about them. Since it sits on a hill near the port, the Quality Hotel offers a lovely view of the bay.

Holiday Inn St. John's
$99
ℜ, ≈, ☺
190 rooms
180 Portugal Cove Rd., A1B 2N2
☎*722-0506*
☎*800-933-0506*
⇄*722-9756*
Located about 15min from downtown St. John's, near a pretty park, the Holiday Inn possesses comfortable rooms with the functional layout typical of North American motels. Amenities include a lovely swimming pool and a very satisfactory restaurant

🎖 Hotel Newfoundland
$129
ℜ, ≈, ☺
Cavendish Square, P.O. Box 5637, A1C 5W8
☎*800-441-1414 or 726-4980*
⇄*726-2025*
The most prestigious establishment in St. John's, a member of the Canadian Pacific hotel chain, is a modern, 301-room hotel in the heart of the city. Its interior decor is a brilliant success: it is both original and inviting. From the lobby visitors can go into the Court Garden, where terraced plant beds are embellished by interspersed waterfalls.

The warmth and brightness of this spot are in singular contrast to the cool, rainy climate that so often shrouds the city. Guest rooms are spacious, charming and comfortable – they have been designed as much to please vacationers as to meet the needs of business trav-

ellers – and most of them offer breathtaking views of the port, the city and the bay.

Tour B: The Avalon Peninsula

Ferryland

Downs Inn
$55 bkfst incl.
sb, tv
4 rooms
Rte. 10, A0A 2H0
☎*877-432-2808*
⇄*432-2659*
Lodging is available about an hour from St. John's at Downs Inn, a pleasant bed and breakfast laid out in an old Presbyterian convent. Erected in 1914, this building was home to about 15 nuns until the 1980s; renovation work has managed to preserve the spirit of the house. Each of the spacious, clean, comfortable rooms is equipped with a fireplace, but none of them have private washrooms.

Trepassey

Trepassey Motel
$59
ℜ, tv
10 rooms
P.O. Box 22, A0A 4B0
☎*438-2934*
⇄*438-2179*
This little motel on the edge of Route 10, at the southern tip of the peninsula, occupies a very quiet setting near the Avalon Wilderness Reserve, a summer habitat for caribou. Although rather indifferently fur-

Newfoundland and Labrador

nished, its rooms are well kept and inviting, and the fare served at the Trepassey Motel restaurant (see p 279) more than meets the mark.

St. Bride's

Bird Island Resort
$49
ℜ, K, tv
20 rooms
Rte. 100, A0A 2Z0
☎*337-2450 or 888-337-2450*
⇋*337-2903*
Bird Island Resort is located in the tiny village of St. Bride's, a little bit away from the ornithological reserve at Cape St. Mary's. This recently built establishment occupies a large grassy property facing Placentia Bay. Its rooms are impeccably clean and some are equipped with kitchenettes.

Placentia

Rosedale Manor
$50 bkfst incl.
4 rooms
Riverside Dr., A0B 2Y0
☎*227-3613*
Guests of the Rosedale Manor, one of the loveliest inns on this part of the peninsula, will feel right at home. Located in the heart of the village, just across from the bay, this pretty historic house offers carefully decorated rooms embellished with antique furniture and equipped with private bathrooms. The owner is both attentive and discreet. If you are interested, she will be happy to fill you in on the local history.

Harbour Grace

Garrison House Inn
$64
pb, ℜ
3 rooms
16 Water St., A0A 2M0
☎*596-3658*
Garrison House Inn, a beautiful Victorian house that dates from the beginning of the 19th century, stands in the heart of the little town of Harbour Grace. At once welcoming and elegant, this very well-renovated home is embellished with antique furniture. All of the guest rooms are equipped with private bathrooms. The Garrison's dining room is the best place for supper in Harbour Grace.

Brigus

Brittoner Inn
$55 bkfst incl.
sb pb
3 rooms
12 Water St., A0A 1K0
☎*528-3412*
One of the prettiest towns in the province, Brigus numbers many Victorian houses, one of which is home to the Brittoner Inn This inn is well situated – in the heart of Brigus, facing the bay – and its rooms are comfortable and well kept. Two of the five rooms offer private bathrooms. A copious breakfast and a warm welcome pleasantly round out a stay at the Brittoner.

Tour C: Eastern and Central Newfoundland

Marystown

Hotel Marystown
$75
ℜ
131 rooms
79 Ville Marie Dr. P.O. Box 487
A0E 2M0
☎*279-1600 or 800-563-2489*
⇋*279-4088*
This modern establishment in the heart of the community of Marystown is the most comfortable on the Burin Peninsula. Its reasonably priced rooms are well maintained and conveniently designed.

The hotel's enjoyable restaurant, TJ Billington (see p 279), serves simple but flavourful, well-prepared cuisine and is a popular meeting place for visitors from the French island of St. Pierre.

Fortune

Fair Isle Motel
$59
ℜ, tv
13 rooms
Main St., A0E 1P0
☎*832-1010*
⇋*832-2229*
Fair Isle Motel, a little blue and white building at the Fortune exit of Route 210, rents a few summarily equipped rooms. Fortune's harbour is the departure point for the ferry to the French islands of St. Pierre and Miquelon.

Grand Bank

Thorndyke B & B
$55 bkfst incl.
4 rooms
33 Water St., A0E 1W0
☎/⇰*832-0820*
This oceanside house was built in 1917 by John Thornhill, a fisherman who was renowned as one of the best seamen in the region in his time. The old two-storey house is architecturally reminiscent of New England and, although its interior is not especially luxurious, it has a pleasant, old-fashioned allure.

Trinity

🛶 **Campbell House**
$80 bkfst incl.
tv, ℜ
5 rooms
High St.
☎*464-3377 or 877-464-7700*
⇰*464-3377*
Campbell House is a bed and breakfast set up in a lovely house that dates from the 1840s. The old-fashioned appeal of this stately residence, which stands in the middle of the town's historic area, has been well preserved thanks to meticulous renovation work. The rooms are charming and prettily decorated. From Campbell House there is a beautiful view of the town and the ocean.

The Village Inn
$52
ℜ, *tv*
7 rooms
Taverner's Path
☎*464-3700*
The Village Inn is, despite its relatively modest size, the largest hotel establishment in Trinity. It has occupied this building in the heart of the village since the beginning of this century. Its rooms vary greatly in comfort and quality. There is a good family restaurant on the premises and whale-watching trips are organized here.

Trinity East

🛶 **Peace Cove Inn**
$69 bkfst incl.
sb pb
5 rooms
Rte. 230, A0C 2H0
☎*464-3738*
⇰*464-2167*
Peace Cove Inn, a pretty house painted beige and green, occupies a beautiful spot on the shores of the bay in Trinity East, a few kilometres from the heart of Trinity's historic area. A few of its inviting, tastefully furnished and decorated rooms are equipped with private bathrooms; excellent breakfasts are served in the morning.

Cape Bonavista

🛶 **Silver Lining B & B**
$65, bkfst incl.
3 rooms
P.O. Box 1497, A0C 1B0
☎/⇰*468-1278*
The Silver Lining B & B stands just next to an adorable church on a

hilltop overlooking the village of Cape Bonavista. This beautiful Gothic-style house was built in 1901 and has very successfully preserved its old-time splendour and allure. Its ground-floor common rooms are all tastefully decorated and adorned with antique furniture, as are the guest rooms. The Silver Lining lives up to its name for visitors who value a peaceful, friendly spot tinged with a touch of elegance.

Port Blandford

Terra Nova Park Lodge
$90
79 rooms
ℜ, ≈, ≡, *tv*
A0C 2G0
☎*543-2525*
⇰*543-2201*
The Terra Nova Park hodge stands on a large lot near the national park and close to an excellent 18-hole golf course. Naturally, it attracts golfers, but also travellers who simply want to enjoy its peaceful setting. This luxurious establishment offers all of the comforts, and the excellent cuisine served in its restaurant adds to the pleasure of staying here.

Newfoundland and Labrador

Gander

Comfort Inn
$75 bkfst incl.
ℜ, K
64 rooms
112 Trans-Canada, A1V 1P8
☎*256-3535 or 888-256-3535*
≈*256-9302*
The recently built Comfort Inn a hotel along the Trans-Canada Highway, offers quality accommodations.

Hotel Gander
$72
ℜ, ≈, tv
154 rooms
100 Trans-Canada, A1V 1P5
☎*256-3931 or 800-563-2988*
≈*651-2641*
One of the many establishments in Gander, Motel Gander rents perfectly suitable, well-kept rooms in a slightly worn-out, two-story building. Its restaurant is among the best in the area.

Grand Falls - Windsor

Mount Peyton Hotel
$78
ℜ
118 rooms
Rd 1., A2A 1P8
☎*489-2251* 800-563-4894
≈*489-6365*
The town of Grand Falls-Windsor, about halfway between the east and west coasts of the island, offers numerous accommodations options. Among these is the Mount Peyton Hotel a quality establishment that offers comfortable, albeit somewhat impersonally decorated, rooms.

Carriage House Inn
$79, bkfst incl.
tv
4 rooms
181 Grenfell Heights, A2A 2J2
☎*489-7185 or 800-563-7133*
≈*489-7185*
One of the best inns on this part of the island, the Carriage House occupies a beautiful, handsomely landscaped property.

Tour D: Western Newfoundland

Port aux Basques

St. Christopher's Hotel
$70
ℜ
54 rooms
Caribou Rd., A0M 1C0
☎695-7034 800-563-4779
≈*695-7034*
St Christopher's Hotel, conveniently located near Port aux Basques' main attractions, contains clean, simple, spacious rooms.

Port au Port

Spruce Pine Acres
$89
ℜ, K, △, ☺
5 rooms
Rd. 460 P.O. Box 219, A0M 1T0
☎*648-9600 or 877-648-9600*
≈*648-9600*
Set on a pretty, landscaped property between Stephenville and Cape St. George on the Port au Port Peninsula, Spruce Pine Acres offers top-notch lodging. Four rooms with private bathrooms are available in the beautiful main building, or guests can stay in a cottage that comprises

two large rooms, a kitchenette and a living room with a fireplace.

Corner Brook

Bell's Bed & Breakfast
$46, bkfst incl.
tv
8 rooms
2 Ford's Rd., A2H 1S6
☎*634-5736*
≈*634-1114*
Le Bell's Bed & Breakfast occupies a comfortable, modern house in a residential neighbourhood overlooking downtown Corner Brook, about 10min on foot from the town's main commercial thoroughfares. Its rooms are spacious and pleasant; each of them has a private washroom. In the morning, delicious breakfasts are served in a sunny kitchen at the back of the house. The welcome is friendly and the owners are both accessible and discreet.

Glynmill Inn
$69
ℜ, tv
81 rooms
1 Cobb Lane, A2H 6E6
☎*634-51881 or*
1-800-563-4400
≈*634-5106*
Glynmill Inn, the most famous hotel in the area, stands in the heart of Corner Brook. This beautiful Tudor building occupies a large, quiet, prettily landscaped, flower-covered property that looks out over Glynmill Pond. The inn's rooms are comfortable and charming; some have recently been renovated. The Glynmill Inn houses

two restaurants, including the elegant Wine Cellar (see p 280), a pleasant bar and conference rooms.

Holiday Inn
$89
≈, ®, ☺
99 rooms
47 W. St., A2H 2Z2
☎*634-5381 or 800-399-5381*
⇄*634-1723*
On Corner Brook's main street, close to its main attractions, this hotel offers spacious rooms that, although very functional, are pretty much typical of this hotel chain. The establishment is comfortable and the service is efficient and courteous.

Tour E: The Viking Route

Norris Point

🏔 **Sugar Hill Inn**
$156
pb, △, ℜ, tv
7 rooms
Rte. 431, P.O. Box 100, A0K 3V0
☎*458-2147 or 888-299-2147*
⇄*458-2166*
As you come to Norris Point, in the southern part of Gros Morne National Park, the Sugar Hill one of the best places to stay on the western half of the island, comes into view on a beautifully landscaped hillside. All of its rooms are charming and equipped with private bathrooms. A

sauna and a whirlpool are at guests' disposal and excellent fare is served in the inn's dining room.

Rocky Harbour

Ocean View Motel
$65
ℜ, tv
44 rooms
Main St.
☎*458-2730 or 800-563-9887*
⇄*458-2256*
offers rooms that are spacious, comfortable and clean, but of no particular charm. This establishment is well kept and houses a good family restaurant.

Cow Head

Shallow Bay Motel & Cabins
$65 bkfst incl.
ℜ, ≈, K, tv, △
34 rooms
P.O. Box 441, A0K 2A0
☎*243-2471 or 800-563-1946*
⇄*243-2816*
At the northern end of Gros Morne National Park, near a beautiful fine-sand beach, stand the few small cottages and buildings of the Shallow Bay Motel & Cabins. This quiet spot offers an excellent view of the Gulf of St. Lawrence. Although they are not particularly luxurious, they are all comfortable. Guests have access to an outdoor swimming pool and a restaurant that serves simple, well-prepared dishes.

L'Anse aux Meadows

Marilyn's Hospitality Home
$40
3 rooms
Hay Cove, P.O. Box 5, A0K 2X0
☎*623-2811*
About 1km from L'Anse aux Meadows, amid the few houses that make up the little community of Hay Cove, lodging is available at Marilyn's Hospitality Home. Marilyn, a very congenial woman who is always ready to share items of local lore, offers slightly over-decorated but well-kept rooms and, come morning, a very generous breakfast. The service is simple and friendly.

St. Anthony

St. Anthony Haven Inn
$72
ℜ
28 rooms
Goose Bay Rd., A0K 4S0
☎*454-9100 or 877-428-3646*
⇄*454-2270*
On a hill overlooking St. Anthony, the St. Anthony Haven Inn contains suitable, although uninterestingly decorated, rooms. St. Anthony is the largest community on this part of the island.

Cape Onion

Tickle Inn
$60, brkf incl.
ℜ
4 rooms
R.R. 1, A0K 4J0
☎/⇄*452-4321*
A little over half an hour off the road from

L'Anse-aux-Meadows and St. Anthony is the Tickle Inn, an appealing little inn in an enchanting setting facing the ocean and surrounded by valley landscapes. This spot is perfect for long walks and for spotting whales and icebergs on the open sea. The rooms are well kept and inviting. The Tickle Inn's dining room serves some of the best cuisine in the area.

Tour F: Labrador

L'Anse-au-Clair

Beachside Hospitality Home
$45
3 rooms
9 Lodge Rd., A0K 3K0
☎*931-2662 or 800-563-8999*
The few villages along the road that skirts the Strait of Belle Isle shelter many bed and breakfasts where visitors will be warmly received; the people of Labrador are known for their friendliness. One of these is the Beachside Hospitality Home, which has inviting, well-kept rooms.

Northern Light Inn
$68
ℜ, *54 rooms*
58 Main St. P.O. Box 92, A0K 3K0
☎*931-2332 or 800-563-3188*
⇋*931-2708*
Also in L'Anse-au-Clair, the largest establishment on the coast, the Northern Light Inn offers motel-type rooms.

Labrador City-Wabush

Wabush Hotel
$90
69 rooms
9 Grenfell Dr., A0R 1B0
☎*282-3221*
⇋*282-3061*
The twin cities of Labrador City and Wabush number a few hotel establishments that offer comfortable rooms with no discernable charm. The most sizeable of these is the Wabush Hotel whose architecture resembles that of large lodge.

Restaurants

Tour A: St. John's

Ches's
$
9 Freshwater St.
☎*722-4083*
726-3434
Ches's is incontestably the king of fish and chips in St. John's! Having occupied the same address on Freshwater Street since 1956, this friendly little restaurant is an institution. Their famous fish and chips, as well as hamburgers and chicken, are served at very reasonable prices in an atmosphere that could not be more jovial.

Although the owner, Ches Barbour, no longer hauls in the catch himself, the ambiance

of those bygone days remains. There are two other Ches's in St. John's: one on Topsail Road and one on Mount Pearl.

Stella's
$
106 Water St.
☎*753-9625*
Stella's is absolutely perfect for a quick bite or for a tea break. This warm and welcoming spot offers a menu made up of fish, chicken and vegetarian dishes, sandwiches, salads and soups. The seafood chowder is especially comforting on a rainy day.

Classic Café
$-$$
364 Duckworth St.
☎*579-4444*
The Classic Café is a charming spot that offers a relaxed atmosphere, an inviting interior decor and summertime outdoor dining. The lunch menu is made up of simple fare such as quiches, salads, fried squid and hamburgers. In the evening the menu lists well-prepared fish, seafood, poultry and meat dishes. It is also possible to sample some Newfoundland specialties here. The Classic Café is open 24hrs a day and serves excellent breakfasts around the clock.

Taj Mahal
$$
203 Water St.
☎576-5500
Taj Mahal lavishly decorated in Victorian style, prepares authentic Indian cuisine. Its elaborate menu highlights various tandoori specialties. The chicken tikka, the tandoori shrimp and the malai tikka fish are especially delicious. The nan bread is succulent, as is the steamed rice. Most of the main dishes cost about $10. A complete dinner for two can be enjoyed here for under $40.

Cellar
$$-$$$
Bird's Cove, Water St.
☎579-8900
One of the best restaurants in the province, the Cellar earns its reputation with an innovative menu that seduces the senses. Whether in a pasta, seafood or meat dish, the originality of the flavours and the freshness of the produce are as impressive as the beautiful presentation. The pleasant atmosphere of the dining room and its low-key lighting are perfect for intimate evenings.

Stone House
$$$
8 Kenoa's Hill
☎753-2380
The magnificent Stone House, built in the 1830s, is comprised of four dining rooms and offers an interesting

menu that mingles nouvelle cuisine with the culinary traditions of Newfoundland. Such as the appetizer of cod tongue, as well as a wide selection of seafood- and fish-based main courses. In addition there is an excellent choice of game, such as caribou, moose, wild goose and pheasant. The wine cellar is well stocked and may be visited upon request.

Tour B: The Avalon Peninsula

Witless Bay

Meghan's Restaurant
$
Rte. 10
☎334-2202
Restaurants are not legion in this part of the Avalon Peninsula coast, but before or after a trip to sea from the port of Witless Bay visitors can restore themselves at Meghan's Restaurant. Simple dishes are prepared here, notably some local specialties such as fish chowder and cod tongue, and few of them cost more than $5.

Trepassey

Trepassey Restaurant
$-$$
Rte. 10
☎438-2934
The magnificent Trepassey Restaurant, in the Trepassey Motel (see p 273) is the perfect spot for lunch. The

dishes on offer, mainly seafood and fish, are simple but well prepared and inexpensive. The layout of the restaurant is inviting and offers a pretty view of the bay.

St. Bride's

Atlantica Restaurant
$-$$
Rte. 100
☎337-2860
Vacationers can stop in St. Bride's, on the way to Cape St. Mary's, for a light meal at the Atlantica Restaurant. The menu lists rather simple dishes, including fish, scallops and fried shrimp. Hamburgers and other fast-food fare are also served.

Tour C: Eastern and Central Newfoundland

Marystown

TJ Billington
$$
☎279-1600
In the warm atmosphere of an English pub, its wall bedecked with a multitude of knick-knacks and framed pictures, TJ Billington cooks up the best food on the peninsula. The menu includes seafood and fish, as well as delicious steaks, ribs and chicken brochettes. Contrary to the standard practice of most Newfoundland restaurants, fresh vegetables are served here instead of canned ones.

Newfoundland and Labrador

Grand Bank

Manuel's
$-$$
Main St.
☎*832-0100*
Manuel is a family restaurant that offers fried chicken and fish, hamburgers and a few other simple dishes.

Trinity

Eriksson
$$
☎*464-3698*
Eriksson simmers up simple dishes composed mainly of seafood and fish in the warm atmosphere of a stately old home.

Village Inn
$$
☎*464-3269*
Village Inn lovingly puts together family-style meals that are not especially original but good nonetheless. The restaurant proves comfortable, the dishes copious, and the atmosphere friendly.

Tour D: Western Newfoundland

Corner Brook

Casual Jack's
$-$$
West St.
☎*634-4242*
In a young, very relaxed atmosphere, Casual Jack's serves pub-style cuisine that mainly constits of chicken dishes, ribs and steaks accompanied by a choice of beers on tap. In lieu of entertain-ment, televisions do full-time duty broadcasting sporting events.

Thirteen West
$$-$$$
13 W. St.
☎*634-1600*
Refined inspired cuisine and a tastefully decorated dining room account for the reputation of Thirteen West as one of the best restaurants in the province. Its lunch menu offers many excellent dishes for under $10 In the evening, the supper selections include a wide variety of main dishes such as seafood au gratin, linguini in clam sauce, chicken breast in white wine and roast lamb. To top it off, an excellent crème caramel and a succulent cheesecake appear on the dessert list. In the summer there is dining al fresco on a lovely patio.

Wine Cellar
$$-$$$
☎*634-5181*
The Wine Cellar, set up in a circular, stone-walled room, is one of two restaurants at the Glynmill Inn (see p 276). This elegant dining room with its plush atmosphere mostly makes steak. The wine list includes an extensive selection of wines and spirits.

Tour E: The Viking Route

Trout River

Seaside Restaurant
$$-$$$
☎*451-3461*
Seaside Restaurant owes its renown to the freshness and quality of its fish and seafood, which make up the greater part of its menu. The cuisine is refined and well-prepared, while the service allows for plenty of time (sometimes a bit too much) to contemplate the fascinating motion of the ocean through the dining room's large picture window.

Rocky Harbour

Fisherman's Landing
$$
☎*458-2060*
An unpretentious family restaurant, Fisherman's Landing offers a menu of seafood and fish, with some meat and poultry items for good measure. The service is courteous, although somewhat businesslike, and the prices are reasonable. In the morning copious breakfasts are served.

St. Anthony

Lightkeepers' Café
$$-$$$
Fishing Point
☎*454-4900*
There could be no better location for a restaurant than that of the Lightkeepers' Café. At the very tip of Fish-

ing Point, it offers a remarkable view of the ocean, an entrancing tableau occasionally enhanced by the slow drift of an iceberg or the to and fro of a whale. This beautiful panorama is happily complemented by excellent fare. The menu lists mainly fish and seafood dishes, including succulent snow crab, and the wine list is quite varied. Sunrise over the sea is a sight that can be enjoyed here starting at 7am.

Tour F: Labrador

Goose Bay

Mary Brown
$
Hamilton River Rd.
☎896-8159
For a bite that won't break your budget, Mary Brown offers satisfying family-style fare. There is nothing extravagant on the menu, but the fried chicken is always tasty.

Labrador Inn (*$$-$$$*; *380 Hamilton River Rd.* **☎896-3351**) and the **Aurora Hotel** (*$$-$$$*; *382 Hamilton River Rd.,* **☎896-3398**) post varied daily menus that are sure to satisfy.

Entertainment

Tour A: St. John's

Newfoundlanders are a festive lot, and is reflected in St. John's' nightlife. There are a good many bars and nightclubs in the city, but more remarkable is the incredible number of Irish, English and Scottish pubs. The best spot for an introduction to nocturnal St. John's is unquestionably **George Street**, home to the longest uninterrupted row of pubs in Canada.

Shopping

Tour A: St. John's

Shopping Centres

The **Avalon Mall Regional Shopping Centre** (*Kenmount Rd.*) is the largest retail mall in St. John's. It encloses about 100 shops,

department stores and supermarkets.

Boutiques

It would seem that **Water Street** was the first commercial thoroughfare in North America. Now it is the site of a few interesting shops. For beautiful woolen clothing, try **Annika's** (*172 Water St.,* **☎754-1146**) or the **Newfoundland Weavery** (*177 Water St.,* **☎753-0496**).

Tour D: Western Newfoundland

Corner Brook

Nortique Speciality Gift shop (*Confederation Dr.,* **☎634-8334**). This lovely shop, near the Corner Brook tourist information office, displays an interesting selection of souvenirs, crafts and beautiful woolen clothing.

INDEX

Aboiteau Beach (Cap Pelé) 108
Acadia University (Wolfville) . . . 162
Acadia University Art Gallery
    (Wolfville) 162
Acadian Coast
    Outdoors 117, 118
Acadian Coast (N.B.) 107
    Accommodations 119
    Entertainment 127
    Exploring 108
    Practical Information 108
    Restaurants 124
    Shopping 127
Acadian Festival (N.B.) 114
Acadian Museum (Caraquet) . . . 114
Acadian Museum of Prince
    Edward Island (Miscouche) . 227
Acadian Pioneer Village
    (Mont-Carmel) 228
Accommodations 38
Advocate Harbour (Nova Scotia) 153
Airports 31
    Moncton Airport
        (Southern N.B.) 78
    St. John Airport
        (Southern N.B.) 78
Aitken Bicentennial Exhibition
    Centre (Saint John) 86
Alberton (P.E.I.) 228
    Accommodations 240
Alberton Museum (Alberton) . . . 228
Alcohol 40
Algonquin Hotel (St. Andrews
    by-the-Sea) 80
Alma (Southern N.B.) 88
    Accommodations 98
American Revolution 17
Amherst (Nova Scotia) 151
    Accommodations 155
Andrew & Laura McCain Gallery
    (Florenceville) 68
Anglican Cathedral of St. John
    the Baptist (St. John's) 257
Annapolis Royal (Nova Scotia) . 163
    Restaurants 171
Annapolis Royal Historic
    Gardens (Annapolis Royal) . 164
Annapolis Tidal Project
    (Port-Royal) 163
Anne Murray Centre (Springhill) 152
Anne of Green Gables Museum
    at Silver Bush (Park Corner) 219
Anse-Amour (Labrador) 268

Antigonish (Nova Scotia) 150
    Accommodations 154
    Restaurants 156
Antique Automobile Museum
    (Saint-Jaques) 64
Architecture 20
Argyle Township Court House &
    Goal (Tusket) 174
Art Gallery of Nova Scotia
    (Halifax) 135
Arts and Culture 25
Atholville (Acadian Coast)
    Shopping 128
Atlantic Salmon Centre
    (St. Andrews by-the-Sea) 81
Atlantic Wind Test Site
    (North Cape) 228
Aulac (Southern N.B.) 91
Avalon Wilderness Reserve (New
    foundland) 259
Baddeck (Nova Scotia) 197
    Accommodations 201
    Restaurants 204
    Shopping 206
Banks 34
Barachois (Acadian Coast) 108
Barbour's General Store
    (Saint John) 86
Barrington (Nova Scotia) 174
Barrington Passage (Nova Scotia)
    Accommodations 182
Bars 40
Bartibog Bridge (Acadian Coast) 113
Basin Head (P.E.I.) 225
Basin Head Fisheries Museum
    (Basin Head) 225
Bath (St. John River Valley) 68
Bathurst (Acadian Coast) 116
    Accommodations 123
    Shopping 128
Battle Harbour Resettled Fishing
    Community
    (Mary's Harbour) 268
Bay Fortune (P.E.I.)
    Accommodations 238
    Restaurants 245
Bay of Fundy (Nova Scotia)
    Accommodations 167
    Exploring 151
    Outdoors 166
    Practical Information 158
Bay St. Lawrence (Nova Scotia) . 198
Baywatch Lighthouse (P.E.I.) . . . 221

Beaches 46
    Aboiteau (Acadian Coast) . . 116
    Basin Head (P.E.I.) 230
    Cabot Beach (P.E.I.) 218
    Caraquet (Acadian Coast) . . 117
    Crescent (Nova Scotia) 176
    Downtown (Acadian Coast) 117
    Escuminac (Acadian Coast) . 117
    Ferguson (Acadian Coast) . . 117
    Île Miscou (Acadian Coast) . 117
    Kouchibouguac (Acadian
        Coast) 117
    Lavilette (Nova Scotia) 199
    Maisonnette (Acadian Coast) 117
    Murray (Acadian Coast) . . . 116
    Panmure Island Provincial
        Park (P.E.I.) 230
    Parlee (Acadian Coast) 117
    Prince Edward Island
        (P.E.I.) 229
    Red Point Provincial Park
        (P.E.I.) 230
    Souris Beach Provincial Park
        (P.E.I.) 225
Beaconsfield Historic House
    (Charlottetown) 214
Beaverbrook Art Gallery
    (Fredericton) 56
Bed and Breakfasts 39
Beechwood
    (St. John River Valley) 68
Beer 40
Belliveau Cove (Nova Scotia)
    Restaurants 171
Beothuk 14
Beothuk village (Grand Falls) . . 264
Betrand (Acadian Coast)
    Restaurants 126
Bicycling 34, 45
    Acadian Coast (N.B.) 117
    Cape Breton Island
        (Nova Scotia) 199
    Fredericton (N. B.) 58
    Halifax (Nova Scotia) 140
    Prince Edward Island 231
    Southern New Brunswick . . . 92
    St. John River Valley (N.B.) . . 70
Bird-watching 47
    Acadian Coast (N.B.) 117
    Cape Breton Island
        (Nova Scotia) 200
    Newfoundland 271
    Prince Edward Island 230
    Southern New Brunswick . . . 93
Blandford (Nova Scotia)
    Accommodations 186
Blowers Street (Halifax) 138

Blue Rock (Nova Scotia) 179
Bluenose II (Nova Scotia) 179
Boating
    Prince Edward Island 232
Bonar Law Historic Site (Rexton) 112
Bonavista Peninsula
    (Newfoundland) 262
Borden (P.E.I.) 216
    Finding Your Way Around . 210
Borden Interpretation Centre
    (Borden) 216
Bottle Houses (Cap Egmont) . . . 228
Boucanières (Cap Pelé) 108
Bouctouche (Acadian Coast) . . . 110
    Accommodations 121
    Restaurants 125
Boyce Market (Fredericton) 57
Boyd's Cove Beothuk
    Interpretation Centre
        (Newfoundland) 264
Brackley Beach (P.E.I.) 221
    Accommodations 237
    Restaurants 244
Bras d'Or Lake (Nova Scotia) . . 195
Bras d'Or Scenic Drive (Bras
    d'Or Lake) 195
Bridgewater (Nova Scotia) 177
    Accommodations 183
Brier Island (Nova Scotia) 164
    Restaurants 171
Brigus (Newfoundland) 261
    Accommodations 274
Burin (Newfoundland) 261
Burin Heritage House (Burin) . . 261
Burin Peninsula (Newfoundland) 261
Burlington (P.E.I.) 216
Bus 33
Business Hours 35
Cabot Tower (St. John's) 258
Cabot Trail (Nova Scotia) 198
    Shopping 206
Cabot, John 13
Campbellton (Acadian Coast) . . 116
    Accommodations 123
Camping 39
Campobello Island (Southern
    N.B.) 82
    Accommodations 95
Canoeing 46
    Acadian Coast (N.B.) 118
    Fredericton (N. B.) 58
    Lighthouse Route
        (Nova Scotia) 181
    Southern New Brunswick . . . 93
    St. John River Valley (N.B.) . . 70
Canso (Nova Scotia) 192
Cap-Egmont (P.E.I.) 228

Index

Cap-Pelé (Acadian Coast) 108
   Accommodations 119
   Restaurants 124
Cape Bonavista (Newfoundland) 263
   Accommodations 275
Cape Breton Island
   (Nova Scotia) 191
   Accommodations 201
   Beaches 199
   Entertainment 206
   Exploring 192
   Outdoors 199
   Practical Information 192
   Restaurants 204
Cape D'Or Lighthouse
   (Advocate Harbour) 153
Cape Enrage (Southern N.B.) . . . 88
Cape Fourchu (Nova Scotia) . . . 165
Cape North (Nova Scotia)
   Restaurants 204
Cape Onion (Newfoundland)
   Accommodations 278
Cape Split (Nova Scotia) 162
Cape St. Mary's (Newfoundland) 259
Car 32
Car Rentals 32
Caraquet (Acadian Coast) 114
   Accommodations 122
   Entertainment 127
   Restaurants 126
   Shopping 128
Cardigan (P.E.I.) 225
   Restaurants 245
Carleton (P.E.I.)
   Finding Your Way Around . 210
Carleton Martello Tower
   (Saint John) 87
Cartier, Jacques 13
Cathedral Church of All Saints
   (Halifax) 135
Cathedral of the Immaculate
   Conception (Edmundston) . . 64
Cavendish (P.E.I.) 219
   Accommodations 235
   Shopping 249
Cavendish Figurines factory
   (Summerside) 227
Ceildish Trail (Nova Scotia) 199
Central and Western Labrador
   (Newfounland) 268
Central New Brunswick
   Woodmen's Museum
     (Newcastle) 113
Centre d'Art de l'Université de
   Moncton (Moncton) 91
Centre La Rochelle (Grand Falls) . 67

Centre Scientifique de Science
   Est (Fredericton) 57
Channel Port aux Basques
   (Western Newfoundland) . . 264
Chapel (St. Andrews) 226
Charlotte County Museum
   (St. Stephen) 80
Charlottetown (P.E.I.)
   Accommodations 233
   Entertainment 247
   Restaurants 240
   Shopping 248
Cherry Brook Zoo (Saint John) . . 87
Chester (Nova Scotia) 180
   Accommodations 186
   Entertainment 189
   Restaurants 189
   Shopping 190
Chester Playhouse (Chester) . . . 180
Chéticamp (Nova Scotia) 199
   Accommodations 203
   Restaurants 205
Children 40
Christ Church Cathedral
   (Fredericton) 57
Church Point (Nova Scotia) 165
City Hall (Fredericton) 54
City Hall (Halifax) 135
Clear Spring (P.E.I.)
   Restaurants 245
Clifton House (Windsor) 161
Climate 36
Clothing 36
Clyde River (Nova Scotia)
   Accommodations 182
Cod 13
Colchester Historical Society
   Museum (Truro) 153
College of Piping (Summerside) 227
Colony of Avalon Archaeology
   Site (Ferryland) 259
Colville, Alex 25
Commissariat House (St. John's) 256
Conception Bay Museum
   (Harbour Grace) 261
Confederation Arts Centre
   (Charlottetown) 212
Connell House (Hartland) 69
Consulates 28
Corner Brook (Newfoundland) . 265
   Accommodations 276
   Restaurants 280
   Shopping 281
Cossit House (Sydney) 195
Courthouse (Fredericton) 54
Covered bridge (Hartland) 68

Cow Head (Newfoundland)
Accommodations 277
Credit Cards 34
Crithlow Harris, William 24
Crocker Hill Garden & Studio
(St. Stephen) 80
Cross-Country Skiing 48
Cruises
St. John River Valley (N.B.) . . 70
Crystal Falls (Labrador) 269
Crystal Palace (Moncton) 91
Cumberland County Museum
(Amherst) 152
Currency 34
Customs 27
Dalhousie (Acadian Coast) 116
Danceclubs 40
De Monts, Pierre 14
De Poutrincourt, Baron Jean 15
Deep-Sea Fishing
Cape Breton Island
(Nova Scotia) 200
Deer Island (N.B.) 82
Deer Lake (Newfoundland) 265
DesBrisay Museum
(Bridgewater) 177
Dieppe (Southern N.B.) 90
Digby (Nova Scotia) 164
Accommodations 168
Practical Information 158
Restaurants 171
Dingwall (Nova Scotia)
Accommodations 203
Restaurants 205
Discovery Centre (Halifax) 135
Diving
Lighthouse Route
(Nova Scotia) 181
Dock Street (Shelburne) 174
Dory Shop (Shelburne) 176
Downhill Skiing 48
Acadian Coast (N.B.) 119
Newfoundland 272
Downtwon Saint John (N.B.) 86
Driver's License 32
Drugs 41
Dune de Bouctouche
(Bouctouche) 111
Dunes Art Gallery
(Brackley Beach) 221
East Point (P.E.I.) 225
East Point Lighthouse
(East Point) 225
East Quoddy Head (Campobello
Island) 82
Echo caves (St. Martins) 87

Ecomusée de la Courtepointe
(Wellington) 227
Edmundston (St. John
River Valley) 64
Accommodations 71
Finding Your Way Around . . 64
Église Notre-Dame-du-Mont-
Carmel (Mont-Carmel) 227
Église Saint-Bernard
(Saint-Bernard) 164
Église Sainte-Cécile
(Île Lamèque) 114
Église Sainte-Marie (Pointe-de-
l'Église) 165
Electricity 41
Elmira (P.E.I.) 225
Elmira Railway Museum
(Elmira) 225
Embassies 28
Emergencies 37
Entrance Formalities 27
Eptek (Summerside) 227
Escuminac (Acadian Coast) 112
Exploring 38
Extended Visits 27
Farmer's Bank of Rustico (P.E.I.) 221
Ferguson Beach (Grande-Anse) . 115
Ferries 33
Ferryland (St. John's) 259
Accommodations 273
Firefighters Museum (Yarmouth) 165
Fisheries Museum of the Atlantic
(Lunenberg) 178
Fishing 46
Prince Edward Island 232
Fishing and Aquatic Culture
Festival (N.B.) 113
Flesché, Jessé 15
Florenceville (St. John
River Valley) 68
Flower pots (Hopewell Cape) . . 88
Foire Breyonne (Edmundston) . . 64
Forestry 20
Fort Howe (Saint John) 87
Fort McNab Historic Site
(McNabs Island) 139
Fort Point Museum
(Nova Scotia) 177
Fortress of Louisbourg
(Louisbourgh) 196
Fortune (Newfoundland) 261
Accommodations 275

Index

Fredericton (New Brunswick) . . . 53
  Accommodations 58
  Entertainment 61
  Exploring 54
  Outdoors 58
  Practical Information 54
  Restaurants 60
  Shopping 62
Fundy Geological Museum
  (Parrsboro) 153
Fundy National Park (Southern
  N.B.)
  Accommodations 98
Fur Trade 14
Gaelic College
  (South Gut St. Ann's) 198
Gagetown (St. John River Valley) 70
  Accommodations 73
  Restaurants 74
  Shopping 74
Gallery 78 (Fredericton) 57
Gander (Newfoundland) 263
  Accommodations 276
Ganong Chocolatier
  (St. Stephen) 80
Garden of the Gulf Museum
  (Montague) 224
Gaspereaux (P.E.I.) 223
Gay and Lesbian Life 38
Geography 11
Georgetown (P.E.I.) 224
Giant axe (Nackawic) 69
Giant salmon (Campbellton) . . . 116
Glace Bay (Nova Scotia) 196
Glenora Distillery (Mabou) 199
Glenville (Nova Scotia)
  Restaurants 205
Golf 47
  Cape Breton Island
    (Nova Scotia) 200
  Prince Edward Island 231
Goose Bay (Labrador)
  Restaurants 281
Government House (St. John's) . 256
Grand Bank (Newfoundland) . . 261
  Accommodations 275
  Restaurants 280
Grand Falls (St. John River
    Valley) 67
  Accommodations 71
  Entertainment 74
  Restaurants 73
Grand Falls Museum
  (Grand Falls) 67
Grand Falls-Windsor
    (Newfoundland) 264
  Accommodations 276

Grand Manan Island
    (Southern N.B.) 84
  Accommodations 96
Grand Parade (Halifax) 135
Grand-Pré (Nova Scotia) 161
Grande-Anse (Acadian Coast) . . 115
Green (Fredericton) 57
Green Family Forge (Trinity) . . . 262
Green Gables House
    (Cavendish) 219
Green Park Shipbuilding
    Museum (Port Hill) 229
Greenock Church (St. Andrews
    by-the-Sea) 81
Grenfell House Museum
    (St. Anthony) 267
Grenfell Mission (St. Anthony) . 267
Haliburton House (Windsor) . . . 161
Halifax 131
  Exploring 132
  Finding Your Way Around . 132
  Outdoor Activities 140
  Practical Information 132
Halifax (Nova Scotia)
  Accommodations 140
  Entertainment 145
  Exploring 132
  Practical Information 132
  Restaurants 143
  Shopping 146
Harbour Grace (Newfoundland) 261
  Accommodations 274
Harris, Robert 25
Hartland (St. John River Valley) . . 68
  Accommodations 72
Health 37
Heart's Content (Newfoundland) 260
Heart's Content Cable Station
    (Heart's Content) 260
Hector Heritage Quay (Pictou) . 151
Henry IV of France 15
Hering Cove (N.B.) 84
Hibernia Platform 20
Hiking 45
  Cape Breton Island
    (Nova Scotia) 199
  Fredericton (N. B.) 58
  Halifax (Nova Scotia) 140
  Isthmus of Chignecto
    (Nova Scotia) 154
  Lighthouse Route
    (Nova Scotia) 181
  Newfoundland 271
  Prince Edward Island 230
  Southern New Brunswick . . 92
Hiscock House (Trinity) 262

Historic church of Saint-Henri-
    de-Barachois (Barachois) . . 108
Historic Ferryland Museum
    (Ferryland) 259
Historic Properties (Halifax) . . . 136
Historic Quaker House
    (Dartmouth) 139
History 13
    Acadia and Early Settlement . 14
    The 20th Century 19
    The Arrival of the Loyalists . . 17
    The Deportation 16
    The Golden Age and
        Canadian Confederation . 18
Hitchhiking 34
Holidays 36
Hopewell Cape (Southern N.B.) . 88
Hotels 39
Hubbard House (Campobello
    Island) 84
Hubbards (Nova Scotia)
    Accommodations 187
Huntsman Marine Science
    Centre and Aquarium
        (St. Andrews) 81
Hydroelectric dam (Mactaquac) . . 69
Hydroelectric power station
        (Beechwood) 68
Iceberg-watching
    Newfoundland 271
Île Lamèque (Acadian Coast) . . . 114
    Accommodations 122
    Restaurants 126
Île Miscou (Acadian Coast) 114
Île Miscou Lighthouse
    (Île Miscou) 114
Imperial Theatre (Saint John) . . . 86
Indian River (P.E.I.) 218
Ingonish Beach (Nova Scotia)
    Accommodations 202
    Restaurants 204
Ingonish Ferry (Nova Scotia) . . . 198
    Restaurants 204
Inns 39
Insurance 37
International Baroque Music
    Festival (N.B.) 114
International Fox Museum
        (Summerside) 227
Irish Festival of Canada (N.B.) . . 112
Iron 20
Irving Eco-Centre (Bouctouche) 111
Isle Madame (Nova Scotia) 194

Isthmus of Chignecto
        (Nova Scotia) 149
    Accommodations 154
    Beaches 154
    Exploring 150
    Outdoors 154
    Practical Information 150
    Restaurants 156
    Shopping 156
James Roosevelt House
        (Campobello Island) 84
Joggins Fossil Centre (Amherst) . 152
Jost House (Sydney) 195
Jost Vineyards (Malagash) 151
Kayak
    Prince Edward Island 232
Kayaking
    Acadian Coast (N.B.) 118
    Cape Breton Island
        (Nova Scotia) 200
    Fredericton (N. B.) 58
    Lighthouse Route
        (Nova Scotia) 181
    Southern New Brunswick . . . 93
Kensington (P.E.I.) 216
Kent County Museum
        (Bouctouche) 111
Kings Landing (Prince-William) . . 69
Kingsbrae Horticultural Garden
        (St. Andrew's by-the-Sea) . . . 81
Kingsclear (St. John River Valley)
    Accommodations 73
King's Square (Saint John) 86
Kirk Presbyterian (St. George) . . . 82
La Have (Nova Scotia) 177
La Vieille Maison (Nova Scotia) . 165
Labrador (Newfoundland) 267
    Finding Your Way Around . 253
Labrador City-Wabush
        (Labrador)
    Accommodations 278
Labrador Straits Museum
        (L'Anse Au Loup) 268
Laudromats 41
Lawrence House (Maitland) . . . 154
Leper cemetery (Tracadie-Sheila) 113
Lieutenant-Governor's residence
        (Charlottetown) 214
Lighthouse (St. John's) 258
Lighthouse Museum (Fredericton) 57

Index

Lighthouse Route (Nova Scotia) . 173
  Accommodations 182
  Beaches 181
  Entertainment 189
  Exploring 173
  Outdoors 181
  Practical Information 173
  Restaurants 187
  Shopping 189
Liscomb (Nova Scotia)
  Accommodations 201
Little Pond (P.E.I.)
  Accommodations 238
Little Rock (P.E.I.)
  Accommodations 237
Little Sands (P.E.I.) 223
  Accommodations 237
Liverpool (Nova Scotia) 176
  Accommodations 183
Lobster Cove Head lighthouse
  (Newfoundland) 270
Lockeport (Nova Scotia) 176
  Accommodations 183
Log Cabin Museum (Murray
  Harbour) 223
Long Island (Nova Scotia) 164
Loomcrofter Studio (Gagetown) . 70
Lord Beaverbrook 25
Louisbourg (Nova Scotia) 195
  Accommodations 201
  Restaurants 204
Loyalist House
  Historic Site (Saint John) 86
Lucy Maud Montgomery
  Birthplace (New London) . . 219
Lunenburg (Nova Scotia) 177
  Accommodations 184
  Restaurants 188
  Shopping 189
L'Anse Au Loup (Labrador) 268
L'Anse aux Meadows
  (Newfoundland) 266
  Accommodations 277
L'Anse-au-Clair (Labrador) 268
  Accommodations 278
Mabou (Nova Scotia) 199
  Accommodations 203
  Restaurants 205
MacDonald Farm Historic Site
  (Bartibog Bridge) 113
Machias Seal Island
  (Southern N.B.) 84
Mactaquac (St. John River Valley) 69
Madawaska Museum
  (Edmundston) 66
Magnetic Hill (Moncton) 91

Mahone Bay (Nova Scotia) 179
  Accommodations 185
  Restaurants 189
Maisonnette (Acadian Coast) . . . 115
Maitland (Nova Scotia) 154
Malagash (Nova Scotia) 151
Malecites 14
Malobiannah Centre
  (Grand Falls) 67
Malpeque (P.E.I.) 218
Marble Mountain
  (Newfoundland) 265
Margaree Salmon Museum
  (Northeast Margaree) 199
Margaree Valley (Nova Scotia)
  Accommodations 203
Marine Centre and Aquarium
  (Shippagan) 114
Maritime Museum of the Atlantic
  (Halifax) 136
Mary March Regional Museum
  (Grand Falls) 264
Marystown (Newfoundland) . . . 261
  Accommodations 274
  Restaurants 280
Mary's Point (Southern N.B.) 88
Mavilette Beach Park
  (Nova Scotia)
  Accommodations 169
  Restaurants 172
McCulloch House (Pictou) 151
McKenna, Frank 19
McNabs Island (Nova Scotia) . . . 139
Meat Cove (Nova Scotia) 198
Meetinghouse (Barrington) 174
Melmerby Beach (Nova Scotia) . 150
Membertou 15
Micmac Village (Rocky Point) . . 216
Micmacs 14
Military Compound and Guard
  House (Fredericton) 54
Military museum (Halifax) 134
Military museum (Oromocto) . . . 70
Mill River Provincial Park (P.E.I.) 229
Miner's Museum (Glace Bay) . . 197
Miquelon, France
  (Newfoundland) 262
Miramichi (Acadian Coast) 112
Miramichi River (N.B.) 112
Miramichi Salmon Museum
  (N.B.) 113
Miscouche (P.E.I.) 227

Moncton (Southern N.B.) 88
    Accommodations 98
    Entertainment 103
    Practical Information 78
    Restaurants 102
    Shopping 105
Moncton Museum (Moncton) . . . 90
Money 34
Mont-Carmel (P.E.I.) 227
    Accommodations 239
    Entertainment 248
    Restaurants 246
Montague (P.E.I.) 224
    Accommodations 238
    Restaurants 245
Montgomery, Lucy Maud 25
Monument (Escuminac) 112
Motels 39
Mount Allison University
    (Sackville) 91
Mount Carleton (N.B.) 66
Murray Harbour (P.E.I.) 223
Murray River (P.E.I.) 223
    Shopping 249
Musée Acadien (Moncton) 90
Musée Acadien (West Pubnico) . 174
Musée de Cire d'Acadie
    (Caraquet) 115
Museum (Grand Manan Island) . . 84
N. S. Fisheries Exhibition and
    Fisherman Reunion
    (Lunenberg) 178
Nackawic (St. John River Valley) . 69
National Historic Sites
    Alexander Graham Bell
        (Nova Scotia) 197
    Cape Spear
        (Newfoundland) 258
    Fort Anne (Nova Scotia) . . . 163
    Fort Beauséjour (Aulac) 92
    Fort Edward (Windsor) 161
    Grand-Pré (Nova Scotia) . . . 161
    Grassy Island (Canso) 194
    Halifax Citadel (Halifax) . . . 132
    Hawthorne Cottage
        (Brigus) 261
    Hopedale Mission
        (Labrador) 268
    L'Anse aux Meadows
        (Newfoundland) 266
    Lefebvre Monument (N.B.) . . 91
    Marconi (Nova Scotia) 197
    Ministers Island (N.B.) 81
    Port au Choix
        (Port au Choix) 265
    Port La Joye - Fort Amherst
        (PEI) 215
Port-Royal (Nova Scotia) . . . 163
Province House
    (Charlottetown) 213
Red Bay (Red Bay) 268
St. Andrews Blockhouse
    (N.B.) 81
Signal Hill (St. John's) 257
York Redoubt (Halifax
    Outskirts) 139
Néguac (Acadian Coast) 113
New Brunswick 49
New Brunswick Botanical Garden
    (Saint-Jacques) 64
New Brunswick College of Craft
    and Design (Fredericton) . . . 54
New Brunswick Museum (Saint
    John) 86
New Brunswick Museum
    (Southern N.B.) 86
New Brunswick Sports Hall of
    Fame (Fredericton) 56
New Denmark (St. John River
    Valley) 68
New Glasgow (P.E.I.) 221
    Restaurants 243
    Shopping 249
New London (P.E.I.) 219
    Restaurants 242
Newfoundland 251
    Accommodations 272
    Entertainment 281
    Exploring 254
    Outdoors 270
    Parks 269
    Practical Information 254
    Restaurants 278
    Shopping 281
Newfoundland Museum
    (St. John's) 257
Newspapers 41
Nicolas Denys Museum
    (St. Peters) 194
Nigadoo (Acadian Coast)
    Restaurants 127
Norris Point (Newfoundland)
    Accommodations 277
North Atlantic Aviation Museum
    (Gander) 264
North Cape (P.E.I.) 228
    Restaurants 247
North Rustico (P.E.I.) 221
    Restaurants 244
Northeast Margaree
    (Nova Scotia) 199
Northumberland Fisheries
    Museum (Pictou) 151

Index

Nova Scotia Museum of Natural
    History (Halifax) 134
Officer's Square (Fredericton) . . . 56
Official Languages Law 19
Old Burying Ground (Halifax) . 138
Old Carleton County Courthouse
    (Hartland) 69
Old City Market (Saint John) 86
Old Government House
    (Fredericton) 57
Old Home Week (Hartland) 69
Old Loyalist Cemetery
    (Fredericton) 57
Old Sow (Deer Island) 82
Old Town Clock (Halifax) 134
Oromocto (St. John River Valley) 69
Orwell Corner (P.E.I.) 222
    Restaurants 244
Orwell Corner Historic Village
    (Orwell) 222
Ottawa House Museum
    By-the-Sea (Springhill) 153
Outdoors 43
Owens Art Gallery (Sackville) . . . 91
Oyster Bed Bridge (P.E.I.)
    Restaurants 244
O'Leary (P.E.I.) 228
P.E.I. Preserve Co.
    (New Glasgow) 221
Panmure Island (P.E.I.) 223
Papineau Falls (Bathurst) 116
Paquetville (Acadian Coast)
    Restaurants 127
Park Corner (P.E.I.) 219
Parks 43
    Argyle Shore (P.E.I.) 221
    Avalon (Newfoundland) . . . 259
    Blow Me Down
        (Newfoundland) 270
    Bore (Moncton) 90
    Brudenell River (P.E.I.) 224
    Cabot Beach (P.E.I.) 218
    Cape Breton Highlands
        (Nova Scotia) 198
    Cape St. Mary's
        (Newfoundland) 259
    Cape St. Mary's Ecological
        Reserve 271
    Caribou (Nova Scotia) 151
    Castle Hill (Newfoundland) . 260
    Cedar Dunes (P.E.I.) 228
    Centennial Park (N.B.) 81
    Chignecto Cape
        (Nova Scotia) 153
    Escuminac (N.B.) 112
    Fundy (Southern N.B.) 88

Gros Morne
    (Newfoundland) 269
Gulf Shore (Nova Scotia) . . 151
Irving (Southern N.B.) 87
Kejimkujik (Nova Scotia) . . . 176
Kejimkujik Seaside Adjunct
    (Nova Scotia) 177
Kouchibouguac (N.B.) 112
Lions (St. Martins) 88
Mactaquac (St. John River
    Valley) 69
Maisonnette (N.B.) 115
Melmerby Beach
    (Nova Scotia) 150
Mill River (P.E.I.) 229
Mount Carleton (St. John
    River Valley) 66
Murray Beach
    (Acadian Coast) 116
Odell Park (Fredericton) 57
Ovens (Nova Scotia) 177
Parlee Beach (N.B.) 108
Point Pleasant Park (Halifax) 139
Prince Edward Island (P.E.I.) 226
Red Point (P.E.I.) 225
Ritchie Wharf Park (N.B.) . . 112
Rockwood Park (Saint John) . 87
Roosevelt-Campobello
    (Campobello Island) 82
Sir Sandford Fleming
    (Halifax Outskirts) 139
Souris Beach (P.E.I.) 225
Strathgartney (P.E.I.) 221
Sugarloaf (N.B.) 116
Tatamagouche (Nova Scotia) 151
Terra Nova (Newfoundland) 269
Victoria (Nova Scotia) 153
Victoria (P.E.I.) 221
Waterfowl (Sackville) 91
William F. de Garthe
    (Nova Scotia) 180
Parrsboro (Nova Scotia) 153
Partridge Island (Saint John) 87
Passport 27
Pays de la Sagouine
    (Bouctouche) 111
Peake's Wharf (Charlottetown) . 214
Peggy's Cove (Nova Scotia) 180
Perkins House (Liverpool) 176
Petit-Rocher (Acadian Coast)
    Accommodations 123
    Restaurants 127
Petit-Témis Interprovincial
    Linear Park (N. B.) 66
Petroleum 20

Pictou (Nova Scotia) 150
    Accommodations 154
    Restaurants 156
    Shopping 156
Pier 21 (Halifax) 138
Placentia (Newfoundland) 259
    Accommodations 274
Plane 30
Plaster Rock (St. John River
    Valley)
    Accommodations 72
Playhouse (Fredericton) 56
Pleasant Bay (Nova Scotia) 198
    Restaurants 205
Point Amour Lighthouse Provincial
    Historic Site
        (L'Anse Amour) 268
Point Prim (P.E.I.) 223
Point Prim Lighthouse
        (Point Prim) 223
Pointe Daly Reserve (Bathurst) . 116
Pointe Wolfe (Southern N.B.) ... 88
Pointe-de-l'Église (Nova Scotia) . 165
Politics and the Economy 19
    New Brunswick 19
    Nova Scotia 20
    Prince Edward Island 20
Poole's Corner (P.E.I.)
    Finding Your Way Around . 210
Pope Museum (Grande-Anse) .. 115
Port au Choix (Newfoundland) . 265
Port au Port (Newfoundland)
    Accommodations 276
Port aux Basques
        (Newfoundland)
    Accommodations 276
Port Blandford (Newfoundland) 263
    Accommodations 276
Port Hastings (Nova Scotia) 194
Port of Charlottetown
        (Charlottetown) 214
Port-au-Port Peninsula
        (Newfoundland) 264
Port-Royal (Nova Scotia) 163
Portage (P.E.I.)
    Finding Your Way Around . 212
Portrait 11
Post office (St. George) 82
Post Offices 36
Potato 12
Prescott House Museum (Starrs
    Point) 162
Prince Edward Hotel
        (Charlottetown) 214

Prince Edward Island 207
    Accommodations 233
    Entertainment 247
    Exploring 212
    Outdoor Activities 230
    Parks and Beaches 229
    Practical Information 210
    Restaurants 240
    Shopping 248
Prince Edward Island Potato Mu
    seum (O'Leary) 228
Prince House
        (Campobello Island) 84
Prince of Wales Tower National
    Historic Site (Halifax) 139
Prince William (St. John River
    Valley) 69
Province House (Halifax) 135
Provincial Legislature
        (Fredericton) 56
Public Gardens (Halifax) 134
Pugwash (Nova Scotia) 151
Quaco Head lighthouse
        (St. Martins) 88
Queen's Battery (St. John's) 258
Quidi Vidi (Newfoundland) ... 258
Quidi Vidi Battery (Quidu Vidi) . 258
Quidi Vidi Lake
        (Newfoundland) 258
Randall House Historical
    Museum (Wolfville) 162
Red Point (P.E.I.) 225
Restaurants 40
Restigouche Gallery
        (Campbellton) 116
Restigouche Regional Museum
        (Dalhousie) 116
Restrooms 42
Reversing Falls (Saint John) 86
Rexton (Acadian Coast) 112
Richibucto (Acadian Coast)
    Accommodations 121
Riverview (Southern N.B.) 90
Robichaud (Acadian Coast)
    Accommodations 119
Rocky Harbour (Newfoundland)
    Accommodations 277
    Restaurants 281
Rocky Point (P.E.I.) 215
Roman Catholic Basilica of
    St. John the Baptist
        (St. John's) 257
Roosevelt House (Campobello
    Island) 84
Rose Bay (Nova Scotia) 177
Roseneath (P.E.I.)
    Accommodations 238

Index

Ross Farm Museum (Chester) . . 180
Ross Memorial Museum
    (St. Andrews by-the-Sea) 80
Ross Thomson House
    (Shelburne) 176
Rossignol Estate Winery (Little
    Sands) 223
Sackville (Southern N.B.) 91
    Accommodations 99
    Restaurants 103
Safety 37
Saint Augustine Church (South
    Rustico) 221
Saint John (Southern N.B.) 84
    Accommodations 96
    Finding Your Way Around . . 78
    Practical Information 78
    Restaurants 101
    Shopping 105
Saint Leonard (N.B.) 66
Saint-Basile
    (St. John River Valley) 66
Saint-Bernard (Nova Scotia) . . . 164
Saint-Henri-de-Barachois
    Historic Church (Barachois) 108
Saint-Jacques (N.B.)
    Shopping 74
Saint-Jacques (St. John River
    Valley) 64
    Practical Information 64
Saint-Joseph-de-Memramcook
    (Southern N.B.) 91
Saint-Pierre, France
    (Newfoundland) 262
Sainte-Anne-du-Ruisseau
    Church (Sainte-Anne-
    Ruisseau) 174
Sambro Lighthouse (Halifax
    Outskirts) 139
Sanctuaire Sainte-Anne-du-Bocage
    (Caraquet) 115
Scuba Diving
    Southern New Brunswick . . . 93
Sea View (P.E.I.)
    Accommodations 235
Seal-watching 47
    Prince Edward Island 232
Settlers Museum (Mahone Bay) . 180
Shand House (Windsor) 161
Shediac (Acadian Coast) 108
    Accommodations 119
    Restaurants 124
    Shopping 127
Shelburne (Nova Scotia) 174
    Accommodations 182
    Restaurants 187
    Shopping 189

Shelburne County Museum
    (Shelburne) 176
Sherbrooke (Nova Scotia) 192
Sherbrooke Village (Sherbrooke) 192
Sheriff Andrews' House
    (St. Andrews by-the-Sea) 80
Ship's Company Theatre
    (Springhill) 153
Shippagan (Acadian Coast) 113
    Accommodations 122
    Restaurants 125
    Shopping 40
Signal Hill Tattoo (St. John's) . . . 258
Silent Witness Memorial
    (Gander) 264
Sir Andrew Macphail
    Homestead (Orwell) 222
Smith's Cove (Nova Scotia)
    Accommodations 168
Smoking 40
Snowmobiling 48
Souris (P.E.I.) 225
    Accommodations 238
    South Gut St. Ann's
    (Nova Scotia) 198
South Rustico (P.E.I.) 221
    Accommodations 237
Southern New Brunswick 77
    Accommodations 94
    Entertainment 103
    Exploring 78
    Outdoors 92
    Practical Information 78
    Restaurants 100
    Shopping 104
Southern Newfoundland
    Seamen's Museum
    (Newfoundland) 261
Spanish 21
Spinnakers' Landing
    (Summerside) 227
Spring Garden Road (Halifax) . 138
Springhill (Nova Scotia) 152
    Accommodations 155
Springhill Miners' Museum
    (Springhill) 152
St. Andrews (P.E.I.) 226
St. Andrews by-the-Sea (N.B.) . . . 80
    Accommodations 94
    Restaurants 100
    Shopping 104
St. Ann (P.E.I.)
    Restaurants 243
St. Anthony (Newfoundland) . . . 267
    Accommodations 278
    Restaurants 281
St. Barbe (Newfoundland) 266

St. Bride's (Newfoundland)
  Accommodations 274
  Restaurants 279
St. Dunstan's Basilica
  (Charlottetown) 213
St. Francis Xavier University
  (Antigonish) 150
St. George (N.B.) 81
St. George (Southern N.B.)
  Accommodations 95
St. John Airport (Southern N.B.) . 78
St. John River Valley (N.B.) 63
  Accommodations 71
  Entertainment 74
  Outdoors 70
  Practical Information 64
  Restaurants 73
  Shopping 74
St. John's (Newfoundland) 254
  Accommodations 272
  Entertainment 281
  Restaurants 278
  Shopping 281
St. Martins (Southern N.B.) 87
  Accommodations 97
  Restaurants 102
St. Mary's Church (Souris) 225
St. Mary's Roman Catholic
  Church (Indian River) 218
St. Patrick's Church (Sydney) . . . 195
St. Paul Church (Halifax) 135
St. Paul's Anglican Church
  (Charlottetown) 213
St. Peters (Nova Scotia) 194
St. Peters (P.E.I.) 226
St. Stephen (Southern N.B.) 78
  Accommodations 94
  Shopping 104
St. Thomas (Acadian Coast)
  Restaurants 125
  Shopping 127
St. Thomas Anglican Church
  (St. John's) 256
St. Thomas University
  (Fredericton) 57
Stanley Bridge (P.E.I.)
  Restaurants 242
Starrs Point (Nova Scotia) 162
Stores 35
Strait of Belle Isle (Labrador) . . . 268
Strathgartney (P.E.I.)
  Accommodations 235
Summer Activities 45

Summerside (P.E.I.) 226
  Accommodations 239
  Entertainment 247
  Restaurants 245
  Shopping 249
Summerville Beach (Nova Scotia)
  Accommodations 183
  Restaurants 187
Sunbury Shores Arts & Nature
  Centre (St. Andrews
  by-the-Sea) 81
Swallowtail Light (Grand Manan
  Island) 84
Sydney (Nova Scotia) 195
  Accommodations 201
  Restaurants 204
Tatamagouche (Nova Scotia) . . . 151
  Accommodations 155
Tax Refunds 35
Taxes 35
Telecommunications 38
The Labrador Coast
  (Newfounland) 268
Thomas Williams House
  (Moncton) 90
Tidal bore (Moncton) 90
Tidal bore (Truro) 153
Tignish (P.E.I.)
  Accommodations 240
Tilley House (Gagetown) 70
Time Difference 36
Tipping 35
Tourist Information 30
Towers & Water Gardens
  (Kensington) 216
Town Hall (Souris) 225
Tracadie Historical Museum
  (Tracadie-Sheila) 113
Tracadie-Sheila (Acadian Coast) 113
  Accommodations 122
Train 33
Traveller's Cheques 34
Trepassey (Newfoundland)
  Accommodations 274
  Restaurants 279
Trinity (Newfoundland) 262
  Accommodations 275
  Restaurants 280
Trinity East (Newfoundland)
  Accommodations 275
Trinity Interpretation Centre
  (Trinity) 262
Trinity Pageant (Trinity) 263
Truro (Nova Scotia) 153
  Accommodations 155
Tusket (Nova Scotia) 174
Twillingate (Newfoundland) . . . 264

Tyne Valley (P.E.I.) 229
    Accommodations 240
    Shopping 249
Tyne Valley Studio
    (Tyne Valley) 229
Université Sainte-Anne
    (Pointe-de-l'Église) 165
University of New Brunswick
    (Fredericton) 57
University Residences 39
Val-Comeau (Acadian Coast) . . . 113
Victoria (P.E.I.) 216
    Entertainment 247
    Restaurants 242
    Shopping 248
Victoria Seaport Museum
    (Victoria) 216
Victorian Playhouse (Victoria) . . 216
Viking Highway
    (Newfoundland) 265
Vikings 13
Village Historique Acadien
    (Caraquet) 115
Water Street (St. Andrews
    by-the-Sea) 80
Wedgeport (Nova Scotia) 174
Wedgeport Sport Tuna Fishing
    Museum (Nova Scotia) 174
West Point (P.E.I.) 228
    Accommodations 240
    Restaurants 246
West Point Lighthouse
    (West Point) 228
West Pubnico (Nova Scotia) . . . 174
    Restaurants 187
Westport (Nova Scotia)
    Accommodations 169
    Restaurants 171
Whale-watching 47
    Bay of Fundy (Nova Scotia)   166
    Cape Breton Island
        (Nova Scotia) 200
    Lighthouse Route
        (Nova Scotia) 181
    Newfoundland 271
    Southern New Brunswick . . . 92

White Point (Nova Scotia)
    Accommodations 183
Wile Carding Mill
    (Bridgewater) 177
Wilnot United Church
    (Fredericton) 54
Windsor (Nova Scotia) 158
Wine 40
Winter Activities 47
Witless Bay (Newfoundland)) . . 259
    Restaurants 279
Wolfville (Nova Scotia) 162
    Accommodations 167
    Restaurants 170
Wood Islands (P.E.I.) 223
    Finding Your Way Around . 210
Wooden Mill (Barrington) 174
Woodleigh (Burlington) 218
Woodstock (P.E.I.)
    Accommodations 240
Woodstock (St. John River
    Valley) 69
    Accommodations 72
    Restaurants 73
Yarmouth (Nova Scotia) 165
    Accommodations 169
    Practical Information 158
    Restaurants 172
Yarmouth Country Museum
    (Yarmouth) 165
York County Courthouse
    (Fredericton) 56
York-Sunbury Museum
    (Fredericton) 56
Youth Hostels 39

Order Form

Ulysses Travel Guides

☐ Atlantic Canada .... $24.95 CAN
$17.95 US·

☐ Bed & Breakfasts .... $14.95 CAN
in Québec $10.95 US

☐ Belize .... $16.95 CAN
$12.95 US

☐ Canada .... $29.95 CAN
$21.95 US

☐ Chicago .... $19.95 CAN
$14.95 US

☐ Chile .... $27.95 CAN
$17.95 US

☐ Costa Rica .... $27.95 CAN
$19.95 US

☐ Cuba .... $24.95 CAN
$17.95 US

☐ Dominican .... $24.95 CAN
Republic $17.95 US

☐ Ecuador and .... $24.95 CAN
Galapagos Islands $17.95 US

☐ Guadeloupe .... $24.95 CAN
$17.95 US

☐ Guatemala .... $24.95 CAN
$17.95 US

☐ Lisbon .... $18.95 CAN
$13.95 US

☐ Louisiana .... $29.95 CAN
$21.95 US

☐ Martinique .... $24.95 CAN
$17.95 US

☐ Montréal .... $19.95 CAN
$14.95 US

☐ Miami .... $9.95 CAN
$12.95 US

☐ New York City .... $19.95 CAN
$14.95 US

☐ Ontario .... $27.95 CAN
$19.95US

☐ Ottawa .... $17.95 CAN
$12.95 US

☐ Panamá .... $24.95 CAN
$17.95 US

☐ Québec .... $29.95 CAN
$21.95 US

☐ Québec and .... $9.95 CAN
Ontario with Via $7.95 US

☐ Toronto .... $18.95 CAN
$13.95 US

☐ Vancouver .... $17.95 CAN
$12.95 US

☐ Washington D.C. .... $18.95 CAN
$13.95 US

☐ Western Canada .... $29.95 CAN
$21.95 US

Order Form

Ulysses Travel Guides

☐ Atlantic Canada .... $24.95 CAN
                                                  $17.95 US
☐ Bed & Breakfasts .... $14.95 CAN
  in Québec $10.95 US
☐ Belize .... $16.95 CAN
                                                  $12.95 US
☐ Canada .... $29.95 CAN
                                                  $21.95 US
☐ Chicago .... $19.95 CAN
                                                  $14.95 US
☐ Chile .... $27.95 CAN
                                                  $17.95 US
☐ Costa Rica .... $27.95 CAN
                                                  $19.95 US
☐ Cuba .... $24.95 CAN
                                                  $17.95 US
☐ Dominican .... $24.95 CAN
  Republic $17.95 US
☐ Ecuador and .... $24.95 CAN
  Galapagos Islands $17.95 US
☐ Guadeloupe .... $24.95 CAN
                                                  $17.95 US
☐ Guatemala .... $24.95 CAN
                                                  $17.95 US
☐ Lisbon .... $18.95 CAN
                                                  $13.95 US
☐ Louisiana .... $29.95 CAN
                                                  $21.95 US
☐ Martinique .... $24.95 CAN
                                                  $17.95 US
☐ Montréal .... $19.95 CAN
                                                  $14.95 US
☐ Miami .... $9.95 CAN
                                                  $12.95 US
☐ New York City .... $19.95 CAN
                                                  $14.95 US
☐ Ontario .... $27.95 CAN
                                                  $19.95US
☐ Ottawa .... $17.95 CAN
                                                  $12.95 US
☐ Panamá .... $24.95 CAN
                                                  $17.95 US
☐ Québec .... $29.95 CAN
                                                  $21.95 US
☐ Québec and .... $9.95 CAN
  Ontario with Via $7.95 US
☐ Toronto .... $18.95 CAN
                                                  $13.95 US
☐ Vancouver .... $17.95 CAN
                                                  $12.95 US
☐ Washington D.C. .... $18.95 CAN
                                                  $13.95 US
☐ Western Canada .... $29.95 CAN
                                                  $21.95 US